Socialism, radicalism, and nostalgia

Socialism, radicalism, and nostalgia
Social criticism in Britain, 1775–1830

William Stafford

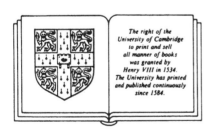

The right of the
University of Cambridge
to print and sell
all manner of books
was granted by
Henry VIII in 1534.
The University has printed
and published continuously
since 1584.

Cambridge University Press
Cambridge
London   New York   New Rochelle
Melbourne   Sydney

Published by the Press Syndicate of the University of Cambridge
The Pitt Building, Trumpington Street, Cambridge CB2 1RP
32 East 57th Street, New York, NY 10022, USA
10 Stamford Road, Oakleigh, Melbourne 3166, Australia

First published 1987

Transferred to digital printing 2002

Library of Congress Cataloging-in-Publication Data
Stafford, William.
Socialism, radicalism, and nostalgia.
Bibliography: p.
Includes index.
1. Great Britain – Social conditions – 18th century.
2. Great Britain – Social conditions – 19th century.
I. Title.
HN385.S762   1987   306'.0941   86–18774

British Library Cataloguing in Publication Data
Stafford, William
Socialism, radicalism, and nostalgia:
social criticism in Britain, 1775–1830.
1. Great Britain – Social conditions –
18th century   2. Great Britain – Social
conditions – 19th century
I. Title
941   HN385

ISBN 0 521 32792 X hard covers
ISBN 0 521 33989 8 paperback

In memory of
Agnes Benton and Ethel Maude Stafford

Contents

Acknowledgements   *page*   ix
1 Introduction   1

Part I Contexts and possibilities
2 General context   11
3 Mental furniture   31

Part II Texts
4 *The Real Rights of Man*, Thomas Spence, 1775   101
5 *An Essay on the Right of Property in Land*, William
       Ogilvie, 1782   107
6 *Enquiry concerning Political Justice and Its Influence
       on Morals and Happiness*, William Godwin,
       1798   121
7 *The Effects of Civilization on the People in European
       States*, Charles Hall, 1805   146
8 *A Lay Sermon Addressed to the Higher and Middle
       Classes on the Existing Distresses and
       Discontents*, Samuel Taylor Coleridge, 1817   164
9 *Report to the County of Lanark*, Robert Owen, 1821   181
10 *A Few Doubts as to the Correctness of Some Opinions
       Generally Entertained on the Subjects of
       Population and Political Economy*, 'Piercy
       Ravenstone', 1821   195
11 *An Inquiry into the Principles of the Distribution of
       Wealth Most Conducive to Human Happiness;
       Applied to the Newly Proposed System of
       Voluntary Equality of Wealth*, William
       Thompson, 1824   214

12 *Labour Defended against the Claims of Capital or the*
     Unproductiveness of Capital Proved with
     Reference to the Present Combinations amongst
     Journeymen, Thomas Hodgskin, 1825   232
13 *Rural Rides,* William Cobbett, 1830   250
14 Conclusion   270
Notes   275
Index   299

Acknowledgements

This book has grown out of teaching the part-time M.A. in History at Huddersfield, and I am grateful to my students, whose comments and questions have led me to develop and clarify my understanding. I owe much also to my fellow members of the History of Ideas panel of the Council for National Academic Awards: their stimulating conversation, in smoke-filled committee rooms and in hotel bars late at night, gave me confidence in the history of ideas as a distinct and valuable intellectual enterprise. My thanks are due to my colleagues, especially those in the Politics section, who arranged for me a year with a lightened teaching load so that I could pursue my research. Searching and detailed criticisms of the first draft were made by Harry Dickinson and by Cambridge University Press's anonymous reader; the book has greatly improved as a result. I have received help on specific points from Peter Wood, David Wright, and Pauline Stafford.

1

Introduction

Between 1775 and 1830 occurred a remarkable flowering of radical social criticism in Britain. The best writings are lively, original, powerful, and moving; when we survey them, we can see the gradual emergence of ways of thinking that have subsequently been labelled 'socialist', but also radical critiques that do not belong under that heading. I propose to examine ten representative texts. Texts, not authors: my concern is the range of socially radical ideas recorded in print, rather than writers and their careers. But let me begin by introducing the books and their authors.

Thomas Spence will always have the fame of a pioneer; for who is there before him? We have to go back a century and a quarter to the Diggers to find anything comparable. *The Real Rights of Man* was first published in Newcastle in 1775; no copy of this edition survives. The earliest we have is from 1779; there were several later editions, with minor changes, under different titles.[1] It is a slight thing, in the quality of its argument and in length—less than three thousand words. Still, it arrests our attention. It calls upon the people, organized in parish associations, to expropriate the landlords. The democratic parishes will lease the land in small parcels, using the rents to pay national taxes and welfare benefits. Spence was untiring in promoting his plan. In 1792 he moved from Newcastle to London, there to be a notorious political activist until his death in 1814. From 1793 to 1795 he published a radical weekly with the immortal title of *Pig's Meat; or, Lessons for the Swinish Multitude*. The government thought him sufficiently troublesome to arrest him several times. Eventually he acquired a small following, some of whom were involved in the Spa Fields riot of 1816 and the Cato Street Conspiracy of 1820.

William Ogilvie's book has one of those long titles so popular at the time: *An Essay on the Right of Property in Land, with Respect to Its Foundation in the Law of Nature, Its Present Establishment by the Municipal Laws of Europe, and the Regulations by Which It Might be Rendered More Beneficial to the Lower Ranks of Mankind.*[2] Published in 1782, it is the only known publication of its author. It contains a vigorous condemnation of the injustice and evil consequences of unequal property in land and argues that every adult male should be allowed to take a farm sufficient to support his family from uncultivated wastes and large estates; in the latter case the landlord would receive compensation. Ogilvie was no egalitarian, but his plan would have entailed a massive assault upon property and was judged visionary and impractical at the time;[3] the 'Scottish Enlightenment' produced no other text of comparable social radicalism.[4]

William Godwin's *Enquiry Concerning Political Justice, and Its Influence on Morals and Happiness* was first published in 1793; a second, much revised edition appeared in 1796 and a third with lesser changes in 1798. I shall consider the last.[5] It is the richest and most substantial of the ten texts, the only one to create a sensation among intellectuals. But its fame was brief. By the late 1790s, Godwin's reputation had fallen, never to recover; ever since, this overlong, repetitive book, written in a clear but formal style, has not received the recognition due to its provocative originality. It argues for anarchism[6] and equality, to be achieved not by violence nor even by political action, but as the culmination of a long period of education and enlightenment. It was not his first book, nor his last; Godwin was a professional writer, publisher, and bookseller who wrote novels and plays as well as works of political theory.

Charles Hall's *The Effects of Civilization on the People in European States* was published in 1805; bound in with some copies of the first edition are his pamphlet of the same year, *Observations on the Principal Conclusion in Mr. Malthus's Essay on Population.*[7] I shall consider the two together. No other work of social theory by Hall is known; but in 1785 he published *The Family Medical Instructor.* Our information about this West Country doctor is exceedingly scanty. It seems unlikely that he was much known even among radical circles of his day, and he has subsequently received minimal attention from scholars. Yet of all the texts we are to consider, his is the most likable and, if we except Cobbett's *Rural Rides*, makes the greatest impact. It sets out a theory of exploitation of the poor by the rich and proposes ways towards equality.

Coleridge's *Lay Sermon Addressed to the Higher and Middle Classes on the Existing Distresses and Discontents* was published in 1817.[8] Though it is the poet's most concentrated work of social commentary, it is only one of a succession of political writings, from the moderately radical lectures of 1795, through the pro-war, anti-French journalism of the first decade of the new century, to the *Constitution of Church and State* of 1830, which speaks against Catholic emancipation and for a conservatism with a conscience. The *Lay Sermon* is by no means egalitarian, but it is predominantly anti-market. It reasserts an idealized, hierarchical, agrarian society that is Christian, organic, and caring. Weighed against this ideal, the landed gentry are found wanting, but Coleridge does not propose to force them into better ways: as befits one speaking from a pulpit, he relies upon an appeal to individual conscience. The *Sermon* calls to mind Carlyle's remark that the poet in his latter days was 'a mass of richest spices putrefied into a dunghill'. There are flashes of deep insight and passages of memorable prose; but the whole is poorly argued and remarkable for the tortuousness of its sentences. His criticisms of his political and religious opponents are unforgivably unsympathetic and intolerant, the pages reek of social and intellectual snobbery, and there is a surfeit of high-minded, antisensual moralizing. Nevertheless the *Lay Sermon* and the later political writings have rightly been admired for introducing and exploring the concept of culture,[9] and for initiating a cultural critique of market society.[10]

Robert Owen's *Report to the County of Lanark*[11] of 1821 has the advantage of being a short work from the pen of a writer who tended to prolixity and repetition. It is only one of his many books and pamphlets, but it is probably the best summary of his main ideas. It recommends cooperation rather than competition as the principle of social organization, it develops Owen's highly optimistic views on the malleability of human character, and it describes his proposed 'utopian' communities, the villages of cooperation or 'parallelograms of paupers', as Cobbett dubbed them. Owen was famous in his day and has been prominent in the history books. He rose from shopboy to wealthy factory owner and manager; he

rubbed shoulders with princes, bishops, and peers. His factory at
New Lanark was internationally renowned for its welfare arrangements. Owen initiated experimental model communities, inspired
the cooperative movement, and was the figurehead of an attempt
to transform society by means of a general union of the working
classes in the early 1830s. It was in Owenite circles that the term
'socialist' first came into currency, in the 1820s and 1830s, as the
opposite of 'individualist'.[12] Yet Owen's writings, when set beside
those of Ogilvie, Godwin, and Hall, appear crude and exaggerated.
This is a salutary warning to intellectuals; the best thinkers are not
always the most influential.[13]

*A Few Doubts as to the Correctness of Some Opinions Generally
Entertained on the Subjects of Population and Political Economy*
is a book whose size corresponds more to the length than to the
modesty of its title. It was published in 1821 by 'Piercy Ravenstone,
M.A.';[14] for the past twenty years it has been established that the
true name of the author was Richard Puller,[15] about whom very
little is known. There is one other work by 'Ravenstone', a much
shorter piece, *Thoughts on the Funding System and Its Effects* of
1824. The first part of the earlier book is designed to demolish the
population theory of Malthus; Ravenstone scores many palpable
hits.[16] The remaining, larger part of the book is a critique of the
'idle' or 'unproductive' classes who live on rents, taxes, and capital.
Capital receives the largest share of venom. Ravenstone is a friend
of the poor and of democracy, but not of social equality. He exhibits
nostalgia for an idealized, rural, paternalistic social hierarchy. He
was not a conservative, for he regarded England as a desperately
corrupt society on the brink of revolution.

William Thompson's *An Inquiry into the Principles of the Distribution of Wealth Most Conducive to Human Happiness* of
1824[17] is a prosy, repetitive work running to more than a quarter
of a million words. It is a synthesis of Godwin, Benthamite utilitarianism, the Hall–Ravenstone critique of capital, and Owenite
socialism. In it Thompson, who was prominent in the cooperative
movement, defends cooperation with more system and argument
than Owen provided. Thompson was an Irish landowner and capitalist, an anarchistic socialist, feminist, teetotaller, and vegetarian.
He had travelled and was acquainted with the works of Sismondi,
Saint-Simon, and Fourier. He wrote three other books: in 1825, a

work advocating equality for women; in 1827, a tract managing to be almost short enough to be termed a pamphlet, taking issue with some points in Hodgskin's *Labour Defended*; and in 1830, a book containing very detailed plans for the setting up of cooperative communities. Marx read him and refers to him in *Das Kapital* and other works.

Thomas Hodgskin's *Labour Defended against the Claims of Capital* of 1825 is a pamphlet of about seventeen thousand words.[18] Hodgskin wrote other works, including *Popular Political Economy* of 1828. In 1822 or 1823 he became a writer for the *Morning Chronicle* and continued as a journalist for the rest of his career. From 1846 to 1857 he worked on *The Economist*, where the leanings of this individualist towards free enterprise became most apparent. But his individualism did not prevent *Labour Defended* from being a powerful critique of the theory of capital of classical political economy, a theory that defended capitalists and the share they took of the nation's wealth. Hodgskin is not content merely to show that capital takes too much: he argues that capitalists, as capitalists, deserve nothing at all. Wealth is produced by labour, especially skilled labour. Justice requires that labour should obtain the whole product. This state of affairs is to be brought about by combinations of workers, sufficiently educated to understand the principles of the economic system. Alexander Gray wrote, 'Among the English forerunners of Marx, it is Thomas Hodgskin . . . who gives most clearly the impression of intellectual eminence and distinction',[19] and the Webbs, in their *History of Trade Unionism*, referred to 'The illustrious disciple of Hodgskin, Karl Marx'.[20] Hodgskin has received more scholarly attention than Ogilvie, Hall, Ravenstone, or Thompson; but to the shame of his countrymen, the two chief studies have been French.[21]

Cobbett's *Rural Rides* was published in 1830.[22] It is a selection, made by himself, from a series of articles that originally appeared between 1822 and 1826 in his weekly *Political Register*. *Rural Rides* is but a small part of Cobbett's total output: he published more than twenty million words. It is a lovely book by a brilliant journalist, a sustained and passionate denunciation of the unreformed political system. It is filled with a deep compassion for the suffering rural poor, and it breathes a nostalgia for a stable and happy countryside, vanishing before the advance of market relationships. Cobbett was no egalitarian; the organic society he idealized was a hierarchical one. But he was far and away the most influential advocate of political and social reform of his day; his writings achieved new publishing records, and his impression was stamped upon working-class radicalism well into the Chartist period.

Several of the texts considered here gave inspiration to the later socialist tradition. For example, Hodgskin's critique of capital anticipates that of Marx and itself continues lines of thought begun by Hall, Ravenstone, and Thompson. Coleridge's rejection of market society belongs to a tradition that includes R. H. Tawney.[23] Cobbett was admired by William Morris[24] and G. D. H. Cole. These apparent continuities should not be allowed to mask the fact that only Owen and Thompson would have been labelled as 'socialists' in the 1820s, when the word first appeared. Hall, Ravenstone, Thompson, and Hodgskin were critics of capital, but Hodgskin was an individualist, and Ravenstone, apparently, a radical Tory. Coleridge was a conservative, Spence and Ogilvie the most radical of land reformers. Godwin, in modern parlance, was an anarchist and an extreme individualist, Cobbett a populist. In talking about the past, we must for the most part use words in common currency today; but we must use them with care. Continuity must not be misread as identity. My list of texts coheres only under the very general description of 'critiques of society'. It is also a highly selective list. I might have considered other works by Owen, Thompson, or Hodgskin. I might have included texts by Thomas Evans, Spence's disciple, or by some of the followers of Owen such as John Minter Morgan; I might have chosen Southey, or John Gray, or John Francis Bray. But these would have added nothing of significance to the stock of ideas; and it is better to analyse a few texts with care, than many with haste.

My discussion of these texts will analyse them critically and will attempt to set them in context. The context will be approached by asking the question, what made radical social criticism *thinkable* at this time?[25] It requires an effort of imagination to pose and answer this question. Because socialism, for instance, is a commonplace doctrine today, it is easy to assume that it was possible as an idea at any time in the past, given a sufficiently original and daring thinker. But this is not the case; all thoughts have not always been thinkable. For example, Lucien Febvre's brilliant study of

Rabelais[26] demonstrated long ago that modern atheism was unthinkable in the sixteenth century. It was not just that sixteenth-century minds did not have at their disposal the theories of geological and biological evolution that enable us to envisage how our world and ourselves have come to be without divine intervention: they also lacked what would enable them to move from what we label 'magical' to 'scientific' conceptions. They lacked certain key abstract terms; they had an imprecise and fluid sense of time; their mathematical reasoning was primitive, their procedures for verifying and disproving hypotheses were, by our standards, wholly inadequate.

One aim of this study, therefore, is to decompose the texts – to lay out for inspection, as it were, the component ideas, propositions, attitudes, and to show how this intellectual furniture is assembled into social criticism. Before the analysis of the texts there is a long chapter that surveys this mental furniture. This order of presentation was not the order of my own investigation of the problem. I began with the texts, allowing them (or more accurately my reading of them) to point the way outwards to the intellectual equipment that conditioned their possibility. The list of things considered in the chapter entitled 'Mental Furniture' is therefore a selective list, and the selection was determined by my reading of the texts themselves. The chapter is also, of necessity, heavily reliant upon the work of other scholars. It is therefore stronger where there is a good and ample secondary literature. Classical economy and eighteenth-century political thought have been much studied, and there are studies of real excellence. Modern works on eighteenth-century religious ideas, by contrast, are thinner on the ground. Eighteenth-century sermons are a copious and important source for the mentality of the age; but they have hardly begun to be exploited in a systematic way. All I can claim to have provided, therefore, is an initial attempt at the question of 'thinkability' in the light of the present state of scholarship. Thinking does not go on in a vacuum; it is a response to events and conditions in the 'real' world. I have therefore provided a chapter on the general context – economic, social, political, and cultural. Once again, this chapter is not meant to be a complete brief survey of Britain from 1775 to 1830: its contents were dictated by what I found in the texts; it considers those events and situations to which the texts are a response. If it is a shorter chapter than the one on mental furniture, this is not because I consider the general context less important than the intellectual, but simply because this book is a history of ideas.

The core of the book is the discussion of the texts in Chapter 4. In each case, I outline the argument and then analyse its structure, attempting to assess what made its point of view possible, what permitted its originality. I also consider the argument critically. If one cares about the subject addressed by a text (and why write about it otherwise?), one wants to assess its strengths and weaknesses. But more important than this, critical discussion is an essential route to fuller understanding. Only by dissecting a text, by probing its methods and assumptions, by testing its chains of argument, does one come to a firmer grasp of it. Just as I have asked what aspects of the general and intellectual contexts made the texts possible, so I have asked whether there were ways in which the available mental furniture limited and weakened the argument, causing it to be, from our point of view, inadequate and unconvincing.

PART I

Contexts and possibilities

General context

I shall consider the general context of social criticism under five
headings: (1) economic structure, (2) social structure, (3) economic
conjuncture, (4) politics, and (5) culture. The sections on economic
and social structure will treat long-term, fundamental changes,
while that on economic conjuncture will deal with short-run
fluctuations.

1. Economic structure
According to the latest estimates, the population of England in 1731
– five and a quarter million – totalled much the same as in 1651.
Then began a sustained and accelerating growth:

1741	5,576,197
1751	5,772,415
1761	6,146,857
1771	6,447,813
1781	7,042,140
1791	7,739,889
1801	8,664,490
1811	9,885,690
1821	11,491,850
1831	13,283,882[1]

Between 1816 and 1826 the annual rate of growth of $1\frac{1}{2}$ percent
was the highest known for England. It may seem small beer beside
the 2, 3, and 4 percent rates of Third World countries today, but
it was sufficient to cause grave social problems. In the middle of
the eighteenth century, Great Britain was a net grain exporter; by
the nineteenth she had become a net importer.[2] There was a danger
that population would outrun the nation's capacity to grow and

buy food. Industrial revolution and rapid economic growth had removed this threat by the end of the 1840s for Britain, but Ireland did not escape the catastrophe of famine.[3] During the period covered by this book, the burgeoning of the population produced a situation in which a bad harvest meant cruelly high prices, and a run of short harvests caused widespread hunger and unrest. In the north, the growth of towns and industry provided, in good years, employment for the surplus rural population; in the south there was a serious problem of overpopulation and unemployment.[4] Here already we find developments that we might expect to provoke anxious thought about economy and society; in the light of these facts, how could an informed and caring observer judge that all was well with Britain? In actuality, late eighteenth-century observers had poor knowledge of eighteenth-century population trends; throughout that century the prevailing view was that population increase was an unmitigated good, for it tended to increase the wealth and strength of the state. But in 1798 Malthus's powerful and dramatic book provided a theory of population showing that overpopulation was a constant threat, and the first census of 1801 appeared to confirm his fears.

The agricultural sector did indeed respond to the rising demand for food. It is well known that in eighteenth-century Britain there was considerable interest in agricultural improvement; but how great the improvement in productivity per acre was is debated among historians.[5] It is probable that the main increase in productivity during the eighteenth century was over by 1760, before the population surge. Thereafter until the end of the period covered by this book, productivity per acre stood still, or advanced very little, or perhaps declined. In the last quarter of the eighteenth century and the first quarter of the nineteenth, the area under cultivation was extended in order to meet the growing demand for food of the growing population. This increased overall production, but lowered productivity per acre. The increase in production failed to keep pace with population growth. In all of this, there was no great technological breakthrough. Mechanization played no significant part, with one exception. After 1780, threshing machines were rapidly adopted, depriving rural labourers of one of their major winter employments. The main technological improvements were the adoption of better rotations and manuring, and these went hand in hand with the enclosures that made them possible.[6] Enclosures, affecting one-quarter of the cultivated acreage of England, were concentrated in the 1760s and 1770s, and from 1793 to 1815. Did they, as has sometimes been maintained, benefit the wealthy landowners and farmers and immiserate the poor? Did they cause a shift to large farms and an extinction of small yeomanry and cottagers? Did they reduce employment and depopulate the countryside? It is difficult to generalize about the effects of enclosures, which varied so greatly from village to village; but recent research has cast doubt on the gloomier scenarios. The legal rights of the lesser fry were on the whole recognized and compensated by the commissioners (though customary rights usually were not). It is true that there was throughout the period a shift towards larger farms, but this was happening independently of enclosures, which merely speeded up the process. Whereas in 1690 there had been two landless labourers to every occupier, in 1831 there were no more than five to every two. English enclosures in this period were not usually designed to remove men in order to make way for sheep and cattle; they were designed to permit improved cultivation, requiring more labour rather than less.[7] And only certain parts of England were affected; for example, large areas of southern England had been enclosed before the eighteenth century, and as Arthur Young and Cobbett observed, the worst rural poverty was found in these old enclosed areas. Distress in the countryside was caused more by population growth than by enclosure. Nevertheless, many contemporary observers did not regard the enclosure movement as blameless. The enclosure of commons and wastes robbed some rural labourers of a marginal resource in times of unemployment and inadequate wages. In parts of Scotland occurred the notorious Highland clearances – enclosures for stock rearing that forcibly drove whole villages of small cultivators from the land. 'Revisionist' histories of enclosures have maintained that they were not the prime cause of rural distress; they have not shown, nor have they attempted to show that they did not contribute to that distress.

In 1800, Britain had ten towns with more than 50,000 inhabitants, and three with 100,000 or more. By 1821 there were fifteen in the former category and six in the latter. The output of iron rose from 68,000 tons in 1788 to 258,000 in 1806. Raw cotton consumed by British industry rose from 30 million lb. in 1790 to 123 million in 1810. The value of British exports rose from £22 million per year in 1792 to £32 million in 1812.[8] To us looking back, it is evident that Britain was in the process of the first industrial revolution, one of the greatest transformations in human history. We might expect this experience to generate radical thought about society in two ways. First, we would expect so great a change to release contemporaries from complacent and somnolent acceptance of things as they are. It becomes difficult to regard the existing order as natural, inevitable, God-given, and eternal when that order is changing before one's eyes. Second, we would expect the unpleasant side effects of rapid change – the extinction of old crafts, the shock of the move from rural to urban environments, the squalor of new towns, the harsher discipline and unhealthy, monotonous character of factory work – to provoke concern. But this raises two big questions. First, how aware were contemporaries of being in an 'industrial revolution', a fundamental shift in the level and nature of productive activity? Second, how disruptive was it, how hard did it bear upon the mass of the people?

The extent to which the majority of Britons, during the period covered by this book, were aware of living through an 'industrial revolution' remains doubtful.[9] Perhaps those living in the environs of Manchester will have had a sense that they were witnessing world-transforming changes; but apart from cotton and iron, many of the growing industries expanded with long-established rather than new technology.[10] Britain did not change in this period from an agricultural to an industrial economy. Agriculture had accounted for less than half the national income before the eighteenth century began: the manufacturing sector contributed no more than 38 percent of the GNP in 1871.[11] It is to be doubted whether the economic changes gave the majority of Britons a sense of living in a new era before the railway age and the Great Exhibition. Still, we would expect at least *some* observers – those with close experience of new, booming industries – to have been liberated intellectually by that experience.

There is a prima facie case for regarding the industrial revolution as grievously disruptive; for we know it was a period of great social unrest, with years of extreme hardship. Some occupations experienced the agony of technological extinction – notably the handloom weavers, who declined from prosperity to ruin between 1800 and 1830. But closer attention to the evidence discourages crude accounts. The hardships of the time were perhaps more due to rising population, war, and bad harvests than to the industrial revolution itself. Was the latter achieved by diverting expenditure from consumption to investment, thus grinding the poor? We must turn to the living standards issue in a moment, but from the investment point of view one recent estimate has shown that the gross domestic investment rose gradually from 7 percent of the gross domestic product in 1780 to almost 12 percent in 1831.[12] What do life expectancy figures tell us about the impact of economic change? It is a commonplace among historians that the population growth of the period stemmed in great part from a decline in the death rate. But if we compare the death rates for urban and rural areas, we discover a dramatic discrepancy:[13]

	Life expectancy in 1837	
	Manchester	*Rutland*
Professions and gentry	38	52
Tradesmen and farmers	20	41
Mechanics and labourers	17	38

In fact, adult mortality rates fell in urban areas (excepting Manchester and Liverpool) as well as rural areas from 1800.[14] However, the growth of towns meant that a higher proportion of the population was exposed to the higher mortality rate of urban environments; and we do not yet have the figures for infant mortality. Evidently, the industrial revolution caused great hardship to certain sections at certain times. Whereas rural workers often had more than one occupation to turn to (farming, plus cottage industry) the growing urban proletariat, tending to consist of workers dependent on one occupation only, was more vulnerable to recessions and layoffs. A consequence of industrialization was that different sectors and regions of the economy became more interdependent, and therefore a recession in one trade or area could spill over into other trades and areas.[15] Still, in all of this allowance must be made for regional and occupational variety; it will not do to talk about the impact of industrialization on 'the working class' as a whole.

The standard of living of the working classes during the early industrial revolution has since the late 1950s been the subject of vigorous historical debate. Because of the difficulty of obtaining reliable and comprehensive statistics on wages and prices, the debate is unlikely to be resolved for some time. The original chief protagonists were Max Hartwell, who argued that real wage levels rose between 1800 and 1850, and Eric Hobsbawm, who argued that they fell between 1790 and 1845.[16] An important article by R. S. Neale on Bath (1966)[17] made two points of method: first, the starting point is crucial. If we measure from the bad year of 1800 we get a more optimistic result than by measuring from the good year of 1790; second, global assessments of the living standard are worthless. Our concern should not be with the standard, but with standards of living, of different regions, occupations, and age cohorts. Neale's own study of Bath yielded a gloomy overall picture. M. W. Flinn's article of 1974 was more optimistic.[18] He argued that, during the spectacular wartime price rise from the early 1790s to 1813, wages largely kept up with prices (though not in the years of peak distress, when harvest failures made food prices astronomical). Then, massive gains were made in the postwar price fall, as wages fell more slowly than prices. Flinn writes of gains of as much as 25 percent. In their 1983 article, Lindert and Williamson declare for optimism, but they doubt whether Flinn is correct in postulating large gains over a very short period. They date the rise in living standards from 1820 rather than 1810 and find a doubling of real wages by 1850.[19] But even their optimism finds no significant gains for any group of workers between 1755 and 1810; and artisans experienced a considerable fall during this period. After 1820 all groups gained, but differentials grew greatly, with white-collar workers surging ahead, and farm labourers lagging behind.[20] An important recent intervention in the debate has been that of Wrigley and Schofield, in their massive *Population History of England, 1541–1871*. They have organized their account of the period covered by this book around a consideration of the classic thesis of Malthus, that population growth chronically tends to exceed the growth of food supply, causing prices to rise and living standards to fall. They conclude that this holds good in the main up to 1780; but between 1780 and 1800 a crucial change occurs. The connection between rising population and falling living standards is broken. Prices cease to rise as fast as population. Population and real wages begin to grow simultaneously, and Britain breaks free of the Malthusian trap.[21]

In tentative summary, therefore, we can say that the *global* figures do not give any clear evidence of a decline in living standards during the industrial revolution, and there may well have been an overall improvement. But the observable trends in real wages between 1775 and 1830 would not have given grounds for a contemporary observer to think that the industrial revolution might solve the problem of poverty for ever; it is only with hindsight that this judgment is possible. And once we move from the general to the specific, it is clear that some groups at certain times suffered severely. Agricultural labourers in the south, and handloom weavers, fell on hard times. Bad harvests and high food prices hurt almost all workers; industrial workers suffered when their trades experienced recession. There was enough distress to provoke searching thought about society. Finally, the standard-of-living debate as I have described it has focussed on real wage levels. But a further issue of great importance is the possibility that, as workers moved from rural to industrial occupations, and from rural to urban environments, standards of accommodation and nutrition deteriorated.[22]

2. Social structure

The bourgeoisie, wherever it has got the upper hand, has put an end to all feudal, patriarchal, idyllic relations. It has pitilessly torn asunder the motley feudal ties that bound man to his 'natural superiors', and has left no other nexus between man and man than naked self-interest, than callous 'cash payment'.

Our epoch, the epoch of the bourgeoisie, possesses, however, this distinctive feature; it has simplified class antagonisms. Society as a whole is more and more splitting up into two great hostile camps, into two great classes directly facing each other – bourgeoisie and proletariat.[23]

These celebrated words from the *Communist Manifesto* of Marx and Engels provide a classic account of the social change occurring in our period – a shift from an organic, paternalistic community to an atomized, individualistic association, a competitive market society, with rivalry and conflict always below the surface and sometimes above it, too. If this interpretation is correct, we have here an aspect of the general context that we would expect to generate reflection about society. But is it correct? That our period was one of considerable and increased social tension is beyond dispute. It is also the case that the character of social protest was changing, away from the food riot of the eighteenth century, towards the industrial strike of the nineteenth.[24] That is to say, social conflict was increasingly between workers and employers, in accordance with the judgment of the *Communist Manifesto*. But in precisely what sense are we entitled to say that the period sees the growth of class conflict? To what extent does class solidarity develop, bridging over the boundaries of particular trades and occupations? Do those who are engaged in strikes, conspiracies, and demonstrations see themselves as engaged in a struggle between the working class and the employing class? Is this the period of *The Making of the English Working Class*?[25] These are hotly debated issues in recent British historiography. A major question concerns the ways in which people thought about society, and we shall have something to say about this when we turn to the texts. But was there an underlying shift from community to individualism in this period?

Peter Laslett, in *The World We Have Lost*,[26] has argued that the deepest social change of this period was from a situation in which, for most people, the home and the place of work were the same place, to a situation in which they were different places. Before industrialization, the major unit of production, in agriculture and manufacturing, was the household. The occupier and some of his family worked there, and the labour he hired – farm labourers, apprentices, servants – lived in. Hence the relationship between employer and employee was a face-to-face one, not unlike that between father and children. The coming of the factory brought new relationships, characterized by distance, impersonality, and lack of emotional solidarity. Even in the countryside living-in declined, as farmers grew more prosperous and aspired to a style of life, patterned on that of higher social strata, that precluded the living together of the old system; in addition the rise in food prices furnished an economic motive for not feeding labourers in the farmhouse.[27] Is it in this change that we find the shift from organic community to individualism? If so, this is not quite the same as the theory of Marx, who thought that the social transformation was caused by the development of capitalism, by the production of commodities for sale rather than for use, labour itself coming to be regarded as a commodity that is bought and sold in the market-place. Furthermore, as Laslett himself suggests, we should not exaggerate or idealize the community that existed prior to industrialization. Preindustrial Britain was not a classic 'peasant' society, in which the extended family was the unit of production, with parents and children owning and working the land collectively. In Britain, children went off to form separate households, and labour was hired in.[28] Indeed, Alan Macfarlane has argued that wage relationships are a salient feature of English society as far back as the High Middle Ages; there may never have been 'peasant communism' to any significant extent in England.[29]

Harold Perkin's *The Origins of Modern English Society, 1780– 1880*[30] postulates a change from traditional society to class society. Traditional society was made up of chains of dependence and patronage; at the top of the chains was the aristocracy, the only group that had any sense of horizontal solidarity. Below, individuals were acutely aware of their relationships with those immediately above and immediately below them, but they had no horizontal class feeling. Rivalry in traditional society was not between classes but between vertical interest groupings. The bond of traditional society was 'friendship' – friendship meant doing good turns to your clients and offering service and gratitude to your patrons. The relationships of this order are described by such words as ranks, degrees, orders; attachment, duty, dependence, charity, deference, subordination, gratitude. In this society, hostility is directed not against 'landlords' or 'capitalists' – face-to-face relationships with employers preclude this. Hostility is directed against bakers who raise the price of bread or Irish labourers who compete for jobs.[31] This society, midway between a formal feudal hierarchy and an impersonal, contractual capitalist cash nexus, is replaced by the latter, Perkin thinks, in the five years after the Napoleonic Wars. A major long-term cause of the change is urbanization, itself permitted by the steam-engine – the old water-powered factories of the countryside involved more paternalism and face-to-face relationships and might often be idealized versions of the old society in miniature.

Perkin's contrast between traditional and modern society is not identical with Marx's; like Laslett, he does not attribute the change specifically to capitalism. Also, his contrast is probably too neat. He notes an important horizontal cleavage in the old society himself – between gentlemen and common people. Capitalist attitudes and vertical antagonisms were surely important long before the Napoleonic Wars – unionism and strikes were on the increase (for example, on the Tyne) from the mid eighteenth century.[32] And the paternalistic attitudes of the old society survived well into the nineteenth century, not only in the countryside but also in industry. The alleged shift from a paternalistic society to a competitive market one may be partly mythical – but if so, the myth was believed by some contemporaries as well as by later historians. This becomes apparent if we consider an alleged phenomenon that G. D. H. Cole and E. P. Thompson, as well as Perkin, have regarded as a major cause of the emergence of class society – an 'abdication on the part of the governors', that is to say, an abdication of social responsibility. At the end of the eighteenth and the beginning of the nineteenth centuries, the fabric of state paternalism was progressively dismantled. The laws that protected workers by regulating wages and apprenticeship were abolished; workers in the affected trades fought unsuccessfully to retain the old paternal system. The 'moral economy' in which the state gave a measure of protection to living standards and expectations by selective regulation of wages and prices was giving way to the free enterprise economy, in which traditional, protected crafts experienced competition and technological extinction, and food prices were governed by the market. It has been argued that this produced, in response, a reactionary artisan radicalism rather than a modern class-conscious proletariat.[33] Artisan radicalism, seeking to restore the 'moral economy', is potentially revolutionary, for it seeks to overthrow the newly emerging social and economic order. Indeed it may be that a revolutionary situation is more likely in the early stages of industrialization, when traditional artisans are destroyed, than later, when an industrial working class seeks, through its organizations (trade unions, co-ops, political parties) to accommodate to and draw benefit from the new economic order that has created it.[34] Some British artisans were indeed inclined to violent action; but the great majority were wedded to legal, constitutional means and more concerned with the interests of their own particular trades than with a broader critique of society.[35] But this period of crisis for the artisan cannot be ignored as a factor setting the stage for radical criticism of society.

A further aspect of the 'abdication on the part of the governors' was the attack being mounted by the privileged classes on the poor laws; Malthus was not the only opponent of poor relief, nor the most extreme. The high-water mark of the campaign was reached in 1817, when a select committee reported in favour of rapid abolition; but the government took fright and convened a committee of the Lords to undo the damage. The upper classes were laissez-faire in their policies when it suited their interests; but when laissez-faire would have harmed them and benefited the poor, they were interventionist. Combination laws were passed to curb trade unions, and corn laws restricted corn importation, in order to keep prices, and hence farmers' and landlords' incomes, high. During the eighteenth century the number of capital crimes was increased, and the game laws that protected the pleasures of the rich became increasingly harsh. The 'abdication on the part of the governors' thesis was not a discovery of twentieth-century historians. It was something of a commonplace at the time; for example, *Blackwood's* magazine was depicting a paternal society betrayed by its aristocratic governors in the late 1820s, and the thesis was repeated by Carlyle in the 1840s. Still, we should approach the thesis with caution; it rests upon the questionable assumption that at some time in the past the upper classes *were* generally kind and caring. To suggest that the thesis is partly mythical is not to deny that there were examples of caring landlords before 1800 and of the naked cash nexus after – no doubt the myth was constructed out of elements of real experience. What is more dubious is the hypothesis that society in general changed, from paternalistic solidarity to harsh individualism. But this book is concerned with the genesis of social criticism, and in this regard it does not greatly matter whether there *was* an abdication; that there was *thought* to be an abdication is the salient fact.

If there was an abdication, it involved the Anglican clergy as well as the landlords. In the late eighteenth century, not only was a large share of ecclesiastical patronage in lay hands, but a large proportion of bishops were of aristocratic and gentry background.[36] There was no gulf between the secular and clerical elites; clergymen shared with squires the leadership of the local communities and were well represented on the bench of magistrates. The word 'squarson' was coined, probably in the early nineteenth century, to refer to the parson who acted as the squire of his village. Although there were many desperately poor curates and even parsons during this period, it is also true that many livings advanced in value through enclosures, favourable commutations of tithes, and the general increase in agricultural prosperity.[37] It has been suggested that Fielding's Parson Adams, poor and close to his flock, gave way to the clergymen of Jane Austen's world, in which a good living was an appropriate provision for a younger son of a gentleman. Pluralism and nonresidence were rife. No doubt there were good clergymen who served their flocks; but the aristocracy and gentry took it for granted that the church was a resource, to be managed for the benefit of their friends and relations.

3. Economic conjuncture

The period under consideration has all the appearance of extreme economic instability. The instability has a special quality, because this is a period of transition. The rhythm of a preindustrial economy is dominated by the goodness or badness of the harvests. An industrial economy moves in accordance with the trade cycle of boom and slump. Britain in the early nineteenth century was in the unfortunate position of being subject to both these rhythms.[38] In addition, the wars with France, lasting with brief respites from 1793 to 1815, had considerable economic consequences, on balance of an adverse nature.

The fluctuations in the agricultural sector have to be set in the context of the rise in population, which dictated a long-term upward trend in farm prices. The upward trend was steady from 1760 to 1793, then rapid, with violent fluctuations, because of the two runs of dreadful harvests, in 1795–1800 and 1808–12. In the bad years, hunger stalked abroad, and social unrest was considerable; but farmers and landlords prospered by the price rises. After the war came a rapid price fall and a period of agricultural depression, at its worst in 1821–3 and 1833–6.[39] Farmers and landlords complained mightily, but historians are not agreed about the gravity of the depression. Prices were much lower than in the peak war years, but still higher than before the war; the hardship experienced by many farmers may not have been absolute, but relative by comparison with their wartime prosperity.[40] However, the psychological effects of the price fall – and the attendant fall in wages – should not be ignored. Even if real incomes declined less than money incomes (or not at all), the fall would be likely to create an atmosphere of gloom and discontent.[41]

Turning to the industrial and trade cycle, the late 1770s witnessed a severe depression, as a result of the war with America and France. On the whole 1781–92 was favourable, but the rest of the 1790s produced an overall depression. The first years of the nineteenth century and the few years into 1810 were years of boom; there were recessions from 1803 to 1808 and from 1811 to 1816. At the end of the war there was a short boom to 1818, followed by a very severe depression; the mid 1820s brought recovery.[42]

The wars with France had very great effects on economy and society. Much of the £1,500 million raised during the war years in loans and taxes was paid to foreign powers as subsidies or spent abroad. In this way, a large chunk of the GNP was going profitlessly out of the country, depressing home consumption and investment. At the time of the Peninsular War, British bullion was flowing abroad in torrents.[43] Throughout these years, economic growth and the industrial revolution were going on apace; but the haemorrhage of national wealth probably slowed the growth down.[44] Only 9 percent of the cost was paid by the income tax; the rest came from loans and consumption taxes, which fell hardest on the working masses. Throughout the war, there was a chorus of complaint about the cost.[45] In 1797 the government, in response to the financial difficulties of the nation, went off the gold standard; the paper currency became inconvertible for the duration, and the quantity of banknotes increased. The real value of the notes fell below their alleged gold value, and this contributed to price inflation. After the termination of the war, the government wished to return to the gold standard and convertibility, and steps were taken to reduce the volume of paper currency. This probably contributed to the catastrophic postwar price fall. Many farmers and landlords had contracted debts when prices, and hence their incomes, were high; but the debts did not go down when prices and incomes did. The effects of government monetary policy should not be exaggerated, however: the Bank of England attempted, with some success, to mitigate the fluctuations in credit.[46] The national debt had risen from £130 million in 1763 to nearly £900 million at the end of the wars; the interest on the debt did not cease with the fighting, and so the burden continued into the peace.[47] The debts and taxes massively redistributed income from taxpayers to holders of the national debt.[48] The wars also skewed the shape of the economy, mopping up labour into the armed forces and causing the growth of industries supplying the army and navy. This skewing was disastrous when the wars ended; disbanded soldiers and sailors were thrown onto the labour market, and the pattern of demand for manufactured goods suddenly shifted.

Our period, then, is one of great economic and social instability; the wheel of fortune turned rapidly. Here is a factor that we would certainly expect to cause the observer to stand back from society and view it critically.

4. Politics

Supporters of the late eighteenth-century British political system would admit that a major mechanism of its working was friendship and connection, the mutual exchange of good offices; radical critics, like present-day historians, insisted that it ran on corruption. The king's ministers obtained the support they needed in the two houses of Parliament by paying for it; they rewarded their friends and allies with titles, pensions, grants of crown land, and places in public employment that might be sinecures.[49] Pitt gave life pensions to Canning, Canning's sisters, Huskisson, and Lord Hawkesbury. Addington gave his son, a schoolboy, a life pension of £3,000 per year.[50] Not only was corruption a principle of cohesion at the top; it was also extensively used in the management of parliamentary elections. In many of the boroughs, with their small electorates, ministers could obtain the election of their supporters by judicious allocation of government contracts and minor government posts, say, in the naval dockyards or in customs and excise. Other boroughs were controlled by local aristocrats and gentlemen, who used bribery and their influence as customers, employers, and magistrates to secure the election of the man of their choice. A great patron like the Duke of Newcastle could use 'his' MPs to obtain office and its spoils. The system was not without its merits. In the absence of strong parties of the modern kind, it was essential if stable majorities in the houses of Parliament, and hence stable government, were to be secured. But it did mean that large sums of public money flowed into private pockets. In the latter part of the eighteenth century, there was a growing demand for reform of this corrupt system, fuelled by the mounting burden of taxation and public debt. The rise in taxation was caused by war rather than corruption; but reform of Parliament was sought as a precondition for imposing economy and retrenchment on ministers. Another source of the rising pressure for reform was the discontent of dissenters. Dissenting religion was tolerated after 1689, but dissenters did not enjoy equal civil status with Anglicans. For example, they were ineligible for municipal honours and government offices. Under William III and the first two Georges, the dissenting interest was quiet, grateful for freedom from persecution. During the reign of George III, gratitude gave way to discontent. Thirdly, events abroad stimulated demand for reform. The loss of the American colonies occasioned severe criticism of the government, and consequently of the political system that allowed such incompetence to go unpunished. The Americans then set an example, by establishing more egalitarian and less corrupt political systems for themselves. But most important of all, the French Revolution that began in 1789 and by 1792 had made France a democratic republic, acted as an inspiration.[51]

The demand for political reform did not cease in 1688; there were 'true Whigs' and country critics of corrupt government in the late seventeenth and early eighteenth centuries. But the movement for reform gained momentum with the Wilkes affair, commencing in 1763. The campaign thus began in the metropolis, always more 'advanced' than the provinces. Then in 1779 a reform movement began in Yorkshire, under the leadership of the Rev. Dr. Christopher Wyvill;[52] other counties soon joined in, and dissenters were prominent. After the commencement of the French Revolution, the reform movement deepened, widened, and became more intense. A sharp polarization developed between the aristocratic governing establishment and the middle-class dissenting interest. The loss of the American colonies and the higher taxation and disruption of trade that went with it had already produced disaffection in this group towards a seemingly incompetent government. From 1787 to 1790, dissenters mounted a campaign for the repeal of the Test and Corporation acts; in the reactionary climate generated by the French Revolution, the government refused, and loyalists began to harry dissenters. The Priestley riots in Birmingham were the most striking example of this persecution. The wars with France, and the later Orders in Council that disrupted trade, helped to generate an alliance of dissent and commerce in favour of peace and reform and against the government.[53] A further development was the involvement of new social groups in the movement for reform. Hitherto the reformers had been of the middle class and gentry; now the first reform associations of working men were founded. Associations sprang up throughout the provinces,[54] and some began to use militant language. With mounting agitation at home and the terrible French example abroad, the government and the ruling classes generally took fright; in the 1790s, reaction and repression set in. New laws were passed to curb political associations and publications; radical reformers were prosecuted; voluntary associations of loyalists intimidated the progressives of their locality. The Conservative reaction was vigorous and nasty; although few were executed, transported, or imprisoned for long terms, many were driven to emigrate. By 1800, the reform movement was crushed and went underground for a few years. There followed a handful of dramatic, conflict-ridden years, with the Spa Fields riots, the Peterloo massacre, and the Cato Street Conspiracy. But the reaction of the 1790s had destroyed and fragmented the forces of reform in Parliament itself; reform had been postponed for forty years.

The reform movement became more radical as it went on; Wilkes and Wyvill were not democrats, but Cartwright and Paine were. More important than the changes in the demands of the reformers, however, is an underlying unity. Their aims were essentially negative. They were not seeking to establish big government on the twentieth-century pattern, carrying out the will of the people, intervening extensively in economic and social affairs in order to promote the public good. Rather, they were seeking to limit and control government, to purge and cleanse it and hedge it round. They wanted government to do less, above all to spend less. This is demonstrated by their specific demands. Abolition of pensions and sinecures is a recurrent theme. Wyvill and the Yorkshire reformers wanted to increase the number of county seats at the expense of boroughs; the county franchise produced relatively large electorates that could not easily be corrupted or influenced. A central demand was for annual parliaments; these would have made modern, active, interventionist government impossible, but they would have been ideal as a way of checking, controlling, indeed, hamstringing the administration.

Britain had had a revolution in the seventeenth century. The ideological debate of that revolution was concerned mainly with politics and religion; but when the conflict turned the world upside down, men's minds were released from the fetters of convention, and some – the Levellers and Diggers – began to speculate about transforming the social and economic order.[55] After the Restoration, there ensued a period of comparative calm, briefly interrupted by the Glorious Revolution of 1688. Political protest revived after 1760, as I have narrated; as the tempo quickens, we would expect to see speculation and criticism spilling over from politics to social and economic arrangements, as it had done in the seventeenth century. We would especially expect this because organizations and activities aimed at redressing economic grievances were growing up step by step with the radical political tendencies. Unionism and strike activity were increasing to such an extent from the mid eighteenth century that in 1799 and 1800 the Combination acts were passed in an attempt to crush them. The Luddite risings between 1811 and 1817 greatly alarmed the government, and large numbers of troops were stationed about the country to keep the populace under control.[56] The periods of acute economic distress brought social turmoil. Was there a political dimension to this economic unrest? May it even be the case that Luddism is merely the tip of a submerged revolutionary conspiracy, linking back to the reform movements of the 1790s and forward to the mass demonstrations of the postwar years? Historians are deeply divided on this issue.[57]

The fiscal and economic effects of the wars with revolutionary and Napoleonic France have already been mentioned. But the wars hurt labouring people in other ways.[58] Recruitment into the armed forces was a source of grievance throughout. Where the poor were concerned, there was scant respect for human rights; the press gangs and crimping houses obtained recruits by force and sometimes indiscriminately. The recruiting system was manifestly unfair; rich people balloted for the militia could buy themselves out. Conditions of service in the armed forces were often inhuman; not until 1797 were commanding officers required to report the dead by name, and even then there was no official system for informing relatives. At first, the families of nonmilitia servicemen got relief only at the same rate and in the same manner as parish paupers. At first also, soldiers were expected to feed themselves, and were given an allowance that proved so inadequate in times of high prices as to promote food rioting among the troops. Ill-disciplined troops were often a menace to the areas where they were quartered. When demobilization occurred, as in 1802 and 1815, there were no policies to ensure employment of returning soldiers and sailors. In 1809, one man in every nine or ten of military age was in the regular forces; if volunteers and local militia are taken into account, one in six. The loss of life among servicemen was proportionately higher between 1794 and 1815 than between 1914 and 1918. The working people of Britain were being called upon to make supreme sacrifices; yet, shockingly and almost incredibly, at the same time the fabric of paternalist regulation was being dismantled and the campaign for the abolition of poor relief was at its height. Poverty was a growing problem in these years. In 1785 the poor rates had stood at £2 million; by 1803, they had risen to £4¼ million, and by 1818 to £8 million.[59] Social welfare policy was very much on the agenda for discussion, and not only the poor law; legislation to control the conditions of work in factories began in the early nineteenth century.

5. Culture

The eighteenth century witnessed an expansion of the reading public, and a great increase in the quantity and range of things for them to read. J. H. Plumb has provided stimulating reflections on these developments.[60] He argues that the combination of an alphabet, plus the technology of printing, has 'explosive social possibilities', but these only began to be exploited fully in the eighteenth century, when there was a boom in literacy; in the printing of books, pamphlets, newspapers, and magazines for a mass audience; and in reading as a pastime. The boom can be demonstrated, for example, by the emergence at the end of the seventeenth century of the first national newspapers and then the proliferation of the provincial press; by the amazing growth of circulating libraries; by the huge print runs of certain items. Apart from newspapers and magazines, the literary product that enjoyed the greatest boom was the novel. The possibilities of the genre were exploited fully for the first time in the 1740s by Richardson and Fielding; once launched, it grew mightily. The novel was the stock in trade of circulating libraries;[61] more than any other product, it helped democratize reading. The rate of novel production increased from roughly seven a year be-

tween 1700 and 1740, to twenty between 1740 and 1770, and forty
between 1770 and 1800.[62]

This new market for literary leisure was largely a middle-class
market. The price of books alone dictated this; new novels, for
example, were expensive at the beginning of the nineteenth century
and they got dearer. The 'cheap' book of the age was the five-shilling
reprint (twenty-five pence) that cannot have been available to the
labouring masses. But for those who had a little spare cash, there
were ways round the prohibitive cost of new books – circulating
libraries, book clubs, the publication of books in cheap installments,
after 1774 reprints of out-of-copyright works. Granted that a mass
reading public (albeit a middle-class one) emerged, what was its
significance? Plumb makes the point that Josiah Wedgwood, who
left school at ten, was reading Voltaire and Rousseau in middle
age; and he insists that this should astonish us, as it is a phenomenon
unprecedented in earlier periods and other cultures. The boom in
reading permits a 'cultural seepage' of ideas down from the educated elite to the masses. It has been suggested that in England there
was no gulf between a high and a low culture, such as we find in
France of the enlightenment.[63] At the crudest level, we can say that
this phenomenon opens up greater possibilities of political and social speculation to more people. The new provincial press was alive
with political debate.[64] Print-run figures demonstrate that some
radical writings – for example, by Price and Paine – reached very
many people.[65] The political nation, those who were interested and
informed about public affairs, was expanding. A more subtle point
is Jack Goody's about the link between literacy and social criticism.[66] He argues that ambiguous and vague statements and in-
consistencies, which may pass unchallenged when merely heard,
are more easily detected, analysed, and rejected when found on a
printed page; hence a book culture will be more critical than an
oral one. Furthermore, whereas listening is social or public, reading
is private; the very privacy of reading opens up possibilities for
independence of mind, freedom of thought, and deviance from the
norms.

One final point on reading. Because of their reliance upon reprints, lower-class readers would tend to read 'classics' and the
works of the previous generation. Hence the lower-class reader of
the early nineteenth century would read especially the Bible, *Pil-*

grim's Progress, Paradise Lost, the eighteenth-century poets (Thomson, Goldsmith, Cowper, Pope, Akenside, Gray, Blair, Collins), *Robinson Crusoe,* the histories of Smollett and Hume, and the essays of Addison, Steele, and Johnson.[67]

Britain at the end of the eighteenth century was a diverse and complex society. There was not a single culture, not one shared *Lebenswelt* – life-world and set of experiences. There was great occupational diversity, on the land, in the professions, in industry and trade. New professions and trades were emerging – the man of letters, the engineer, the factory manager, the factory proletarian. Occupational diversity caused diversity of life-styles. Britain embraced many different environments, from the southern countryside to highland Scotland, to market towns, ports, spas, industrial and commercial cities. There was the great cleavage between the established church and nonconformity, the latter being reinvigorated at this time by the tide of evangelicalism. Britain at the end of the eighteenth century had many subcultures. A society like this could not easily be free of political and social dissent and criticism. Only when there is a shared *Lebenswelt* can we expect ideological consensus. In late eighteenth century Britain we must expect a plurality of opinions and points of view, corresponding to the plurality of experiences. Here was a fertile seedbed for social criticism.

3

Mental furniture

If radical criticism of society is to be possible, the critic must be able to rise above the society in which he or she would otherwise be immersed and view it as if from outside; to think of it as something that is not natural, inevitable, and eternal. It is a matter of creating a space within which to talk about society, a distance between subject and object, observer and observed. The general context sketched in the preceding chapter encouraged and permitted this distancing. But economic, social, and political factors do not act independently of intellectual ones in causing individuals to think in certain ways. The wider context has to be experienced before it can be a cause of doctrines; and this experience is mediated and shaped by our mental furniture, our stock of attitudes, assumptions, concepts, and theories. We can only think what our mental furniture allows us to think. The aim of this chapter, therefore, is to survey, in the light of modern scholarship, aspects of the generally available mental furniture that made radical social criticism possible. The topic is discussed under eight headings: (1) ideas of human nature and the individual; (2) conceptions of society and of the ways in which individuals do and should relate to one another; (3) economic theory; (4) moral discourse; (5) political thought; (6) religious ideas; (7) conceptions of time and change; and (8) methodology and epistemology, the methods of arguing and proving theories, and the conception of truth. These divisions are sorting-boxes whose purpose is to aid orderly presentation, rather than a systematic set of categories. They represent a dividing-up of the terrain of knowledge from the point of view of one living in the late twentieth rather than the late eighteenth century. Today, we divide and separate what was then kept together. The modern disciplines of ethics, sociology, economics, political science, and history lived side by side, barely if at all differentiated, sometimes under the heading of 'moral philosophy'.[1] Above all, it was not usual to distinguish factual and evaluative questions in the way we do. Modern discipline boundaries have much that is arbitrary about them. Discourses of the late eighteenth century do not fall within them in any natural or easy manner. For example, the topics I have separated under the distinct headings of 'moral discourse' and 'political thought' are not obviously separable now and were less separable then. But I have not attempted to array my material under headings that would have been used in the late eighteenth century, because the boundaries on the map of knowledge were shifting then, and to recover them in their movement is a major historical task, only just begun. In any case, it is impossible simply to take off our present-day conceptual spectacles, and to put on those of another period. Our task is to try to understand the past from the vantage point (not necessarily higher) of the present.[2]

1. Human nature and the individual

In this first section I look at conceptions of the components of society, namely, individuals: to what extent were individuals valued as such, and what was the leading theory of the nature of the individual, of human nature? In the next section I move on to conceptions of how individuals cohere in society.

The term 'socialism' is first used in the 1820s to refer to the opposite of 'individualism'; it asserts cooperation and community instead of selfishness and competition.[3] Yet a condition of the possibility of modern egalitarian and libertarian socialism is a respect for individual persons, a recognition of their identity and dignity and a belief in their ultimate value. It is this that distinguishes socialism from fascism, and perhaps western democratic socialism from eastern totalitarian communism. Many cultures have not had this conception of individuality:

> In primitive societies the training of the child is usually directed to his learning the traditions of his tribe, so that he may find his identity, not in anything peculiar to himself, but in the common mind of his people.[4]

The ideal of equality rests upon the belief that every person matters, that it is wrong to sacrifice or ignore the many or even a minority or one for the sake of the splendid few or the public good.[5] By this standard British society at the end of the eighteenth century, if weighed in the balances, would be found wanting. Individualism is often dated to the Reformation or Renaissance; it is almost certainly older: 'The discovery of the individual was one of the most important cultural developments in the years between 1050 and 1200'.[6] Western Christianity has always been Janus-faced, on the one hand playing collectivist themes about the community of saints and all the faithful, and on the other being deeply concerned about the infinite worth of each soul in the sight of God,[7] proposing a direct relationship between the individual and God and the necessity of self-scrutiny in matters moral and religious. Whenever the high evaluation of individuals originated, it was certainly an old and established belief by 1775.

Theories of human nature can be powerful distancing devices. For they may provide a handful of first principles that can help us to analyse behaviour and social structure systematically. By the late eighteenth century, a theory of human nature with great potential for social criticism had been developed. Conservatives have perennially replied to social reformers with the jibe, 'But you can't change human nature'. Associationism provided an answer to this jibe; for it purported to show that human characters and abilities were not fixed and unchanging, but malleable.[8] The development of the theory begins effectively in the late seventeenth century in the philosophy of John Locke. He argues that the child is born with an empty mind, like a blank sheet of paper, on which experience subsequently writes. All the knowledge an individual possesses is furnished by experiences received through external and internal senses. Locke suggested that, just as we are born without knowledge but acquire it in the course of our lives, so we are born without character dispositions but learn them also. Later thinkers elaborated a theory out of Locke's hints. By the middle of the eighteenth century, Gay, Hume, and Hartley had evolved the theory of the association of ideas. Simple sense data are built into complex ideas in accordance with principles of association. For example, as a result of frequently experiencing, simultaneously or in succession, a particular set of ideas of colour, shape, feel, and scent, we associate these into the idea of a rose. We learn behaviour in the same way. A child sees a candle flame, is attracted by the brightness, reaches out, and burns its hand; experience has taught it to associate that brightness with pain, and such behaviour is avoided thereafter. By an identical process, character traits such as sympathy arise. The suffering of others – their cries and writhings – affect our senses disagreeably, and so we lend succour in order to remove the source of our discomfort. Originally we seek our own ease; but over the course of time, we come to associate the happiness of others with our own happiness and to desire their welfare for its own sake.

The implications of associationism for social and political theory are boldly and wittily unpacked by Helvétius in 1773.[9] He addresses the phenomenon of unequal abilities and insists that all, except the grossly deficient physically and mentally, are born essentially alike. Inequalities are not innate, but fostered by education and environment. There are no natural aristocrats, no born hewers of wood and drawers of water. Even genius is not inborn, but is stimulated by chance experiences. For example, M. Vaucanson became a great mechanical inventor because as a child he was left by his pious mother every day in the clock chamber adjoining the cell of her confessor. Shakespeare became a great playwright because he stole deer from a nobleman's park and had to flee to London, abandoning Stratford and the wool trade of his father. He tried acting as a profession, but his acting was so bad that he was driven to write plays. Corneille was a lawyer who developed his talent for literature when he tried his hand at writing verses for his mistress. Even Newton was inspired by the sight of a falling apple. Helvétius is convinced that the characters of individuals are powerfully affected by their religious, social, and political environments. Religious indoctrination impairs the reasoning powers; social and political inequality begets softness and pusillanimity in the rich, servility in the poor. Helvétius's is an extreme statement; in more moderate versions the theory was widely diffused. For example, Adam Smith wrote that the child of a street porter is not born inferior to the child of a professor; if they turn out differently, this is entirely the consequence of differing environments.[10] The associationist tradition from Locke to Hartley played an important part in the education provided by dissenting academies, and Joseph Priestley was a notable late eighteenth-century exponent.[11] It was taken on board by the philosophic radicals of Bentham's circle and restated with great vigour by James Mill.[12] Its importance for social theory is evident. It supports the view that men are not born doomed to inequality, some to be wise and some foolish, some virtuous and some vicious, some to be leaders and others followers. Inequality is not an ineluctable genetic fact, but an adventitious product of circumstances, removable by education and social engineering. The doctrine opens up glorious vistas of an improved future human race. It even enables Helvétius, Condorcet, and Mary Wollstonecraft to argue that the inferiority of women is not natural. If the roots of the doctrine go back a hundred years to Locke, in its developed form, with its critical potential unleashed, it is an achievement of the late eighteenth century.

2. Conceptions of human relations and society

I have argued that an aspect of individualism – its insistence upon the value of each person – is a component and condition of socialism. But another strand in individualism is the opposite of socialism, and in our period provokes social criticism both of a socialistic and of a nostalgic kind. I refer to accounts of human conduct in terms of self-interest. The growth of commerce may have played a part in making self-interested action seem normal and legitimate.[13] With more certainty it can be asserted that the political conflicts of the seventeenth century provided the arena for the rise of self-interest in propaganda and theory. Before the seventeenth century, political discourse did not recognize the legitimacy of private interest; the public good and the commands of cosmic natural law were paramount, and they required self-abnegation. This was challenged, in the seventeenth century, in the process of challenging monarchical absolutism. The public good, it came to be argued, cannot be utterly opposed to private interests, but must in some way include them.[14] This development in political discourse was accompanied by the rise of egoistic explanations of human nature. The classic, extreme example is the philosophy of Hobbes, which reduces all motivations to selfish ones. La Rochefoucault and Helvétius in France, and Mandeville in Britain, continue Hobbesian arguments. Mandeville, like Hobbes, is cynical about professions of benevolence and public spirit; such professions are but masks. Egoism is appealing as a theory; it brings neatness and system, permitting the explanation of all behaviour in terms of a single cause. But in other respects it is obviously unattractive, and the eighteenth century witnessed a lively debate over the issue. Benevolence was defended by Butler, Shaftesbury, Hume, and Adam Smith. It was not only a matter of reinstating a kindlier view of human nature. Hobbes also represented seventeenth-century rationalism and depicted wise human beings making calculations about their conduct, working out with cool detachment what would best serve self-interest in the long run (fools, by contrast, rush to their own destruction). A benevolist like Hume reacts not only against the selfish system but also against excessive rationalism. Reason is but the slave of the passions; we are not moved to act, nor are we often directed by her clear light, but by the opaquer forces of habit and sentiment.

Halévy, in his classic *The Growth of Philosophic Radicalism*, places this debate at the centre of social and political theory in the period we are considering. Even the staunchest defender of benevolence acknowledged the power of self-love, and hence the problem was how to contain this apparently disruptive and antisocial urge; how to bring basically selfish individuals to live in harmony. Halévy identified three main solutions to this problem.[15] First, the principle of the fusion of interests. This counters egoism with sympathy. We are so constituted as not to be purely selfish; we also delight in the happiness of others and abominate their misery. Under favourable circumstances, sympathy can control self-love. This is the theory of Hume, and also the moral theory of Adam Smith. Second, the principle of the natural identity of interests. This accepts the egoistic thesis, but maintains that if everyone pursues self-interest, the outcome will be the public good. The universe is so wonderfully arranged as to bring public benefit out of private vices. This is the theory of Mandeville, and the economic theory of Adam Smith and Bentham. Third, the principle of the artificial identification of interests. This also accepts the egoistic thesis, but is not prepared to leave it to the good order of the universe to bring favourable outcomes from general selfishness. The state must create an artificial situation in which antisocial conduct is contrary to self-interest, because it leads to punishment. This is the theory of Hobbes himself, also the legal and political theory of Bentham. Such in outline is Halévy's classic account. It still has value as a way of understanding the thought of the age, but it needs some qualification and amplification before we can use it. Some of his judgments of major figures require modification; and his scheme is too simple to reflect the range of ideas in play.

In the first place, it is doubtful whether any great thinker gave unqualified adherence to the principle of the natural identity of interests, even in the limited sphere of economic activity. Even Mandeville saw the need for a statesman to keep the ring;[16] and Adam Smith thought that governments should use the law to create an institutional framework in which the pursuit of private interest would lead to the public good. 'Natural' harmony required 'artificial' support.[17] To be sure, Smith often refers to a 'natural' order that is benign; but his thought as a whole is ambiguous. Only certain 'vulgar' economists, popularizers of classical economy in the early nineteenth century, held an unqualified faith in natural harmony. Halévy's thesis generates an 'Adam Smith problem', namely, a conflict between the principle of the 'fusion of interests' in his *Theory of Moral Sentiments* and the principle of natural harmony in *Wealth of Nations*. If there is a conflict, it is not as stark and irreconcilable as the Halévy thesis implies. The *Theory of Moral Sentiments* does not disregard or dispraise self-love; self-love embraces many valuable qualities and is to be approved provided that it is subordinated to justice. And the economic agents of the *Wealth of Nations* do not seek purely private, material gain; they also desire the admiration and sympathy of others.[18] The Halévy thesis also generates a Bentham problem – a conflict between natural harmony in his economic theory and artificial harmony in his legal theory. Once again, this is probably incorrect; Bentham is not in principle opposed to state intervention in the economy.[19] Rather, he is suspicious of existing incompetent and corrupt states, and there are some ends (e.g., abundance) that he doubts the ability of any state to promote. But other ends, such as basic subsistence for all, are within the state's competence.

Secondly, we can usefully divide each of Halévy's three principles into two. The first, the fusion of interests, can be interpreted in two significantly different ways. I may serve my fellows out of sympathy, because I love them; or out of habit. In the latter case we live amicably and harmoniously together because social behaviour through custom has become 'natural'. Both sympathy and habit are invoked by Hume. The second principle, the natural identity of interests, may also have two interpretations. It may be that selfish behaviour leads to the public good as an unintended consequence, as Mandeville and Adam Smith thought. In pursuing my own good I unwittingly do good to others. Alternatively, selfishness may lead by plan and intention to the public welfare. Prudent egoists may calculate that only by aiding others can they create an environment for their own comfortable living. There are hints of this in Hobbes. Finally, the artificial identification of interests may be produced by private action as well as state action, through contracts. A contract is a device whereby self-seeking agents create a relationship for mutual aid: *do, ut des,* I give that you may give.

The three solutions identified by Halévy constitute a radically inadequate set of concepts for thinking about society. The trouble is that they are too psychological, too unsociological. They postulate individuals being born with a fixed set of motives, selfish or sympathetic; or all developing such a set in the course of growing to maturity. They fail to recognize that our behaviour may be determined, not by some species-universal inner drives, but rather by social and cultural norms that vary from society to society and that we internalize as a kind of second nature. It may not be the case that we start out as individuals with motives, and then form social bonds out of love or by contract. It may rather be that when we begin to act in relation to others we are already socialized, already saturated with the norms and expectations of our culture, already bonded to our fellows by a shared pattern of beliefs, values, and behavioural dispositions.[20] If this conception, classically expressed in sociology by Durkheim, is correct, then it undermines the standard eighteenth-century antithesis of private interest versus public good, for it denies that a person *can* have any purely private interest; interests and desires are given or shaped by social conditioning and they may be such as are conducive to the survival of the social whole. In fact, this theory of society and culture was beginning to form in the eighteenth century. Hume's emphasis upon habit is a move in that direction; Burke develops the ideas yet further. Scottish philosophical history, developing the insights of Montesquieu, had begun to investigate the ways in which human motivation, behaviour, and interaction were modified by environment. Arguably Adam Smith stands somewhere between Hobbes and Durkheim.[21] But these promising beginnings were checked in early nineteenth-century Britain; liberal and radical thought, the thought of the Edinburgh and Westminster Reviews, returned to a simpler, more static conception of human nature.[22] As a result, the crucial final steps towards a theory of culture are taken not in Britain, but in Germany; Herder is the great progenitor whose insights are explored by a host of followers.[23]

Awareness of one's own society as *a* society, having its own character, is made possible by awareness of other, different societies. The knowledge that societies can vary is of the utmost importance in enabling thinkers to distance themselves from their own society; recognizing that it is not the universal, 'natural' form of human association. Contrasting societies may be located elsewhere, or in another time. In this period, four areas of contrast are important; societies of the Old Testament; societies of classical antiquity; 'savage' societies of the new world;[24] and the past of western societies, especially the Middle Ages. None of these contrasts is new in the late eighteenth century, nor is it a novelty of the period to prefer other societies to one's own; the high prestige of classical antiquity is as old as Christian Europe itself, the myth of Anglo-Saxon liberties dates back well into the Middle Ages.[25] Admiration of the savage or primitive, as in Ferguson, Rousseau, and Herder, *is* new, however. And, above all, the eighteenth century develops an increasing awareness of societies as wholes, having their distinct characters or spirits. The work of Montesquieu is seminal in this regard; but it is also a pervading concern of thinkers of the Scottish enlightenment such as Ferguson, Hume, Adam Smith, and Millar, and it is not absent from the pages of Gibbon's great history. Scottish thinkers of the eighteenth century were especially well placed to observe the contrast between 'feudal' and 'commercial' societies.

Finally, the concept of society gains in sharpness by being contrasted with an imagined presocial state, the 'state of nature' of Hobbesian and Lockean political theory. The classical ideal, Anglo-Saxon liberties, and the theory of social evolution will be taken up again in later sections of this chapter; at this point, however, I want to consider the emergence of the belief that the Middle Ages, or feudal society, were characterized by organic solidarity and benevolent paternalism, caring relationships rather than the cruel, impersonal cash nexus. This belief is more or less a commonplace in literate circles by the 1820s, for it pervades the pages of the popular novels and poems of Sir Walter Scott. This goes not only for his

novels about the Middle Ages, but also for those set in the recent
past of the Scottish highlands, such as *Waverley* and *Guy Man-
nering*. These depict a society in the last stages of feudalism. It is
easy, then, to establish an end point, by which a conception of a
period of 'feudal, patriarchal, idyllic relations' has become established. But when does this conception emerge? What are the stages
by which the uncomprehending hostility of the enlightenment towards the feudal era comes to be replaced with sympathetic interest
and enthusiasm? From Scott we can trace it back to writers of the
German Sturm und Drang with which he was familiar. The Catholic
John Lingard's *History of England* (1819–30) argues that medieval
monasteries cared better for the poor than the modern poor law.
Sir Frederick Morton Eden's *The State of the Poor* of 1797 asserts
medieval paternalism; Sir John Cullum's *History of the Antiquities
of Hawstead and Hardwick* of 1784 argues that the labouring
classes lived better under Edward III or Henry IV.[26] Potentially, the
idea is present in Adam Smith's *Wealth of Nations*; he describes
feudal societies as characterized by close personal bonds between
lord and retainer.[27] Smith does not admire feudalism, which he
thinks was disorderly and hostile to freedom; but it is an easy matter
to accept Smith's description and change his evaluation. Smith's
teacher Ferguson described feudal societies in a similar way and
evaluated them favourably in 1767.[28] Ferguson did not use Scotland
as an example, but there can be little doubt that his nostalgia is for
the Scottish clan system that was so quickly destroyed after the
1745 rebellion in support of 'Bonnie Prince Charlie'. The 'Gothick'
literature that becomes fashionable in the second half of the eighteenth century – the Gothick novels, 'Ossian', the poems of Chat-
terton, Percy's collection of old ballads – depicts relationships of
care and loyalty rather than calculating self-interest. This tracing
back may appropriately be ended with Bishop Hurd's *Letters on
Chivalry and Romance* of 1762:

> Look there, said he, on that fine room (pointing to the HALL, that
> lay just beneath them); and tell me if you can help respecting the
> HOSPITALITY which so much distinguished the palaces of the great
> in those simpler ages. . . . The same bell, that called the great man
> to his table, invited the neighbourhood all around, and proclaimed
> a holiday to the whole country. . . . Hence the weight and influence
> of the old nobility, who engaged the love, as well as commanded
> the veneration, of the people. . . . Chivalry was employed in rescuing
> humble and faithful vassals, from the oppression of petty lords.

So, from the middle of the eighteenth century, a conception of feudal society was available that challenged rationalistic and egotistic accounts of interpersonal relations.

Were there, in this period, changes in the ways people felt about one another? Does the literature of the age throw any light on this? The rise of the novel was mentioned in the previous chapter; and it may be that the growth of a novel-reading public is a most significant phenomenon. One of the main enjoyments of novel reading is vicarious living. We empathize with the heroes and heroines, we see through their eyes and live through their experiences. Empathic responses are elicited by novels of a certain type, a type pioneered by Defoe and above all Richardson. Richardson explores individual consciousness to produce an intimate, intense identification with his heroines. Diderot, in his *Eloge de Richardson* (1761), describes how he became so involved in *Clarissa* that it was as if her tragedies were happening to him. The epistolary form of Richardson's novels is well adapted to achieving this result. All novels do not exhibit these characteristics to the same degree. We do not empathize with the hero of a picaresque novel (e.g., the heroes of Smollett) to any great extent, nor is the character and consciousness of such a hero the focus of attention. The hero is rather the site on which all manner of colourful and amusing events occur.[29] But, overall the rise of the novel leads to a growth of empathy, which may have been revolutionary in its implications. Novel reading enables us to imagine ourselves in a greatly extended range of situations. It either requires or produces readers capable of imaginatively stepping into the shoes of others different from themselves, and into situations they have never experienced in their own lives. It is the opening up of an infinite vicarious universe, and it may break down the barriers between people, increasing understanding of and sympathy for those unlike ourselves. In this way it may change the character of social relationships. Furthermore, empathic, vicarious living makes the reader aware that his or her life experience is not the only one, shattering the frame of mind that sustains a traditional society in which patterns of life appear to be ordained.[30]

The 'spring thaw of sentiment' is a striking feature of eighteenth-century literature. In the novel, paradigmatic examples are Sterne's *Sentimental Journey* of 1768 and Mackenzie's *The Man of Feeling* of 1771. But the cult of benevolence and sympathetic responses is

not confined to overtly sentimental literature, and it goes back earlier. Fielding, unlike Richardson, is not concerned with the minute
exploration of feelings, but benevolence is accorded a high value
in his works. Such popular books as Goldsmith's *Vicar of Wakefield*
(1762) and Ann Radcliffe's *Mysteries of Udolpho* (1794) reek of
sentiment. The same tendency can be discerned in the poetry of
Thomson, Collins, Shenstone, Young, Gray, and Goldsmith. Nor
are these developments confined to literature. The ethical and aes-
thetic theories of Shaftesbury, Hutcheson, Hume, and Adam Smith
lay increasing emphasis upon the emotions.[31] In religion, the evangelical revival fosters a warm religion of the heart.

What is the significance of all this? The boldest claim one could
make would be that it caused a change in the way people responded
and related to one another: but such a claim is hardly believable
without severe qualification. More modestly, it might be claimed
that the growth of sentiment in literature merely *reflects* changes
that were going on independently in the structure of feeling. This
would accord with the stimulating arguments of Lawrence Stone,
who thinks there was in this century a raising of the emotional
temperature associated with a shift in social relationships from low-
gradient affect (loose bonds and relatively weak emotional ties
within a wide circle of kin and acquaintances) to steep-gradient
affect (intense emotional ties within the nuclear family).[32] In the
early modern period there were 'many adults whose primary responses to others were at best a calculating indifference and at worst
a mixture of suspicion and hostility.'[33] During the eighteenth century, there is a growth in the capacity for intense emotional involvement with others. In literature, for example, it is expressed in
the idealization of romantic love and the growing insistence that
such love should be the basis of marriage. Stone's thesis has drawn
much criticism, and is almost certainly much exaggerated.[34] But
even if we doubt that the way people felt about each other was
different in the late eighteenth century from what it had been in
the sixteenth, the growth of sentiment in eighteenth-century literature is still significant. At the very least the literature demonstrates
that the life of the emotions has come to loom larger in prevailing
conceptions of self and society: the recording of sympathetic responses has become expected and admired.

The zeal for social reform – for example, the campaign against slavery – has often been linked with this growth of sentiment. The connection between sympathy and social concern seems obvious. Here is Mary Wollstonecraft in her *Vindication of the Rights of Men* of 1790:

> Hell stalks abroad; – the lash resounds on the slave's naked sides; and the sick wretch, who can no longer earn the sour bread of unremitting labour, steals to a ditch to bid the world a long good-night – or, neglected in some ostentatious hospital, breathes his last amidst the laugh of mercenary attendants.[35]

The connection is demonstrated by the Jacobin novels, of Holcroft and Mary Wollstonecraft, which combine political radicalism, concern for the poor, and effusive emotionalism. The conservative Jane Austen was suspicious of them, and satirized socially disruptive 'sensibility'. But the link between the cult of feeling and genuine social concern is not a necessary or universal one. So often, the man of feeling seems to be searching out occasions for weeping; his tears matter more than the distress that bade them flow. We feel this about Sterne's Yorick and Mackenzie's Harley, those 'epicures of feeling'.[36] The orientation is towards the subjective response of the artist, not towards the objects that elicited this response.[37] Even where there is genuine concern, this need not imply any criticism of the social order. Intense and sincere sympathy may go with acceptance of the status quo. Misery may be regarded as an individual rather than a social problem, to be relieved by charity rather than reform. The pages of Fielding do contain criticisms of the behaviour of the aristocracy and gentry; he was undoubtedly a benevolist and had a real compassion for the poor. But he was no egalitarian;[38] he had no desire to subvert the social order, and as a magistrate he exhibited a strong hostility to vagabonds and beggars.[39]

Still, it remains the case that the floods of tears in eighteenth-century literature are typically poured out over the unfortunate poor. Gray's *Elegy* defends 'The short and simple annals of the poor', weeping over the graveyard where 'The rude forefathers of the hamlet sleep':

> Some village-Hampden, that with dauntless breast,
> The little tyrant of his fields withstood;
> Some mute inglorious Milton here may rest,
> Some Cromwell guiltless of his country's blood.

Thomson's *Winter* sorrows over frozen peasants; Goldsmith's
Traveller and *Deserted Village* lament the plight of simple folk,
driven from their homes by enclosures:

> The good old sire the first prepar'd to go
> To new-found worlds, and wept for others' woe;
> But for himself, in conscious virtue brave,
> He only wish'd for worlds beyond the grave.
> His lovely daughter, lovelier in her tears,
> The fond companion of his helpless years,
> Silent went next, neglectful of her charms,
> And left a lover's for her father's arms.
> With louder plaints the mother spoke her woes
> And bless'd the cot where ev'ry pleasure rose;
> And kiss'd her thoughtless babes with many a tear,
> And clasp'd them close, in sorrow doubly dear;
> Whilst her fond husband strove to lend relief
> In all the silent manliness of grief.

During the eighteenth century, the focus of attention in literature
shifts downwards in society, and social criticism becomes more
common.[40] The Augustan Age was not one of radicalism in literature. Writers such as Dryden and Pope write for a small, highly
cultivated, mostly metropolitan coterie;[41] they had aristocratic patrons. The nature of the audience was such as to encourage wit and
to discourage earnestness and enthusiasm. But in the second quarter
of the eighteenth century the club–coffeehouse coterie broke up,
authorship increasingly became a profession, and the audience expanded to mass proportions. It has been argued that the new kind
of professional writer was often in touch, in a real and personal
way, with the degradation of poverty;[42] hence the cast lists of eighteenth-century novels and plays are full of deprived and unfortunate
people. Even in the Augustan Age there was a literary fashion, at
the end of the seventeenth and the beginning of the eighteenth centuries, for crime and roguery – *Moll Flanders*, the *Beggars' Opera*
– and this may represent a deep vein of hostility towards the social
and political establishment. Hogarth's immensely successful prints
continue the assault on the upper classes. Once again, the novel is
important here. Classical art – Greek, Renaissance, seventeenth-
century French classicism – made a class distinction with respect
to genre.[43] Tragedy, serious art, was always about public people,
aristocratic or royal; common people were fit subjects only for com-

edy. The novel breaks with this, taking the inner life of ordinary people seriously. This 'democratic' tendency in the novel has Christian roots; the exploration of the moral life of the individual in the novel follows the similar examination of conscience in the spiritual autobiographies of dissenting Protestantism.[44] From the middle of the century, social concern and reformist sentiment become prevalent in the arts. 'The most obvious feature common to all the arts of Western nations after 1750 was the refusal to validate the contemporary social world.'[45]

So we find in literature abundant evidence of a change in the way people thought about human relationships, an apparent burgeoning of sympathetic responses, and an increased focus of attention upon the poor. In conclusion to this section, we need to say a little about attitudes to the country and the town. No image of contrasting societies and ways of life was more common in the literature of the age. So often, the idealization of the rural seems to be an idealization of the lowly, a concern for them, a lament over their exploitation, a rejection of the corrupt and oversophisticated rich. Before we draw too tidy a link between the pastoral idyll and social reformism, we need to attend to the salutary remarks of Raymond Williams.[46] The general drift of his argument is towards the conclusion that the contrast between country and town 'promotes superficial comparisons and prevents real ones'. In much pastoral literature, there is a tendency to mythologize rural life, casting a rosy glow over it, depicting rural enjoyments, peace, and harmony while ignoring the sweat and labour. 'God made the country, and man made the town' denies or ignores the fact that rural labourers continually remake the countryside by the sweat of their brows. The contrast between town and country suggests that, as opposed to the hectic corruption, luxury, and selfishness of the town, all is well in the country, thus ignoring rural exploitation:

> [T]here is . . . throughout, an ideological separation between the processes of rural exploitation, which have been, in effect, dissolved into a landscape, and the register of that exploitation, in the law courts, the money markets, the political power and conspicuous expenditure of the city.[47]

As the century advances, the contrast between country and town tends to give way to a closely related contrast between past, lost country (idealized) and present country, destroyed by commercial

pressures. Goldsmith's *Deserted Village* is a lovely expression of
this, but it, too, involves deception, suggesting that the old rural
order was benevolent and nonexploitative, that all the blame rests
on the new men. It ascribes 'to social decay what was actually the
result of social and economic growth'.[48] Crabbe protests against
the idealizations in *The Parish Register* (1807). Williams, in conclusion, is critical of eighteenth-century humanitarianism. It exhibits care and sympathy, but its protest is that of the priest and
doctor. It cares for the soul and body *within* the framework of the
existing order. It is deeply moralistic, but moral critique is divorced
from critique of the economic relationships that cause the problems.
It seeks scapegoats (e.g., enclosures). Finally, its charity is a charity
of consumption, not of production; it looks to an order in which
the labourers sit down at the groaning table to enjoy the feast, but
it fails to tackle the more fundamental issue of exploitation in the
relationship between employer and employee. Williams's argument
is powerful; but it does not entirely eliminate the importance of the
rural idyll. To focus attention on simple folk and to idealize them
at least prepares the way and provides materials for more adequate
social criticism, as our study of the texts will reveal. Barrell has
argued that from about 1790 *The Deserted Village* came to be
regarded as a radical and socially dangerous poem, depicting a
pastoral idyll destroyed by grasping landlords. Crabbe disliked it
for this reason: it suggested that rural workers could, if they held
their own lands, live a life of some work, much leisure, and considerable enjoyment. Crabbe believed that the poor should rather
recognize that hard labour was their necessary lot.[49]

The rural idyll, though it becomes so prominent in eighteenth-
century poetry, is much older. It is popular in the Graeco-Roman
world from Alexander onwards. Perhaps the longing for a simple
life emerges whenever a certain level of complexity of civilization
is reached; and classical culture is a culture of cities.[50] The myth
goes into oblivion in the Middle Ages, to be revived in the sixteenth
century, having thereafter a continuing existence.

3. Economic theory

The economic theories of the Scottish enlightenment and the classical economists are of the utmost importance for *social* theory. If radical social criticism requires for its existence the establishment of a

space, a distance, between the commentator and the object, then classical political economy does this in its very nature. For it is an attempt to construct a science or general theory of economy and society as if looking from the outside. In order to do this, it develops its own abstract terms, and proposes laws. The science of Adam Smith, whose *Wealth of Nations* came out in 1776, does this in a different way from that of Ricardo, whose *Principles of Political Economy and Taxation* was published in 1817.[51] Arguably it is anachronistic to refer to Smith as an 'economist', for this label encourages us to carry back into the late eighteenth century a conception of economics as a distinct discipline, clearly marked off from ethics, sociology, politics, and history. The *Wealth of Nations* embraces all of these fields and does not draw sharp discipline boundaries.[52] Society is not separated from economy, nor moral reflection from scientific; the possibility of social critique is built into its very structure. Therefore it is not sufficient to study Smith as the first, or one of the first, great economists, setting him in the context of an evolving science of economics, finding important predecessors in such thinkers as the physiocrats in mid eighteenth-century France and his friend Hume in Britain. Smith must be placed in other traditions as well. For example, his work challenges the classical tradition of civic virtue, without repudiating it entirely. More important, recent studies have shown how the *Wealth of Nations* belongs to the natural jurisprudence tradition.[53] This mode of discourse about law, politics, and society stems from classical antiquity and has as its central concepts natural law and (from the later Middle Ages) natural rights. Natural jurisprudence will be treated more fully in the next section on moral discourse, but at this point we should note the problem it set for Smith. If the earth was originally the common possession of humanity, and if every individual has a right to subsistence, then how can private property be justified? One answer to this problem is to say that the rights of private property must be restricted, and on occasion overborne, in order to save the poor from starvation. The issue was sharply raised in the European grain trade debates of the 1760s. Should there be a free trade in grain, or should the supply and the price be controlled for the sake of the poor? Smith argued for free trade. One of the main aims of the *Wealth of Nations* is to show that the conflict between the rights of property and the right of the poor to subsistence can be transcended. The growth of commerce and of the division of labour increases the wealth of nations and is the best route out of poverty; but economic growth requires freedom and security for property. Following Locke, Smith argues that property and inequality have benefited the poor:

> ... and yet it may be true, perhaps, that the accommodation of a European prince does not always so much exceed that of an industrious and frugal peasant as the accommodation of the latter exceeds that of many an African king, the absolute master of the lives and liberties of ten thousand naked savages. (I, 11)

If Smith is, from a modern standpoint, a moralist and historian as well as an economist, Ricardo's *Principles* looks much more like an economics text. Its range is far narrower.[54] Smith's is an encyclopaedic survey of economy and society; Ricardo constructs a theoretical model of the dynamics of the economic system, showing how it distributes wealth, how it grows and declines. There is much less in the way of explicit moral reflection. Some commentators have seen this as an advance;[55] with Ricardo, economics breaks free from moral philosophy and at last becomes a science. Others have viewed it as a degeneration; the terrain of humane knowledge is reduced to 'balkanised fragments',[56] the study of society is divided and thereby disabled. But Ricardian economics still has much to offer the social critic, as we shall see. And Ricardo, just as much as Smith, is a *political* economist, ready to cash his theories into policy prescriptions, advice to governments.

The ability to stand apart from and grasp the economy as an object is enhanced by the use of statistics. Statistical analyses of population and mortality, wealth and economic activity, began in the second half of the seventeenth century, with William Petty and Gregory King, and became increasingly familiar during the eighteenth. The first census was taken in 1801, and Patrick Colquhoun's *Treatise on the Wealth, Power and Resources of the British Empire* was published in 1814. Such statistical information enabled commentators to talk about society with greater precision and comprehension.

Turning now from general characteristics of political economy to specific doctrines that helped to generate social criticism, the following will deal mainly with Smith, Ricardo, and Malthus's *Essay on the Principle of Population*, which first appeared in 1798.

These three are the most celebrated, but not the only significant economists of the period. For example, James Mill and McCulloch are followers of Ricardo who add their own contributions. As for the general public, few, in all probability, mastered Ricardo's difficult treatise; but the works of Smith and Malthus were at once more accessible, and brilliantly written. Above all, we should remember the work of popularizers – McCulloch's article in the *Encyclopaedia Britannica*, the magazine articles of Harriet Martineau.

It is appropriate to begin with Malthus's theory about the most fundamental economic factor – population. No doctrine has been more suited to generate heated debate about society. The essay is written as a reply to the optimism and reformism of Condorcet and Godwin, and it apparently demonstrates that any hopes for a better future are destined to be extinguished by growing population continually pressing against food resources. More precisely, Godwin and his like are crushed, like nuts in a nutcracker, between the two mathematical ratios. Malthus maintained that population, if unchecked, has the capacity to increase geometrically, doubling itself every twenty-five years, that is, in the ratio of $1:2:4:8:16$. . . . He believed this contention could be supported by evidence, for example, the population statistics of the American colonies, where owing to an abundance of land, population grew without check. What about food resources? In areas like Europe, which lacked an expanding frontier, he suggested that food production could not increase faster than in an arithmetical ratio, that is, in periods of twenty-five years according to the ratio $1:2:3:4:5$. . . . He does not prove this, but offers it as an opinion few will challenge; most will think that a rise in productivity of this order is a good result. Now it was obvious that population in developed countries was not increasing geometrically; furthermore, the slower growth of food output meant that it could not so increase. What was happening? Malthus argued that checks must be operating to curb the power of procreation. He lists these checks under the headings of misery and vice: misery in the form of epidemics, famine, and late marriages; vice in the form of wars and 'vicious customs with respect to women'.

Malthus is quick to draw reactionary conclusions from this elegant theory. The present distribution of property at least means that some are free from want. If property were equalized, soon all would starve. Suppose, he suggests, Godwin's utopia is established: property is equal and poverty eliminated; benevolence and harmony reign. Very quickly all this will be destroyed, for the newly prosperous inhabitants of utopia will take the opportunity to have more children. Desperate conflict for food will ensue, and benevolence will go out of the window. Poverty may be mitigated but can never be cured, and the attempt to cure it, by destroying wealth, will destroy art, learning, and culture. Civilization would descend to barbarism. Ricardo follows Malthus, concluding that the existing poor laws are iniquitous. Relief to the starving encourages breeding and hence greater shortages:

> The clear and direct tendency of the poor laws, is in direct opposition to these obvious principles; it is not, as the legislators benevolently intend, to amend the condition of the poor, but to deteriorate the condition of both poor and rich; instead of making the poor rich, they are calculated to make the rich poor, and whilst the present laws are in force, it is quite in the natural order of things that the fund for the maintenance of the poor should progressively increase, till it has absorbed all the net revenue of the country. (126)

All this is bad news to the kindhearted; it is a standing challenge to construct an alternative theory. Moreover Malthus adds insult to injury, appearing at times to relish the gloomy picture he has painted:

> The power of population is so superior to the power of the earth to produce subsistence for man, that premature death must in some shape or other visit the human race. The vices of mankind are active and able ministers of depopulation. They are the precursors in the great army of destruction; and often finish the work themselves. But should they fail in this war of extermination, sickly seasons, epidemics, pestilence, and plague, advance in terrific array, and sweep off their thousands and ten thousands. Should success still be incomplete, gigantic inevitable famine stalks in the rear, and with one mighty blow levels the population with the food of the world. (118)

Classical economy marks an important stage in the emergence of the theory of class. Smith writes:

> The whole annual produce of the land and labour of every country . . . naturally divides itself . . . into three parts; the rent of land, the wages of labour, and the profits of stock; and constitutes a revenue to three different orders of people; to those who live by rent, to those who live by wages, and to those who live by profit. (I, 230)

The first sentence of Ricardo's book is

> The produce of the earth – all that is derived from its surface by the

united application of labour, machinery, and capital, is divided
among three classes of the community; namely, the proprietor of the
land, the owner of the stock or capital necessary for its cultivation,
and the labourers by whose industry it is cultivated. (49)

So the economists propose that society is divided into three classes
– rentiers, capitalists, and labourers – defined by economic function. To us this seems an old and familiar story, but it would be a
mistake, an anachronism, to regard it as obvious in 1776.[57] Historians have shown that this tripartite economic class division was
by no means generally employed at the end of the eighteenth century.[58] Other terms of social classification were used. Society might
be divided into gentlemen and the rest, or into the people (i.e., the
respectable) and the mob; into the lower and higher ranks, or orders; into higher, middle, and lower classes; into interests (landed,
farming, commercial, manufacturing). These older modes of classification are not without value; some of them recognize that social
distinctions are based upon status and power as well as upon economic function. But the class analysis of the economists has greater
precision and is based upon a theory of society. In fact, Smith employs another classification, which he borrows from the physiocrats. He divides society into the productive and unproductive
classes. In physiocratic theory, the productive classes were those
who worked the land, the farmers and labourers, because they provided the food and raw materials on which all lived. The rest –
landlords, soldiers, manufacturers, traders – were unproductive,
parasitic as it were. Smith does not use the distinction in quite this
way. He regards all producers, both agricultural and manufacturing,
as productive, and also traders. All these contribute to increase the
wealth of the nation. The unproductive ones are the idle rich and
their servants, and also those in the pay of government. Money is
spent productively when it hires productive labourers – that is to
say, when it hires a labourer who produces a commodity that can
be sold at a profit. This kind of labour and this kind of expenditure
is self-perpetuating, self-sustaining; for the initial outlay in wages
is replaced and more than replaced when the commodity is sold.
Hence the employer can continue to employ a productive labourer,
and has not diminished his power so to do. The reverse is true of
unproductive expenditure and unproductive labour. Money is spent
unproductively when it goes on labourers or consumption goods

in such a way that at the end of the day the spender is not left with
a commodity for sale – for example, when he spends money on
servants. The money that a man lays out in this way is not returned
to him – it is gone for good – and hence it does not confer upon
him the capacity to employ labour in the future. In other words,
productive expenditure is that portion of a man's revenue that goes
to replace a capital; unproductive is the portion that is consumed.
Looking at the economy as a whole, if the portion going to capital
increases, employment opportunities will grow; but if the portion
going to consumption increases, employment contracts. Smith believed that private individuals, anxious to maintain their position,
would not squander their revenue-earning capital on consumption.
The greatest threat to the capital stock came from the exactions of
government, for all government spending was unproductive. This
classification of social groups and modes of expenditure into productive and unproductive is not a purely scientific one, but is tainted
with moral considerations, and highly questionable ones at that. It
has dropped out of economic theory; but it is tailor-made for the
social critic.[59] Colquhoun's widely read statistical survey of 1814
employs it as an organizing principle. But the economists' division
of society into landlords, capitalists, and labourers also has great
critical potential; for they use it in constructing theories of the distribution of wealth and have something to say about class conflict.

According to Smith, the wages of labour will be highest in an
expanding economy; for expansion will lead to an increased demand for labour. But when an economy declines, job opportunities
contract; labourers compete for work, and wages fall. Economic
expansion also benefits landlords; in buoyant times, labourers, receiving good wages, can pay more for food and therefore rents can
be raised. So, the prosperity of both workers and landlords is best
served by growth; their interests are 'strictly and inseparably connected with the general interest of the society' (I, 230). But the same
cannot be said of capitalists. If an economy expands, a surplus of
wealth is produced that seeks investment. If there is plenty of money
seeking outlets, interest rates are low. But if an economy is in decline, then the amount of wealth available for investment will be
small, and capitalists will be able to charge high rates of interest.
The interests of other sections of the bourgeoisie do not always

coincide with the general good. Smith tells us that men of commerce
are the shrewdest moneygetters. They spend their time plotting and
planning for profit, and acquire an accurate knowledge of what
will serve them best. They easily outwit labourers, and even the
landed interest, for landlords devote their energies to pursuits other
than getting rich; to Parliament, the bench of magistrates, hunting.
Consequently traders often deceive the landed interest that holds
political power and obtain laws favourable to themselves rather
than society at large. For example, they restrict trade, so there will
be less competition:

> The proposal of any new law or regulation of commerce which comes
> from this order ought always to be listened to with great precaution,
> and ought never to be adopted till after having been long and care-
> fully examined, not only with the most scrupulous, but with the most
> suspicious attention. It comes from an order of men whose interest
> is never exactly the same with that of the public, who have generally
> an interest to deceive and even to oppress the public, and who ac-
> cordingly have, upon many occasions, both deceived and oppressed
> it. (I, 232)
> People of the same trade seldom meet together, even for merriment
> and diversion, but the conversation ends in a conspiracy against the
> public, or in some contrivance to raise prices. (I, 117)

Smith also has acid things to say about master manufacturers in
their dealings with their employees. The wages of labour are fixed
in a contract, a bargain between workers and masters. Both sides
combine (the workers in a union, the masters in an employers'
association) in order to get the best of the bargain. Smith has no
doubt that the masters will always win at this game. Being fewer
in number they combine more effectively; the law does not prohibit
their combinations, but it does those of the workers; the masters,
having greater resources, can last longer in a strike. Smith disap-
proves of the violence and tumult of workers' combinations and
industrial action; but he also writes:

> We rarely hear . . . of the combinations of masters, though frequently
> of those of workmen. But whoever imagines . . . that masters rarely
> combine, is as ignorant of the world as of the subject. Masters are
> always and everywhere in a sort of tacit, but constant and uniform
> combination, not to raise the wages of labour above their actual
> rate. . . . Masters, too, sometimes enter into particular combinations
> to sink the wages of labour. . . . These are always conducted with

the utmost silence and secrecy, till the moment of execution, and when the workmen yield, as they sometimes do, without resistance, though severely felt by them, they are never heard of by other people. (I, 59)

The *Wealth of Nations*, therefore, has a good deal to say about the distribution of wealth between classes (in fact, Smith is confused and unsatisfactory here); it exhibits an awareness of class conflict, and considerable suspicion of the capitalist bourgeoisie. Smith cannot be read as a complacent defender of the status quo, and certainly not as an unqualified bourgeois ideologist.[60] This is illustrated by the curious and contradictory assimilation of physiocratic doctrines into his text. The French physiocrats – e.g., Quesnay, Turgot – reacted against the mercantilist and Colbertist policies of the government that favoured industry and commerce. They argued that the true source of a nation's wealth is agriculture, which should always be given preference. Smith, too, argues that the agricultural sector is most productive, and that if the supply of capital is limited, it should be invested first in agriculture and only afterwards in manufacture and trade (I, 327). Yet in other passages he defends trade against the physiocrats (I, 401).

Ricardo is more favourably disposed towards capitalists than Smith; but his work, even more than Smith's, opens the way to a theory of class conflict. He insists that the distribution of wealth is the central issue of economics:

> [I]n different stages of society, the proportions of the whole produce of the earth which will be allotted to each of these classes, under the names of rent, profit, and wages, will be essentially different. . . . To determine the laws which regulate this distribution is the principal problem in Political Economy. (49)

Ricardo's theory of distribution, contrasting with Smith's, is clear, elegant, and consistent. It is worked out under the aegis of Malthusian population theory. Ricardo argues that, if wages rise, profits must fall, and vice versa; for if the labourers take an increased share of the finished product, there will be that much less left for the capitalist. In this sense, the interests of capital and labour are opposed; class conflict is written into the very heart of the distribution theory. As Malthus had shown, population will tend to rise faster than food output. The demand for food will increase, and food prices will rise. More land will be brought into cultivation. But as the more fertile lands are cultivated first, the extension of cultivation will entail recourse to less fertile land. However, because food prices have risen, the cultivation of such 'marginal' lands will become an economic proposition. If a farmer can gain a living on land of low fertility, then on more fruitful soils, farmers can produce a living, plus a surplus income. This surplus constitutes the rent that goes to the landlord. As population continues to grow, and as less and less fertile land is brought into cultivation, so the surplus income produced on the more fertile lands augments, and rents increase. Meanwhile the level of real wages does not keep pace with food prices, and so the labourers suffer as the landlords prosper. Still, money wages *will* rise to an extent. Wages tend to be around subsistence level and cannot easily be forced below it; so, when the cost of subsistence rises, money wages follow. But, as we noted at the outset, a rise in wages reduces profits. So there is a tendency for rents to rise, profits to fall, and wages to fall in real terms while they rise in money terms. The beneficiary of the process is the landlord, who gains this windfall without earning it. In Ricardo's theory, the landlord appears to be the enemy; but capitalists and labourers also have opposed interests.

Apparently, then, class conflict was not invented by Marx; it is to be found in Adam Smith and even more in Ricardo. But we need to enter some provisos. Both Blaug and O'Brien have argued that the main body of economists were embarrassed by the ideas of class conflict in Ricardo and sought to play them down or contradict them.[61] Berg goes further. She argues that Ricardo's attack is directed against the corn laws, which aimed to keep corn prices and hence rents high and which, if successful, would in Ricardo's opinion have caused a fall in profits and real wages, as explained above. Berg thinks that Ricardo was not arguing against the agricultural interest and rentiers as such, not arguing that conflict between rentiers and the rest of society was inevitable; such conflict would occur only if the corn laws were maintained. If, on the other hand, food prices could be kept down, domestically produced grain being supplemented by imports in times of dearth, then population increase and economic growth could go hand in hand, and landlords, capitalists, and workers could prosper together.[62] The strongest attack on the interpretation of Ricardo as a theorist of class conflict and a precursor of Marx has been mounted by Samuel Hollander.[63] He maintains that if other economists read Ricardo in this way, then

they misread him; but in fact Hollander thinks there is little evidence
for such a misreading. Post-Ricardian political economy did not
need to repudiate a Ricardo who had given comfort to socialism,
for the so-called Ricardian socialists borrowed little from him, or
were hostile to his theories. Berg and Hollander are probably correct
in arguing that Ricardo did not think class conflict desirable or
necessary, and he was not hostile to landlords. But his disciple James
Mill readily turned his theories to the defence of the middle classes
and against aristocracy.

Classical political economy, as every schoolboy knows, has a labour theory of value, and this theory, suitably modified, is the cor-
nerstone of Marxian economics. If we wish for an overview of
the history of the theory, we must start with Locke.[64] Locke does
not, with Marx, see labour as the determinant of value and hence,
indirectly, of price; but he regards labour as the main agent in producing things useful to human life, and as the source of property
right.[65] He says that the earth was originally common property;
private property is created when individuals mix their labour with
the earth. For the product of a man's labour ought to belong to
him. But, one might object, the value of a piece of land is made up
of two components. First, there is the value of the land as it was
originally, in a wild, unimproved condition; in that state it was
common property. Second, there is the value added by labour.
Granted that men are entitled to the fruits of their labour, why
should the added value outweigh the original value, turning the
whole piece of land from common to private property? Locke's
reply is that the added value is vastly greater than the original; a
piece of cultivated land is perhaps worth one hundred times as much
as it was when uncultivated. The greater part of the wealth of the
world is produced by labour. Locke's argument for the right to the
fruits of one's labour will only work if it is possible to identify what
one's labour has produced. He finds no problem here, because of
the way he thinks of labour. For him, the paradigmatic labourer is
the self-employed craftsman who undertakes a whole task, takes
responsibility for it and carries it through to completion.[66] It is
much more difficult to see how his argument is relevant to situations
in which it is impossible to identify the product of the labour of a
particular worker – for example, when a number of workers undertake the productive task together, on a building site or in a

factory – when there is elaborate 'division of labour', as Smith calls it. Even if Locke's argument is relevant to his own day, we may doubt whether it can apply to a modern industrial situation. But Lockean thinking lingers on, as we shall see.

Adam Smith also places great emphasis upon labour. Perhaps the most significant aspect of the *Wealth of Nations* in this regard is the fact that he insists that the wealth of a nation is the annual product of its labour – not the stocks of gold or the value of its land and movables. Locke, Petty, and the physiocrats anticipate him in this. He also attributes the growth of national wealth to the expansion of the division of labour. If workers specialize – one farming, another fishing, another making shoes, another cloth – greater production is possible than when each tries to produce everything he or she needs. Going a stage further, if a productive operation is divided into a number of distinct tasks, each undertaken by a labourer who specializes in that task, productivity will be vastly greater than when one labourer undertakes the whole job. His famous illustration is the manufacture of pins. One man could make 20 per day; 10 men dividing up the task between them make 48,000. Finally we come to the theory of value in Smith. The value of an item is determined by what it costs to produce. Here he draws a distinction between primitive and modern economies. In a primitive economy, the value of an article is determined by the amount of labour required to make it. In a modern economy, labour is not the only factor going into its production. There are three cost factors: the cost of the labour, the cost of hiring the capital (machines, tools, factory, etc.), and the cost of renting the land employed in production. The value of an item is determined by the sum of these components. But although labour is not the sole determinant of value, it is still, Smith maintains, the best measure of value. If I want to know the value of a thing, the most stable and meaningful way of assessing it is in terms of the amount of labour I would need to do in order to make or obtain it. In this sense Smith has a labour theory of value.

Ricardo goes further than Smith. He argues that the value of a commodity is determined by the amount of labour required to make it, in modern as well as in primitive economies. Or at any rate, he begins his chapter 'On Value' by arguing this. Later on, he admits that the value of an item must make some allowance for the length of time a capitalist has his capital tied up in producing it – in other words, like Smith, he is allowing that value is determined by other costs as well as labour costs. Only Marx, of the great economists, is bold enough to maintain that labour and labour alone determines value. But the distance between Ricardo and Marx is not great here; Ricardo thinks that by far the greater part of the value of a commodity is determined by labour, and that we can largely ignore other factors. Classical economy up to Ricardo, therefore, is favourably inclined towards labour; McCulloch writes eulogies of it.[67] This is a ready resource for critics of capitalism.

According to Smith, productivity is proportioned to the division of labour. The greater the degree of specialization, the greater the output. But Smith acknowledges that the division of labour has unfortunate side effects.

> In the progress of the division of labour, the employment of the far greater part of those who live by labour . . . comes to be confined to a few very simple operations. . . . The man whose life is spent in performing a few simple operations, of which the effects are perhaps always the same, or very nearly the same, has no occasion to exert his understanding or to exercise his invention. . . . He naturally loses, therefore, the habit of such exertion, and generally becomes as stupid and ignorant as it is possible for a human creature to become. . . . The uniformity of his stationary life naturally corrupts the courage of his mind, and makes him regard with abhorrence the irregular, uncertain and adventurous life of a soldier. It corrupts even the activity of his body, and renders him incapable of exerting his strength with vigour and perseverance. . . . But in every improved and civilized society this is the state into which the labouring poor . . . must necessarily fall, unless government takes some pains to prevent it. (II, 263–4)

By direct and indirect channels, this feeds into Marx's concept of alienation; Smith himself could have learned it from his teacher Ferguson.[68] It opens the way to a profound critique of industrial society.

The *Wealth of Nations* is Janus-faced. Book I attributes wealth to labour, and its increase to the advance of the division of labour and growing skill: Book II, by contrast, emphasizes the importance of the accumulation of capital to the growth of output. Since Smith wrote, capital has been at the centre of the debate about society. As an account, explanation, and defence of capital, *Wealth of Nations* is radically defective, and its weaknesses linger on, in Ricardo and in the early socialists. Smith distinguishes fixed and circulating capital. Fixed capital is tools, machines, buildings, roads, canals, ships, land: circulating capital is the stock of raw materials used in production, and the funds for the payment of wages. Smith's theory places most emphasis upon circulating capital. When he writes about the accumulation of capital that makes increased production possible, he seems to be mainly thinking of circulating capital. Maybe this was a reasonable attitude in a preindustrial economy; in Adam Smith's Scotland, by far the largest manufacture was the linen trade, carried on on a domestic basis.[69] It may even have been reasonable in early industrial society; later stages of industrialization, however, most notably the development of railways, required considerable fixed capital. Marx did not make Smith's mistake:

> The bourgeoisie, during its rule of scarce one hundred years, has created more massive and more colossal productive forces than have all preceding generations together. Subjection of nature's forces to man, machinery, application of chemistry to industry and agriculture, steam navigation, railways, electric telegraphs, clearing of whole continents for cultivation, canalisation of rivers, whole populations conjured out of the ground – what earlier century had even a presentiment that such productive forces slumbered in the lap of social labour?[70]

In addition, Smith has no satisfactory answer to the question, how does capital accumulation come about? He does praise parsimony, saving – but plainly this is no explanation on its own. An ordinary labourer could never save enough of the fruits of his own labour to build a factory; there must be some additional element in the equation. How do some men become rich enough to be great capitalists? What is the origin of inequality? The only answer to be found in *Wealth of Nations* is *conquest* – in the remote past, invaders and conquerors dispossessed the defeated, establishing the gulf between rich and poor. But this is an explanation of unequal possession of *land*; its relevance is by no means obvious to an industrial or capitalist system. Ricardo gives no better defence of capitalists: capital, in his account, is essentially accumulated labour (67), which sounds very much like selling the pass to the enemy. The economic theories of Smith, Malthus, and Ricardo have an early industrial, even preindustrial flavour; significantly (if we accept the orthodox interpretation of him),[71] Ricardo's abstract model of economic evolution is a *corn* model, concerned with changes in the production and distribution of that particular commodity.

The greatest achievement of classical economy is its explanation of the workings of the economy in terms of the self-regulating mechanism of the market.[72] The classic example is Smith's account of how production of black cloth adjusts itself to demand. If demand suddenly rises (because of a public mourning), then supply will be inadequate; competition among buyers will push up prices. Hence, the profits to be got out of the manufacture of black cloth will rise, and capitalists will rush to invest in the activity. Supply will be increased, competition between buyers will give way to competition between sellers, and the price will fall back to its old level or below. Smith uses this idea of a self-regulating system to explain trends in population, wages, and profits as well as prices; to explain flows of bullion in and out of the country; and to account for changes in the pattern of international trade. Self-regulating mechanisms justify the laissez-faire policies recommended by Smith and his disciples. If statesmen step in and by laws attempt to decide where capital should be invested and what industries set up, at best they will bring no benefit and at worst will reduce production below what it would otherwise be. If capitalists are left free to invest their money as they wish, they soon discover the most profitable and productive outlets:

> Every individual is continually exerting himself to find out the most advantageous employment for whatever capital he can command. It is his own advantage, indeed, and not that of society, which he has in view. But the study of his own advantage naturally, or rather necessarily, leads him to prefer that employment which is most advantageous to the society . . . he is in this, as in many other cases, led by an invisible hand to promote an end which was no part of his intention. (I, 398, 400)

The weight of Smith's fire is directed against mercantilism, the system that seeks to foster domestic industries by excluding foreign imports. To do this will always diminish the wealth of the nation. Free trade is justified by the benefits of division of labour; by extending the market it permits an international division of labour. Each country can then invest its capital in what it does best, thus maximizing productivity:

> By means of glasses, hotbeds, and hot walls, very good grapes can be raised in Scotland, and very good wine too can be made of them

at about thirty times the expense for which at least equally good can be brought from foreign countries. Would it be a reasonable law to prohibit the importation of all foreign wines merely to encourage the making of claret and burgundy in Scotland? (I, 402) Is Smith then an advocate of complete governmental laissez-faire in the realm of economics? Does he believe in a natural and benign economic order? Certainly the *Wealth of Nations* has often been read in this way, from Smith's own day up to the present.[73] The weight of modern scholarship, however, tends to qualify this interpretation.[74] Smith was ready to countenance many measures of government intervention, where projects of public benefit would not be undertaken by private individuals (e.g., building roads) or in order to achieve public goods other than prosperity (e.g., popular education). More fundamentally, it has been argued that Smith thought that self-regulating economic mechanisms would work for the public good only if the state provided an appropriate artificial framework of law and regulation. For example, the top rate of interest might be fixed in order to encourage loans to productive investors rather than to wealthy prodigals. It remains the case, however, that Smith often refers to 'natural' mechanisms; at the very least, there is in the *Wealth of Nations* an incipient tension between 'nature' and 'artifice'.

What kind of thing is a self-regulating economic mechanism in Adam Smith's thought? The well-known 'invisible hand' passage suggests some divine teleology at work, eliciting the greater good from the tangled web of self-interested action. But Smith, in his methodological reflections, repudiates explanations in terms of final causes or purposes; and the mechanisms he describes can all be understood in terms of efficient or antecedent causes. There is no need to invoke God to explain how supply adjusts itself to demand, how capitalists tend to invest their money in activities most conducive to national wealth, and how each country, under a system of free trade, adopts those industries to which it is best suited.[75] Nevertheless, his generally optimistic stance may be a residue of religious attitudes; the good God has assembled a world that will work well.[76] His optimism is illustrated by his faith in progress. He believes there is solid evidence to demonstrate advance in the general wealth of the nation, and in the living standards of the masses. It is true that he does not think economic progress will go on for ever; eventually, all investment opportunities will be exhausted, and the economy will attain a stationary state. But this condition is probably a long way off, and in any case is likely to be reasonably prosperous and happy. A rosy vision? Yes – but it has its less appealing aspect. The unfortunate side effects of the division of labour have already been mentioned. Additionally, the theory of the self-regulating natural order is built upon the premise that each individual largely pursues self-interest; the public good is an unintended consequence:

> But man has almost constant occasion for the help of his brethren, and it is in vain for him to expect it from their benevolence only. He will be more likely to prevail if he can interest their self-love in his favour, and show them that it is for their own advantage to do for him what he requires of them. . . . It is not from the benevolence of the butcher, the brewer, or the baker that we expect our dinner, but from their regard to their own interest. We address ourselves, not to their humanity but to their self-love, and never talk to them of our own necessities but of their advantages. (I, 13)

Benevolent commentators might think that if a free market society fosters such attitudes then it is not altogether perfect.

The benefits of the minimally regulated order become even more questionable in the theories of Malthus and Ricardo. Smithian optimism turns to grim Malthusian pessimism. Malthus's theory of population is yet another application of the idea of a self-regulating market mechanism, which shows how the level of population continually adjusts itself to food supply, growing until starvation levels are reached and then falling back. Ricardo shows how this tragic rhythm may govern the evolution of the economy as a whole. As population grows, food prices rise. Wages follow, but more slowly. As the share of the product taken in wages grows, so the share of profit falls. Eventually, population pushes food prices and the wage share so high, that the level of profits is insufficient to sustain and encourage investment; economic growth ceases and the system changes gear from progress to decline. Only when starvation has brought population down can growth be resumed. As I have already indicated, most economists were deeply embarrassed by the gloominess of Malthusian and Ricardian economics, and the attempt to combat such pessimism was a central concern in economics in the 1820s. Berg has shown that even Ricardo thought that economic decline was not inevitable, or was a long way off, provided that governments did not restrict the importation of cheap food. According to Samuel Hollander, the orthodox reading of Ricardo that has been presented here is mistaken; Ricardo was an optimist.[77] Still, a gloomy reading of Ricardo has always been possible, and enough question marks hung over the alleged benefits of the free market system to provoke discussion of alternatives. Even the optimism of Smith is an optimism of the long run rather than the short. The economic machine is self-regulating in the long term; eventually, production adjusts itself to demand, and population to resources and jobs. In the short term, there may be severe and tragic dislocations as the system rights itself. Malthus and Ricardo recognized this when they observed the catastrophic shifts in trading and employment opportunities caused by such factors as war and the introduction of labour-saving machinery.

This brings me to the last aspect of classical economics that influenced social critics – the problem of monetary policy, and the closely related question as to whether the government should intervene to stimulate the economy, increasing demand and promoting full employment. The issue was raised, starkly and urgently, by the trade cycle – by the phenomenon of recession, when the market was glutted at once with goods that could not be sold and with labourers who might like to buy those goods but were unable to do so because they were unemployed. Would it not be desirable for the government to stimulate the economy, perhaps by putting more paper money into circulation, providing jobs, and mopping up the surpluses? Or should the state regulate the economy, ensuring that overproduction, with its attendant crisis of unemployment, did not occur? The theoretical basis for interventionist policies like these was worked out later than our period, by Sismondi, Marx, and Keynes. Sismondi and Marx explained that gluts resulted from the 'stickiness' of the economy – the miscalculations of capitalists investing in particular products for which demand was insufficient and the subsequent difficulty of moving resources (capital and labour) into more promising productive activities. Keynes showed that capital, and hence labour, might be underemployed because entrepreneurs, lacking confidence in the state of the market, might exhibit 'liquidity preference' – might hold on to cash balances rather than investing them. Consequently a priming of the pump by government might be required to release the flow of investment.

In the first half of the nineteenth century there was a major debate about underconsumption, government intervention, and monetary policy. One side, following Ricardo, argued that the economy should be left to work its own way out of recession and that the government should pursue a 'sound money' policy by returning to the gold standard. On the other side, underconsumptionists argued that there was a danger that demand would fall short of supply, even in the long term, and representatives of the 'banking school' called for the issue of paper money to stimulate the economy out of recession. The underconsumptionists, with the exception of Malthus, were lightweights, and even he did not really anticipate Keynes. Malthus argued that because the bulk of workers would be at subsistence level and unable to buy refined manufactures, there would be a chronic shortage of demand unless there was a rich class of rentiers, able and willing to buy luxuries, thus mopping up the surplus. Malthus's argument is intended to defend the wealth of the landed class. The orthodox answer to Malthusian underconsumption was Say's law, or (as James Mill called it) the 'law of the markets'. According to Say's law, demand cannot chronically fall short of supply, for a supply is at the same time a demand. Any commodity brought to market increases the supply; but since its vendor wishes to exchange it (through the medium of money) for some other commodity, it also adds to the demand. This argument has greatest plausibility from a long-term point of view; in the short term, there might be insufficient demand for certain commodities (e.g., for bicycles, if people stopped riding them). If several commodities happened to be in excess supply simultaneously, this might cause a general collapse of confidence and recession. All that Say's law does is to claim that general, long-term gluts are impossible. But from this it does not follow that in the long run capital will be fully employed; because of 'liquidity preference' and 'stickiness', capital may be *chronically* underemployed. Even if Say's law were right, it would not mean that there would necessarily be full employment; all it would mean is that supply would create its own demand. But this might be at a level of economic activity insufficient to provide work for all.

But were the banking school and the inflationists correct in recommending the issue of credit and paper money to stimulate the economy and promote full employment? In the first place, with the exception of the financial collapse at the end of the Napoleonic Wars and the deflationary attempts to return to gold, it does not appear that there *was* a shortage of money in our period; the banks were not tightly regulated, and if credit was wanted, they found it.[78] But further, it is debatable whether inflationist policies would have cured underemployment and promoted prosperity at the beginning of the nineteenth century. For there was in this period a recurring problem of dearth; extra money in working-class pockets might simply have gone into buying food, thus pushing up food prices. It would not necessarily have created demand for manufactured goods, leading to new employment in industry. Finally, it has been argued[79] that there was unemployment in this period, not because capitalists were holding on to cash balances and investing less than they might. The problem was a deeper one, more akin to that of Third World countries today; it was a problem of undercapitalization, of a radically insufficient stock of productive capital in relation to the size of the population, a problem that could not be rectified in the short term by mere pump-priming.

4. Moral discourse
Moral discourse is an obvious and ancient way of creating a distance between observer and observed actuality. It is critical in its very essence, for it rests upon the distinction between what is and what ought to be. But this critique need not be social critique. Moral criticism may be directed solely at the failings of individuals. Indeed, moral conscience can be conceived as an internalization of those rules of conduct that secure the stable continuance of society as it is.[80] In the period with which we are concerned, however, moral principles are turned against the perceived failings of society; it is therefore necessary to identify the moral ideas that lent themselves to such employment. There is a large and rich eighteenth-century literature on moral philosophy, but we can ignore much of it. A major topic of debate was the psychology and logic of moral judgment; what kind of utterance is a moral judgment, how do we come to make it, and how can we 'prove' it? This fascinating debate is not relevant to our study of social criticism: our concern must rather be with substantive moral principles and ideals. The main part of this section will be organized around a discussion of three moral principles that were important at the time and that have become

established topics in the academic discussion of morality. I shall consider them in order of seniority: first, the principle of justice; second, natural rights; and third, the principle of utility. These three are alike, first in that they are readily applicable to the judgment of political and social arrangements, and second in that they are potentially critical doctrines. All three have been developed into sophisticated philosophical theories. But the theories, and the principles themselves, are explorations and formalizations of more basic and enduring moral ideas – of impartiality, respect, desert, happiness, and harm, of the components of individual well-being such as individuality and fulfilment. I shall give attention to these basic elements as well as to more systematic theories.

Justice is a moral concept of great antiquity. Modern philosophical analysis has identified several different kinds or aspects of justice,[81] but this study can content itself with the consideration of two only: procedural or formal justice, equity; and desert-based justice. The principle of formal justice or equity is summed up in the maxim, 'treat like cases alike'. The original forum for the exercise of this principle is the court of law; but its application can readily be extended to other contexts, including those where the distribution of good things – food, wealth, power – is at issue. Justice, in this sense, is typically done to individuals; when we say that a person has performed a just or unjust act, we think not of his or her treatment of society in general, but of what has been done to particular individuals. The person who is treated unjustly feels angry, but it is anger of a special kind, and its peculiar character reveals much about the nature of procedural justice. The victim is angry because injustice hurts; but also the sense of pain is moralized, made righteous and impartial, because injustice is offensive not only to the sufferer but also to truth and reason.[82] For example, to punish an innocent is, as well as harming him, to tell a lie about him, to say that he is guilty when in fact he is innocent; the *truth* has been harmed. To take another example, to discriminate – to say that blacks or women will not be considered for jobs as, say, bus drivers – is to behave arbitrarily, in a way offensive to reason; there is no good reason for such differential treatment. Or alternatively, it is to tell a lie – to say that there is a significant and relevant difference between white males, on the one hand, and blacks or women on the other, when in fact none exists. Justice, then, means rational, truthful dealing with persons; honest, impartial, fair, nonarbitrary conduct. This has clear implications for the discussion of society. For a person to receive more wealth or power than others, because of accident of birth or because he or she is favoured by prince or minister as a sleeping partner, is offensive to reason. If, in addition, such privilege is defended on the grounds that the rich and wealthy are superior persons, this may be regarded as an affront to truth – especially if, as was increasingly the case in the eighteenth century, the prevailing theory of human nature maintains that all are born alike. If, at the same time, hard-working and virtuous labourers and peasants die of poverty, the injustice will seem flagrant. The connection between procedural justice and socialism is very strong; much socialism has embodied the belief that the distribution of society's goods should not be arbitrary and accidental, but rather based on reason. It demands that society's arrangements should be planned and moralized.

It has been argued that the principle of procedural justice, when applied to society, is not in itself egalitarian.[83] For, it is said, the maxim 'treat like cases alike' would require us to treat people equally only insofar as they are equal. If people or 'cases' are different, then different treatment may be appropriate. The question is, what counts as a relevant difference; and the principle of procedural justice gives no guidance on this. When allocating wealth or power, why not differentiate according to ancestry, skin colour, or occupation? We may not like the apartheid laws of South Africa; but surely it is possible for us to distinguish between equitable and inequitable applications of those laws. If a law excluding blacks from certain jobs is enforced equally against all blacks, then according to this interpretation, procedural justice has been respected. The principle of equity would be an egalitarian principle only if people were alike in every respect; in fact they are infinitely differentiated, by birth and social situation. These arguments are not negligible;[84] but if we look at the mental furniture of our chosen period, we find a number of ideas that enabled, even encouraged, people to interpret the principle of formal justice in an egalitarian way.[85] I have already referred to some of these. First, associationist psychology maintains that virtually all individuals are essentially equal at birth; if the social and political environment subsequently makes them unequal in knowledge and virtue, then that environment itself may be judged unjust. Second, Christian doctrine asserts the equal worth of every human soul in the sight of God. Third, an influential tradition in the political thought of the age begins its argument by abstracting individuals from society, where they are different and unequal, and imagining them starting out all on a level, all alike and equal, all simply human beings. This is the theory of the social contract made in the state of nature, a theory classically set forth by Hobbes, Locke, and Rousseau, a theory that is assumed as the basis of the American Declaration of Independence and the French Declaration of the Rights of Men and Citizens. In all these ways, there is a strong tendency in late eighteenth-century thought to regard inequalities as less than skin deep:[86] artificial, not natural, accidental, not essential; and therefore probably unjust.

Desert-based justice is the doctrine that people should be rewarded or punished according to their deserts. What counts as being deserving is the obvious problem here, but we need not explore it; for our purposes, it will be sufficient to refer to those ways in which justice as desert showed socially critical potential in our period. Coupled to some of the ideas I have discussed under the heading of the labour theory of value, desert-based justice readily offers a challenge to landlords and capitalists. If the wealth of the world is produced by labour, if labour is the source of value, if capital is stored-up labour, then the great wealth enjoyed by landlords and capitalists looks difficult to defend from the standpoint of justice. From a religious context comes another possible challenge to the justice of the existing order. Christianity has always been concerned with the worthiness of people – do they deserve to be saved or damned? English puritanism, with its stern moralism and condemnation of fleshly indulgence, presents the issue sharply. What are we to think of the justice of a nation that loads sinners, profligates, and luxurious livers with wealth, honour, and power, while excluding the saints from public life?[87]

Is the principle of justice that recommends that we reward the deserving an egalitarian principle? It might be argued that it is not; that it looks on life as a race, in which the fastest runners take the prizes. It is the principle of meritocracy, of equality of opportunity rather than equality.[88] But as we found with the principle of formal justice, when we set justice as desert in the intellectual context of the time, we find that it can lend itself to egalitarian arguments.

For the principle of desert is not only, or chiefly, used in competitive situations. Take, for example, the religious context just mentioned. When we ask whether men and women are deserving in the sight of God, we do not rank them in order from first to last; we divide them into the saved and the damned. And in a court of law, it is not a question of deciding whether the accused has won the race of wickedness, whether he has been the worst burglar or murderer. Whether or not he deserves punishment depends on whether he is innocent or guilty. Similarly, therefore, when the issue is the distribution of wealth, the principle of desert may not be applied to recommend a system of unequal rewards. The question may rather be framed like this: 'Has this landlord, or capitalist, laboured? If not, he does not deserve riches. Has this labourer earned his bread with the sweat of his brow? If so, he does not deserve such scanty and irregular fare.' In an economy where there is much division of labour, where many workers cooperate in the process of production and where therefore it is impossible to assess what any one individual has contributed to the final product, it is arguably easier to apply the principle of justice as desert in this way than in an inegalitarian, competitive way.

The natural rights tradition in moral discourse is easier to discuss than justice, for we are blessed with excellent studies, both analytical and historical. The concept of natural rights is rich and ambiguous, and historical work has revealed how different meanings emerged in the course of the evolution of the concept.[89] Our first distinction is between 'objective' and 'subjective' conceptions of right. The objective conception is when we say 'this is right', the subjective appears in 'I have a right'. Only the subjective corresponds to our modern conception of *a* right. The objective is older; when does the subjective emerge? The idea that individuals have rights probably emerged in the twelfth century. *Individuals* have rights; just as justice is typically done to individuals, so it is individuals who have rights. The second distinction to note is between active and passive interpretations of rights. A passive right is the correlative of a duty; it is a duty seen from the receiving end. If I have a duty to honour my father and mother, then they have a right to be honoured by me. In this sense, the term 'right' is redundant; the moral relationships referred to here could be described in the language of duties without loss. There are still those who argue for the complete redundancy of 'rights', but I think this is a mistake, a mistake that can only be made if one ignores important elements in the concept of rights. This brings us to the active rights interpretation. An active right is a property that individuals possess. Rights conceived in this way cannot be translated without loss into duties; they imply something more than being on the receiving end of a duty. Rights in this sense are claims *that we are entitled to assert*; they are 'especially sturdy objects to "stand upon",. a most useful sort of moral furniture'.[90] If I say that I have a right not to be imprisoned arbitrarily, but to be tried by due process of law, I am not merely saying that the law enforcement agencies have a duty to try me properly; I am in addition saying that I am entitled to *demand* or *require* a fair trial, that the law is bound to respect me in this way, and recognize me as 'a person with standing to protect his basic needs'. To have a right to something is quite different from deserving to get something by the charitable act of another. I cannot require a charitable stranger to buy me a drink – whether he does so is entirely up to him – but I can require that the state pay me a pension, because that is my right: 'There is something great and virile in the idea of right which removes from any request its suppliant character, and places the one who claims it on the same level as the one who grants it'.[91]

A third distinction, which at first sounds like the previous one but in fact is quite different, is the distinction between rights of action, or liberty rights, and rights of recipience. Liberty rights are those such as the right of free speech and worship; the right to vote; the right to associate in clubs, unions, and parties; the right to own property; the right to choose one's partner, job, and place of residence; the right to travel freely. Liberty rights are major components of individual freedom. The possessor of a liberty right can be thought of as a mini-sovereign, with authority to govern his or her own conduct in certain areas. The demand for such rights grows out of the sense that one is a person, capable of conceiving and implementing purposes, not merely a thing, to be used by others:

> . . . for every individual in nature is given an individual propriety by nature, not to be invaded or usurped by any . . . for everyone as he is himself hath a self propriety – else could he not be himself – and on this no second may presume without consent; and by natural birth all men are equal, and like born to like propriety and freedom, every man by natural instinct aiming at his own safety and weal.[92]

Rights of recipience are rights to receive certain goods – food, shelter, health care, education. They are parts and conditions of the rights to life and the pursuit of happiness. They derive from the belief that all human lives are valuable and should be respected. There is a potential conflict between liberty rights and the right of recipience, a conflict of the utmost importance to this study of social criticism.[93] The conflict arises from the liberty right of property. If property right is absolute, then may this not endanger the right to subsistence of the propertyless? Medieval natural law insisted that the poor be not allowed to starve. Aquinas in the thirteenth century, for instance, thought that in times of dearth goods necessary to subsistence became common property; that is to say, private property was not absolute. In the seventeenth century, this issue was taken up, in the language of rights, by Grotius, Pufendorf, and Locke. They inherited a way of talking about property, which began with the postulate that the earth was originally common property, held and enjoyed jointly by the whole of humanity. How then did this original 'positive community' give way to private property right, and how could private right be squared with the universal right to subsistence? Grotius and Pufendorf, and probably Locke,[94] significantly modified the theory they had inherited by insisting that the earth was originally in common, not as a 'positive community' – not held as a joint property – but as a 'negative community' – that is to say, it belonged to no one, but could be used by all. Grotius and Pufendorf thought that private property, essential to the order and prosperity of society, originated in consent. Grotius conceded that the necessitous had a right to help themselves to the property of the rich, but only in exceptionally dire circumstances. Pufendorf weakened the rights of the poor more decisively. He interpreted property right as an active right, but the right of recipience as a mere passive right. That is to say, the rich had a duty to relieve the starving, and the starving had a claim on the rich. But the property of the rich was at their disposal, they were entitled to bestow or withhold; the poor had no right to take. Still, in Pufendorf's theory, private property originated in consent, and this was a weakness from the point of view of defenders of property. If consent could be given, perhaps it could be withdrawn. Locke showed how property right originated, through the mixing of labour, without consent.[95] Locke's theory does acknowledge the rights of the needy.

He begins his account of property by asserting the right to receive subsistence, and he sets limits on what an individual may accumulate as a private holding. These limitations are designed to protect the universal right of subsistence; but no sooner does Locke assert them than he shows how they may be overcome, and in practice he sets no limit on accumulation. The grounding of property right in labour would seem to imply an egalitarian society of property-holding peasants and artisans; but Locke defends the right of inheritance and thereby the possibility of cross-generational accumulation. Even more significantly, he assumes without discussion the right to buy, to hire labour and hence to labour by proxy, as it were; a man can thus acquire property in the turfs that his servant has cut, for example. Having opened the door to inequality, even extreme inequality, how does Locke solve the problem of the right to subsistence? He argues that private appropriation makes for more efficient cultivation, and hence increases the stock of subsistence goods. Property and inequality are not in conflict with, but consonant with, the right to life. This solution was taken up and developed further by Adam Smith. The achievement of seventeenth-century natural jurisprudence, therefore, was to provide a more secure defence of private property. But embedded within that defence lay the possibilities of a radical critique of established property. In its very structure, the doctrine of rights has immense critical potential, for it can be used to mount a moral condemnation of any society that denies liberties and the satisfaction of basic needs. The critical aspect is encapsulated in the idea of *natural* rights; to appeal to rights of nature is to appeal to a moral order that transcends particular social and political arrangements. The language of natural rights continued to be important throughout the eighteenth century. Locke's arguments were repeated and developed by Priestley, Price, and Paine,[96] by American and French revolutionaries, by conservatives such as Blackstone in his *Commentaries on the Laws of England*. Natural jurisprudence was taught in the Scottish universities. At the beginning of the eighteenth century, Gershom Carmichael taught the theories of Grotius, Locke, and especially Pufendorf; Francis Hutcheson, Adam Smith's teacher, continued the tradition.

I have said that justice is typically done to individuals; it is in this sense an individualistic moral idea. In fact, there is another

conception of justice that is not individualistic at all. This organic
conception of justice is concerned with the just arrangement of the
community, in order to achieve efficiency and harmony; its aim is
the balance and 'health' of the whole, and it regards the interests
of individuals as subordinate to the public good. The conception
of justice in Plato's *Republic* is of this kind. The Chinese term for
'unjust' translates as 'against public harmony'. Rights, on the other
hand, are rights *of individuals*; or if an attempt is made to extend
their attribution to particular groups, then these groups assert their
rights against the community as a whole.[97] Marxists have argued
that individualistic conceptions of justice and rights are 'bourgeois
ideology'; they regulate the dealings between individuals who have
conflicting interests, they are required by competitive market society. Socialist societies, by contrast, would not need these moral
languages; for under socialism, rational administration would secure the common good. Social conflict would cease; fraternity and
love would replace competition and hostility. Pre-Marxian socialists, if they base their case upon an appeal to rights or justice, are
trapped in bourgeois concepts, and this must weaken their
arguments.[98]

   This Marxist dismissal is unconvincing. Individualist conceptions
of justice and rights are older than market society. And to suppose
that in socialist societies there would be no conflicts – that individuals would never need to demand justice or the recognition of
their rights – is surely naive. Only in a simple, traditional society,
where all think alike and where there is no rational, critical thought,
could such solidarity be possible. In a complex modern society, with
a plurality of points of view and ideals, some disagreement and
conflict is inevitable. If utopia is an ideal society beyond the bounds
of possibility, then in this respect Marxism is utopian. Not only
the possibility, but also the desirability of a society without individualistic justice and rights is questionable. It is good to be treated
with love and care, but they can be stifling and crippling unless
associated with respect.[99] Recognizing an individual's rights is according respect to that individual. It is more dignified to demand
justice and one's rights, than to receive charity. Insofar as social
criticism in our period is based on these individualizing conceptions,
this should be regarded as a strength, not a weakness.

   Utilitarianism, by contrast with rights and justice, is concerned with the good of the whole – the 'greatest happiness'.[100] What matters is not any particular individual, but the sum total, the aggregate of happiness; individuals can and should be sacrificed if the happiness of the whole body is greater than it would be without such sacrifice. This aggregative characteristic of utilitarianism brings it into conflict with justice and rights.[101] Utilitarianism is a consequentialist ethics. Actions, institutions, and social arrangements are to be judged solely with reference to their consequences. If on balance they produce good consequences, or the best possible consequences under the circumstances, then they are right. What count as good consequences, what as bad? According to eighteenth-century British utilitarianism, happiness is alone good or desirable in itself, unhappiness is alone evil in itself. By making happiness the test of the goodness of states of affairs, utilitarianism is a secular doctrine. In its Benthamite form, it is a doctrine with scientific pretensions. Bentham aspires to take all doubt and imprecision out of moral judgments, making them an affair of objective calculation.[102] Totals of pleasure and pain (Bentham prefers these terms to happiness and unhappiness) are to be added and compared; if the pleasure total outweighs the pain, then we have a good state of affairs. Sometimes, like Hutcheson, he asserts that an action is right if it promotes the greatest happiness of the *greatest number*. In other words, we can only judge a state of affairs good if more people are happy than unhappy. Utilitarianism is, as it were, democratic or egalitarian in this formulation;[103] the majority may never be sacrificed for the sake of the greater happiness of the few. Utilitarian moral theory is an eighteenth-century creation, the work largely of British thinkers – Hutcheson, Hume, Priestley, Paley, and Bentham – with important continental inputs, for example, from Beccaria, Helvétius. Some of its component ideas are much older in moral thinking – the idea that we judge actions by their consequences, the idea that pleasure is good, pain bad. What is new is the pulling together of a number of ideas – aggregation, consequentialism, happiness, calculation, and a measure of egalitarianism – into a systematic theory that claims to supersede all other moral theories or to be the core of good sense at their heart.

Bentham's work reveals the great critical potential of the theory. He uses the principle of utility to cut swathes through English law, showing that many of its prohibitions and punishments are irrational and barbaric in that they do not promote the greatest happiness. Utilitarianism has no respect for the age or pedigree of a law or institution; if it does not on balance produce happiness, then it should be consigned to oblivion. The resolute consequentialism of the doctrine is the essence of its critical power. We may feel reverence for monarchy and aristocracy because they are institutions of great antiquity and splendour; but this is irrelevant in judging them. All that counts is, do they produce good consequences? Bentham fearlessly applies his principle to property; should wealth be redistributed so as to make it more equal? In an ideal situation, he thinks, property would be nearly equal.[104] For there is a law of diminishing returns from the acquisition of extra portions of wealth. An additional pound brings more happiness to a poor man than to a rich one. But Bentham argues there is little the legislator can rightly do to promote equality. For security is even more valuable. Only if they feel their property secure will individuals work hard and produce wealth. The threat of forcible redistribution would dry up the springs of wealth creation. Therefore the most Bentham is prepared to contemplate is some amendment to the laws of inheritance – for example, the abolition of primogeniture so that great estates will be shared among children. He hopes that such measures will, over time, bring greater equality.[105]

5. Political thought

The doctrine of natural rights is of enduring importance in eighteenth-century political thought.[106] Rights were considered in the previous section; here we need to look further at their application to political questions in our period. Locke casts a long shadow over eighteenth-century discussions. In politics, Locke, though he asserts the equal natural rights of all, is no democrat. He draws back from the radical, egalitarian possibilities of his own principles. Other Whiggish thinkers such as Sydney and Tyrell followed him in this and under the Hanoverians Whig political thought tended to become even more conservative.[107] But after the middle of the eighteenth century, a growing number of thinkers, mostly outside the circle of power, resumed Lockean arguments and began to take them to more radical conclusions. By the mid 1770s, reformers like Major Cartwright were demanding a democratic franchise. Dissenters (from old dissent rather than new, Methodism, which tended

to Toryism) like Priestley and Price were important in the radical-
ization of the natural rights tradition. The culmination of the process is Tom Paine's influential book, *Rights of Man*. Paine defends
the main liberty rights – to associate, speak freely, vote, and so on
– and also, like Locke, insists on the right to receive subsistence.
In the second part of his book, he proposes a set of welfare measures
– free education, pensions, family allowances, unemployment benefits – in order to protect the right to life. These are to be paid for
by a progressive income tax. But Paine's proposals are not intended
to subvert private property, to introduce equality or to change in
any way the employer–employee relationship. He detests aristocracy, but is prepared to contemplate nothing against it beyond the
abolition of primogeniture.

Utilitarianism, in the hands of the 'philosophic radicals', also led
to radical and democratic conclusions. The central statement is
James Mill's *Essay on Government*, which first appeared in
1821.[108] Mill combines the utilitarian principle in its egalitarian
form – that we must promote the greatest happiness *of the greatest
number* – with a Hobbesian psychology, which proposes that most
individuals, most of the time, will pursue self-interest. Therefore if
political power is entrusted to a minority – say, an aristocracy –
that group will rule in its own interest, to the detriment of the rest.
If the interests of all are to be secured, then all must have some
hold upon political power; representative democracy is the best way
of obtaining this.[109]

There has been a tendency in recent years to play down the importance of Locke and the natural rights tradition in British political
thought of the eighteenth century and to draw attention to other
ways of discoursing about politics. The diminution of Locke and
natural rights is mistaken, but the other traditions are undoubtedly
influential. One of them is the appeal, not to natural but to traditional rights – the ancient British liberties embodied in the constitution, liberties that have been realities at certain times but sup-
pressed by tyrannical governments in others.[110] On this view,
British political history has been a dialectic of liberty and tyranny,
with sharp breaks. A major version of it is the myth of 'the Norman
yoke'[111] – the belief that Britain was free, perhaps democratic and
egalitarian, in the Anglo-Saxon period and that liberty was sup-
pressed by the Normans. Magna Carta was a limited recovery of

lost freedoms; the Tudors and Stuarts brought a return to despotism; liberty was reasserted in the revolutionary period 1640–60 and at the Glorious Revolution of 1688. Since then, the power of the crown and its ministers has grown overmighty. The myth of 'the Norman yoke', according to Christopher Hill, is a rudimentary class theory of politics, having a continuous history from early in the Middle Ages themselves. In the eighteenth century, widely read statements are to be found in Mrs. Macaulay's *History of England*, which appeared from 1763, and in the anonymous *Essay on the English Constitution* of 1771. Major Cartwright based his case for parliamentary reform upon it. The appeal to a traditional constitution could be used by conservatives as well as radicals. In the seventeenth century, conservatives could argue that all that was good in British institutions had its origin in the violence of the Norman conquest. Tories like Brady maintained that Saxon times were times of tyranny and oppression. In the eighteenth century, Whigs were increasingly inclined to argue that liberty was attained at the Glorious Revolution of 1688 and had not existed earlier; there was no need to go back further. This was Hume's opinion. Burke denied that liberty had been successively lost and reasserted; the British constitution, and the liberties it embodied, had exhibited an unbroken continuous evolution. He denied that the events of 1688 had constituted a revolution, a judgment shared by Tories and by many Whigs in the first few decades after 1688. But behind the dissensions of conservatives and radicals lies a widespread structural agreement, a shared belief that the present order is to be validated or invalidated by reference to the past. Priestley and Price, appealing to abstract, ahistorical rights after the manner of Locke, begin to break with this traditionalism. Paine and his followers (e.g., the Norwich reformers) repudiated the myth of the ancient constitution and preferred to appeal to reason and natural rights. But even if Paine and his followers were sceptical about Alfred and Anglo-Saxon liberties, extinguished by Norman despotism, they could at least take the notion that the present order of power and wealth had its origin, at some point, in conquest, theft, and expropriation:

> The English Government is one of those which arose out of a conquest, and not out of society, and consequently it arose over the people; and though it has been much modified from the opportunity

of circumstances since the time of William the Conqueror, the country has never yet regenerated itself, and is therefore without a constitution.[112]

Another pervasive mode of conceptualizing politics is the classical republican tradition, which is explored and summed up in J. G. A. Pocock's *The Machiavellian Moment*.[113] The genealogy of this tradition begins with Polybius in the second century B.C. In the modern period, Machiavelli gives a classic restatement of Polybian political thinking. In Britain, the key figures are Harrington (a 'neo-Machiavellian') and Shaftesbury (a 'neo-Harringtonian'). Polybius's ideal is the balanced polity; but balance is continually threatened with corruption and decay. In Machiavelli, the threat to balance is *fortuna*; fortune must be resisted by *virtus*, by masculine and military qualities, by strenuous effort and citizen militias. The classical republican tradition, which admires Sparta and the Roman republic, is a political theory of active participation in the polis, as opposed to philosophies and attitudes that seek fulfillment in Christian contemplation, or private life, or the extrapolitical pursuit of gain. Harrington adopts the language of Machiavelli and adapts it to meet British needs. Balance can be preserved only if the landed freemen are strong and independent of the crown. If they are weakened or subordinated, the state degenerates into tyranny, corruption, and weakness. Shaftesbury's neo-Harringtonianism has a more aristocratic emphasis; it is not the small freeholders, but the landed aristocrats who are the defenders of virtue and independence. During the eighteenth century, a significant transformation occurs; the role of *fortuna* in causing imbalance and corruption comes to be occupied by credit and commerce. There had always been a germ of this in the language of the myth; luxury had always been regarded as a cause of enfeeblement and dependence. When citizens pursued wealth rather than the good of the polis, balance could not long be maintained. The classical republican language marries readily with the homegrown court–country contrast. Increasingly in the eighteenth century the problem seems to be how to control an extravagant, corrupt, warmongering executive, strengthened by its connections with the new monied interest – joint stock companies, the holders of the burgeoning national debt – and by its large standing army. In classical language, the court (and London) is the seat of luxury and decadence; it corrupts the industry, simplicity, honesty, and patriotism that can only be found in the country. This is a common literary theme, in Swift, Pope, Gay, Fielding, Thomson, and Goldsmith.

The classical republican ideal undergoes important modifications at the hands of representatives of the 'Scottish enlightenment'.[114] Ferguson is, for the most part, in the neo-Machiavellian mainstream. The fact that he is sometimes called the 'Scottish Rousseau' reminds us that both he and Rousseau derive their preference for simplicity and military virtues to luxury and sophistication from this tradition.[115] Hume and Adam Smith, however, are critics of it, defending commercial society. They follow Montesquieu in thinking that

> Spartan, Roman or Gothic virtue . . . was inhumanly harsh, and that it was only with the spread of commerce and the arts that humanity became socialized into the capacity for trust, friendship and Christian love.
>
> [A] society with no wealth but its land – Gothic England, contemporary Poland, or the Scottish Highlands – would lack both liberty (the tenants being subject to their lords) and culture.[116]

They favour civil liberty rather than political – the freedom of the subject to engage in private concerns, rather than the ability of the citizen to participate in political affairs. Civil liberty, they believe, is better secured in modern monarchies such as that of France than in classical republics. In spite of this reappraisal, even Smith does not completely emancipate himself from classical republican language and attitudes. He is suspicious of luxury, conspicuous consumption, and, as we have seen, distrusts the commercial classes. He recognizes that economic advance, through the division of labour, brings losses as well as gains, undermining the vigour and intelligence of the labouring classes, unfitting them for war.

Classical republicanism was almost always socially inegalitarian. The classical republics of Sparta and Rome were based upon slavery, and in the early eighteenth century their Scottish admirer Andrew Fletcher of Saltoun advocated a system of domestic servitude.[117] The repudiation of the ideal by Hume and Smith can be interpreted as a defence of the poor; their well-being is more important than civic virtue. Nevertheless, the ideal is a rich resource of concepts and themes for political and social criticism. It is fundamentally opposed to uncontrolled, arbitrary power. In its Harringtonian version especially, it is antiaristocratic in its rejection of patronage and dependence and idealization of the small freeholder. In the eighteenth century it uses the concepts of corruption and decadence to criticize commercial society, and is usually deployed against the Whig establishment.[118] Like Marxism, it refuses to draw a sharp line between society and politics, seeing them rather as interdependent. It discusses the moral quality of societies and their manners.

Mention of Harrington reminds us that there was a utopian strand in British political thought. Utopianism is of great antiquity in western culture. As the enduring appeal of classical republicanism reminds us, educated people in eighteenth-century Britain read deeply in the Latin classics, which were the basis of the school and university curriculum. In Vergil, Ovid, Lucian, and Plutarch, and also in Greek classics such as Homer, they read about the lost Golden Age.[119] Modern utopias – those of More, Bacon, Harrington, Swift – were well known. Utopia is always contrasted with the here and now, to the detriment of the latter; the Age of Gold is a reproach to the Age of Iron. But this is not always a criticism of *society*; utopianism can be a satire on human nature, its vices and weaknesses. For most of its history, the utopian tradition has not been constructive and practical; there has been no sense that its ideal societies could and should be brought about. Utopia, usually, is not located in the future, near or remote; utopia is no place, out of time.[120] At the end of the eighteenth century and the beginning of the nineteenth, however, all this changes; utopias – those of Spence, Owen, Cabet, Fourier, Saint-Simon, Weitling – become blueprints for a better world. Which brings us back to the problem posed in the introduction: what makes it possible to conceive of and to propose the radical transformation of society?

To what extent does eighteenth-century political thought conceive of and advocate 'big government' – an active, interventionist state, vigourously promoting a good society? Continental 'enlightened despotism' is moving this way, but what about Britain, where such foreign ways are feared? The importance of the language of rights has already been noted, and rights of recipience – to food, education, care in sickness and old age – might require an increase in government activity. This conclusion is not drawn from the language of rights until the second part of Paine's *Rights of Man*, which proposes an embryo 'welfare state'.[121] Outside the natural rights tradition, the crucial figure is Bentham.[122] The principle of utility will favour big government if that is conducive to the greatest happiness, and by the end of his life in his *Constitutional Code*, Bentham envisages, for the future if not for the present, an extensive bureaucratic state. His final doctrine thus anticipates late nineteenth-century state collectivism. But in late eighteenth-century and early nineteenth-century political discourse, there are powerful forces pulling the other way, and even Bentham's thought is subject to some of these contradictory pulls. The classical republican tradition, for instance, may demand participation in politics, for evil flourishes when good men keep silent; but as the tradition is interpreted in Britain, political participation is aimed at achieving negative goals. A man should not become embroiled in politics in order to do something positive, to create something new; he enters the arena to arrest corruption, stopping others – the ministers – from doing too much. Bentham is deeply suspicious of such corrupt influence. The talismanic word of radical eighteenth-century political discourse is liberty; eternal vigilance is required to protect liberty against tyranny. The doctrine of natural rights reinforces this emphasis. This is especially so because for most of the eighteenth century liberty rights are asserted rather than rights of recipience. The negative thrust of eighteenth-century political thought is buttressed by the laissez-faire doctrines of classical economy. As has been shown in an earlier section, Adam Smith was no defender of complete laissez-faire, even in the purely economic sphere; but he was widely interpreted in that sense, and his influence swayed Bentham for a time against state activity. The myth of 'the Norman yoke' and the classical republican tradition do not encourage a vision of politics as a means to achieve improvements, social reforms; their aim is simply to restore the polity to its pristine condition, or to balance.

So there are many influences working for a limited conception of government activity. Furthermore, the prevailing idea of *politics* is a restricted and inadequate one. There is in Britain at this time no Rousseauist conception of politics as a process in which the will of the people is formulated and implemented. There is no view of politics as a creative, innovative activity. There are only the beginnings of a conception of politics as a continuous process of bargaining, conciliation, and compromise, in which people and groups with rival interests and ideals settle their differences.[123] The naive and oversimple antithesis of private interest versus public good precludes this conception. If only the system can be made to work to secure the public good – by the recovery of Anglo-Saxon liberties or by the restoration of the balance of the constitution – if only private interests can be checked by appropriate constitutional machinery, then all will be well; the purpose of politics will be achieved. Thereafter, politicians could pack up and go home, were it not for the continual tendency of arbitrary power and private interests to reassert themselves. This defensive and negative way of thinking ignores the possibility that there may not be a 'public good'; that even honourable men and women may disagree, that differences may not only result from the cosmic war of good against evil, and that therefore the dynamic and creative activity of politics must go on indefinitely.

6. Religious ideas

R. H. Tawney thought that socialism was Christianity in practice; certainly there is much in the Bible that can be enlisted in support of social reformism and even egalitarianism. Jesus' earthly father was a carpenter, and his chief disciples were fishermen; he went about preaching and administering to the poor. In the Sermon on the Mount, he advised, 'Lay not up for yourselves treasures upon earth, where moth and rust doth corrupt, and where thieves break through and steal'. He told the rich young man to sell all he had, give to the poor, and follow him; for it is easier for a camel to pass through the eye of a needle than for a rich man to enter into the kingdom of heaven. This message is more vividly presented in the parable of Dives and Lazarus. In the parable of the vineyard, all labourers receive equal wages, even though they have worked unequal hours. There are passages in the Acts and Epistles recommending equality and communism. Finally and most deeply, there is the doctrine that all are children of one heavenly father; in subsequent centuries this becomes the assertion of the equal value of every human soul. In heaven there will be no class divisions.

But not all of this is necessarily socially radical. As eighteenth-century prelates pointed out, the Christian duty of charity is only possible if there are both rich and poor. According to Bishop

Pretyman of Lincoln in 1794, Christianity is fundamentally a religion of inequality dependent upon the exercise of compassion,
gratitude, and humility – these virtues could not be exercised without a diversity of ranks.[124] Jesus himself said, 'The poor you have always with you'; and the episode that evoked that utterance – the
annointing of his feet – made the point that there are things more
important than the relief of poverty. Against the parable of Dives
and Lazarus may be set the parable of the talents, which can so
easily be interpreted as an endorsement of go-getting economic enterprise. The tenth commandment is 'Thou shalt not covet'. The
values of meekness, humility, and resignation do not encourage
social revolt, nor does the prevailing otherworldliness of the New
Testament. Many forms of Christianity have postulated so deep a
rift between this vale of tears and the world of spirit, that practical
social criticism seems irrelevant. Finally, Christians have often argued that since the world is under the guidance of God's providence,
since in Burke's words we have been marshalled by a divine tactic,
therefore the existing order is ordained by God. But to descend
from generalities, how did the official and leading spokesmen of
different denominations speak on social issues in our period?

The eighteenth- and early nineteenth-century Church of England
has deservedly had a very bad press over its social attitudes. In
Chapter 2 I referred to the close links between the church and the
landed ruling class. Viner, in a survey of eighteenth-century charity
school sermons, finds 'a dominating complacency with respect to
the eighteenth century *status quo*'.[125] The poor were regarded in
such sermons as an inevitable part of the social landscape; it was
quite wrong to attempt to change things, or to give them ideas above
their station. Charity was indeed a Christian duty, but must be
exercised with discretion. According to Viner, more generous attitudes are hard to find; before 1776 only William Law among
clergymen recommends heroic charity, and Bishops Butler, Stil-
lingfleet, and Shipley and a few dissenters are alone in urging a
more liberal educational provision.

R. A. Soloway paints a similar picture in greater depth and detail.
Most eighteenth-century clerics were not hostile to the poor, but
they were complacent about poverty. Richard Watson's sermon of
1793, 'The Wisdom and Goodness of God in Having Made Both
Rich and Poor', is unusual only in the amount of attention it gives

to the question. The episcopate did not transcend the attitudes of the class from which it sprang, and it participated in the growing harshness towards the poor of the years after the French Revolution. No bishop criticized the authorities over Peterloo. The absence of any difference in attitudes between church and establishment is nicely illustrated by the manner in which churchmen shared the fashionable enthusiasm for political economy and Malthus.[126] During the second decade of the nineteenth century, when the fiercest assault was being launched upon the poor laws, the bench of bishops could not raise a protest. One hopes that Bishop Whately of Durham's suggestion to Nassau Senior in 1832 is not typical of episcopal compassion:

> Pray suggest, in your report on paupers, that any female receiving relief should have her hair cut off; it may seem trifling, but *hae nugae*, etc. . . . . A good head of hair will fetch from 5/– to 10/–, which would be perhaps a fortnight's maintenance. . . . Indirectly, the number who would exert themselves to save their hair is beyond belief.[127]

There were honourable exceptions. Bishop Copleston, before he became swept up in the harsh Malthusianism of the Peterloo period, spoke as 'a Tory clergyman still attached to a pastoral social system heavily encrusted with at least the ideal of gentry paternalism';[128] and the same can be said of Bishop Law of Bath and Wells, who defends the *right* of the poor to aid. Law, when Bishop of Chester, had modern factories in his diocese; he visited them and presented the petition for legislation restricting child labour in the House of Lords. But in general the best that can be found in the ranks of the episcopate is dislike of political economy, a critique of the 'abdication of the governors', and a reassertion of hierarchy and paternal responsibility. This is not socially revolutionary; its values are charity, dependence, gratitude, and humility, and it often goes with the denial that the poor have any *right* to charity.

These are the conclusions of Viner and Soloway; but perhaps we need to distinguish between the considered opinions, the final judgments of churchmen on social issues, and the implications, the critical potential of some of their Christian principles. For our concern is not to count up the numbers who favoured a transformation of society, but rather to identify those ideas that made such a transformation thinkable. Take, for example, William Paley, Archdeacon of Carlisle, wealthy pluralist clergyman and influential writer.

He is certainly a social conservative, and a smug and complacent one, as we see in his 'Reasons for Contentment addressed to the Labouring Part of the British Public'.[129] But his defence of charity, in his *Moral and Political Philosophy* of 1785, is strong and generous; the poor have a right to charity, deriving from their right to life and therefore to subsistence, and from the original common ownership of the earth. He insists that the rich do not provide for the poor, but the poor, by their labour, provide for the rich; it is the rich who are dependents.[130]

So far, in looking at the established church, I have omitted an important aspect of the story – evangelicalism. Soloway's judgment is unfavourable; he thinks it causes harsher and less sympathetic attitudes. Whereas previously the prevailing view may have been that poverty was no sin, evangelicalism, with its sense of sin and personal responsibility, takes the contrary view. Poverty is a sign of vice and depravity; if a man is poor, it is his own fault.[131] I believe this is a harsh and crude judgment; evangelicalism is deeply ambiguous on social questions. Without doubt some of its characteristics lend themselves to social conservatism: the focus on the individual soul rather than on social improvement, the tendency to explain evils in terms of individual responsibility rather than social disorder. The evangelical onslaught on the loose manners of the age is a way of interpreting social troubles in terms of sin and indeed the perceived loose manners are often those of the poor. Evangelicalism exhibits a mixture of philanthropy and conservatism; the duty of charity, so strongly enforced (in 1801 Wilberforce gave away £3,000 more than his income to relieve hunger),[132] does not conflict with the belief that poverty is divinely ordained and does not challenge the established order. Evangelicalism often went with distaste for participation in secular affairs; it sharply draws the distinction between the realm of grace and this world and urges believers to fix their hopes on heaven. Wilberforce, the friend of Pitt, was a political conservative who voted for repressive measures and defended the authorities over Peterloo. The patronizing attitudes of Hannah More and her sister in their charitable work in Somerset are well known,[133] as is her *Village Politics*, a popular tract written to advocate political quiescence to the labouring classes.

This is one side of the coin; there is another. There can be little doubt that evangelicalism entails greater attention to the problem of the poor, for the central aspect of it is the desire to save souls, now sunk in sin. One consequence of this was a desire that the poor should be sufficiently instructed to recognize the depth of their depravity, to be able to read the Bible and thus, perhaps, attain salvation – hence the enthusiasm for Sunday schools. Evangelicals were deeply committed to popular education, and were on occasion criticized by those who saw this as potentially subversive.[134] On many issues they were socially progressive – not only on the abolition of the slave trade, their greatest glory. Wilberforce supported the law against chimney boys, favoured factory regulation, and opposed the press gang. Obsession with sin could be turned against rich as well as poor; both Wilberforce and Hannah More write in deeply critical vein of the loose manners and morals of the great.[135] Those who are obsessed with a sense of personal sinfulness are ever on the lookout for things about which they can feel guilty; the poor were a never-failing resource. But most important of all is the evangelical mission to save souls, because all are equal in the sight of God – or rather, the difference between souls is ultimately measured, not by wealth or birth, but by the virtue of their lives and the liveliness of their faith. Since this is a doctrine primarily to do with future rewards, other-worldly things, it is not inevitably and immediately socially radical. But it could have egalitarian implications in this world, as is proved by the fact that there were those who attacked it on this score. The Duchess of Buckingham criticized the preaching of George Whitefield with famous words: it was 'strongly tinctured with impertinence and disrespect . . . towards superiors, in perpetually endeavouring to level all ranks, and do away with all distinctions'; it was monstrous 'to be told that you have a heart as sinful as the common wretches that crawl on the earth'.[136]

Much of what has been said about evangelicalism in general is true of Methodism in particular; but a brief, separate consideration of Wesley is justified. The evangelical focus of attention upon the poor is classically evident in his case; so is the possible link with the alleged growing benevolence of the age, for his Methodism was a 'heart' religion. Though he was a political conservative he espoused ideas that were socially radical, or at least potentially so in their implications. Riches were a great danger. Those who sought and loved them were almost certainly neglecting spiritual things.[137] No man was entitled to live in luxury, nor in idleness on the labour of others. All things belong to God; we are merely the stewards of our possessions, and must use them according to His will, not ours. Anything we have over and above our basic needs must be given to the poor.[138]

> May not this be another reason why rich men shall so hardly enter into the kingdom of heaven? A vast majority of them are under a curse, under the peculiar curse of God: inasmuch as in the general tenor of their lives, they are not only robbing God, continually embezzling and wasting their Lord's goods, and by that very means, corrupting their own souls; but also robbing the poor, the hungry, the naked; wronging the widow and the fatherless, and making themselves accountable for all the want, affliction, and distress, which they may, but do not remove.[139]

In his eighth discourse on the Sermon on the Mount, he recommended the communism of the early church as a pattern for Methodists.[140] He rejected the status system of the world.

> Weigh thyself in another balance; estimate thyself only by the measure of faith and love which God hath given thee. If thou hast more of the knowledge and love of God than he, thou art on this account, and no other, wiser and better, more valuable and honourable than he who is with the dogs of thy flock. But if thou hast not this treasure, thou art more foolish, more vile, more truly contemptible, I will not say, than the lowest servant under thy roof, but than the beggar laid at thy gate, full of sores.[141]

'New' dissent embraces Methodists and other dissenters affected by the evangelical revival. 'Old' dissent comprises Presbyterians, who in the second half of the eighteenth century evolved into Unitarians, Quakers, and Congregationalists and Baptists unaffected by the evangelical revival. The social pattern of old dissent is clear.[142] Before their final political defeat in 1660, the dissenting denominations had members from the highest levels of the social hierarchy; after 1660 these gradually withdrew. Old dissent, in our period, tends to be antiestablishment and antiaristocratic. But it was not lower class; its social composition tended to be higher than that of the new dissent. Hence, though it was often politically radical, this usually went hand in hand with a measure of social conservatism.[143] The manufacturing interest was well represented in

the Quakers, the Unitarians, and the Baptists,[144] and so, for example, these denominations were divided over the factory acts; they
could not afford to alienate manufacturers in their congregations.
   Coming to detail, let us glance at so-called rational dissent – the
Unitarians. Price, Priestley, and Cartwright, all Unitarians, were
prominent in political reform, but were not social reformers. Price
is typical; he was conservative with respect to property, but coupled
this with hostility to hereditary honours. Priestley's commitment
to economic laissez-faire – in his view a natural corollary of religious freedom – goes hand in hand with distrust of charity. He
often uses the metaphor of the race to describe human life.[145] Perhaps it is wrong to regard Priestley's as simply a hard-faced capitalist attitude.[146] Charity goes with dependence, deference, gratitude; it is not altogether anti-poor to say that it is better if they
stand on their own feet, that they be free from nauseating patronage.
Not all were as reluctant to help the poor as Priestley. The Norwich
Unitarian William Taylor disliked both Malthus and evangelicalism
– 'the rich man's smug device for keeping the poor in order'.[147]
And above all, as we noted with respect to Paley and Wesley, the
fact that they were social conservatives is by no means the end of
the story. We have to observe also the radical potential of their
doctrines, the critical possibilities they did not exploit, but that
others might. To eighteenth-century old dissenters, freedom of conscience was sacrosanct, and the duty to think for oneself in religion
led to the duty to search for new truth in other spheres. Their
attitude of mind is corrosive of respect for authority, tradition, and
established opinions. So Priestley writes:

> Establishments, be they ever so excellent, still fix things somewhere;
> and this circumstance, which is all that is pleaded for them amounts
> to, is with me the greatest objection to them. I wish to see things *in
> a progress* to a better state, and no obstructions thrown in the way
> of reformation.[148]

Priestley and Price admire *independence* – having one's own religious convictions, thinking for oneself, deferring to no priest or
social superior. In part, this is simply Protestantism carried to its
logical conclusion; it is also, no doubt, an attitude that appeals to
the segment of society where rational dissent was strong – the middle classes, opponents of aristocracy. Price writes:

> But to be obliged from our birth to look up to a creature no better

than ourselves as the master of our fortunes and to receive his will
as law – what can be more humiliating? What elevated ideas can
enter a mind in such a situation?[149]

These remarks are aimed against monarchy; but they could so easily
be turned against social inequality:

> Jesus Christ has established among Christians an absolute equality.
> He has declared that they have but *one* master, even himself and
> that they are all brethren and, therefore, has commanded them not
> to be called masters and, instead of assuming authority over one
> another, to be ready to wash one another's feet.[150]

The shock of the French Revolution, and the economic and social
upheavals of the time, provided a perfect seedbed for a reawakening
of millennialist ideas. The myth of the millennium is a way of coming to terms with and explaining appalling chaos and insecurity.[151]
According to the millennialist vision, the world is on the point of
a great transformation. The troubles of the time demonstrate that
the reign of antichrist is nearing its climax, or perhaps more accurately its nadir. When things are worst, antichrist will be over-
thrown, and a thousand-year rule of the saints here on earth will
begin. In its attitude to the present, its hopes for the future, and its
conceptions of time and change, millennialism has vast radical potential. It exhibits in extreme form something that is characteristic
of dissent, but present to a degree in much Christian thought,
namely, a tendency to think in sharp antitheses – God versus the
devil, good versus evil rather than greater or lesser degrees of imperfection, black and white rather than shades of grey. Apply millennialist language and assumptions to society, and a possibility
emerges of drawing a sharp contrast between the present, utterly
depraved order and a future of total perfection. Millennialism is
difficult for a modern, scientific, sceptical intelligence to understand; but at the beginning of the nineteenth century such ideas
enjoyed a brief flourishing. It is tempting to view it as an enthusiasm
of the poor and unlettered; in fact, it caught on extensively in respectable and educated circles as well.[152] So to the poor followers
of Richard Brothers and Joanna Southcott, we must add Hartley
and Priestley. Even some bishops, thrown off balance by the French
Revolution, leaned towards millennialist explanations (Napoleon
being antichrist) – Bishop Porteus of London, Bishop Horsley, and
Van Mildert before he became bishop of Durham. Naturally bishops do not use millennialist images and language in proposals to

turn society upside down – they use them *against* Jacobins and democrats. But the myth of the millennium is a two-edged sword.

I hope I have demonstrated that the religious culture of the age provided a mass of combustible materials. If we comb through the ranks of the Church of England, Methodism, new and old dissent, we find scarcely anyone we would denominate a radical social critic. But if we look at beliefs and doctrines, with an eye for their latent potential, we find copious ammunition for foes of the established order. To find social criticism rooting itself in religion is not incompatible with the assertion of a divergent thesis; that the thinkability of social transformation and improvement was aided by growing secularization. During the eighteenth century, the conception of the universe as an ordered hierarchy, a 'great chain of being',[153] with God at the top and the lower ranks arranged by his command, was losing power. Increasingly, there were those who looked for happiness and fulfilment in this world rather than the next. To such minds, poverty and suffering could be regarded, not as part of God's plan, not as the due reward of sin, but as the result of bad social arrangements.

One final footnote: the appeal to 'Nature', so common in eighteenth-century arguments, is a secular alternative to the appeal to God's will; but Nature is often conceived in an essentially religious fashion. Adam Smith's *Wealth of Nations* typifies this. There are natural laws governing social and economic life; if we obey them, we will prosper. Things are so wonderfully arranged that if every individual pursues self-interest, the general good will result. This is divine providence under another name.

7. Conceptions of time and change

Our consideration of conceptions of society, economic theory, and political and religious discourse has revealed a range of ideas about time and change. In order to systematize our survey of this topic, we might ask the following questions: what directions of change were supposed; what was thought about the speed and quality of change; what were perceived as the agents of change; and what, precisely, was thought to be the subject of historical change?

Where the direction of change is concerned, the age of enlightenment is usually thought of as an epoch in the emergence of the belief in progress; increasingly heaven was located, not in another dimension of existence, but in the future.[154] Faith in progress was greatly sustained by enthusiasm for science and its advances:

> Thus all knowledge will be subdivided and extended; and *knowledge*, as Lord Bacon observes, being *power*, the human powers will, in fact, be enlarged; nature, including both its materials and its laws, will be more at our command; men will make their situation in this world abundantly more easy and comfortable; they will probably prolong their existence in it, and will grow daily more happy, each in himself, and more able (and, I believe, more disposed) to communicate happiness to others. Thus whatever was the beginning of this world, the end will be glorious and *paradisiacal*, beyond what our imaginations can now conceive.[155]

But faith in progress is counterpointed by lament over decline. Primitivism, the myth of a past age of noble simplicity and goodness, is another eighteenth-century fashion, classically represented by Rousseau and important in literature. Tales of progress and decline do not exhaust the repertory. Traditionalisms – the appeal to the ancient constitution, the assertion of traditional English liberties, the myth of 'the Norman yoke' – imply a pattern of superficial change over underlying continuity. The classical republican paradigm of Polybius, Machiavelli, and Harrington offers yet another conception.[156] It is teleological and organic, thinking of change in terms of growth to maturity and then decline. It is pessimistic in temper, having an overriding concern with the danger of the balanced, mature polity suffering corruption and fall. For time is the dimension of instability; given time, all good states come to ruin. Once a state has fallen, the immensely difficult task is to restore it to health. Hence this conception of time and change is cyclical – a cycle of fall and renovation.

With respect to thinking about the pace and character of change, progressivism, since it sets so much store by the accumulating advance of science, is often gradualist. At the opposite pole is millennialism, which maintains that the coming changes will be cataclysmic, revolutionary: the seventh seal will be opened, there will be fire and sword, and an abrupt transition from absolute evil to absolute good.[157]

What are the agents and mechanisms of change proposed by these various conceptions? Polybius and Machiavelli find the threat to stability in time itself; the tendency to grow old, to decay, is part of the very nature of things. But change can be resisted, and a fallen state restored, by *virtus* – by individual initiative and heroic action. There is thus a tension in the perceived dynamics of change. Bad changes result from impersonal forces, good ones from human intentional agency. Classical republicanism, therefore, though a pessimistic doctrine, is not a quietistic one. Nor is the myth of 'the Norman yoke'. Liberty was destroyed by conquerors, driven by greed and ambition: it can be restored by political action. Millennialism sees change resulting from the action of transcendent forces of good and evil. It is therefore more passive than classical republicanism: we can but wait in faith and hope. Theories of progress can be 'idealist' or 'materialist' (or, more usually, as in Condorcet, a mixture of the two). 'Idealists' think in terms of the advance of knowledge and its technological payoffs. Credit for this advance may be given to great inventors (Newton topping most lists), but there is also an interest in the contribution of impersonal factors – the development of printing, changes in the intellectual temper of nations and ages.

But what is perceived as the subject of historical change? Does eighteenth-century thought identify and discuss *social* change? Millennialism does not; the actors in the drama are transcendent forces of good and evil, working through human individuals. Traditionalisms focus upon politics rather than society. The theory of progress is originally a doctrine about knowledge. But increasingly in the second half of the century, there is hope that intellectual progress will result in economic, political, and social progress. Classical republicanism also insists upon the interaction of economic, political, and social factors in the process of change. Of greatest interest to us are those accounts of progress that study the relationships between society and economy.[158] Montesquieu distinguishes 'savage' and 'barbarous' nations; a savage nation is one that gets its living by hunting, a barbarous by keeping flocks and herds. Different modes of subsistence generate different institutions and manners. After Montesquieu, this approach is developed in both France and Scotland. One of the most sophisticated versions of it is the four stages theory, according to which societies evolve from hunting to pasturage to agriculture to commerce – social, political, and cultural changes going hand in hand with economic. This theory, to be found in the writings of Adam Smith and Millar, had great influence in the last two decades of the century. It has been interpreted as a 'materialist' theory of evolution similar to the Marxist; but it is not a one-way economic determinism, giving the economic sphere a constant priority. Rather it is interested in the interaction of different spheres – economic, social, political, military – and it also pays attention to the role of individuals in the unfolding of social development.[159] Its importance for social criticism is obvious; it constructs 'society' as an object and traces its evolution, placing emphasis upon property and production.

The result of our survey of available conceptions of time and change is to show how rich and diverse were the stocks upon which contemporaries could draw. Not as rich as ours, nor yet as those available to Marx: late eighteenth-century Britons lacked the powerful dialectical theory of change that was being worked out in Germany at this time, culminating in the philosophy of Hegel. Nor of course could they possess the theory of evolution by functional selection that we associate with Darwin. Nor were there any thoroughgoing historical relativists, prepared simultaneously to recognize massive social and cultural transformations, while refusing to evaluate those transformations in terms of progress or decline. Conceptions of time and change in the period under study are saturated with moral content. But still, for them as for historians today, the main problem was not any shortage of conceptions of change, but rather how to organize the rich stock of ideas into coherent accounts: how to recognize and reconcile vast impersonal forces with individual agency, material with intellectual factors, long-run determinants with short-run opportunities.

8. Methodology and epistemology

Eighteenth-century arguments often make appeal to 'Reason' and 'Nature'. These are rich, protean, polysemic terms. Often they serve as ultimate but unexamined courts of appeal. In other ages, God's will was invoked as the final validation. In this way 'Reason' and 'Nature' are abstract, bloodless alternatives to 'God', secular rhetorical devices for closing arguments. Looked at in another light, reason and nature take on greater significance; for they may be seen as assertions of contemporary standards of method, argument, and proof. The appeal to nature often signifies a requirement that conclusions be based upon a systematic and comprehensive survey of the evidence, the *facts of nature*. The technique of the social survey and increased use of statistics are manifestations of this empirical methodology, prestigious since Bacon. The appeal to reason frequently goes hand in hand, in this period, with rejection of tradition. It symbolizes a drive towards rationalized consistency in opinion and practice. Often it means the adoption of a detached and impartial point of view – free from passion, prejudice, and interest. The disinterested observer of Adam Smith's moral philosophy epitomizes this ideal. Finally, reason may mean theory – the systematic analysis and explanation of phenomena in terms of fundamental laws or principles. Associationism is a paradigmatic example of the application of theory to explain humanity and society. It opens up the possibility of explaining all human behaviour and variety in terms of the regular operation of a few simple principles, a handful of original characteristics of the human organism. The methodological ideals symbolized by 'Nature' and 'Reason' are not without consequences for social criticism. Insofar as they are realized or approached, they liberate the observer from prejudice, from immersion in the given. They enable and encourage the observer to conceive of him- or herself as set apart from the object of study, viewing it from outside, from a detached vantage point; they permit, in fact, the achievement of a space, a distance, between observer and observed, subject and object.

Distancing is also promoted by the acquisition of abstract concepts, which in the history of languages are latecomers. Take such key concepts as state, society, property, and economy. Quentin Skinner argues that the concept of the state emerges in the period of the Renaissance and Reformation.[160] The precise definition of property as absolute individual ownership is, according to Aylmer, a seventeenth-century achievement.[161] Bossy,[162] following Raymond Williams,[163] identifies two main meanings of 'society'. The first and older meaning is companionship, fellowship; something that individuals possess in their relationships with one another, an activity rather than a condition. 'Society' as a term to denote the objective entity, 'the body of institutions and relationships within which a relatively large group of people live', is not to be found before the seventeenth century. According to Williams, 'The decisive transition of *society* towards its most general and abstract sense . . . was an C18 development'. The concept of the economy, meaning the system of the production and distribution of wealth, is an achievement of eighteenth- and early nineteenth-century economic theory.[164] A proviso needs to be entered here. To have abstract conceptions of the state, of the economy, and of society does not require the use of those precise words. Other words or phrases may designate the entity that has been conceived in thought, as we shall see when we look at the terms used in the texts to refer to 'society'. That these words begin to be used is a sign of the arrival of the concepts rather than a cause or necessary condition.

If one is to criticize society and seriously propose Utopia, it helps to be certain that one is right. Conversely, doubt sits well with conservatism and cautious moderation. Distrust of the powers of reason is at the core of Burke's conservatism:[165] it is better to leave things as they are, than to trust to feeble and fallible human contrivances. Burke's assault upon reason is so urgent and heartfelt precisely because he has witnessed unbounded faith in the progress of knowledge going hand in hand with political radicalism. Confidence in the power of intellect was encouraged by prevailing conceptions of the nature of knowledge. Historians of seventeenth- and eighteenth-century thought have divided epistemological theories into rationalist and empiricist ones. Rationalism offered the promise of watertight certainty, attained by the deduction of truths from self-evident axioms. The great age of rationalism was the seventeenth century, the age of Descartes, Hobbes, Spinoza, and Leibniz; but the rationalist methodology, though challenged, continued to be employed in the eighteenth. For example, Richard Price constructed a rationalist ethics. But already Hume had begun to develop the critique of rationalism that forms the basis of our present-day doubts about its claim to furnish indisputable truth.[166] The conclusions of logical deduction are indeed certain, but logic is concerned with relations between our ideas, not directly with real relations in the material world. Reality may not embody logical or rational relationships. Empiricist methods, by contrast, *are* concerned with the real world. Eighteenth-century empiricism stems from Locke. According to Lockean epistemology, knowledge comes into the mind from without in the form of sense data. For the most part, the mind is a passive receiver, a mirror, accurately receiving a picture of the external world. The images recorded in the sensorium correspond in all important respects to external reality.[167] So, we have an external world, and then a first copy of it in the form of the images it has thrown via the senses. We go on to construct a second copy, a copy of the sensual images, in language. We attach names to the images, and hence to the real external objects they represent. Provided that the names correspond with sufficient accuracy to the images – provided that we properly distinguish those things that are different, naming all the minerals, all the varieties of buttercup, all the species of animals – then the account we give of the world in language is a true one. Language copies our sensations, which copy reality.[168] Unfortunately, language has led humanity astray in the past; for insufficient care and method have been employed in observing and classifying. Also, under the guidance of superstition, some have let their imaginations run away with them, producing magical rather than scientific accounts of the world. Or they have become imprisoned in dogmas, received views, and hence are unable to see the way things are. But now, open-minded, sober, and methodical researchers are building up a true knowledge of the order of things.

This 'copy' theory of knowledge does not convince us today. We suspect that the mind does not simply receive information, passively, like a mirror; we suspect that knowing and thinking are more active, that the mind imposes a pattern, an organizing structure, upon what it receives. We suspect that words and concepts do not simply record and communicate what we already know; they also structure, mould, enable, and limit our knowledge.[169] We can therefore be less confident of our own rectitude than were some – though not all[170] – of our eighteenth-century forebears. They, or some of them, were sure that there was a truth, and that they could lay hold of it; we are sure of neither proposition, especially when the object of our discourse is humanity and society. One of the forms our doubt takes is the theory of ideology, which maintains that our conception of the human world is shaped and coloured by our own social position.[171] Was there in Britain between 1775 and 1830 any dawning of awareness of ideological distortion, and if so did it significantly weaken the epistemological optimism of the age? The answer is yes to the first question and no to the second. Puritans, accustomed to the careful examination of the state of their own souls, well knew how passion and interest could hide the truth from the eyes of the sinner. The enemies of priestcraft, on the other hand, pointed to the way in which religion filled the minds of the masses with superstitious terrors in order that they might contribute more readily to the coffers of the church. But these obstacles to truth were not insurmountable; they were veils that could be drawn back.

This completes my survey of ideas that made radical social criticism possible. Possible, not inevitable; these doctrines, ideas and assumptions are amenable to inclusion in other ideologies. Let us take by way of example the traditions of moral discourse. Natural rights language has perennial radical possibilities; today it is used by oppressed minorities (and majorities, in the case of women). But it has also been used to defend the status quo, especially to defend property against socialism. It was used in this way by the U.S. Supreme Court in the early years of this century.[172] G. D. H. Cole thought that the theory of natural rights had evolved from a left-wing theory in the eighteenth century to a right-wing one in the twentieth.[173] Robert Nozick has recently used natural rights as the foundation stone of an extreme defence of private property against socialism and social welfarism.[174] A similar point can be made about utilitarianism. When we think of it, Bentham looms large in our minds, and this encourages us to forget that in the eighteenth century utilitarianism was used to defend the status quo as much as to criticize it. Hume and Paley were both social conservatives. Bentham and James Mill themselves were enthusiastic defenders of capitalism. The concept of justice is no different. Modern analysts have distinguished conservative and prosthetic justice;[175] conservative justice interprets 'to each his or her due' to mean that each should be treated in accordance with established expectations and institutions. Desert-based justice is a form of prosthetic, not conservative, justice; but the doctrine that we should reward the deserving has at times been used to defend inequality and capitalism.

Structuralism has been a fashion in recent years. Its proponents are interested in the ways in which language, methods, and assumptions – the structures of discourse – determine knowledge. The approach of this book is not totally dissimilar from that of structuralism. But some structuralists show a tendency to abolish the author, believing that a text is produced more by the available discourses than by the man or woman whose name appears on the title page.[176] But if the available discourses (for example, the language of ethics) can be mobilized in defence of widely differing ideologies, then surely the creative originality of the writer of the text cannot be ignored. In the next chapter, I want to analyse precisely this: the manner in which my chosen authors took the available mental resources and used them to lay the foundations of a new radicalism.

PART II

Texts

The Real Rights of Man, Thomas Spence, 1775

Spence begins by asserting a natural and equal right to land and liberty. In a state of nature, land is held in common. The equal right to land is justified because to deny it is to deny the right to sustenance and therefore to life. No people is entitled to alienate its land, for to do so would be to deprive posterity of the sustenance that is their right. This is the natural state of affairs; and society, we may presume, was created in order to safeguard these original rights. But if we look at existing nations, we do not find these natural rights established; for in the past land was claimed, or rather usurped, by a few lords, and their claim was not challenged. Consequently they became the possessors not only of the land, but also in effect of the resident animals and even men, who depended upon the lords for their livelihood. 'Thus were the first landholders usurpers and tyrants' (2);[1] they have transmitted this unjust property to their descendants, causing misery for the majority and a continuing violation of natural rights. This is the present state of affairs; Spence now proposes a plan for a better arrangement. He imagines the inhabitants of a country, 'after much reasoning and deliberation', assembling in their parishes and setting up parish corporations. The parishes then retake all land into the possession of the people. Henceforward the parish is the landlord, but it does not have the authority to alienate land. The parish lets the land in small farms to the inhabitants; this creates both employment and abundance. The rents are used to pay taxes to the national government, to relieve the poor and provide public works; no other taxes are collected. Parishes are democratically governed, and voting is secret in local and national elections. National government leaves the parishes alone, unless they violate public good or the rights of individuals. A man acquires membership of a parish by a year's residence; nonmembers who fall ill or into distress are supported out of the rents, and the cost deducted from the sum paid to the national exchequer. The parishioners form a militia, and there is no professional army. It will be a condition of plenty and freedom, and once established it will stand for ever. The example will spread, 'and thus the whole earth shall at last be happy, and live like brethren' (5).

This is Spence's plan, of which he was proud. As a piece of social and political thinking, it is feather-light, but historically it is of the utmost significance. To find anything approaching its social radicalism we have to go back to the Diggers. But the plans of the Diggers were conceived in the midst of a social and political revolution, when the world was turned upside down: their context permitted and encouraged new departures. Whatever the tensions of late eighteenth-century British society, the social pyramid stood securely on its base; and Spence's plan was formulated fifteen years before the shock of the French Revolution. Here is an absorbing historical problem: what made Spence's plan possible?

Was it a natural outgrowth of the intellectual climate of the 1770s? Was Spence simply working out the implications of current ideas – doing something that, sooner or later, someone else would have done had he not got there first? When we set about analysing the intellectual conditions of the possibility of Spence's text, we have to beware of a dangerous temptation. The Newcastle lecture makes no explicit acknowledgement of its intellectual ancestry. But later products of his pen quote and refer to other writers. It is tempting, but illegitimate, to infer that he had read these before 1775. For example, his *History of Crusonia* (1782) and the *Description of Spensonia* (1795) prove that he was working within the tradition of utopian writing. *Pig's Meat* quotes Harrington and Swift, and he was influenced by More's *Utopia*. The utopian genre is specifically and consciously concerned with *distancing* – putting a space between existing society, and the writer or reader. Those who have drunk deeply at this literary fountain are well prepared to be social and political radicals. But we cannot be certain that Spence had read utopian works before 1775. It is true that the lecture contains remarks that could have been inspired by Harrington. Harrington's independent landed gentlemen have been translated and reduced into peasant farmers, leasing their land from the democratically elected parish corporation; but they exhibit the same virtues of freedom and incorruptibility, and they defend their independence by forming a militia: '[A]s all have property alike to defend, they are alike ready to run to arms when their country is in danger ... each man has a vote in all the affairs of the parish, and for his own sake must wish well to the public' (4). Spence could have arrived at these ideas without reading Harrington, for they were a commonplace of 'left of centre' political culture.

Locke's influence, similarly, may have been direct or indirect. Whichever way it was, the doctrine of natural rights is fundamental to the argument of the lecture. This is the moral ground upon which Spence stands, the vantage-point from which he criticizes his society and proposes a better. Though he asserts the right to liberty, the main job of work is done by the most important recipient right – the right to the sustenance required to maintain life. This doctrine that every individual has the right to life and therefore to sustenance was deeply rooted in western political culture by the late eighteenth century. Spence infers from this the right to land: 'For, as I said before, there is no living but on land and its productions, consequently what we cannot live without, we have the same property in, as in our lives' (1). If this were a valid inference, then Spence's case for the ownership of land by all would be powerful and persuasive. Unfortunately it is not. The right to life implies the right to sustenance; but the right to sustenance does not imply the right to hold a share of the land, for sustenance can be got in other ways. To deprive individuals of a share of the land is not necessarily to deprive them of life.

Spence's doctrine of rights, like Locke's, is embedded in a distinction between a state of nature (where individuals enjoy natural rights) and a civil state, where those rights may not be recognized. This distinction, however implausible historically, is of great critical importance, for it permits a comparison of the existing order with an original condition that acts as a benchmark, or reference point. Spence formulates this contrast in the precise words 'state of nature' versus 'society'. The word 'society' is used several times, and its meaning appears to be that captured by the common eighteenth-century expression 'civil society' – a term that designates specifically the political condition that may be contrasted with the prepolitical state of nature. 'Society' as Spence employs it here could not be used in the plural. He would not write of '*a* society' or '*many* societies'. Instead, he refers to particular 'nations' or to 'any country'.

One or two other intellectual sources may be guessed at. His assertion that the land, originally common property, was later usurped by a few lords, may be an echo of 'the Norman yoke' myth; but if so, it is a strange echo. The usurpation apparently succeeded, not because it was supported by force of arms, but because the majority did not bother to challenge it (2). There may also be biblical and religious influences. We know that the young Spence had contact with the Glassites, who maintained that church members, like the apostles, should regard their property as a trust, always available for the needy.[2] The odd phrase, 'sincere friends to truth', 'as the truth here is of such importance to be known, let it be boldly sought out' (1) is reminiscent of dissenting sermons of the day. The final paragraph may have a millennialist ring to it:

> But what makes this prospect yet more glorious is, that after this empire of right and reason is thus established, it will stand for ever. Force and corruption attempting its downfall, shall equally be baffled, and all other nations struck with wonder and amazement at its happiness and stability shall follow the example, and thus the whole earth shall at last be happy, and live like brethren. (5)

Incidentally, the fact that we have to be so tentative about the religious influences points up a difference between Spence's lecture and Digger tracts. Digger writings are saturated with biblical quotations and allusions and with contemporary religious themes. Their social philosophy is evidently formed and conditioned by a religious culture.

With caution, then, we can suggest the intellectual sources of Spence's plan. But what is remarkable is that there is nothing new to the realm of ideas here. These intellectual materials were available for the greater part of the period between the Diggers and Spence's lecture. The *Real Rights of Man* was not inspired by fresh intellectual departures, it does not bear the stamp of the radical enlightenment. Certain ideas (especially of rights) were necessary conditions of Spence's radicalism, but, after we have listed them, we still do not feel that we understand how Spence could be so radical in 1775. We are driven, therefore, to consider the broader context out of which the lecture sprang.

A striking feature of Spence's plan is its advocacy of a society built upon parishes as the main economic and political units. Two possible sources in his experience may be suggested. First, he belonged to the congregation of the Rev. James Murray.[3] Murray, originally a Presbyterian, came to assert the Independent doctrines of congregational autonomy and democracy. Here in long-established dissenting practice is a model for Spence's self-governing, democratic parishes. Second, Spence (with Murray) was deeply involved in the Newcastle town moor dispute.[4] In 1771 the oligarchic, co-opted town corporation decided to lease part of the common for enclosure. The freemen of the borough organized themselves to resist this: they broke the enclosure fence, fought the issue in court, and won. In 1774 an act of parliament was obtained, limiting leasing of the moor to 100 acres and to terms of seven years. The profits of leasing were to be used for the relief of poor townsfolk. A congregational church, and a local enclosure dispute; these two items of Spence's experience probably provided him with his strategy for transition, as well as with his vision of a meliorated society. Just as a group of believers could decide to set up an independent congregation, just as the freemen of Newcastle could assert their right to the town moor, so the inhabitants of each parish would come together and resolve to take over the land from the landlords. Unfortunately for Spence's plan, the cases are not sufficiently similar. After the civil war of the seventeenth century, independent congregations were (usually) tolerated. The Newcastle citizens were not attacking a landlord in 1771–4; they were establishing through the courts their own legal rights. These are not precedents for depriving all landlords of land to which they were legally entitled.

The lecture also grows out of the agitation for political reform. One of the benefits Spence claims for his plan is that it will cleanse elections of corruption. He is vehement against government expenditure and taxation. In the society he proposes,

> [T]he government, which may be said to be the greatest mouth, having neither excisemen, custom-house men, collectors, army, pensioners, bribery, nor such like ruination vermin to maintain, is soon satisfied, and moreover, there are no more persons employed in offices, either about the government or parishes, than is absolutely necessary; and their salaries are but just sufficient to maintain them suitably in their offices. (4)

National politics aroused great interest in Newcastle in the 1770s.

Spence's friend James Murray was deeply involved in the related campaigns for removing the political disabilities of dissenters, against the American war and for reform of Parliament. Newcastle newspapers reported the Wilkes affair, radical periodicals and political clubs were established. In the town moor dispute, the freemen retained the legal services of Serjeant Glynn, radical MP for Middlesex and Wilkes's partner in that constituency.[5]

The phenomenon of popular involvement in radical politics gives a clue to what made Spence's lecture possible. Let us think for a moment about who he was and what he did. His origins were utterly humble; his father was a small shopkeeper. Spence himself was an autodidact who became a teacher and then turned to writing and selling political tracts. In 1775, the year of his lecture, he published *The Grand Repository of the English Language*, which proposed a phonetic alphabet in order to make learning to read easier. The tracts he wrote and sold, later in London, were cheap, costing a few pence or even just one penny.[6] The title and nature of his periodical *Pig's Meat* is significant. It was written for the 'swinish multitude',[7] and it provided them with *meat* – intellectual food. Most of it consisted of extracts from political classics – Harrington, Locke, Swift, Priestley, Godwin.[8] The books from which the extracts were taken would be beyond the pockets of most of Spence's readers; but *Pig's Meat*, in weekly penny numbers, gave them access to important ideas. Spence's life and activities are utterly bound up with the explosion of the reading public. Throughout the eighteenth century, readership had been extending downwards from the elite.[9] This expansion of readership was also an expansion of the political community – of those who took an interest in political affairs. Daily and weekly newspapers, reaching a wide audience, were a late seventeenth- and mainly eighteenth-century creation.[10] The spread of societies in the provinces – discussing science, politics, and general questions – was part of the same phenomenon. Significantly, Spence's lecture was prepared for the Newcastle Philosophical Society, newly founded in 1775. One may speculate, therefore, that its social radicalism was possible because individuals like Spence, viewing society from the bottom, had been drawn, by a communications explosion, into political debate. The intellectual materials were not new; what *was* new was the viewpoint, and the ability to express it.

5

An Essay on the Right of Property in Land, William Ogilvie, 1782

Ogilvie builds his argument on two foundations: natural right and utility. The argument from natural right owes its conceptual framework to natural jurisprudence, and Ogilvie was no doubt familiar with classic seventeenth-century treatments of property within that tradition, such as those of Pufendorf and Locke.[1] Ogilvie's treatment, however, is more radical and egalitarian than theirs. Property right can be derived either from occupancy or labour. The right of occupancy is a right to a share of the earth equal to that enjoyed by all other 'occupants', that is to say, individuals, members of the human race (subsequently, Ogilvie slips into interpreting 'individuals' as male heads of households) (93n).[2] This right is a recipient right – a right to receive what is necessary for the maintenance of life. A right to receive subsistence is also asserted by Locke in the opening sentence of his Chapter 5 on property, but Locke does not infer from it a right to receive an allotment of land. Both Locke and Ogilvie begin by stating that the earth was originally given to all humankind (Locke says by God, Ogilvie does not mention the donor). But whereas Locke interprets this to mean an original situation with no individual holdings, from which private holdings were subsequently carved by labour, Ogilvie supposes an original or natural situation of equal, privately cultivated, privately enjoyed shares (7). The right of labour, according to Ogilvie, is the right to enjoy the fruits of any improvements to the land created by one's labour and that of one's ancestors (11). This is an active or liberty right – a right to do as one wishes with what one has made oneself. It, too, is asserted by Locke, but in a significantly different form. Locke argues that a man acquires a property right in a natural resource – say, a piece of land – when he mixes his labour with it, because that labour contributes more to the value of the finished commodity – say, a harvest of wheat – than unaided nature could. Furthermore, once a property right in a piece of land has been created by such a mixing of labour, a man may retain that right for the rest of his life and transmit it to his heirs. Ogilvie makes no such claim; the right conferred by labour is only to the value of the improvement created by labour, say, in clearing or draining the land. How are the claims of the two rights – of life or occupancy and of labour – reconciled? In Locke's account, the right deriving from labour moves to centre stage, prevailing over and annulling the original common ownership. Potentially this creates a situation in which some own land and some do not. How, in this situation, is the right to life of the latter to be guaranteed? Locke introduces provisos or limitations on the amount that individuals may acquire through labour, in order to ensure that subsistence is available to all. Ogilvie adopts a different solution. He proposes that the value of any piece of land be analyzed into three parts: the 'original' value of the land; the 'accessory' or additional value resulting from improvements made by past and present owners; and the 'contingent' or further value it is capable of receiving through improvements in the future. In terms of this analysis, the owner of a large estate is entitled to the full 'accessory' value produced by his labour and that of his ancestors; but he is entitled to the 'original' and 'contingent' value only of as much land as would fall to him if the land of the state were shared equally among the citizens (14–15).³ He believes that the state should take from large landowners as much of their property as exceeds their entitlement in terms of this analysis and redistribute it among the landless (53). His conclusions concerning the right of property are evidently very different from those of Locke, who is generally interpreted as a defender of the existing distribution. In essence, the difference is this. Locke assumes that the existing distribution is just, being based upon the right of labour, or regulated by positive law to which the citizens have consented. The right of all, including the landless, to subsistence remains, but Locke assumes that right can be satisfied without ensuring that everyone has a share of the land. Ogilvie, by contrast, supposes that every man has a birthright to a private share of land; this right is 'indefeasible' (9) – it cannot be taken away, though a man may alienate it of his own free will. This birthright applies today, as it did 'originally', even though the great majority have been denied their shares; justice requires a restitution. Ogilvie's argument is less elaborated than Locke's and is not without its difficulties; but to anyone who finds justification of property in terms of natural rights persuasive, it may be recommended as not inferior.

The argument from utility maintains that a situation in which every man could become an independent farmer if he wished (and Ogilvie believes the overwhelming majority would choose this) would promote the greatest happiness (21). Though he initially equates 'utility' with 'happiness', subsequently it becomes clear that he identifies the main components of utility rather differently: 'to promote cultivation and the fertility of the soil, to favour the increase of population, and to improve the manners and virtues of the great body of the people' (119). He is troubled by no Malthusian fears; population increase is a good, and he very plausibly suggests that if the right of each man to a farm were granted, then the age of marriage would tend to be lower, and population growth higher. He looks forward to an ideal state, when the earth shall be filled with as many independent cultivators as can be supported in comfort (32).

Having established the principles on which property in land ought to be based, Ogilvie turns his attention to the evils of the present unequal distribution. It has caused poor cultivation, which fails to tap the productive potential of the land (32). It has produced poor human beings – the great majority lack 'that degree of strength and comeliness, which nature seems to have intended for the human race' (27). It has made the lower orders mean-spirited and servile, cunning, fraudulent, hypocritical, and envious: the rich it has made luxurious, vain, and arrogant (33). Because of their monopoly, landlords can enforce an unfair bargain; they reap the benefit of improvements made by the labour of their tenants, they deprive the poor of some share of their just reward.

> Whoever enjoys any revenue, not proportioned to such industry or exertion of his own, or of his ancestors, is a freebooter, who has found means to cheat or to rob the public, and more especially the indigent of that district in which he lives. (34)

Here is the beginning of a theory of exploitation, which was to have so distinguished a history after Ogilvie; those who own the means of production are thereby enabled to seize the fruits of other men's labour. This move in the argument, momentous and radical, follows readily from Locke's grounding of property in labour.

The stage is now set for Ogilvie's remedy: an agrarian law, under which any adult male is entitled to claim, from the wastes or large estates of his village or neighbourhood, a farm of forty acres, to be occupied by himself and his heirs in perpetuity. The landlord from whose estate the farm is taken will receive a fixed rent, assessed by arbitrators at a level sufficient to compensate him for the improvements made by the labour of himself and his ancestors. These bare bones of the agrarian law are fleshed out with detailed practical regulations (92–100). The law may be criticized for failing to come to grips with the injustice created by exploitation, exposed in the preceding stages of the argument. If the present race of landlords is receiving the value created by improvements to the land made by the labour of exploited tenants and hands, then why should these landlords receive compensation for the loss of that value? Ogilvie appears to forget this, and so there is an imbalance between the fierce radicalism of his critique and the mildness of his practical proposals. The rest of the book is concerned with problems of implementation. He recognizes that the landed interest will resist his law, and so he explores the possibility of introducing the law at first in a small way: he suggests a trial run in Ireland, India, or America; he speculates about the forms of government and political circumstances under which an experiment would be feasible (106–16).

We have now established the public or overt argument of the book – what Ogilvie himself would have regarded as the main thrust, the chain of reasoning that gives the book its shape. We have seen that its social radicalism is achieved by making minor but important adjustments to natural jurisprudence theories of rights and property and by employing the critical potential of the concept of utility. There are two further tasks to perform. We need to investigate the hidden or half-buried arguments – those things that are taken for granted, assumed without question. We must also explore more fully how social criticism was *possible* for Ogilvie and why his critique took precisely this form.

It is evident from the text that Ogilvie knew a great deal about agriculture and was much interested in agricultural improvement.

Independent confirmation is given by the little we know of his life history.[4] He was born in 1736, the only son of the laird of Pittensear near Elgin in northern Scotland. Though he sold the family estate in 1772, he leased back the mansion house and manor farm until his death in 1819. In 1773 he bought a property near Aberdeen for £1,500. He spent £1,910 improving it – draining, trenching, and blasting – evidently with success, for he sold the property in 1808 for £4,000. So he was an improving landlord; his concern in his book with the optimum size and mode of landholding may be seen as an extension of the interest in agricultural improvement that he shared with a small but significant number of his class. His proposal to analyse the value of any piece of land into three parts – the original, accessory, and contingent values – points clearly to his context. Land surveys were an increasingly frequent occurrence in late eighteenth-century Scotland as a result of enclosures; the growing number of professional land surveyors testifies to this. The assessment of the contingent value of a piece of land – that is, of the additional value it might acquire if improved – is irrelevant to the purpose of compensating a landlord from whose estate allotments are to be carved. The reason why Ogilvie mentions it at all must be his intense interest in *improvement*; and improvement looms large as an issue for many of his educated contemporaries because they perceive Scotland as a backward country when compared with England.[5] His interest in agrarian reform is easy to understand; but given his background, his verbal assaults upon landlords at first seem nothing short of remarkable. Not only was he a laird; he was closely connected with the aristocracy. He was descended from the earls of Findlater and Seafield and was deeply indebted to the patronage of one of them. One of his five sisters married the factor of the duke of Gordon, and in 1798 he borrowed £2,000 from the duke to finance his agricultural improvements. Yet he insists that the incomes of landlords are a greater evil in the state than tithes, or the robbery of public funds through political corruption. By their oppression, 'the happiness of mankind has been for ages more invaded and restrained, than by all the tyranny of kings, the imposture of priests, and the chicane of lawyers taken together' (27). Yet, as already remarked, these verbal assaults are not matched by correspondingly radical proposals; the landlords are to enjoy compensation that will enable them to maintain the standard of life to

which they are accustomed (82, 92n), and the tendency of his
scheme is to increase the number of independent cultivators rather
than to achieve equality. At the end of the day, he is no traitor to
his class. So, if he does not propose to rob the rich, how can he
suppose that his agrarian law will bring that enhanced comfort to
the poor that he so obviously and sincerely desires? The circle is to
be squared by the greatly enhanced productivity that will ensue
(23n, 119). But nowhere does he demonstrate that the division of
the earth among small independent farmers will promote efficient
agriculture. The idea of an agrarian law to promote independent
cultivation is not unique to Ogilvie in the eighteenth century. It can
be found in Mrs. Macaulay's popular *History of England* published
in 1766–83, and before that in Hutcheson's *System of Moral Philosophy* of 1755. In the early eighteenth century, Andrew Fletcher
proposed that landlords be compelled to sell uncultivated lands to
those willing to cultivate them.[6] Harrington's *Oceana* is a seventeenth-century precursor. But the ultimate source, to which Ogilvie
himself refers, is the agrarian laws of the Gracchi, who were officers
of the Roman republic in the second century B.C. He also draws
inspiration from the Bible – the 'Mosaic Law', on which he proposed to write a treatise, and the practice of the jubilee.

But to trace the source of ideas in Ogilvie's argument – natural
right, utility, agrarian law – is at best only half an answer to the
question of what made radical commentary possible for him. At a
deeper level lies the problem of how he was able to regard the
economic and social order as challengeable; not to be accepted as
inevitable, but to be coolly appraised as one of a number of possible
social orders. At this level, the issue is not what made his specific
arguments and proposals possible, but what made radical criticism
of any kind possible. Why, in 1782, did it seem sensible and timely
to advocate social transformation, not as a mere utopian fantasy,
but as a soberly practical plan? To answer this question, we may
start by looking, not at arguments, but at words – words that crop
up repeatedly, words that indicate a state of mind so habitual to
the author that he never feels the need to explore and defend it.
On page 1, he contrasts 'prejudice' with 'men of enlarged and in-
quisitive minds'; he speaks of an unspecified past age as 'not deserving to be extolled for legislative wisdom'. On page 2, he writes
of 'free and speculative disquisition', the 'free exercise of his

thoughts in speculative inquiries', and appeals to the 'candid'. On page 3, he refers to himself as 'thinking freely', and deplores the consequences of 'stagnation of inquiry' and 'silent acquiescence'. On page 4, old laws are judged 'absurd and pernicious'. In a footnote on pages 7 and 8, he remarks that the bulk of mankind are so ignorant and unreflecting that they accept the laws of their own country as 'permanent and immutable . . . fixed by the destination of nature'. On page 44, he says that 'free discussion which every subject now receives gives reason to hope that truth and utility will always triumph' and on the following page that 'many errors have been rectified in theory'. On page 50 there is a reference to 'that magnanimous and comprehensive turn of mind', and on page 82 to 'speculative men of enlarged views'. In a footnote on page 92 he appeals to 'unbiassed reasoners'. Similar examples could be multiplied; these words and phrases mark him as a representative of the Scottish Enlightenment – the very word 'enlightened' is in the text.[7] To propose radical social reform seems timely to Ogilvie, therefore, because he has an image of himself and others like him standing at a turning point in human affairs. Before there was silent acquiescence; now there is free and speculative disquisition. Some of the words we have picked out are pregnant with meaning – take, for example, 'candid', 'theory', 'prejudice', and 'enlarged'. 'Candour' is a quality much favoured by eighteenth-century rational dissenters.[8] The word refers to the courage of nonconformists who are prepared to defy the law for the sake of their religious convictions. But 'candour', coming from the lips of Price or Priestley, refers to this original act of religious courage, generalized to an intellectual temper; the candid man will fearlessly pursue an inquiry wherever it may lead and speak what he believes to be the truth, no matter how disturbing or unpopular, no matter whether his zeal for truth adversely affects his worldly prospects. 'Theory' signifies the attempt to systematize and order knowledge; to explain particular events by reference to general laws, to judge institutions in the light of ultimate moral principles – just as Ogilvie tests the institution of property against natural right and utility. 'Prejudice' contrasts with free inquiry; the prejudiced person is mentally asleep, fettered in thought to the status quo. 'Enlarged' views – or magnanimous and comprehensive thinking – contrast with bias and partiality. Men of enlarged minds stand above the prejudices and partialities of class, sect, and nation; their ideal is to see things dispassionately and from every angle. These words denote different aspects of the ideal of intellectual freedom; Ogilvie's book is an attempt to realize that ideal in his chosen field of study. One other aspect of this 'enlightened' frame of mind deserves mention – the drive to rationalized consistency. Every opinion is to be probed and tested; contradictions and woolly, unfounded beliefs are not to be tolerated. Accordingly, Ogilvie exposes the inconsistency of those who attack state pensions and sinecures while defending the incomes of landlords that are similarly unearned (33, 34, 111n).

In the context of his life history, Ogilvie's enlightened frame of mind is in no way surprising. He entered King's College Aberdeen in 1755 and graduated in 1759. This was not the end of his formal education; he attended Glasgow University in 1760 and 1761 and Edinburgh University in 1761 and 1762. At this time Adam Smith was lecturing at Glasgow, and Adam Ferguson at Edinburgh. In November 1762 Ogilvie took up a post as Assistant Professor of Philosophy at King's College Aberdeen; in 1765 he was elevated to Professor of Humanity. His kinsman, Lord Deskfoord, played an important part in gaining him these posts. He continued to pursue his academic career until 1817. The Professor of Humanity gave lectures on natural history, among other things; Ogilvie was deeply interested in this branch of the science of his day. He established a collection of fossils and minerals at the university and pressed unsuccessfully for the creation of a botanical garden. The enlightened frame of mind was greatly inspired and formed by the methods and triumphs of natural science.

This frame of mind is responsible for a major weakness of the book – its epistemological overoptimism.[9] Ogilvie, like so many of his contemporaries, has been led astray by his acceptance of an oversimple contrast between unthinking prejudice on the one hand, and enlightenment on the other. This contrast suggests that the alternatives are error or truth; and of course Ogilvie believes he possesses the latter. He ignores the possibility that, instead of one 'truth', there may be many reasonable and defensible opinions on the subject of land ownership. 'To all unbiassed reasoners', he confidently proclaims,

> [I]t will probably appear that no right whatever can be better founded than that which every man willing to employ himself in

agriculture has, to claim a certain proportion of the district in which
he happens to be born, he becoming bound to make just compensation to those by whose labour that spot of ground has been fer-
tilized. (92n)

But the argument of his book is not as obvious and indisputable
as he thinks, even to unbiased reasoners. Both his foundations –
natural right and utility – are contested today and were contested
when he wrote. His account of happiness is, as we shall see, a special
and debatable one – it is certainly not Bentham's, for example. And
it is open to question whether he is right in claiming that his agrarian
law would achieve universal comfort and prosperity; Malthus
would not have been persuaded.

This, then, is the fundamental weakness and overoptimism of the
book – the assumption that, when once we have emancipated ourselves from prejudice, final answers are within our grasp. The book
cannot be charged, however, with excessive optimism concerning
the difficulties of persuading landlords to overcome self-interest and
accept the agrarian law. Throughout the argument, private or sec-
tional interests are counterposed to the public good. Private interest
versus public good – these are key concepts of eighteenth-century
social thought.[10] Hobbes, Mandeville, and their critics explore these
concepts and the relationships they seek to grasp. Classical political
economy discusses society with their aid. One of the jobs of 'utility'
is to assert the public good and to attack laws and institutions that
benefit only the few.[11] But 'private interest' is, without further elab-
oration, vague and unspecific. How does Ogilvie interpret it, and
how does he propose to mediate between private interest and public
good? In his book, private interest means the interest of a section
– the landed interest being his major concern. The language of
'interests' is not to be equated with the Marxist language of 'class'.
He does not have a single and systematic set of concepts for analysing society. He refers to ranks, orders, the lower and higher
classes, the labouring poor, and the mendicant poor. To speak in
terms of private interest versus public good is in itself to inhabit a
different conceptual universe from the Marxist; for Marx, interests
are class interests and there is no public good as such. Ogilvie is
thoroughly aware of the difficulty of combatting 'private interest';
much of his book is devoted to the problem of how to counter it.
Three lines of thought should be considered. First, he sometimes

suggests that the landlords are *mistaken* in pursuing a supposed
private interest to the detriment of the public good. The agrarian
law would benefit them also (82, 85). In other words, he is proposing a natural identity of interests in the form of a prudent, rational egoism.[12] But since he fails to show how this is so, we must
judge it to be no more than a pious hope, the result of a tender-
minded unwillingness common to the age, to face the fact that rival
interests may in fact be irreconcilable. Second, he sometimes appeals
to landlords to be magnanimous, to sacrifice private interest for the
sake of public good (52–3). This is to try to extend the enlightenment ideal of dispassionate and impartial reason from the realm
of thought to the world of practice; a variant upon the hypothesis
or recommendation of a fusion of interests. That Ogilvie has little
faith in such altruism is demonstrated by the fact that he places
most reliance upon an artificial identification of interests – impo-
sition of the agrarian law by a government that can afford to ignore
the wishes of landlords. There are not too many candidates for this
role, but he hopes that imperial governments might try out the
scheme in their colonies, or that some enlightened despot – specifically Frederick the Great – will lead the way (49, 73). We cannot
charge Ogilvie with overoptimism on this issue, then, but neither
can we judge this aspect of his thought particularly successful. The
simple contrast between private interest and public good has considerable critical potential, but it cannot compensate for the lack
of an adequate set of concepts for the analysis of society, nor does
it lend itself to convincing strategies for social reform.

The shape of Ogilvie's social criticism and proposals for reform
is heavily influenced by his values. This brings us to an issue we
have sidestepped more than once; his interpretation of 'utility' and
'happiness'. The first point to make is that his utilitarianism, like
Bentham's, has a strongly egalitarian flavour. What counts is the
happiness of the mass of the common people; military glory and
power are featherweights in the balance by comparison (71). 'If he
be asked what is the most natural state of human kind, it may be
replied, that in which the whole tribe or race approach near to one
common standard of comeliness and strength' (20n, 18). This is
partly what he means when he uses those stock terms of the age,
'humane' and 'humanity'. The object of our concern should be *all*
humankind, the humble as well as the elevated. The term 'humane'

also implies a general benevolence. His book does not dwell on the sorrows of the poor, after the manner of 'sentimental' literature of the day, but we cannot doubt that his sympathy for common people is genuine and that he values a benevolent disposition (8n), admiring 'the friends of mankind' (43, 71).

'The happiness of individuals . . . is nearly in proportion to their virtue' (19). The second point to make is that what Ogilvie values is not really *happiness*, but *virtue*. What constitutes virtue? It is most to be found among yeoman farmers; a virtuous life is one of independence, simplicity, and modest comfort, fostering honesty, industry, and manliness (19, 71). Vicious lives are characterized by luxury, frivolity, and dissipation in the case of the rich (58n) and by mean-spiritedness, servility, cunning, fraud, hypocrisy, and malignant envy on the part of the poor. His ideal of virtue is a familiar eighteenth-century theme; it is based upon the myth of the classical republics of Greece and especially Rome, with its public-spirited farmer–soldiers, 'that virtuous and laborious class of men, of whom the severe Roman has said with delight that they are viri fortissimi – milites strenuissime – et minime male cogitantes' (83, trans. the strongest men, the toughest soldiers, and the least likely to think of evil doing). The classical republican ideal, as we have seen,[13] can be an aristocratic ideal, as in the writings of Shaftesbury; more usually it idealizes the independent gentleman. It can even, as in the case of Andrew Fletcher, find advantages in the institution of servitude. Ogilvie employs its vocabulary and subscribes to its values, while presenting it in egalitarian form. The ideal polity will be one in which all exhibit the virtue that stems from independence and simplicity. No doubt he owes a good deal to Ferguson. Like Ferguson, he criticizes luxury, advocates a militia, and hints at the corruption produced by the division of labour in manufacturing: 'Their industry is not like that of the labouring manufacturer, insipidly uniform, but varied, – it excludes idleness without imposing excessive drudgery' (19). Rural occupations are more 'natural' (10); we detect more than a hint of Rousseauist or Fergusonian primitivism (20). Ogilvie was deeply familiar with the classical sources of the rural idyll and the republican myth. The main duty of the Professor of Humanity was to teach classical history and literature. One or two of his pupils have left us a few scraps of evidence; they inform us not only that he was a most stimulating teacher, but also

that his translations of classical authors were very fine. One particularly remembered his translation of Vergil's *Eclogues*, poems
that paint a lost rural golden age. Ogilvie can criticize his society
severely, in part because his classical studies have furnished him
with the captivating image of a better one.

There are still a number of questions to ask about the structure
of his social thought. What is his conception of historical change,
and is it the product of conscious human agency or impersonal
forces? Correspondingly, what is the status of the given? How do
things come to be as they are, and how permanent is the status
quo? What is the extent and nature of his awareness of past times
and other societies? We have already noted his admiration of classical republics and simple societies. Yet the language of the text
does not carry a primitivist message. The terms 'progress', 'perfection', 'improvement' are regularly employed; he writes of the
'present advanced state' (8). There is a tension here; he is aware of
progress in some areas, such as commerce and public order; he also
recognizes that progress has entailed loss. But he has hopes for the
future; arrangements are possible that will combine the benefits of
progress without its costs. The phrase 'gradual progressive innovation' (3) indicates his conception of the nature and tempo of
change; he does not think of sharp breaks or revolutions. When we
consider his conception of how change has occurred, again we find
a tension. The present, unsatisfactory state of affairs was never
intended by anyone; evils do not result from malice but have arisen
in 'the course of things' (18). The present unjust conduct of landlords is to some extent excusable, as they are determined by their
situation; they do not have any clear perception of alternatives. His
explanation of the present, therefore, emphasizes environmental
determination and impersonal forces; but his hopes for future improvement are couched in terms of conscious intention and planning. 'This consummate prosperity cannot be thought to exceed the
compass of human wisdom duly applied' (26). Either this is a confusion, or it implies a belief that human affairs are at a turning
point: hitherto we have been in the grip of forces beyond our control, but now, because of enlightenment, we may direct the historical process. Certainly the present order of things appears to Ogilvie
to have no inevitability or permanence. He can regard it in this way,
as he tells us himself, because he is aware of historical change (43)

and also because he has knowledge of other nations.[14] Such knowledge frees its possessor from the conviction that the institutions of his own country are 'permanent and immutable . . . fixed by the destination of nature' (8). As we have seen, he has reflected upon the states of classical antiquity and is interested in land tenure arrangements described in the Bible. He knows about contemporary agriculture in Ireland, France, Spain, Prussia, Hungary, Poland, Russia, Egypt, America, and India. There are hints of a theory of the historical past of the British Isles echoing the theories of Hume, Ferguson, and Smith.[15] 'In the progress of the European system of landed property', he tells us, 'three stages may be distinguished – the domestic, the feudal, and the commercial' (43n). He seems nearer to Ferguson than to Hume and Smith in that he sees advantages in feudalism, lost in a commercial age. In a feudal order, lord and vassal are united by bonds of mutual need and service, 'But in the present times there is no reciprocal dependence' (44n). The final clause of the agrarian law states that

> [e]very person who has acquired an allotment of land in this manner shall pay to the lord of the manor certain aids and services of a feudal nature, so regulated as to produce that degree of connection and dependence which may be expedient for preserving order and subordination in the country without danger of giving rise to oppression and abuse. (99–100)

Here the reader may feel cynical; Ogilvie, apparently, has emerged in his true colours, at bottom a landed gentleman with the prejudices of his class. But the footnote that explains this clause indicates that the regulation is intended to ensure mutual concern and assistance; it reminds us of an earlier passage, in which he insists that 'the situation of a proprietor is more allied to that of a prince than that of a merchant, and requires some degree of those generous sentiments, and that benign demeanour, which ought to adorn the highest station' (8n). This may reflect the interests of a landlord; but the conception of a landlord and his role has been refined and idealized. He does not, like Hume and Smith, criticize the feudal age for its lack of freedom; he recognizes, however, that it was warlike and turbulent and that 'the present advanced state' has the advantage of order and security. He favours, under certain circumstances, sumptuary laws to restrain luxury (38–9); but apart from this he is a perfect Smithian in rejecting restraints upon commerce and industry (21–2). He stands poised between primitivism and progress; he wishes 'to unite the essential equality of a rude state, with the order, refinements, and accommodations of cultivated ages' (41).

In summary, Ogilvie has distanced himself to a considerable degree from the society of his day, creating a space for social criticism. Distancing has been achieved by means of an extensive awareness of other times and places and a conception of the outlines of historical evolution. These have emancipated him from any sense that his society is natural, permanent, or inevitable. Second, criticism has been encouraged by the enlightenment ideals of free inquiry and 'humanity'. Third, the concepts of natural right and utility have provided the essential dialectical weapons. None of these distancing devices is new, all are part of the enlightenment's stock-in-trade. But he employs them with courage and originality. Turning to the weaknesses of the book, he lacks a set of clear and systematic concepts to describe and analyse social structure and relationships and he has no coherent theory of social change. He does not use evidence in an orderly way – as he ought to have done to sustain or qualify his contention that small, independent farms are favourable to agricultural improvement. These weaknesses cannot be blamed entirely on the inadequacies of the intellectual equipment of his age; better analyses of society had already been provided by Smith and Millar, both of whom have theories of historical change. But the profoundest weakness – overconfidence in the possibility of moving from 'error' to 'truth' and arriving at final answers – is not at all unusual in the 1780s. The book may strike the postindustrial revolution reader as a mere museum-piece, because of its almost exclusively agrarian focus. In defence of Ogilvie, if he could have foreseen the industrial revolution in 1782, he would have been the most remarkable prophet of his age; and he lived in a part of the British Isles not remarkable for industrial development. Nevertheless it remains the case that in 1782 less than half the population of Britain was engaged in agriculture.

Enquiry concerning Political Justice and Its Influence on Morals and Happiness, William Godwin, 1798

Not all of *Political Justice* is relevant to this study. As its title indicates, much of it deals with politics rather than society. Furthermore it is a wide-ranging book, with long sections on mind and ethics. In spite of its length and range, its argument is coherent, though not well organized. The work is divided into eight books. The first three lay the groundwork, treating human nature, ethics, and general principles of government. Book 4 is a miscellany, but it contains arguments against revolution and for political change by means of education and enlightenment. Book 5 discusses politics under the traditional headings of monarchy, aristocracy, and democracy, looking forward to the 'euthanasia of government' in the (probably remote) future, recommending representative democracy in the meantime. Book 6 is a defence of free thought and discussion, Book 7 a critique of punishment, which Godwin hopes will one day be abolished. Book 8, our main concern, defends equality of property.

Whereas Ogilvie signified his adherence to the creed of enlightenment in passing, referring occasionally to the spread of science and decline of prejudice, Godwin shouts the faith from almost every page. He makes it abundantly clear to the reader, not only that 'enlightenment' has made radical criticism possible for him, but also that he has taken the ideal of enlightenment on board to such an extent as to regard the fearless and iconoclastic pursuit of truth to be one of the highest duties. He has 'the jealous eye, of a man habituated to the detection of errors' (72)[1] and 'the courage to strike into untrodden paths' (285). He brings 'the piercing search of truth' (256) and counsels us to submit ourselves to 'the guidance of truth, however unexplored might be the regions, and unexpected the conclusions to which she conducted us' (548). Prejudice is bad: scepticism, investigation, speculation are good. Not only is free inquiry a duty; it is also one of the highest pleasures:

> Sublime and expansive ideas produce delicious emotions. The acquisition of truth, the perception of the regularity with which proposition flows out of proposition, and one step of science leads to another, has never failed to reward the man who engaged in this species of employment. (298)

As with Ogilvie, an associated ideal is impartiality; the free inquirer is to be liberated from the distorting spectacles of self-interest and passion, exhibiting a godlike detachment (173–4). Furthermore, fearlessness in seeking truth must be accompanied by fearlessness in imparting it – Godwin's word for this is 'sincerity'. We must not be deterred from speaking what we know to be true by social and political pressures, nor by the fear of causing offence (333). So Godwin is a striking, even exaggerated, product of the enlightenment. Further confirmation of this is provided by his references to his reading; as a good scholar and honest man, he acknowledges his intellectual debts. So we discover he has read Locke, Shaftesbury, Swift, Butler, Mandeville, Hutcheson, Hume, Adam Smith, Paine, Voltaire, Rousseau, d'Holbach, Helvétius, Beccaria, and many others.

His advocacy of 'enlightenment' very often sounds as if it emanates from and idealizes a specific occupational and social position. It is the ideal of the free-floating intellectual, which Godwin was, to his glory and cost.[2] He inherited no secure and comfortable niche in society; his father was a dissenting minister, and the son, trained also for that profession, lost his intended career when he lost his faith. If he had lived today, Godwin would no doubt have been an academic, enjoying a steady salary and a solid reputation. As it was, from the time when he left the ministry in 1783 until his receipt of a government pension in 1833, he was forced to live by his pen – and a precarious living it was. Appropriately enough, the pattern of life of his anarchist ideal resembles his own life, without the insecurity. It will not be a life of incessant manual labour; there will be much leisure for intellectual pursuits. But it will not be a life of extravagant riches and luxury: 'Soundness of understanding is connected with simplicity of manners, and leisure for intellectual cultivation' (78).

If *Political Justice* bears the imprint of the enlightenment on every page, it is also saturated with ideas and assumptions from a different source – from the culture of dissent, in which Godwin was trained.[3] As we shall see, for example, the system of values of the book is intelligible by reference to this context. To be born a Congregationalist, an Independent, as Godwin was, meant a birthright of social marginality; his subsequent career pushed him further towards the fringe. In 1767 he went to school at Hindolveston, where his schoolmaster, Dr. Samuel Newton, was a Sandemanian. Sandemanianism, the English branch of the Scottish Glassites, was a small sect, close to Congregationalism, espousing a number of socially radical ideas and seeking to return to a pure and strict Calvinism of a rationalist kind. From 1773 to 1778 Godwin completed his education at Hoxton College. Though financed by Congregationalism, Hoxton, like other dissenting academies, was liberal and progressive, priding itself on its rationalism, free inquiry, and scientific education. Altogether, this was no bad training for a critic of society. For Protestant dissenters, freedom of conscience was the holy of holies, an attitude that combined readily with the enlightenment faith in free inquiry. The last stage of Godwin's religious upbringing came in 1783, when he read Priestley and 'veered to Socinianism' or unitarianism, of all branches of eighteenth-century British Christianity the most rationalist. I have emphasized the affinities between his religious culture and the enlightenment; but what he inherited from Congregationalism and Sandemanianism gave a peculiar colouring to his radicalism, as we shall see. If our list of the major cultural areas from which he drew inspiration is to be complete, mention must be made of the classics. Like all his educated contemporaries, he is steeped in classical literature and history; indeed he refers to the histories of Greece and Rome more than to any other history, even of the British Isles.

Before finally coming to grips with the arguments of the text about society, it is useful to observe the book's method, the method Godwin thinks appropriate for the conduct of an inquiry. *Political Justice* is an exceedingly abstract exercise. Its 700-odd pages contain no statistics and virtually no factual evidence of a specific kind. That his watchwords are 'reason' and 'truth' rather than 'experience' or 'facts' is unsurprising. Truth is to be attained by methodical procedures, that is to say, by establishing 'premises and fundamental positions' (72) and reasoning from them. Hence the third edition begins with a 'Summary of principles established and reasoned upon in the following work' (75). If he thinks his premises and fundamental positions need demonstration, his method is to establish them *discursively* – that is to say, by discussing them, along with rival principles and objections, until, he hopes, we are convinced. The road to truth, therefore, runs not via experience but via *theory*, that is, order and system, and via an appropriate attitude of mind – courageous, sceptical, and speculative. Now the main principles from which he reasons, his utilitarian conception of justice and his theory of the plasticity and improvability of human nature, are expounded in Books 1 and 2.

No utilitarian has ever bound together more strongly the principle of utility and the principle of benevolence. Benevolence can overcome selfishness, it often does, and it always should. Benevolence is accompanied by pity; the benevolent person ever has a tear at the ready: 'Humanity weeps over the distress of the peasantry in all civilized nations' (728). Sympathy should not be partial; we should concern outselves for the welfare of all mankind, be 'friends of . . . the human species' (408). Our pity extends even to animals:

> Every animal, however minute, has a curious and subtle structure, rendering him susceptible, as it should seem, of piercing anguish. We cannot move our foot without becoming the means of destruction. . . . These petty animals are capable of palpitating for days in the agonies of death. It may be said, with little licence of phraseology, that all nature suffers. (401)

Still, the happiness of our fellow humans must be our main concern, for they are capable of levels of felicity far above the mere animal. The best illustration of this is Godwin's four-stage scale of happiness. At the bottom come the brute sensual pleasures of the labourer or peasant, who 'slides through life with something of the contemptible insensibility of an oyster', but who, it is grudgingly admitted, 'is happier than a stone'. The next level is the refined sensuality and social amusements of 'men of rank, fortune and dissipation'; but such are still 'only a better sort of brutes'. The third level marks a considerable advance; the 'man of taste and liberal accomplishments' enjoys also the intellectual pleasures of science and art. Godwin reserves his eloquence, however, for the fourth level, represented by the man of benevolence and virtue (393–5). This scale deserves some comment and amplification. It is critical of merely sensual pleasures, of luxury and indulgence. It favours, therefore, a measure of simplicity: but it is not primitivist. Felicity does not mean a return to a basic mode of existence, for intellectual pleasures rank very high. Accordingly, Godwin insists that equality must mean a levelling up rather than a levelling down (395–6). At the top of the scale come the pleasures of benevolence, which enable Godwin to square the circle. Benevolence can triumph over self-love, because enlightened men and women will realize that benevolent conduct in fact brings the most exquisite and lasting happiness to the agent:

> There is no true joy but in the spectacle and contemplation of happiness. There is no delightful melancholy but in pitying distress. The man who has once performed an act of exalted generosity knows that there is no sensation of corporeal or intellectual taste to be compared with this. . . . No man reaps so copious a harvest of pleasure as he who thinks only of the pleasures of other men. (395)

Where does this system of values come from? Several sources may be suggested. The role accorded to benevolence and pity echoes both the philosophical critics of Hobbes and Mandeville – Butler, Shaftesbury, Hume – and the 'sentimental' literature of the day. The attack on luxury and assertion of the value of independence is reminiscent of the classical republican ideal, as modified for English consumption by Harrington and his successors; certainly *Political Justice* contains eulogies of classical republics. But Godwin is no unqualified 'classical republican'; he has no admiration for military 'virtues' (84) and he thinks that the *political* equality of republicanism is of no worth without social and economic equality (745). A more obvious source of these values lies in his dissenting background; disdain for sensual pleasures and glorification of 'independence' are wholly natural to one trained for the Independent ministry. Finally, this set of values has a striking social content; it is critical of the life-style of the rich without idealizing that of the poor. Its beau ideal is the life of the intellectual middle classes.

A further aspect of the moral theory bears the strong imprint of Calvinist dissent. The Calvinist doctrine of the calling prescribes that it is a man's duty to labour in the station to which God has called him; he is answerable for every scrap of time, every thought and deed. He is merely the steward of his time and possessions, held as a solemn trust from God; at every moment he must be directed not by inclination but by duty. Accordingly Godwin asks, 'But how much am I bound to do for the general weal, that is, for the benefit of the individuals of whom the whole is composed?' and answers 'Everything in my power. . . . If the extraordinary case should occur in which I can promote the general good by my death more than by my life, justice requires that I should be content to die' (174). Godwin is a strict, even a heroic moralist; his is a code for saints or angels. I must never spend time, money, or effort on my own concerns if I can promote more happiness by devoting them to others. Here we have the seeds of contradiction; Godwin, the intense puritan moralist, is often more concerned with making his fellows virtuous than with making them happy.

Godwin's social thought is built not only on utility, but also on concepts of justice and rights. What he says about rights can best be expounded in the context of his discussion of property; but justice requires preliminary treatment. As the title of the book indicates, its importance to him is paramount. Justice to him means impartial nonarbitrariness; in modern terms, what we call procedural justice:[4]

> . . . to put ourselves in the place of an impartial spectator, of an angelic nature, suppose, beholding us from an elevated station, and uninfluenced by our prejudices (173–4).
>
> Justice requires that I should put myself in the place of an impartial spectator of human concerns, and divest myself of retrospect to my own predilections. (76)

When discussing Ogilvie we noted the close similarity between this ethical ideal of impartiality and the intellectual ideal of enlightenment. This similarity is even clearer in Godwin's case. Both ideals perhaps express a yearning for freedom, the freedom that comes with detachment – freedom from passion and prejudice, freedom from overmuch concern and anxiety over one's own affairs:

> The man who vigilantly conforms his affections to the standard of justice, who loses the view of personal regards in the greater objects that engross his attention, who, from motives of benevolence, sits loose to life and all its pleasures, and is ready without a sigh, to sacrifice them to the public good, has an uncommonly exquisite source of happiness. When he looks back, he applauds the state of

his own affections; and when he looks out of himself, his sensations are refined, in proportion to the comprehensiveness of his sentiments. He is filled with harmony within; and the state of his thoughts is uncommonly favourable to what we may venture to style the sublime emotions of tranquillity. (383)

When discussing procedural justice in Chapter 3, I noted that it does not necessarily imply equality. For if individuals vary in merit, it may be inferred that justice requires they be given varying rewards. Godwin sometimes says this. The most notorious passage in the book is the little parable of Fenelon (a French moralist much admired by Godwin) and his valet. Suppose there is a fire, and I can rescue Fenelon or his valet: whom should I save? There can be no doubt – Fenelon must be rescued, both because he is likely to do more to promote the good of humanity and because 'being possessed of higher faculties, he is capable of more refined and genuine happiness' (169). To emphasize this passage, however, would be to miss the main drift of his thoughts on justice, which are strongly egalitarian in implication. The maxim 'treat like cases alike' becomes in his hands a principle of equality, through the instrumentality of an extra input; the claim that all human beings *are*, essentially, alike – all equally capable of reason and happiness.

> We find by observation that we are surrounded by beings of the same nature with ourselves. They have the same senses, are susceptible of the same pleasures and pains, capable of being raised to the same excellence and employed in the same usefulness. (381; see also 183, 231, 249, 749)

This is not to say that all are actually equal in merit here and now; it is, rather, an assertion that all can become equal in excellence. This is made clear by his fine answer to those who argue that the emancipation of slaves is unnecessary, because slaves are too degraded to resent their condition:

> Are they contented? I am not contented for them. I see in them beings of certain capacities, equal to certain pursuits and enjoyments. It is of no consequence in the question that they do not see this, that they do not know their own interests and happiness. They do not repine? Neither does a stone repine. That which you mention as an alleviation furnishes in my conception the portrait of their calamity. Abridged as they are of independence and enjoyment, they have neither the apprehension nor spirit of men. I cannot bear to see human nature thus degraded. It is my duty, if I can, to make them a thousand times happier than they are, or have any conception of being. (393)

Where does he get his egalitarian premise from? No doubt the Christian doctrine of the equal worth of every human soul is important. Egalitarianism is also built in to the approaches and assumptions of the enlightenment – the pervasive drive to explain complexity and diversity in terms of simple and uniform basic elements, the drive, in other words, towards the application of scientific method – as then understood – in all fields of inquiry. This leads naturally to the other principle from which the argument of *Political Justice* is reasoned – the principle of malleability.

Political Justice develops an associationist psychological theory, quoting Locke, Hume, Hartley, and Helvétius.[5] Like Helvétius, Godwin argues that mental and moral inequalities are not natural and inevitable but environmentally engendered. Consequently, better human beings can be produced by improving education and environment. Also like Helvétius, he lays great stress upon the social and political dimensions of the environment:

> It is beyond all controversy that men who live in a state of equality, or that approaches equality, will be frank, ingenuous and intrepid in their carriage; while those who inhabit where a great disparity of ranks has prevailed will be distinguished by coldness, irresoluteness, timidity and caution. . . . Political institution, by the consequences with which it is pregnant, strongly suggests to everyone who enters its sphere what is the path he should pursue. Under a government fundamentally erroneous, he will see intrepid virtue proscribed, and a servile and corrupt spirit uniformly encouraged. (113–14)

Godwin is no tame and unoriginal follower of Helvétius, however. Whereas the latter thought that the ruling passion was and always would be self-love, Godwin believed that human beings could be reared up to the most perfect benevolence. And something that is uniquely his own – Godwin sets great store by the possibility of improving men and women by reasoning with them; frankly showing them the error of their ways, pointing out to them the paths of truth, virtue, and happiness:

> Sound reasoning and truth, when adequately communicated, must always be victorious over error: Sound reasoning and truth are capable of being so communicated: Truth is omnipotent: The vices and moral weakness of man are not invincible: Man is perfectible, or in other words susceptible of perpetual improvement. (140)

He devotes a long chapter to the thesis that reason can always prevail over passion; we need never be 'carried away'. Considerations presented to the faculty of reflection will annihilate lust (131). And perhaps we may be able to disarm an assassin who comes against us with a sword, not by force but by reasoning (642– 3). Such faith in the unbounded power of reason over conduct was unusual even in the age of enlightenment; Pope's judgment was more typical:

> On life's vast ocean diversely we sail,
> Reason the card [i.e., map], but passion is the gale.

It is an afterecho of the Sandemanianism of Godwin's youth. Sandeman wrote to refute the 'heart' religion of revivalism and especially Methodism. The main issue in the debate was the manner in which conversion occurred and a sinner became saved. Wesley maintained that conversion took the form of a turning of the heart away from the world and towards Christ, a shattering emotional experience deeper than reason. Revivalist preaching, therefore, was dramatic, designed to achieve this emotional impact. Sandeman had considerable distaste for the ecstatic physical manifestations of revivalism and for preachers who stimulated such frenzies. By contrast, he argued that the change that constitutes conversion and secures salvation occurs not in the heart but in the understanding; a man is saved when he hears, understands, and believes the gospel. The sustained argument in *Political Justice* for the power of reason and truth should be seen, therefore, as a consequence of the debate between Sandemanianism and Methodism – Godwin suggests as much himself.[6]

This completes the survey of the principles upon which his argument is based – the moral theory and values, faith in reason and passion for enlightenment, the doctrine of malleability. Before turning to our main concern, his critique of property and aristocracy, we can briefly sketch his main political conclusion. Government stands condemned; its constant concern is for order, stasis, and hence it obstructs the progress of knowledge. It controls, not by reason, but force. Of its very nature it curbs independence, prescribing to citizens what they should do and avoid, instead of leaving them to think and decide for themselves. And it is unnecessary. By good education, through reason, men and women can be made benevolent, wise, and virtuous; such improved beings will not need to be coerced and restrained, but will live in peace and love.

Godwin's theory of property is expressed in the language of

rights. His analysis of rights presents some difficulty. He begins by distinguishing active and passive rights: passive rights, the 'right we possess to the forbearance or assistance of other men' (191), are simply the correlatives of duties. I argued in Chapter 3[7] that in this sense, the term 'rights' is redundant; any statement about rights of this kind could be translated into the language of duties without loss, and the duties are prior, the rights derivative. For Godwin does not intend that the possessor of a passive right should be regarded as having the power to compel the performance of the corresponding duty; in a perfect society without government there would be no legal enforcement of the duty. Active rights accord more nearly with what we normally understand by the term 'rights'. They are 'the right in certain cases to do as we list' (191), that is to say, they demarcate areas of conduct over which the possessor of such rights is sovereign and can choose to do as he or she pleases. Godwin peremptorily denies that we have any such rights. His reasoning is that at any moment, or any point of decision, there is never more than one course of action that we may rightly choose. For we must always seek out and do that which will promote the greatest balance of happiness; we are not entitled to do that which will make two people happy if we could instead make three equally happy. To suppose we had the right to choose the former would be to suppose we had the right not to promote the greatest happiness, that is to say, the right to do wrong, and 'There cannot be a more absurd proposition than that which affirms the right of doing wrong' (196).

> Few things have contributed more to undermine the energy and virtue of the human species than the supposition that we have a right, as it has been phrased, to do what we will with our own. . . . We have in reality nothing that is strictly speaking our own. We have nothing that has not a destination prescribed to it by the immutable voice of reason and justice. (194)

A preliminary assessment might therefore come to the conclusion that he rejects rights: for he denies any 'active rights', that is, rights as usually understood, and accepts only 'passive rights', which are arguably redundant, merely the correlatives of duties. In fact this would be a false conclusion; he *does* believe in active rights, and is merely confused when he denies this. For it is clear that he is deeply opposed to coercing individuals to perform their duties:

[E]ach must have his sphere of discretion. No man must encroach upon my province, nor I upon his. He may advise me, moderately and without pertinaciousness, but he must not expect to dictate to me. He may censure me freely and without reserve; but he should remember that I am to act by my deliberation and not his. . . . Force may never be resorted to but in the most extraordinary and imperious emergency. (198)

Now if this faculty of exercising a discretion that may not be infringed by my neighbour is to have any sense, it *must* mean that on occasion others may not interfere even when I do wrong; if I should only be left free when performing my duty, I would have no discretion at all. Godwin has fallen into the trap of confusing the objective and subjective senses of 'right';[8] doing *right* and having *a right*. If we may take it upon ourselves to sort out his confusion, what he really intends is to say that we ought always to do right, but we also have a right to govern our own conduct, except in 'the most extraordinary and imperious emergency', and of course the exercise of this right will sometimes involve us in doing wrong. This *must* be what he means:

According to the usual sentiment, every club assembling for any civil purpose, every congregation of religionists assembling for the worship of God, has a right to establish any provisions or ceremonies, no matter how ridiculous or detestable, provided they do not interfere with the freedom of others. (196)

There is no problem in interpreting this to mean that it would not be right for a club or congregation to establish ridiculous ceremonies; but to regard it as meaning that they *have no right* to establish such ceremonies – that is, that individuals, or the state, may stop them – would be to interpret this passage in a manner contrary to the whole tenor of *Political Justice*. Godwin therefore, in spite of his confused use of the language of rights, should properly be regarded as a passionate enthusiast *both* for seeking out and doing, at every moment of every day, the right; *and* for active or liberty rights, rights to the greatest possible area of individual discretion and choice. Only if both of these points are borne in mind can we make sense of his theory of property.

And here with grief it must be confessed that, however great and extensive are the evils that are produced by monarchies and courts, by the imposture of priests and the iniquity of criminal laws, all these are imbecile and impotent compared with the evils that arise out of the established administration of property. (725)

This is one of a number of passages reminiscent of Ogilvie, which need occasion no surprise as Godwin acknowledges his debt to this 'ingenious inhabitant of North Britain' whose reasonings 'have sometimes considerable merit' (729n).[9] In answer to the question 'what made radical social criticism possible for Godwin?' one immediate answer is 'Ogilvie's book'. Ogilvie may have had little *direct* influence; indirectly, some of his ideas were broadcast in Godwin's bestseller. The starting point of Godwin's critique of property is a firm conviction that poverty is evil:

> What a contrast does this scene present to the present state of society, where the peasant and the labourer work till their understandings are benumbed with toil, their sinews contracted and made callous by being for ever on the stretch, and their bodies invaded with infirmities, and surrendered to an untimely grave? What is the fruit they obtain from this disproportioned and unceasing toil? In the evening they return to a family, famished with hunger, exposed half naked to the inclemencies of the sky, hardly sheltered, and denied the slenderest instruction. (730)

The contrast between this and the luxury of the rich is intolerable, especially as that luxury is a cause of the contrasting poverty: 'When we see the wealth of a province spread upon the great man's table, can we be surprised that his neighbours have not bread to satiate the cravings of hunger?' (483–4). The good things of the world may be divided into four classes (703): the means of subsistence; the means of intellectual and moral improvement; inexpensive gratifications; and luxuries, which can only be produced with considerable labour. It is this fourth class of things, enjoyed only by the rich, which causes so many to be in want (704). The inequality and deprivation caused by the pursuit of luxuries on the part of the rich also serves to keep down population, as the poor are forced to restrict their breeding; thus the value of all those lives and all that happiness is lost (734).[10] Two remarks may be made about the argument up to this point. First, it depends on Godwin's precise variant of utilitarianism. He criticizes inequality by invoking standards of welfare and happiness that belittle the amount of genuine enjoyment to be obtained from luxuries, locating true felicity instead in modest comforts and mental improvement. Second, the argument is excessively abstract. Important factual claims are made – that the luxury of the rich causes the wretchedness of the poor, that inequality retards population – but are not adequately argued or substantiated.

The main discussion begins by distinguishing three kinds or degrees of property (710). The first and highest is the right each has to those things that will bring more happiness if used by him or her than if used by anyone else. Remembering the division of good things into four classes, this must mean that each has a right, first to the means of subsistence; second to the means of intellectual and moral improvement, provided that the exercise of this right does not deprive anyone else of subsistence; and third to inexpensive gratifications, with the same proviso. This degree of property is referred to repeatedly as a *right*; it is a right of recipience, a right to receive basic, and under certain circumstances not so basic, goods. The second degree of property is the right every man has to dispose of the produce of his own industry. Godwin hastens to add that this does not imply that the producer is morally entitled to consume all he has produced. It may be that some of it will bring more happiness if consumed by another, to whom he must therefore give it. A man is only the steward of whatever wealth he possesses, and 'Every shilling of his property, and even every, the minutest, exertion of his powers have received their destination from the decrees of justice' (711). Here is a striking illustration of that strenuous and all-embracing conception of virtue that characterizes his utilitarianism; I must not spend a shilling on myself if it could be better spent on another. How many of the rich would be acquitted, when tried by this standard? Godwin indicates the biblical roots of this doctrine of stewardship, citing the verse from St. Mark where Jesus advises the rich man, 'go thy way, sell whatever thou hast, and give to the poor', and the verses from the Acts that tell how the apostles held their goods in common, allocating according to need. So far, so good; but now we come once more to confusion over the concept of rights. A man is only the steward of his possessions, 'But still he is the steward'. Though it may be his duty to give his goods to the poor, neither the poor, nor the State, may compel him to do so. For independence is the essence of excellence; each must be sovereign over his own actions, including the disposal of his property. 'And here it is only necessary that we should recollect the principle on which the doctrine of property is founded, the sacred and indefeasible right of private judgement' (722). This is a liberty right, a right of action; and how, if it is indefeasible, can it always be reconciled with the right of others to receive the means of subsistence, mental and moral improvement, and so on? The third degree of property is that 'by which one man enters into the faculty of disposing of the produce of another man's industry'.

> It is a gross imposition that men are accustomed to put upon them-selves when they talk of the property bequeathed to them by their ancestors. The property is produced by the daily labour of men who are now in existence. All that their ancestors bequeathed to them was a mouldy patent which they show as a title to extort from their neighbours what the labour of those neighbours has produced. (711–12)

Here, as in Ogilvie, is a theory of exploitation beginning to crys-tallize, but not yet fully formed. The rich, 'by fraud or force, have usurped the power of buying and selling the labour of the great mass of the community' (713). Evidently his thought on this issue was developing as the book went through its three editions. In the first edition, he looks forward to the day when 'the labourer will receive entire whatever the consumer may be required to pay, with-out having a middleman, an idle and useless monopolizer, as he will then be found, to fatten upon his spoils'. In the second edition, 'middleman' has become 'capitalist' (793).[11] And in the third edi-tion, a long passage is added to Chapter 9 of Book 6 in which we are told:

> The higher and governing part of the commuunity are like the lion who hunted in concert with the weaker beasts. The landed proprietor first takes a very disproportionate share of the produce to himself; the capitalist follows, and shows himself equally voracious. (622)[12]

Here is the suggestion that different economic classes – landed pro-prietors and capitalists – exploit in different ways. But nowhere does Godwin explain how the rich have obtained these powers to enter into the fruits of the labour of the common people, nor the mechanisms by which exploitation operates.

Inequality, as well as causing physical harm to the poor, violating utility and rights, and resting on exploitation, is also corrupting; it corrupts rich and poor alike, damaging the moral fabric of society. The rich become overbearing, insolent, dictatorial, and tyrannical; since they do not have to exert themselves, since everything is done for them by servants, they become soft and indolent. They imbibe 'the poison of flattery and effeminate indulgence' (471). The poor are filled with envy and resentment, they learn to be servile towards their 'betters', and they lack opportunities to develop intellectual capacities. The rich, holding political power, reduce oppression into a system by legislation; the state itself becomes corrupt (92). Justice is bought and sold; theft, which only the poor are tempted to commit, is treated as a capital crime and punished inhumanely, while the rich legislate patents and monopolies for themselves. Workers' combinations are forbidden, and game laws passed to protect the rich man's sport (93–4). Ever-increasing consumption taxes lay the burdens of the state upon the poor. But worst of all, inequality corrupts the moral sense, as wealth comes to be esteemed more than integrity, virtue, understanding, and industry (92). The evil is cumulative. When men are esteemed because they are rich, love of distinction, a universal human characteristic, drives them to indulge in ostentation and extravagance, so that all will perceive their opulence. In order to indulge their taste for luxuries, the rich lay ever greater burdens of work upon the poor. A disproportionate share of society's wealth is in the hands of a few, and they continually seek ways of spending it, ways that multiply rather than reduce labour (746).

> The country-gentleman who, by levelling an eminence, or introducing a sheet of water into his park, finds work for hundreds of industrious poor is the enemy, and not, as has commonly been imagined, the friend, of his species. (712)

In a state of equality without luxury industries, all would live in comfort on half an hour's labour a day (746). Godwin is no enthusiast for what has since been dubbed the 'capitalist work ethic'; how much better, he thinks, if all had leisure for intellectual pursuits. Here again, we get a sense of a theory of exploitation in process of formation, but not yet clarified. Is luxury an effect, or a cause, of the extremes of inequality? Finally, inequality brings on a state of war. The poor become criminals in their attempt to redress the balance, the rich protect the status quo by force. Envy, malice, and revenge become prevalent. By contrast,

> In a state of society where men lived in the midst of plenty, and where all shared alike the bounties of nature, these sentiments would

inevitably expire. The narrow principle of selfishness would vanish. No man being obliged to guard his little store, or provide, with anxiety and pain, for his restless wants, each would lose his individual existence in the thought of the general good. (732)

Much of this argument about the socially corrupting effects of inequality – the vain pursuit of ostentation, the false set of values, the cruel burdens upon the poor, the state of social warfare – is strongly reminiscent of Rousseau's *Discourses*; to note this resemblance is to point to the roots in the classical republican image of corruption and social decadence.

One final aspect of the critique of inequality in *Political Justice* deserves to be heavily stressed. It is not a critique of inequality in the abstract, but of the form of inequality in eighteenth-century British society; that is to say, of aristocracy and a hierarchical system of connection, patronage, and dependence. Five of the basic principles we have already noted play an important role in this argument; the malleability theory, justice, the ideal of independence, the concept of rights, and the intense, demanding moralism that regards no action as indifferent and that makes virtue the ultimate good. Godwin's hatred of aristocracy rises to passion:

> It is not satire, but a simple statement of fact, when we observe that it is not easy to find a set of men in society sunk more below the ordinary standard of man in his constituent characteristics than the body of the English, or any other, peerage. (468)

He is unable to conceive of any justification for an extreme, institutionalized inequality – revealingly, he has sympathy for Satan in *Paradise Lost*, because 'he saw no sufficient reason for that extreme inequality of rank and power which the creator assumed' (309). In the light of the malleability theory, hereditary preeminence is a deep insult to reason and justice. The new-born son of a peer does not have upon him the marks of genius, understanding, virtue, and honour; the son of a mechanic is not born with callous hands and an ungainly form.

> We have been told indeed 'that nature will break out', and that
> 'The eaglet of a valiant nest will quickly tower
> Up to the region of his sire;'
> and the tale was once believed. But mankind will not soon again be persuaded that the birthright of one lineage of human creatures is beauty and virtue, and of another, dullness, grossness and deformity. (467)

Aristocracy flagrantly violates the impartial nonarbitrariness required by justice when it awards wealth, power, and esteem in accordance with the accident of birth. Every uncorrupted mind recognizes that in the race of life, all should start fair, and the prizes should be awarded to virtue, talent, and achievement (184, 242, 472, 474–5). Godwin loathes charity, which corrupts him that gives and him that takes. It is degrading to beg and implore, to depend upon the whims of another. And, as the argument about property has demonstrated, it is morally unnecessary; the needy have a right to subsistence, the rich have an absolute duty to bestow their wealth where it will create most happiness.

> Observe the pauper fawning with abject vileness upon his rich benefactor, speechless with sensations of gratitude, for having received that which he ought to have claimed, not indeed with arrogance, and a dictatorial and overbearing temper, but with the spirit of a man discussing with a man, and resting his cause only on the justice of his claim. (725–6; see also 176, 461, 699–700, 708)

Persons should relate to one another, not on the basis of charity and dependence, but on the basis of justice and right; this alone is compatible with human dignity. This passionate protest against hierarchical and deferential society reminds us again of Godwin's nurture in the culture of religious dissent, in Independency: 'even in the petty institution of Sunday schools, the chief lessons that are taught are a superstitious veneration for the Church of England, and to bow to every man in a handsome coat' (614). In the light of this we can understand what is often regarded as one of Godwin's eccentricities: his total rejection of gratitude. Gratitude is conventionally thought the fit response to a favour; we feel and show it towards one who has done us a good turn which he need not have done, a gracious act of charity to which we have no strict right. But this, says Godwin, is an immoral situation; every moment of a man's time, every shilling of his wealth, must be employed to promote the greatest happiness. If the charity done to me would have promoted more happiness by being done to another, then I ought to blame my benefactor rather than be grateful. If on the contrary the charity was conducive to utility, then I have no cause to be grateful; the benefactor has simply done his duty, which he would have been blamable for omitting (171). This is a significant argument. Eighteenth-century moralists – Hume, Hutcheson,

Adam Smith – lay great stress on the virtue of gratitude. To cite gratitude as one of the chief virtues would not be an obvious thing for a twentieth-century western European to do; clearly the eighteenth-century moralists are reflecting the structure of their own society, which was built upon patronage and gratitude. Gratitude was a cement that glued the social fabric together. Godwin's rejection of it as a virtue is a central element of his repudiation of inequality.

An ideal society, then, will be without government, and egalitarian. Enlightened individuals will have too much regard for justice to seize the fruits of the labour of others, and so much regard for utility that they will give to the poor all they possess over and above what is necessary to a life of simple comfort. Godwin has little to say about the detailed arrangements of his utopia, but on one general issue he has a distinctive and fascinating point of view – the issue of interpersonal relations in an improved society. What is so special is the thoroughgoing way in which he attempts to combine perfect altruism with a jealous safeguarding of individuality. His sense of what the individual owes to the whole is in no way bounded or lukewarm: '[W]e are but one. . . . Each man is but the part of a great system'. (178). Yet, as we have seen, he also regards independence as an essential condition of all human excellence, intellectual and moral. He takes the defence of independence to the point of criticizing many normal forms of cooperation. Symphony concerts are condemned because the musicians slavishly and mechanically play together (760); cohabitation and marriage cannot escape censure, for when we live constantly with other people, we continually adapt our pattern of life, our pursuits, and even our opinions to suit them (761). Cooperation in the division of labour is similarly a threat to independence, and he looks forward to the day when, with the aid of improved machines, one man will be able to undertake any productive task on his own (766–7).

> How may the peculiar and independent operation of each individual in the social state most effectively be preserved? . . . How may the individuals of the human species be made to contribute most substantially to the general improvement and happiness? (79)

As we have seen, he insists both that we are under a stern duty to use every moment for the general good and that no one may coerce us to do this, that we must act in accordance with our own decisions:

> [I]t is necessary that we should distinguish two sorts of independence, one which may be denominated natural, and the other moral. Natural independence, a freedom from all constraint, except that of reasons and inducements presented to the understanding, is of the utmost importance to the welfare and improvement of mind. Moral independence, on the contrary, is always injurious. (754)

A celebrated distinction in social thought is between those societies that are organic, whose members pursue a common good and are motivated to do so nonrationally, by affection, instinct, and habit, and those societies that are individualistic, whose members pursue self-interest and govern their conduct by rational calculations of advantage.[13] Godwin resolutely rejects both these forms of social cohesion. Admittedly he places great store by benevolence and thinks that in an equal society this emotion will be strengthened (288, 317, 388). But benevolence must work under the guidance of reason, and he has no time for habit. We can say, therefore, that he subscribes to the principle of the fusion of interests,[14] but we must add that he gives his own distinctive slant to it. He does not follow Hume, who based altruistic motivation on sympathy reinforced by custom. At the other extreme, he can find nothing to admire in a situation where individuals work together out of a regard for rational self-interest. Significantly, he repudiates the use of contracts; the contract is the paradigmatic form of a social relationship in which each participant does a service for others, solely with a view to the advantage he has been promised in return (220, 222). Godwin's attempt to reconcile devotion to others with independence is at the heart of *Political Justice*; it is a strenuous, noble, and inspiring ideal and gives the book much of its appeal. To many readers it has seemed altogether *too* high an ideal, and hence it has contributed to earning the book its reputation as a visionary, impractical work. But it constitutes his best claim to originality and enduring interest. This conception of human relationships, as we have seen, is possible for him because of his roots both in dissenting culture and in the thought of the enlightenment.

One large topic remains to be considered – conceptions of time and change. The idea of progress is shouted from almost every page and is one of the principles listed at the beginning of the book: 'The extent of our progress in the cultivation of knowledge is unlimited. Hence it follows . . . That human inventions, and the modes of social existence, are susceptible of perpetual improvement' (77). This is it, in essence; progress is conceived, primarily, as progress in knowledge; but this will generate social advance. It is possible, as some eighteenth-century thinkers illustrate, to combine a belief in progress with a nostalgia for primitive virtues; but Godwin, for the most part, is single-minded in his rejection of the 'noble savage'. Pre-political societies present a sorry spectacle; they lack order and security, which are prerequisites of science, technology, and literature (723). Primitives may have been innocent, that is, not corrupted by luxury; but innocence is not virtue:

> Virtue demands the active employment of an ardent mind in the promotion of the general good. No man can be eminently virtuous who is not accustomed to an extensive range of reflection. . . . Ignorance, the slothful habits and limited views of uncultivated life, have not in them more of true virtue. (153)

Rousseau argued correctly that in primitive societies, there was infinitely less inequality, hence an absence of the contrast between the misery of the poor and the corruption and effeminacy of the rich. Mandeville and Hume were also right in arguing that progress in art and science stemmed from a departure from this primitive equality; indeed, inequalities of property were perhaps necessary incentives to the unfolding of the powers of mind (181, 721, 750). But this does not mean we are faced with an unattractive choice between equality and progress; both may be combined in the future. A conception of how progress has occurred has to be assembled from slight, scattered references in *Political Justice*; though the result is a mere sketch, it is a sketch with a clear outline. Progress began with the invention of language, which has since advanced, becoming more copious and refined (158). Then came writing; first picture writing, then the superior alphabetical writing. Progress has accelerated in the last three centuries, especially since the fall of Constantinople to the Turks in 1453, which 'dispersed among European nations the small fragment of learning . . . shut up within the walls of this metropolis' (397). Printing was invented at about the same time; it has multiplied books, thus safeguarding Europe against any lapse into barbarism, such as overtook Greece and

Rome. One of the most promising aspects of his own day, Godwin thinks, is the diffusion of knowledge that has resulted from the use of the printed book. Books are now very cheap, and there is a mass readership (398). Another cause of progress was the Reformation, 'which gave an irrecoverable shock to the empire of superstition and implicit obedience. From that time, the most superficial observation can trace the improvements of art and science' (397). His faith in progress is evidently sustained by an awareness of and enthusiasm for the advance of science (273, 279). This account of progress is strikingly intellectualist; there are no more than a few badly assimilated references to those economic changes that played so important a part in the theory of progress of the Scottish historical school, a theory that was echoed in Ogilvie's book.[15] Nor does the account of progress rely in any way upon detailed knowledge of societies at different levels of development, past and present. The debate over primitivism and progress has clearly had a great influence upon him, but he engages with that debate in a superficial and abstract way. The concept of 'society', however, is more developed in his text than it was in Spence's or Ogilvie's. In *Political Justice* the term is not synonymous with 'civil society', as it was in *The Real Rights of Man*: a society is quite distinct from the state and could exist apart from it. Godwin regularly uses 'society' as an abstract term to refer to the condition in which large groups of individuals form stable institutions and relationships. Like Ogilvie, he uses such terms as 'nation', 'country', and 'community' to refer to particular societies; but he also uses 'a society', 'societies', to do this job, which Spence and Ogilvie do not. He is very much alive to the fact that societies differ, though his discussion of social differences is taken almost entirely from Hume (146–56).[16] But his precise conception of society does not prevent his from being an 'idealist' account of progress. This accords with the unbounded faith in the power and instrumentality of mind that we find throughout *Political Justice*. We are reminded of that curious appendix (which, it must be granted, he insists is no more than a 'deviation into the land of conjecture') entitled 'Of health, and the prolongation of human life' (770). It contains speculations about the influence of the mind over the body, suggesting that illness is very often caused by mental disorder, and looks forward to the day when we will be able to extend our conscious control over all bodily

processes, including aging. Perhaps, when reason and enlightenment have advanced far enough, we shall become immortal.

How is society to be improved? As we would expect, he opposes
the use of legislative and political methods of change. Because of
the value he places upon independence and 'truth', not only does
he reject monarchy and aristocracy; he also has grave doubts about
democracy. To be ruled by majority opinion is not necessarily desirable; for the majority may be ignorant and misguided. In a representative assembly, decisions are taken by vote; but a proposal
that wins in the lobbies is not therefore right (260, 547). His repudiation of political strategies for change is epitomized by his rejection of legislation. 'Legislation . . . is not an affair of human
competence. Immutable reason is the true legislator, and her decrees
it behoves us to investigate' (236). In other words, we are not entitled to create, through political activity and legislation, an order
of society that pleases us or that achieves a compromise between
conflicting interests; all we may do is discover, by the exercise of
reason, the order that is eternally and universally right. But having
discovered it, may we not pursue political means to bring it about
and employ legislation to enforce it? His emphatic answer is no;
and his main ground for this refusal is summed up in a saying he
quotes repeatedly – 'Government is founded on opinion'. He interprets this saying – which he borrows from Hume – in the following way. If opinion is not universally in favour of a state of
affairs, then legislating it into being will involve coercion of the
dissenting majority or minority; and this is always wrong. But if
opinion *is* universally in favour, then legislation is not required; the
state of affairs will spontaneously come about, by the unforced
actions of the whole community. Reason and enlightenment are the
only justifiable way forward. In a striking image, he asks us to
imagine ten thousand sane men, brainwashed into thinking they
are mad, shut up in a madhouse under the supervision of three or
four keepers. Gradually, the truth dawns, until eventually all realize
they have been deceived.

> The prisoners are collected in their common hall, and the keepers
> inform them that it is time to return to their cells. They have no
> longer the power to obey. They look at the impotence of their late
> masters, and smile at their presumption. They quietly leave the man-
> sion where they were hitherto immured, and partake of the blessings
> of light and air like other men. (149)

Political Justice therefore rejects the strategies of revolution, of political associations, to achieve change (283, 287–8). Inequality is a great evil; but, since coercion has been ruled out, inequality may not be rectified either by private or public force (716). This argument appears unsatisfactory.

Godwin has already argued that inequality is maintained by force; the rich use the law and the state apparatus to protect their privileges, and to seize the fruits of the labour of others. Why then may we not use force against force? If coercion is employed to remove a coercive state of affairs, can this conceivably be wrong if at the end of the process there is less coercion than before? He insists that revolution will undermine all security, and without security, 'nothing good or excellent can be accomplished' (717). This may be a good argument against revolution; it is not obvious that it works against reform, against gradual and moderate legislative measures to reduce inequality. Godwin nowhere suggests that inequality might be mitigated through taxation policy; an omission explicable, no doubt, in terms of the evil reputation of 'old corruption'. 'If we had neither foreign wars nor domestic stipends, taxation would be almost unknown' (625; see also 621, 623). But to the modern reader this is not too promising; he has ruled out revolution and reform by legislative or fiscal means. He has put all his eggs into the basket of enlightenment. His position is only tenable because of his massive faith in the power of truth to win out in the end. Yet even Godwin, sometimes, doubts (248). Why has truth not triumphed hitherto? Part of his answer is that error has had power on its side (490, 563). But this traps us in a vicious circle. We may not use force to bring about a better order, we must rely upon showing our opponents the truth. But truth cannot prevail over error institutionalized, error backed by force. This reminds us of the chapter on education, in which he concedes that 'political education', that is to say, the bad influence of an unequal social and political system, is the most powerful kind of education, that enlightened teaching is futile in a bad environment (113–15).

If we begin our assessment by asking how successful Godwin has been in distancing himself from his society, we have to conclude that his achievement is remarkable. He manages to put much to the question – not only the economic, social and political order, not only work and the family, but also the everyday, taken-for-granted practices we use in relating to one another – practices such as promising and making contracts, responses of charity, deference and gratitude, all forms of cooperation. *Political Justice* is still a radical and challenging book. As we have seen, its distance from late eighteenth-century England is made possible by a synthesis of cultures or intellectual styles – that of the enlightenment and that of dissenting religion. Naturally Godwin does not address himself to our question, of how he can be so radical; but if he had done so, he would have had little difficulty in giving the answer. He himself points to the intellectually emancipating effects of the Protestant Reformation and of science; he directs our attention to the diffusion of letters by printing. He knows how free inquiry is facilitated by the private study made possible by a culture based upon the printed book (256). *Political Justice* was also prompted by the world-shattering experience of the French Revolution, but the subsidiary importance of this event, when compared with the intellectual milieux already referred to, is indicated by the fact that neither the events in France nor the reaction in England made much difference to his attitude of hostility to political strategies for the achievement of change. Secondly, *Political Justice* is powerful as a moral critique; it mobilizes the intense moralism of dissent, concepts of utility, rights and justice, and values such as independence and benevolence derived from dissenting culture and eighteenth-century moral argument. Much of this is very successful; but Godwin gets into a tangle over rights, and he is open to the charge that his moral ideal – an uncompromising synthesis of independence and altruism – is too high for humanity. Thirdly, *Political Justice* is able to deploy against aristocratic society an excellent psychological theory. Associationism, without which *Political Justice* would be a completely different book, was the result of a century's debate and discussion about the mechanisms of mind. Fourthly, a related point, the critique of the status system of an aristocratic society is devastating.

If, however, we consider the theory of society in *Political Justice*, we are likely to be somewhat less impressed. Most of Godwin's artillery is concentrated on a moral critique of status. He is working towards a conception of economic exploitation, but has not discovered the mechanisms of that exploitation. Here he provides only hints and beginnings. There are also the beginnings of a theory of ideology. He has a sense of the ways in whi:ʰ the structure and relationships of a society shape the way its members think. But this awareness is not carried through in the analysis. There is a deep and unresolved conflict between the optimistic psychological theory, which opens before our eyes a vista of future generations of immeasurably improved human beings, and the pessimism of the ideological theory. In the light of these hints at a theory of ideology, the recurring message that present evils result from error and will be banished by truth seems amazingly naive. The conceptions of time and change are, if anything, even weaker. A belief in progress plays a major part in making the radical critique of the book possible; but progress is conceived one-sidedly, as intellectual progress. The history exemplifies a general characteristic of the book; its method of argument is extremely abstract, and very little reference is made to concrete evidence. As a result of these weaknesses, the proposals for a way forward to a better society are highly unconvincing. *Political Justice* is disabled yet further by its firm repudiation of political action. This failing is pardonable; what hopes could any progressive late eighteenth-century Englishman place in politics, with the spectacle of old corruption before his eyes? And if he happened to have been reared a dissenter, he would have additional reasons for wishing the state to be curbed rather than enlarged. Finally Godwin, like Ogilvie, like so many men of the enlightenment, confides too readily in the idea of an incontrovertible 'truth', which all will eventually accept, and whose glorious light will usher in the new day.

7

The Effects of Civilization on the People in
European States, Charles Hall, 1805

Hall tells us that his book is not concerned with the splendid few, but with the mass of people in civilized states. He draws a contrast between civilization and savagery; European states are civilized, the American Indians are his usual example of savages. When we contrast civilization with savagery, we are immediately struck, he claims, by the greater inequality in the former. He estimates the average family income of the labouring poor in Britain at £25 per year; that this is insufficient is proved by the lower average life expectancy of the poor. His estimate that the rich have twice the life expectancy of the poor is not unreasonable for the time. The higher mortality among the poor – and little children are worst affected – is caused mainly by inadequate diet; but overcrowded, unsanitary housing and working conditions hazardous to health are contributory factors. The mental and moral condition of the poor is even worse than the physical. They lack the means and leisure for instruction; and he quotes Adam Smith on the degrading effects of the division of labour. He takes issue with those who have argued that the poor are as happy, though in a different way, as the rich.[1] Such a judgment is possible only from those who are ignorant of the state of the poor.

There had been food shortages and high prices from 1795 to 1801; and though the immediate cause of this was a run of bad harvests, Hall argues that the root cause – which makes famine inevitable in bad seasons – is that an insufficient proportion of the population is employed cultivating the land for food: 'the quantity of the produce of it [the land] will be, the degree of fertility of it being given, as the number of hands or the quantity of labour bestowed upon it' (35).[2] If we divide the population of a country into three –

namely, cultivators, manufacturers and traders, and those who are idle – we can say that the adequacy or otherwise of the food supply will depend on the proportion of cultivators to the other groups; evidently in England this proportion is too low. Those engaged in manufacture may be divided again, into those producing 'gross' manufactures – that is, basic necessities – and those producing refinements and luxuries. It would seem reasonable to suppose that only those who can be spared from producing foodstuffs and basic goods would be employed making luxuries; yet food shortages prove that this reasonable allocation of labour does not occur. This cannot be by choice; man is by nature an outdoor, hunter-gatherer animal, who does not take kindly to being cooped up in factories and mines. So what has caused this unnatural state of affairs? We come to Hall's pivotal idea, his definition of wealth. A man is wealthy if he possesses the means of production – primarily land (43–4). In civilized states, the means of production are possessed by a few, the rich. Now the mass of the people, the poor, can only live if they can gain access to these means of production. They are therefore constrained to work for the rich, on terms imposed by the rich. A bargain is concluded, which is bound to be a bad one for the poor (44). Their labour produces everything, they receive but a part of its fruits; the rest is taken by the rich (70). 'Wealth, therefore, is the possession of that which gives power over and commands the labour of man; it is, therefore, power, and into that, and that only, ultimately resolvable' (48). Having defined wealth in this way, a way involving a simple and clear theory of exploitation, Hall can now explain why too few are employed cultivating the soil to produce adequate food for all. Because the rich take so large a share of the fruits of the labour of the poor, they have a large part of the spending power and can therefore dictate what kinds of goods will be produced. They cannot spend their surpluses on food; generally speaking, food consumption is limited by the capacity of the stomach. In feudal societies, surpluses were spent on multitudes of servants and retainers. But with the progress of civilization, these surpluses have increasingly been devoted to the purchase of luxury goods. Luxuries make it possible for a rich man to consume and destroy infinitely more of the produce of other men's labours than he would be able to do if only foodstuffs and basic necessities were available. Much more labour can be embodied in a piece of lace than in a coarse coat:

> We have heard of great men's cooks boiling down several hams, several legs of beef, many joints of veal, fowls, etc. to make a pint or two of soup; which, after all, makes but a small part of the dinner of their masters. The art of the fine manufacturer and that of the cook have precisely the same effect, viz. the bringing together and reducing the bulky matters to their quintessences, as it were; by which means, the great man can consume and destroy, in a very short time, the works of months and of years. (85)

The power of wealth is the only way of oppressing a whole people. It is greater than the power of the most absolute monarch. Indeed, political power is often founded on wealth. Power may be based on opinion, military force, or wealth; from the point of view of the masses, the last occasions greatest suffering (185–6). Hume and Adam Smith were wrong to regard feudalism as more oppressive than commercial society (52). The legal bondage of serfdom has been replaced by a dependence more onerous, cruel, and irresistible. Rich and poor have become enemies: 'The situation of the rich and the poor, like the algebraic terms *plus* and *minus*, are in direct opposition to, and destructive of each other' (67). The rich owe everything they have to the labours of the poor; but 'The rich man has truly nothing to give the poor man; the money, as well as the bread that was bought with it, the poor man's hands had before produced' (103). The social system, then, is one big, bad bargain; the poor can never make the bargain fair, because the rich, having political power, prevent workers' combinations. And even if combinations were allowed, strikes would not succeed; the poor do not have the resources to win in a fight.

The wealth of the rich, and the misery of the poor, increase in strict proportion. Hall notes three areas in which wealth has been increasing; rents have risen, so has the stock of capital, and so has the public debt. To call a debt wealth may seem paradoxical, but of course to the *creditor* it is wealth, just as rents and capital are; all three are to their possessors so much credit, so much potential spending power that can be used to command the labour of the poor. As wealth in these forms grows, so do the claims upon the labour of the poor increase, and the poor are compelled to spend more time producing luxuries for the rich, less time making necessaries for their own use. This gives pause for thought; Hall is arguing that the poor would be better off if there were fewer claims on them, that is, *less capital*; civilized states are, to use a modern term, *overcapitalized*. Hall also condemns foreign trade, which he believes to be chiefly in luxuries. Statesmen are wrong to regard trade as an index of the wealth of a nation; it is rather an index of the poverty of the masses. Furthermore, trade is a device whereby the rich of civilized states extend their power over the labour of the world. When Europeans trade in luxuries with India, what this means is that thousands of millions less bushels of wheat are grown in Europe and thousands of millions less bushels of rice in India.

> The bulk of the people, on both sides, have been most miserably despoiled by this system of trade, the most pernicious and destructive to the human race, that ever was invented. (89)
>
> Trade knows no friends or kindred – Avarice no compassion – Gain no bounds. (189)

How did this state of affairs come about? Originally, land was held in common; private ownership by a few in large blocks originated in conquest. The leaders of the German tribes that overwhelmed the Roman empire shared the lands they seized among their chief followers. This is the disreputable origin of modern wealth (53, 57). Because of this monopoly of land, agricultural labourers can be compelled to accept a bad bargain. But what about manufacturing labour? Hall suggests we think of it in the following way: the master manufacturer (or tradesman, as Hall calls him) possesses capital, that is to say, stocks of finished manufactured goods. These he can sell to the landowner, in return for a quantity of the necessaries produced on the land – food and so forth. The poor need these necessaries, and so the master manufacturer can grant or withhold them in order to obtain their labour at a rate advantageous to himself. It is as if the master manufacturer participates in the landlord's power over vital natural resources (71).

Using government statistics and estimates by writers on economics, Hall attempts to calculate the distribution of wealth between the rich and the poor. His conclusion is that the rich, the top 20 percent, consume about seven-eighths of the products of labour; the labourers themselves, the remaining 80 percent, are left with one-eighth of the produce they have created. Modern estimates suggest that the inequalities, though striking, were not as desperate as this: in 1803 the top 10 percent consumed about two-fifths.[3] Hall's estimates are partly based upon his assessment of the average family income of the labouring poor at £25 per year. This may have been near the mark for agricultural labourers in the south with which Hall was familiar, and handloom weavers were to fall even lower than this over the next few decades; but agricultural wages in northern England were higher, and so were the wages of many industrial workers. Furthermore, the social pyramid was not as steep as Hall suggests. Describing a situation in which a small class of rich face a huge mass of poor, he ignores the substantial middle strata that present-day economic historians identify as a salient feature of the social landscape of early industrial England.

There is one more large item in Hall's bill of indictment against the rich – war. The rich, who hold political power, go readily to war – understandably enough, as they do not themselves 'go' to the field of battle. Wars are entered into for the sake of trade, as part of the business of ransacking the world for luxury items. War, indeed, is often welcome to the rich; it gives a good excuse for a larger standing army, which can be used at home to keep the masses in their place. All the burdens of war are borne by the labouring poor. They are seized by press gangs, forced into the militia and torn away from their families, many to die in action or from disease; the rich, by contrast, buy themselves off if drafted. What is more, the labourers who are left behind have to pay for the war. 'War operates in a twofold manner; first, by taking off the men the army consists of from agriculture; and then, by occasioning the necessity of supplying these men with provisions, clothes, etc.' (165).

Hall's remedies for the social ills he has so graphically described are legislative and fiscal. Taxation should be progressive; there should be a steeply rising income tax. Primogeniture should be abolished; if this were coupled with a law prohibiting marriages between two people both having, or likely to inherit, land, then the great concentrations of wealth and power would gradually be broken up. But above all, luxury goods – 'refined manufactures' – should be prohibited, or subjected to punitive taxation: '[T]his would be drawing the venom from the jaws of the serpent, and depriving him of the power of destruction: this would prove an effectual cure, and that in a manner safe, peaceable, and constitutional' (218). So, gradually, the power of the rich over the poor will be eroded, and a greater degree of equality will prevail. These are the remedies that

Hall thinks are readily practicable. But he goes on to speculate about an ideal situation, in which an agrarian law distributes property equally. There will be little in the way of luxury and refinement, and no trade. This ideal condition will not entail a reversion to savagery – savages are disorderly and warlike, because of their hunting way of life. Rather it will be the adoption of a middle state between savagery and civilization. In this state, when men enjoy the full fruits of their labour, they will need to work only one-quarter to one-third as much as they presently do; in the absence of great riches, there will be little intemperance, and the abundant leisure will be devoted to study and intellectual improvement, hence the sciences will record faster advances.

The book concludes with a passage reminiscent of what Cobbett was to write sixteen years later in his *Cottage Economy*. Hall discusses the ways of making land more productive; the prime requirement is to put more labour into its cultivation. But he also reveals learning in the improved agriculture of the day, advocating thorough manuring, deep digging, sowing in drills, hoeing, draining, and improved crop rotations. Hall is an enthusiast for good compost; human manure should not be wasted, and there is even a hint that to bury corpses six feet under is a loss of good compost material. He describes how a small holding of three and a half acres might be farmed so as to support a family of five, and on this basis he calculates that England could easily support a population of ninety million. Such are Hall's proposals. Like Ogilvie and Godwin, he is utterly convinced of the truth of his analysis and the appropriateness of his remedies. So why are his views so uncommon? Only the rich, he insists, have the leisure and education for speculation about society, and they are biased in their opinions by their interests:

> Men can very rarely employ their thoughts intensely on any subject which is of no concern to them. On the other hand, in case our interest is against any discovery, if any thoughts arise in the mind concerning it, they are unattended to, or are soon suppressed, as useless or disadvantageous; and this often passes in the minds of people unobserved, and without their being conscious of this their seemingly unfair and uncandid mode of proceeding. (230)

But Hall still has hopes that when the rich have the truth brought home to them, by books such as his, they will be irresistibly impelled by conscience and humanity to set things right.

The appended pamphlet on Malthus is a passionately angry work. 'And for whose benefit are the poor to remain single, to be abstemious and continent? For those, I say, who wallow in waste and luxury, sensuality and lust' (342). The argument is economical and effective; Hall offers four points against Malthus. First, the predicted time when population will outrun the capacity of the land to feed it is far off in England. Hall's estimate of how many England will sustain, which was ninety million in the book, is one hundred and forty million in the pamphlet. Therefore, even if Malthus's ratios are correct, even if the population of England doubled every twenty-five years, there could be a period of eighty years of happiness before the crisis. But second, the crisis is preventable, by measures such as delayed marriages and emigration (for most of the world is barely cultivated). Hall is prepared to contemplate compulsory emigration if necessary, the émigrés to be chosen by ballot. Third, in a state of equality, the Malthusian crisis would have some of its evils mitigated. For the starving would not experience the added sting of seeing others living extravagantly, others whose wealth was (as Hall has demonstrated in the book) the immediate cause of their misery. In a state of equality, the evil of overpopulation would be accepted as natural and inevitable, according to the will of God rather than produced by the actions of men. Fourth, if, as was argued in the book, the labouring poor do everything for the rich, and the rich do nothing for the poor; and if the rich, by diverting labourers from agriculture to refined manufactures, cause the dearth of foodstuffs; therefore in the event of a crisis of subsistence, the idle rich should in justice go short rather than the labourers:

> It is not true that he has *doomed himself*, or that nature has doomed *him, and his family, to starve*; that cruel doom is brought on him by the rich. If any are to be treated in this cruel manner, it is those who have been rich, and who have never produced any part of all they have consumed.

Hall, kindhearted as he is, concludes, 'But none ought to receive such hard usage' (341). In the book an additional point is made in answer to Malthus. God, benevolent as he is, cannot have intended that the poor should starve. So perhaps the day when population finally and irretrievably outruns the capacity of the earth to supply food is intended by God to be the end of the world.

Such is the outline of Hall's argument; our task now is to investigate more thoroughly its structure, and in particular the conditions of the possibility of so radical a critique. That it is primarily a moral argument is evident; explicit references to formal moral *theories* are, however, few. The property theory of Locke has cast its shadow over Hall as well as Ogilvie. The earth was originally possessed in common (37, 53) and individuals are born with a natural right to subsistence, and therefore to a sufficient portion of land on which to raise that subsistence. Ogilvie and Hall differ in part from Godwin here. Godwin, on utilitarian grounds, proposes that each individual is entitled to subsistence, which others should give him if he has been unable to obtain it for himself. Ogilvie and Hall advocate a right to subsistence and a corresponding right of access to natural resources. Godwin's is an entitlement to consume, Ogilvie's and Hall's a right to produce. Hall also advances the right to enjoy the full fruits of one's labour. He anchors these rights in God's will. God made living creatures and the earth to support them:

> It is evident, therefore, that the Creator intended the land for the use of the creatures he has put on it. Consequently, that no creature ought to be cut off from the possession of some part or other of the earth, and that in such quantity as to furnish him with the necessaries of life. (107–8)

Another moral theory is invoked when Hall answers Hume's and Paley's defences of property and inequality on grounds of utility. What utilitarian justification can there be for institutions that bring poverty and misery to the many without making the few rich truly happy? He adopts Hume's account of happiness as consisting of a combination and balance of activity, relaxation, and pleasure. The happiness of the rich is deficient because, doing no work, they are insufficiently active. Hall briefly and effectively dismisses the utilitarian arguments for inequality on grounds of incentives. The rewards go to the idle; the incentive to wealth creation would be infinitely greater if the labourers could expect the full fruits of their labour. Finally, inequality is condemned on the grounds of justice; but this line of argument is barely developed.

A further aspect to the moral critique of the book is the images of contrasted good and bad societies and the evaluations that support this sorting into good and bad. Hall's critique of civilization frequently resembles Rousseau's, but there is no direct evidence he

had read Rousseau, and the resemblances could be due to the
sources on which both drew. Like Ogilvie, Hall offers a version of
the classical republican ideal, with its hostility to luxury and trade,
and its emphasis upon simple rural independence, virtue, and
patriotism.

> [Civilization and manufactures] . . . debase the species: they lessen
> the stature of man: they misshape his body: they enervate, and di-
> minish his strength and activity, and his ability to bear hardships:
> and with all these effects on his body, they depress the spirit and
> vigour of his mind, and thus, in every respect, unfit him for war.
> (157)

In view of the fact that in other places Hall paints the horrors of
war and looks forward to its disappearance in a more equal society,
this appeal to the military virtues is a testimony to the enduring,
and imperfectly assimilated, influence of the republican ideal. There
are also allusions to the classical myth of the ages of gold and iron.
Civilization, with its inequality, struggling, and jostling, is very
much an age of iron. Hall's egalitarian golden age is to be one of
simple, homely, unheroic comfort – a medium state. His account
of the appropriate regime for a nursing mother may be quoted as
a fair indication of his image of the good life: '[T]he woman should
be well fed with a full proportion of animal food; perhaps some
quantity of good beer; live in good houses; good air; be employed
in wholesome and pleasant exercises; and void of care' (14). How
different this is from the value system of Malthus, whose greatest
fear is not the want and misery that the laws of population inflict
upon the mass of people, but that an excess of charity might destroy
the rich, and with them all art, learning, and splendour: Malthus
who justifies God's providence in devising so cruel a natural order
on the grounds that the struggle for subsistence is an incentive to
improvement.

   Though Hall's book is deeply moral, we cannot really say that
his social criticism, the distancing he has achieved from the status
quo, has been made possible by moral theories, for moral theory
does not interest him much. Is the key to be found in his conceptions
of time and change? His awareness of other societies is not unusual
for an educated man of his age. He is familiar with Greek and
Roman history and literature, from which he has gleaned an ideal
of a golden age of rural simplicity; Sparta in particular provides a

model for the system of equality. The history of the Jews in the Old Testament provides, he thinks, another example of an egalitarian society, ordained by God himself. America looms large for him; its aborigines, whom he admires, furnish his conception of the savage condition. Its white settlements demonstrate how happy and prolific the human race can be when natural resources are not monopolized by the few – but he fears America is moving towards the European pattern. China is for him an example of a society[4] reduced to the last dreadful extremes of poverty by an excess of trade and civilization. His knowledge of China appears to come entirely from Adam Smith's *Wealth of Nations*. It goes without saying that as far as the history of European civilization is concerned, he does not perceive a pattern of progress. In one area, science, he has no doubts about advance; but in the lot of the mass of the people he sees only declension. The decline stems from one initial, catastrophic act of wickedness: conquest, and the resultant monopoly of land by a few. Once that had occurred, the deterioration in the lot of the labouring poor advanced steadily and inevitably, by spontaneous economic processes, as the wealth of the rich increased and a greater proportion of labour was diverted away from agriculture and into manufactures. This overview of European history is vital to his argument; but as a historical theory it is crude, especially by comparison with the achievements of the Scottish historical school. The levels of explanation and the modes of historical agency are mixed and confused; we begin with a natural order of harmony and equality, which is suddenly disrupted by a violent act of aggression, motivated by greed, which is itself a natural human characteristic. Then the natural economic processes set to work to drive Europe towards the civilized state. Civilization is to end, and equality is to be reinstated (at a higher level than the original) by conscious human agency; the rich and powerful, converted by the arguments of those such as Hall, will employ legislative remedies.

We are left with the feeling that, in looking at moral theories and conceptions of time and change, we have not come to the heart of Hall's position. I would suggest the core, the essence of what made this radical book possible, is to be found in three areas: first, Hall's experience, and the manner in which he responded to it; second, science; and third, science's offshoot in the field of social theory, classical political economy. Hall was a West Country doctor. So

he tells us; but we would know anyway, for his pages are replete
with the experience and learning of his profession. As a doctor, he
had intimate knowledge of the living conditions of the poor and of
the diseases nurtured by inadequate diet, bad housing, and dangerous working conditions. The opening chapters, which record this
experience, are vivid and moving. He experienced the contrast between the sickrooms of the rich and the poor:

> [W]e are frequently entreated to visit the child or children of a poor
> man, in the same illness; several of them generally lying in the same
> bed; heated by and heating each other, in a small room, corrupted
> by the exhalations of the whole family; disturbed by one another's
> cries; their wakefulness and restlessness, the effects of the disorder,
> increased by the vermin and hard beds, covered by filthy clothes;
> having nothing proper to use from the cellar, the kitchen, the garden,
> or apothecary's shop; no attendants but the poor mother, worn out
> by watchings, anxiety, etc.; the father from home, obliged to leave
> it to get their daily bread. (15)

Hall is one of a number of medical men – men like Dr. Thomas
Percival and Dr. Aiken of Manchester, Dr. Currie of Liverpool, W.
P. Alison of Edinburgh, Kay-Shuttleworth, Thomas Wakley, and
Thomas Southwood Smith – who at the end of the eighteenth and
the first few decades of the nineteenth century led the way in drawing attention to these problems and pressing for solutions. Hall had
also seen how his patients bore the burdens of war and how their
sufferings were aggravated in times of dearth. These experiences
evidently formed his mind. But there had been suffering poor and
doctors to observe them before; there had been wars and bad harvests. Yet these similar experiences had not produced a similar
book. Experience is not just received passively. Experience is an
affair of responding, grasping, apprehending: it is taken, seized,
and the manner of its taking is largely determined by the mental
furniture of the person who is having that experience. Hall responds
to and grasps his experience with all the austere seriousness and
feeling of the late eighteenth century. In his book, the sentimentalism of Sterne, Mackenzie, Gray, and Goldsmith has blossomed
into powerful social criticism. His compassion flows spontaneously
and with indubitable sincerity. He thinks that any other response
would be improper – inhumane, as he puts it, a word that implies
'contrary to human nature', attributing to sympathetic feelings a
timeless, static quality, obscuring the way in which patterns of re-

sponse change and evolve. Godwin also placed great emphasis upon benevolence; but if we compare him with Hall, we are left with the impression that he is rationally convinced of the importance of benevolence, while Hall's very being is dominated by the compassion he has felt for his poor patients. The character of Hall's response is evidenced by such remarks as 'The reflection . . . is too sad for a human heart to dwell on' (168) and 'these being too obvious and affecting to need a representation to people of any observation, and endued with any sensibility' (31), and also by some of the recurrent words − for example, those used to describe the situation of the poor: distress, misery, cruel, long languishing sufferings; or, to describe the responses of the observer: regret, sad, lament, grievous, affecting, sensibility, compassion, commiserate, humanity, pity. It is at this level rather than at the level of theory that the pervasive moral argument of the book operates. The perennial moral intuitions, that pain and distress are bad, happiness and comfort good, are given an intensity and a direction by the sentimentalism and concern for humble people of preromanticism.

One of the handful of facts we know about Hall's career leads us to expect him to be a man of science; he obtained the degree of M.D. from the University of Leyden, with a thesis on pulmonary consumption. The pages of the text substantially confirm this expectation. Hall regularly appeals to 'facts' and 'observation', and describes the activity in which he is engaged as 'discovering the cause', drawing 'effects and consequences from physical and moral causes'. As we have seen, he regards human history as a tale of decline, not progress; but he makes science an exception. Not only does he reveal considerable medical knowledge; he is also deeply interested in agricultural technology. He makes the greatest efforts to provide a sound foundation of evidence for his argument and as a result his book has a wholly different flavour from that of Godwin's abstract philosophical disquisition. He is not content with the unsystematic citation or supporting facts; he also invokes statistical analysis wherever possible − for example, about the death rates of different classes, the distribution of wealth between classes, and crime rates and to calculate what population England could support. His book shows how scientific methods facilitate social criticism. For the scientist's business, Hall's language and practice imply, is to test superficial and received opinions against the facts, properly observed and analysed. The hunger of the poor is not something to be passively noticed and acquiesced in, but is to be investigated, quantified, explained. Whether or not the poor must always be hungry is a question to be resolved not by conventional wisdom, but by science. There is a further dimension to his scientific attitude. For him, as for Newton, Locke, and Priestley, science and religion, nature and God's providence, are not opposed, but mutually supporting. To explain natural processes, and to understand God's purposes, are one and the same activity (107–8, 273, 336). If for Godwin the ultimate court of appeal was reason, for Hall, it is the facts of nature, or God's commands – these different expressions do not designate different things. The underlying assumption is of a divinely ordained natural order, regular, purposive, and benevolent. Suffering is therefore a state of disorder, unnatural, and contrary to God's will; a state of affairs produced by human wickedness.

Without classical economy, Hall's book would have been impossible. Sections of it are debates with Lauderdale and Adam Smith, and Smith is quoted and cited more than any other author. The whole of the appended pamphlet is a debate with Malthus. Hall demonstrates familiarity with some of the concepts and modes of analysis of political economy; the ultimate success or failure of his argument, in fact, depends to a high degree on the quality of its economic thought. This was not true of Ogilvie, Spence, or Godwin. Some of the debates with and debts to classical economy may briefly be noted. His reply to Malthus has already been described; in passing it should be mentioned that his victory over Malthus's geometric rate of population increase is but a partial one. Hall largely accepts this, suggesting delayed marriages as a remedy: Malthus would readily have classed these as a form of 'misery'. Second, Hall's hostility to manufactures and trade, and insistence that more effort should go into agriculture, sounds like a debt to the physiocrats; but we need not suppose that Hall had read them. He could have known of their doctrines from Smith's *Wealth of Nations*, which contains a statement of their position. Both the physiocrats and Smith, as we have seen, draw a distinction between productive and unproductive labour, the physiocrats arguing that only agricultural labour is productive, Smith extending the honour to manufacturing operations, because they produce a 'vendible commodity'. Hall does not explicitly employ this distinction, but his theory is evidently a development of this theme, and his position is closer to that of the physiocrats than to that of Smith. Smith argued that only productive expenditure created jobs and only productive labour added to the wealth of a nation. For Hall, this is to miss the point. The mere creation of jobs and the production of goods may bring no benefit to the mass of the people who make up the nation, if that wealth takes the form of expensive luxuries. Third, there can be little doubt that Hall owes to classical economy his ability to perceive – and hence criticize – an economic and social *system*, to stand back from it and apprehend it as a whole. Fourth, Hall's book should be set against the debates, in the second half of the eighteenth century, about the trade in grain.[5] Mercantilist economics sought to regulate this trade, in order to secure subsistence for the mass of the people. The physiocrats and Adam Smith rejected intervention. Smith thought that the lasting cure for poverty was economic growth, which would best occur under conditions of freedom of trade and enterprise. Hall does not agree with Smith; the growth of commerce has deteriorated the condition of the poor, not improved it. But he does not propose a return to state regulation as the solution, except in the one case of sumptuary laws. He defends free trade in grain in the best Smithian manner. His analysis of the problem goes radically beyond the mercantilist–free trade debate.

As already noted, the central idea of Hall's argument is his definition of wealth. 'Wealth . . . is the possession of that which gives power over . . . the labour of man.' It is no mean achievement; this idea was to be fundamental to subsequent early critiques of capital in Britain, fundamental also to the thought of Marx. Hall arrives at his definition by giving the slightest twist to a similar one provided by Adam Smith himself. Smith proposed that the best measure of the value of a person's wealth is the amount of labour he can save himself, or, to put it another way, the amount of labour he can purchase or 'command' with it. Smith defines wealth as the power to purchase labour, and leaves it at that; Hall defines it as *power over labour* and proceeds to unpack the implications of the definition through the greater part of his book. The original wealth or power is the monopoly of land by conquerors; later, manufacturers and tradesmen, through the agency of their capital, come to share in it. The main category of Hall's economic analysis is *wealth*, and capital is sketchily explained in terms of it. This is shown by his insistence that the essential social division is between rich and poor; landowners, churchmen, lawyers, professionals are essentially the same because all are rich. Now it is no doubt an important achievement to point out the similarity between capital and other sorts of wealth as forms of power over labour; but he fails to recognize and explore the differences between the exploitation of a peasant by a landlord and the exploitation of a proletarian by a capitalist. Both sorts of wealth – landed and capitalist – and the power they confer upon their possessors are understood as monopolies. Hall thinks he knows how landed monopoly arose; it came about through conquest. But how does the capitalist's monopoly originate, and then maintain itself? The text has no answer. Furthermore, Hall does not consider the different aspects of capital – buildings, machinery, raw materials, the fund for the payment of wages; indeed, he defines the tradesman's capital as a stock of finished articles, which he can exchange with the landlord for food and raw materials. Hall's critique of inequality is vulnerable to an opponent arguing for the benefits of capital. 'The rich man has truly nothing to give the poor man; the money, as well as the bread that was bought with it, the poor man's hands had before produced' (103). But, the defender of capital might reply, the rich man has accumulated a stock of raw materials and provisions that will keep his workmen alive, and in business, until the finished articles are sold; this is an essential service in advanced market economies, where the periods of time between commencing a productive task and receiving payment for the finished article, are often long. Also, he has provided machinery that enhances the productivity of labour. Therefore the capitalist performs real services, for which he deserves a reward. Not only does Hall furnish no satisfactory answers to such arguments; it is to be doubted whether he has faced up to the issues involved. As already remarked, he suggests that the plight of the poor in his day is partly caused by too much capital, that is, too many claims upon the fruits of their labour. But the rise in popular living standards since Hall's day has gone hand in hand with capital accumulation.[6] Hall has argued that the miseries of the poor result from the fact that too many of them are kept busy, making luxuries, and too few allowed to be employed in agriculture.

This may have seemed plausible in the times of full employment during the war; but how could Hall's argument be squared with the high unemployment that followed the war? Still, however *inadequate* Hall's analysis of capital and exploitation, at least he has provided a *clear theory* of exploitation and its origin. Hall's theory is too simple, but it marks a new departure. It is a theory of *economic class* exploitation; he does not use the older systems of classification – ranks, orders, interests; gentlemen, people, mob. Whereas Godwin was more interested in status than in economic class, Hall virtually ignores status.

What about his economic remedies? It is not easy to share his faith in laws prohibiting luxury manufactures. He claims that luxuries are a necessary condition of inequality and exploitation; but what if the luxury of the few is a *consequence* instead of a *cause* of their unfair share of wealth? After all, as he noted himself, in the feudal period, when luxury goods were not as available, lords could spend their surpluses on servants and retainers instead. Hall cannot propose convincing remedies, because his diagnosis of the sickness – his analysis of the specific essences of landed and capitalist exploitation – is inadequate. Secondly, his proposals for increasing the productivity of the soil have two aspects; putting more labour into the land and adopting improved methods, including manuring, drainage, and rotations. His *legislative* proposals – abolition of primogeniture, prohibition of luxury goods – are designed to achieve the first of these. But how can we be certain that putting more labourers on the land would be accompanied by the adoption of improved technology? The good practices that Hall recommends had made slow progress during the eighteenth century. What assurance could there be that the adoption of his legislative proposals would not lead to a situation like that of England in the thirteenth century, when a large proportion of the population was engaged in cultivating the soil, but the soil was overworked, 'plough-sick', because too many crops had been taken out of it, and insufficient heart put back in?[7]

In conclusion we may say that Hall has made effective use of one or two concepts and methods adapted from political economy; but he has made little use of the rest of its conceptual and theoretical apparatus. In spite of the debt to Smith, Hall's book is utterly different from the *Wealth of Nations*, in kind as well as in conclusions.

Whereas Smith is primarily concerned with economic description and analysis, to which moral reflections are added, Hall is first and foremost a moralist, who draws upon the language and insights of social science (42).

Before we sum up and assess Hall's achievement, a few further points are in order about his proposed strategy for change. The good society, the 'medium state' of modest comfort, is to be achieved by legislation and progressive taxation. Is Hall therefore a precursor of the modern Labour Party? Hall and the Labour Party are worlds apart; and one reason why this is so is that he envisages no sustained legislative effort, no continuing state management of economy and society. The implication is that once monopoly has been destroyed, and near equality and a return to the land brought about by a few simple laws, then legislation and taxation will no longer be necessary. Second, Hall does not think that the poor themselves will play much of a part in bringing on the great change. His remedy

> may be safely committed to the hands of such persons as are dis-
> interested and dispassionate. To obtain such persons, they should
> be taken not from the aggrieved party; for from that quarter they
> would not probably be cool and temperate. . . . It would be better
> therefore that the redress of the grievances of the poor should orig-
> inate from the rich themselves. (216)

This, as well as being unconvincing, does not square too well with the argument of the rest of the book. We have already been told that the rich and the poor are as opposed as plus and minus and that the opinions of the rich are systematically biased and distorted by their interests. It is just as in Ogilvie and Godwin: powerful pages have been devoted to the analysis of conflict; the evil effects of selfishness have been exposed; then on a sudden we come to the great change, when benevolence breaks out. Just like Ogilvie and Godwin, Hall weakly suggests that the rich, in trying to *remain* rich, have misperceived their true interests; they would be happier in a state of equality because they would be able to engage in in-vigorating work, and there would be less crime.

The manner in which Hall has distanced himself from his society is captured in the phrase 'this cruel system' (24). The word 'cruel' signals the emotional temperature of the book; critique, carried to the height of passion, stems from sympathetic identification with the poor. The word 'system' signals the fact that Hall, owing much to classical economy, has looked at his society as a whole and got a handle upon it by means of a simple but clear theory. This is his achievement, his new departure unanticipated in Ogilvie and Godwin. He uses a simpler moral apparatus than those two writers, but this does not detract from his effectiveness; Hall, the scientist, has a due regard for properly marshalled and analysed evidence, and consequently the factual basis of his argument is better. He pays greater attention to industry than Ogilvie, but at the end of the day the same agrarian emphasis emerges. This is wholly natural, given the rural ideal, derived from classical literature, which they share; and it would be anachronistic to blame either for failing to foresee the industrial revolution. One of the main weaknesses of Hall's text is that he has not made even more use of classical economics; in particular, the discussion of capital is too thin. Another major inadequacy is that the theory of historical change is sketchy and incoherent. It is therefore unsurprising that Hall cannot see clearly forward, cannot persuade his readers that he has identified a pathway to a better society.

*A Lay Sermon Addressed to the Higher and
Middle Classes on the Existing Distresses
and Discontents*, Samuel Taylor Coleridge,
1817

The *Lay Sermon*, as its title reveals, addresses the social turmoil of
1817. After an introduction, Coleridge embarks upon a consideration of those 'who have hitherto prescribed for the case, and are
still tampering with it' (142)[1] – that is to say, the radicals and
'demagogues'. His targets are not mentioned by name, but there
can be little doubt that they include Burdett, Hunt, and Cobbett.
He attacks these men with an intolerance and scurrility reminiscent
of the *Anti-Jacobin* newspaper of the war years; in ten pages he
reveals a rich repertory of abuse and defamation. One of the milder
passages will illustrate the style:

> . . . when we hear persons, the tyranny of whose will is the only law
> in their families, denouncing all law as tyranny in public – persons,
> whose hatred of power in others is in exact proportion to their love
> of it for themselves; when we behold men of sunk and irretrievable
> characters, to whom no man would entrust his wife, his sister, or
> his purse, have the effrontery to propose that we should entrust to
> them our religion and our country; when we meet with *Patriots*,
> who aim at an enlargement of the rights and liberties of the people
> by inflaming the populace to acts of madness that necessitate fetters.
> . . . (149–50)

This sustained character assassination is larded with biblical references, taken especially from the prophetic books. This is a continuation of the argument of a lay sermon of the previous year, that
the Bible is the best guide to political skill and foresight. There are
echoes here of the millenarian writings of the war years, which
sought to show that the Bible had prophesied the turbulent events
of the time.[2] But Coleridge's claim is not that the prophets foretold
the late eighteenth-century revolution, rather that they provided an
eternally valid anatomy of the fiendish reptilian incendiary. Coleridge takes issue with the radical argument that the distresses of

the time are largely caused by excessive taxation and could be removed by the savings resulting from the abolition of government
pensions and sinecure places. Government expenditure, he maintains, does not detract from public prosperity; indeed, by stimulating the economy it may enhance wealth and general well-being.
What is more, the radicals know this too. Their proposed remedies
are a pack of lies, designed to persuade the unfortunate that economic ills are removable, that agitation is worthwhile. True friends
of the people would demonstrate to the poor that distress is inevitable, though perhaps temporary: they would teach resignation.
For the 'true proximate cause' is the cessation of the war and of
the buoyant wartime demand for goods. This economic cause is
reinforced by a moral one.

The sudden and hectic prosperity of the war engendered exaggerated expectations in those who profited; but now the bubble has
burst, and those who rose high have fallen hard:

> I leave to your own experience and recollection the assemblage of
> folly, presumption, and extravagance, that followed in the proces-
> sion of our late unprecedented prosperity; the blind practices and
> blending passions of speculation in the commercial world, with the
> shoal of ostentatious fooleries and sensual vices which the sudden
> influx of wealth let in on our farmers and yeomanry. (161)

This leads him to long-term and fundamental causes of distress.
He identifies the 'OVERBALANCE OF THE COMMERCIAL SPIRIT IN CON-
SEQUENCE OF THE ABSENCE OR WEAKNESS OF THE COUNTER-WEIGHTS'
(169). In a footnote he adds that he is not against commerce itself,
for commerce has favoured liberty as well as prosperity. But trade
should not dominate national life. Three 'natural counter-forces to
the impetus of trade' are identified (170). The first is 'the ancient
feeling of rank and ancestry' (Coleridge is not an unqualified admirer of aristocracy). The second is the neglect of 'austerer studies'
– that is to say, philosophy. Not just any philosophy will do; he
derides eighteenth-century empiricism and prefers the Platonism of
the Renaissance and Reformation period. Dante, Petrarch, Spenser,
Sir Philip Sidney, Algernon Sidney, Milton, and Barrow were all
Platonists, he informs us. The third and most important is religion.
Philosophy and religion can counterbalance the commercial spirit,
because they draw the mind away from sensual, material things,
facilitating control of the passions, especially the passion of greed.

But just as not all philosophy can do this, so not all religion can elevate and spiritualize a society. Religion must fill the whole being of a believer; it must not be a mere Sunday affair. It can act in this pervasive way on the upper and middle classes who give a nation its tone, only if it absorbs and exercises their understandings. In the sixteenth and seventeenth centuries, deep and intense theological investigation and discussion were commonplace, and not only among the higher and middle strata. But since the shallow eighteenth century, the received view has been that Christianity is plain and simple, accessible in the form of a few easy doctrines to the meanest understanding at first hearing (177). Coleridge attacks the Bible society for distributing the Bible without notes or commentary. It is not sufficient merely to enable the poor to read the Bible; they need theological instruction too. He turns on the simple rationalism of the Unitarians, to which he subscribed as a young man. But his rudest remarks are reserved for the Quakers. They provide the perfect test case. Theirs is a religion of the utmost sincerity. Their respectability is exemplary, and they repudiate all the tinsel vanities of the world. But they are unencumbered with theological learning:

> That species of Christianity I mean, which, as far as knowledge and the faculties of thought are concerned, – which, as far as the growth and grandeur of the *intellectual* man is in question – is to be learnt extempore! A Christianity poured in on the catechumen all and all at once, as from a shower-bath. . . . (191)

And what is the result? Quakers are typically engaged in commerce, and their religion fails to temper commercial avidity:

> [T]he distinguished world-honoured company of Christian Mammonists appear to the eye of my imagination as a drove of camels heavily laden, yet all at full speed, and each in the confident expectation of passing through the EYE OF THE NEEDLE, without stop or halt, both beast and baggage. (191)

This is Coleridge's anticipation of the 'religion and the rise of capitalism' thesis. His version differs significantly from those of Weber and Tawney. The precise aspect of Protestantism that is to blame is the strand that insists Christianity is unesoteric. Capitalism is to be checked, not by the social discipline of the Middle Ages, but by theology of a Platonic and neo-Platonic kind.

So the spirit of trade is rampant, and there is little to check it.

Coleridge claims to prove his thesis by reference to economic and social conditions. A major symptom of the disease of excessive commercialism is the trade cycle. Upswings are caused by greed; slumps follow inevitably as speculative mania overreaches itself. This feverish activity has, in the long term, augmented the national wealth; but its side effects have been dire. Public honesty has been eroded by the widespread and unscrupulous striving after a fast buck. Slumps have had a dreadful effect upon the health and welfare of the 'labouring poor'. In the prevailing use of this expression to designate those who labour Coleridge finds a melancholy reflection on the spirit of the age. Chronic unemployment and the practice of paying less than a living wage have thrown labourers upon poor law relief. Their self-reliance and moral respectability have been destroyed: unable to provide for themselves, they have become improvident.

A nation's economy has two sectors, trade and agriculture. The two should be regulated by distinct principles. In commerce, self-interest and the pursuit of profit are, in the main, appropriate (215, 220). But the ends of agriculture are public as well as private. The ends of agriculture are coterminous with the three positive functions of the state as a whole: to secure subsistence for each individual; to secure the hope of betterment to each citizen for himself or his children; and to promote the rational and moral qualities that are the specific excellences of humanity (216–17). Therefore the landlord must regard his estate as a trust. He has no absolute and unqualified right to do as he wishes with his property. His rights are limited by the rights of nonpossessors to subsistence, hope, and moral growth. To this extent, the Spenceans are right: their errors are dangerous precisely because they are half-truths. Because of the overbalance of the spirit of trade, agriculture is increasingly run on commercial lines. To such an extent have the true ends of agriculture been forgotten, that landlords complain of a superabundant harvest (with attendant low prices) as an evil. The day of capitalist landlords and farmers has arrived. Price inflation during the war encouraged this; to keep up their standard of living and consequent standing in the world, landlords pushed up rents. The level of rents depends upon the productivity of farms, and so landlords favoured as tenants large farmers with plenty of capital to invest in improvement.

Hence farm has been united to farm, smaller tenants and cottagers squeezed out, and the countryside depopulated. Now far too many live and are fed in towns from the produce of fields on which they do not labour. The point is vividly illustrated by reference to the Highland clearances. Formerly, a laird could march off to battle supported by an army of his tenants and labourers. These have now been marched off the land and replaced by sheep. The new arrangements may produce more wealth. Coleridge has been told by a political economist that 'If three were fed at Manchester instead of two at Glencoe and the Trossacs, the balance of human enjoyment was in favour of the former'. He replies:

> I have passed through many a manufacturing town since then, and have watched many a group of old and young, male and female, going to, or returning from many a factory, but I could never yet persuade myself to be of his opinion. Men, I still think, ought to be weighed not counted. Their *worth* ought to be the final estimate of their value. (211)

What is to be done? What is required is that the spirit of trade should be confined to its proper channels and therefore excluded from agriculture. The nation needs 'a healthful, callous-handed but high-and-warm-hearted Tenantry, twice the number of the present landless parish-paid labourers' (218). He applauds a report by Lord Winchilsea, which recommends that labourers should be leased, along with their cottages, allotments on which to grow food and keep a cow. But all of this should be done by private initiative. He emphatically repudiates legislative interference with landed proprietors: it would be folly to propose and worse than folly to attempt (217). When it comes to the crunch, the *Lay Sermon* remains a sermon, relying on an appeal to conscience. The reader may feel some surprise at this conclusion. Coleridge has insisted that absolute property right is more appropriate in the commercial world than in the agricultural; yet while he refuses to countenance legislation compelling landlords to treat their estates as a trust, he demands that 'Our manufacturers must consent to regulations' (229), and he supported the Factory Bill moved by the first Sir Robert Peel. Finally, he believes that the troubles of the time can ultimately be cured only by a turning of the upper and middle classes to the 'austerer studies' of philosophy and theology. In the introduction he proposed that the privileged position of the upper and middle classes could only be justified by their ability to understand the ultimate principles of knowledge and conduct. This alone fits them to rule and guide.

The mental furniture that permits and shapes Coleridge's social criticism has much in common with the texts already considered; but there are new emphases and also some items not encountered hitherto. His theory of human nature is not made explicit in this sermon, but it is implicit and pervades the argument. As a young man, he had been an associationist and determinist, naming his first son Hartley after the Christian associationist philosopher. But by 1817, he had come to reject associationism and also to subscribe to the doctrine of the freedom of the will. This emancipation from the philosophy of his youth – that of Hume, Priestley, and Godwin – was achieved with the aid of his study of Kant. The abandonment of associationism had major consequences for his social theory. Associationism, as we have seen, easily lends itself to egalitarian and optimistic beliefs. Coleridge, after his conversion, no longer has this glad confidence in the future. Furthermore, his rejection of determinism goes hand in hand with a reassertion of human sinfulness. Therefore, though evil may be reduced, it can never entirely be eradicated. Coleridge does not believe in the malleability of humanity; but he *does* have a theory of environmental conditioning, inspired, like his rejection of associationism, by German sources. But his theory – celebrated by J. S. Mill as the philosophy of human culture of the Germano-Coleridgean school – has conservative rather than radical and reformist implications. Whereas Godwin thought that vicious characters were produced by bad environments and would disappear in good, Coleridge believes that the propensity to vice is eternal and ineradicable. Society does not corrupt; it is the constant function of the institutions and culture of a nation to impose social discipline and training. In the introduction he points out that, though the upper and middle classes have ceased to be deep students of sound philosophy and religion, they are saved from absolute depravity by the great blessing of being born English. The English way of doing justice, the torrent of moral sermons, the earnestness and respectability of dissent, the social hierarchy, and interdependence of economic life all serve to buttress and support good character. This is his conception of 'culture', and it breeds a great respect for time. He looks upon a culture as a system of social discipline that is the hard-won fruit of centuries. Therefore radical reform is too dangerous to contemplate: it may disrupt the elaborate and delicate fabric that controls the beast in man. This conception of culture is at the opposite pole to Godwinism in that it does not regard reason as the only or the best means of controlling conduct. Instead, it takes into consideration all manner of opaque, nonrational factors: habits, practices, and institutions. The conception views society[3] as a kind of living organism, with a character of its own, a national character, of which the individuals are the results or expressions rather than the creators. A society is not an artificial construction, but has grown. This conception, pioneered by Burke and Coleridge in Britain, cuts the ground from under the easy and unhistorical optimism of Godwin and Owen. Marx, no stranger to this way of thinking, was compelled to dismiss Owen as a naive utopian and to set about constructing a socialist theory that paid due attention to time and the social and cultural whole.

This conception inevitably transforms the way in which interpersonal relations are conceived. All of the texts considered so far have, in keeping with ruling ideas of the eighteenth century, discussed the issue in terms of the forces of self-love versus the public good. Chapter 3 indicated the range of eighteenth-century theories of how the public good could come about in spite of human selfishness.[4] A great merit of Coleridge's conception of culture is that it at once undercuts and transcends this antithesis. For we can no longer think in terms of individuals, pre-constituted, as it were, outside society, all torn between the rival motivations of self-love and benevolence and needing to be brought together, somehow, into mutually advantageous association. We now have to think of an a priori unity, a *culture*, with its social bonds and ligaments already built into its practices, attitudes, and beliefs; a culture that produces 'individuals' already prepared for society (we have to put the word in inverted commas, for in pure versions of this theory the true *individual* is the social organism; 'individuals' are parts or expressions of it). Owenite socialism, as we shall see, lacked concepts and theories to provide a convincing account of how individuals could be united into a cooperative whole; it could usefully have drawn upon Coleridge's insights. But his way of thinking about society was not incorporated into indigenous socialist theory until *Fabian Essays in Socialism*, seventy years later.[5]

Coleridge argues in his sermon that the community that its members love and serve has been undermined by the development of commercialism. This is illustrated with reference to the Scottish Highland clearances. He 'reports' the words of a highland widow:

> Yes, Sir! One hundred and seventy-three Christian souls, man, woman, boy, girl, and babe; and in almost every home an old man by the fire-side, who would tell you of the troubles, before our roads were made; and many a brave youth among them who loved the birth-place of his forefathers, yet would swing about his broadsword and want but a word to march off to the battles over sea. . . . Well! but they are gone, and with them the bristled bear, and the pink haver, and the potatoe plot that looked as gay as any flower garden with its blossoms! (210)

The lairds have cleared their lands of the dependents who would formerly have rallied in arms to their support. Here, then, Coleridge's social theory appears to reflect the economic and social changes of his time. Coleridge is witnessing the passing away of a face-to-face, organic, caring society, and its replacement, in Carlyle's words, by 'cash payment the sole nexus' between man and man. But as was argued in Chapter 3,[6] this alleged transformation may be partly mythical. Coleridge's report of the words of the highland widow is not merely history, faithfully recording the facts: it is literature, fine writing, designed to evoke a certain emotional response in the reader. The image of peasants rallying behind their laird is reminiscent of Scott's *Waverley*. The remembering of the settlement, once so full of life and colour but now cleared for sheep and the lament over the simple poor call to mind Goldsmith's *Deserted Village*. Fashionable nostalgia helps to make the real agony of the highlands visible and deplorable, sustaining social criticism, but of a conservative and inegalitarian kind.

The sermon has a powerful – perhaps too powerful – moral flavour. In the main the moral ideas do not correspond to those of the texts so far discussed. The apparatus of utilitarian theory is not employed; Coleridge was a critic of utilitarianism, which he regarded as a philosophy for pigs. There is little use of the language of rights. He denies to landlords absolute liberty rights over their land; it is entrusted to them and must be used for public purposes.

Conversely, he claims recipient rights for the poor; they have a right
to subsistence and to the hope of betterment. For persons are not
things, they are ends and not means: an employer is not entitled
simply to treat his employees as a factor of production having the
same moral quality as his machines or raw materials. If they are
to be employed as means, they must at the same time participate
in and consent to the end. The Christian roots of this use of rights
are discernible. The relationship of the landlord to his land is one
of Christian stewardship, and the poor have rights by virtue of the
value of all souls in the sight of God.

But more pervasive and more important in the moral discourse
of the sermon is a contrast between animal appetites and the discipline of duty. Here again, a source is no doubt the perennial
Christian theme of the war between flesh and spirit. But it is developed with a special intensity and reiteration in this sermon. Such
an emphasis would not be surprising in an evangelical: in an intellectual Anglican like Coleridge it calls for some explanation. It is possible that an aspect of the Christian tradition has become of central
importance to Coleridge because of his personal history. We know
that he was notorious among his friends and family for lack of will-
power: he was almost incapable of meeting a deadline or finishing
a task. He often helped his writings to completion by extensive
plagiarism. From early manhood he was addicted to laudanum. One
dependence led to another: he would often take large quantities of
brandy to settle his stomach after the drug. Frequently he lay in
bed until midday. As is common among addicts, he practised lying
and deception. He spent money his family needed on laudanum and
brandy. He did these things and was deeply ashamed of them.[7] In
this light we can duly weigh the significance and courage of his
denial of determinism and defence of free will. It represents a refusal
to find an excuse in a comfortable and fashionable philosophical
doctrine, a resolute acceptance of responsibility for his own failure.
In this light the moral stance of the sermon is intelligible. He writes
of 'unclean and animal passions' (127), 'all those whose own malignant passions have not rendered them blind and deaf and brutish'
(143), 'worthless persons . . . not seldom profligates, with whom
debauchery has outweighed rapacity' (144), 'blind practices and
blending passions . . . ostentatious fooleries and sensual vices'
(161), 'the tyranny of the present impulse' (224), 'the drunken stu-

por of a usurious selfishness' (208). He evidently writes from agonized and tragic personal experience. This moral perspective has important consequences for his social and political thought. It gives an edge to his demand that something should be done to remedy the deprived and insecure lives of the poor. How *can* they be better than animals, how can they exercise human qualities of foresight and self-discipline, if recession wrecks all their plans and grasping landlords blight their hopes? The conduct of the rich is condemned in the same terms; their brute appetites have blinded them to their duties. It is interesting that he advises the higher and middle classes to turn their minds to philosophy and theology as antidotes to sensual allurements. It is possible that his own turning from poetry to philosophy was part of a strategy to combat his addiction. But the main consequence of this moral stance is in terms of the solution it leads him to propose for the ills of the time. If the root cause of the trouble lies in human wickedness – the unbridled pursuit of gain and the gratification of appetite – then the remedy is to be found, not in legislative measures or institutional changes, but in the moral regeneration of private individuals. His message is not addressed to the state, but to the consciences of his readers. Obsession with human sinfulness engenders radical criticism in the moral sphere, but political conservatism. This joining of moral radicalism and political conservatism is characteristic also of evangelicalism; representative evangelicals such as Wesley or Wilberforce bear this out.

The discourse of the sermon about economy and society takes shape, like that of Hall, in a relationship of agreement and disagreement with classical economy. It is at the same time a response to dramatic contemporary events – 'the existing distresses and discontents'. Coleridge correctly attributes much of the trouble to the effects of the war and its termination.[8] He remarks that the war acted as a universal stimulant; it increased demand for manufactures, both directly and by the capture of overseas markets. Prosperity in manufacturing led to prosperity in agriculture. Roads, railways, docks, and canals were made, population and national wealth increased together. And then the war, instead of ending slowly by gradual exhaustion, '*plunged* to its conclusion' (159); the collapse of demand put the economy in reverse, and the returning soldiers and sailors swelled the ranks of the unemployed. Not only

does he identify the one-off problems of war, he also describes the
recurrent problems of the trade cycle, likening its curve to the flight
of Icarus (203):

> Alarm and suspicion gradually diminish into a judicious circum-
> spectness; but by little and little, circumspection gives way to the
> desire and emulous ambition of *doing business*; till Impatience and
> Incaution on one side, tempting and encouraging headlong Adven-
> ture, want of principle, and Confederacies of false credit on the other,
> the movements of Trade become yearly gayer and giddier, and end
> at length in a vortex of hopes and hazards, of blinding passions and
> blind practices, which should have been left where alone they ought
> ever to have been found, among the wicked lunacies of the Gaming
> Table. (204)

The description is striking, but as economic analysis it is worthless.
The trade cycle is condemned in purely moral terms. Perhaps greed
is the ultimate cause; but to say this is not to explain the mechanism
of the cycle.

He has interesting remarks on taxation. They are occasioned by
the radicals' insistence that high government spending and taxation
have caused the troubles. Coleridge argues that taxation in itself
need not be harmful to the economy; it all depends on how revenue
is spent. Public expenditure can be as beneficial as private and may
stimulate the economy. He likens a well-directed system of public
finance to a system of irrigation. He is surely right here, and his
remarks provide a useful corrective, not only to the radicals, but
also to the hostility to government spending of Adam Smith, who
regarded it as the most frequent cause of the impoverishment of
nations. But this part of the sermon does not deserve more than
mild applause. Coleridge fails to discuss what kinds of government
spending are beneficial and what harmful. There are no grounds
for regarding him as a precursor of Keynes: he has no theory of
the ways in which an economy tends, or fails to tend, towards full
employment of its resources. On taxation, he furnishes assertion
rather than analysis. His reply to Malthus is on the same level. An
increase of population leads to corresponding increase of the means
of subsistence: and 'I must content myself with observing, that I
have never heard it denied, that there is more than a sufficiency of
food in existence' (169). This may have sounded plausible in 1817,
when farmers were complaining that they could not get a decent
price for a superabundant harvest, but it is no answer to Malthus's

arguments. One is reminded of J. S. Mill's remark: 'In political economy especially he writes like an arrant driveller, and it would have been well for his reputation had he never meddled with the subject'. This is unduly harsh; and Mill adds in a footnote, 'Yet even on this subject he has occasionally a just thought, happily expressed'.[9] The passage Mill quotes is indeed one of the best things in the sermon. It comes after the account of the trade cycle. Political economists, he notes, look on the bright side; they see the economy as a wonderful self-regulating machine, and a crash is to be regarded as a natural rectification of a disturbed balance. All things find their level:

> Thus instead of the position, that all things *find*, it would be less equivocal and far more descriptive of the fact to say, that Things are always *finding*, their level: which might be taken as the paraphrase or ironical definition of a storm. . . . But Persons are not *Things* – but Man does not find his level! . . . After a hard and calamitous season, during which the thousand wheels of some vast manufactory had remained silent as a frozen water-fall, be it that plenty has returned and that Trade has once more become brisk and stirring: go, ask the overseer, and question the parish doctor, whether the workman's health and temperance with the staid and respectful Manners best taught by the inward dignity of conscious self-support, have found *their* level again! (206–7)

And he rams the point home with the pathetic illustration of half-starved children he had witnessed in Dorset. This is more than a moral response to an economic theory. Coleridge has taken on the central doctrine of Adam Smithian optimism and laissez-faire, the theory of the self-regulating market: he has drawn attention to the fact that, at best, 'things find their level' only in the long run, and that in the short term an unregulated process may have unacceptable consequences. At worst, the process of adjustment may entail perpetual instability.

Coleridge's sermon contains at least one striking contradiction and one important ambiguity. We have already noted the contradiction. He has argued that the commercial spirit – the selfish pursuit of gain – has its place in industry and trade; but it must be kept out of agriculture, for agriculture must serve public as well as private purposes. Yet he supports state intervention in industry, while refusing to contemplate it in agriculture. The ambiguity is to do with his theory of culture, which Mill, Leavis, and Raymond

Williams have rightly recognized as his main achievement in social thought.[10] His concept of culture is slippery, shifting between the anthropologist's neutral, descriptive sense, and an evaluative one.

To a modern anthropologist, all societies have a culture or cultures, and all individuals participate in one or more of the cultures of their society. In this sense, there cannot be a distinction between cultured and uncultured human beings. To be uncultured would be to be something other or less than human – to be a highly inadequate animal, like the wild boy of Aveyron. In the anthropologist's sense, a culture is a shared pattern of beliefs, conceptions, and practices that enables the members of a society to talk and live together, binding them into one community, acting as a kind of social glue. If, however, a society does not have one culture but many, then it may lack coherence and stability.[11] The evaluative use of culture is quite different from this. It is concerned with *high* culture – intellectual excellence, the fine arts, perhaps a certain refined, liberal, and noble style of thinking and behaviour. In this sense, not all societies are cultured, and many individuals are uncultured. The question here is not whether a society has a *common* culture, but what is the quality of its culture?

Coleridge shifts between these two meanings of the term. It is my contention that the contradiction concerning the role of the state and the muddle about culture can be explained in terms of the ideological stance of the sermon. We can approach this by studying the language he uses to refer to social structure. We find the occasional use of the term 'capitalist', but the sermon does not usually employ the vocabulary devised by classical economy to describe the workings of a capitalist system. The sermon's language is more traditional and does not derive from economic theory. So, we find higher and middle stations, higher and middle classes, rank, inferior classes, mass, multitude, men of noble race, poor, agriculturalist, manufacturer and tradesman, lower farmers and peasantry, labouring classes, lawyers and tradesfolk, learned class, gentry, and tenantry. When alongside this vocabulary we place references to men of noble rank serving their clients and dependents (125n), to the gentry and their natural clients and dependents (229), and to the rounds of the social ladder, it becomes evident that he is thinking of a hierarchical society of many strata, the levels being determined by economic function and profession, but also by birth and learning.

Not only does the vocabulary describe a hybrid society between feudalism and capitalism; it also endorses it. The sermon is redolent of social snobbery. The radical leaders are described as 'worthless persons of little or no estimation for rank, learning or integrity' (144). He sneers at 'the buffoonery and red-lattice phrases [i.e., alehouse language] of the canaglia' (154) and refers to 'the higher and middle classes' as 'the people at large, as distinguished from the mere populace' (164). The social gospel of the sermon calls upon the privileged to fulfil their duties to their inferiors, but in so doing it defends and justifies their position. Of the utmost significance are his remarks that the demagogues 'affect love to all and shew pity to none' (149) and that they are 'sycophants to the *crowd*, enemies to the *individuals*' (148). These remarks need to be taken together with the injunction at the end of the sermon that the wealthy man should '*act personally and in detail*' (230). As the editor remarks, this was a lifelong theme of Coleridge's. He first developed it as a critique of Godwin's call for universal benevolence.[12] This Godwin-Coleridge debate is replete with social meaning. Godwin rejects the dependency system: we should give, not as an act of charity, but in accordance with impartial justice. We should not favour our friends, nor should we expect gratitude. Coleridge, by contrast, defends the dependency system. Individual charity is the appropriate way to deal with social ills, and gratitude the appropriate response (149). So, for the most part, the sermon rejects political action and legislative remedies; and the few occasions when government action is called for, such as factory acts, are exceptions that prove the rule. The defence of taxation and government expenditure is a defence of the landed ruling class that benefited from such expenditure. Coleridge is an advocate for landed, aristocratic society. In all honesty and consistency, he could not be otherwise: all his life he depended on the patronage system. His father owed his job as schoolmaster and curate to a local gentleman; the same gentleman contributed largely to Coleridge's education at Christ's Hospital and Cambridge. Throughout his life, the greater part of his income came from wealthy benefactors and from a state pension.

Not only does the sermon defend the position of the landed elite: it also defends the intellectual elite, which had such strong links with the gentry, and to which Coleridge himself belonged. Often when he refers to 'men of rank' he adds 'and learning'. The Quakers have gone wrong because

> they excluded from their system all ministers specially trained and educated for the ministry, with all professional Theologians: and they omitted to provide for the raising up among themselves any other established class of learned men, as teachers and schoolmasters for instance, in their stead. (190)

Coleridge himself was originally intended for the ministry, and more than once thought of becoming a schoolmaster: he became instead a professional sage. His oldest son, after failing to be confirmed as a Fellow of Oriel, became a teacher. The learning that Coleridge respects is 'austerer studies'; the humane learning in the classics that he (and the gentry) had acquired. He is scornful of technical knowledge, 'physical and psychological empiricism':

> I feel assured, that if Plato himself were to return and renew his sublime lucubrations in the metropolis of Great Britain, a handicraftsman, from a laboratory, who had just succeeded in disoxydating an Earth, would be thought far the more respectable, nay, the more illustrious person of the two. (171)

The sermon presents itself to the reader as the work of a man of letters: it is larded with classical quotations and allusions, there are learned footnotes. The language, doctrines, and very style of the sermon have to be understood as expressions and defences of a particular social position.

This, I would suggest, is the cause of the ambiguity in Coleridge's theory of culture. He is confused because he is trying to do two things. One is to develop the concept of culture as a shared pattern of beliefs that creates and maintains a community. The other is to defend the position of an intellectual elite, through an ideal of high culture. We should not be surprised that the same muddle is to be found in the writings of Matthew Arnold, T. S. Eliot, and F. R. Leavis, for the social viewpoint of these men has points in common with Coleridge's. The intellectual is not always as *freischwebende* – free-floating – as Mannheim would have us believe.[13]

Coleridge's conception of history accords with this social viewpoint. He had read and admired Harrington, and his overview of British history is another variant of the neo-Harringtonian paradigm. The polity must be balanced: it undergoes corruption and decline when that balance is disturbed. In recent centuries, the balance has been upset by the growth of commerce, which has not

sufficiently been counterbalanced. But the remedy he proposes is
not merely an economic and social one. It is not just a matter of
strengthening the landed interest at the expense of commerce. The
medicine must also be intellectual – a revival of the austerer studies
to counterbalance the ethos of trade. His conception of change is
partly materialist, partly idealist – the vision of an intellectual having links with the landed class. He is no admirer of primitivism
(217), but neither does he agree with the radical enlightenment's
conception of progress as an ever-ascending escalator. The high
point in British and perhaps European history was the period from
the Renaissance until the late seventeenth century (172). That was
a period of deep and serious learning, of Platonic philosophy and
systematic theology. Since then, there has been a decline into materialism and shallow empiricism, encouraged by the growth of the
commercial system after the Glorious Revolution of 1688 (195).

The ultimate foundations of the social philosophy of the sermon
are religious and metaphysical. Religious ideas were present, half-
submerged, in the texts of Ogilvie, Godwin, and Hall; but in Coleridge's *Lay Sermon* the religion is, appropriately enough, explicit
and all-pervading. The pages are filled with biblical references and
quotations. The metaphysics on the other hand is implicit; but with
the help of other texts by this author it can readily be identified as
Platonism or Neoplatonism uneasily reinforced by a Kantian critical
apparatus and epistemology. The discussions of Ogilvie and Godwin sought to demonstrate that those thinkers, overconfident in the
power of Reason, failed to grapple adequately with the problem of
persuading others to agree with them. Coleridge is not confident
that the truth he has found can readily be diffused, for it is elusive
and difficult. He is thus rescued from naive Godwinian flights of
optimism. But in the end, the foundations of his theory are no more
satisfactory. The reader must believe, not only that the Bible contains divinely inspired wisdom but also that Coleridge's often
strained interpretation of it is correct. His mixture of Plato and
Kant is so obscure and ill-defined as to defy rational discussion.

If we employ Mannheim's concepts, we can say that while the texts
of Ogilvie, Godwin, and Hall were primarily utopian, Coleridge's
Lay Sermon is mainly ideological. It provides an idealized depiction
and justification of landed aristocratic society and of the role of

the intelligentsia within it. This ideology is constructed with diverse materials: the Platonic ideal of the philosophic ruler, the Christian antithesis of flesh and spirit, the neo-Machiavellian theory of the balanced polity. With the help of this conceptual apparatus, the troubles of the postwar period are experienced and interpreted. Several of the underlying assumptions of the text – the conception of human nature; the theory of culture; the image of a lost, responsible society; the moral language – all permit a deep and devastating social critique. But at the same time they dictate a particular solution to the problem, in terms of individual moral effort rather than social reform. These assumptions even affect the economic analysis, which is largely conducted in moral rather than neutral and scientific terms. As a sustained argument, the sermon is poor. There is little that deserves the title of reasoning: there is no systematic surveying of evidence. Everything is done by assertion, backed up with vivid examples and conveyed in prose that is sometimes striking and poetic. For all its failings, the piece has real merits. Coleridge reasserts the principles of Christian charity in an age when many clergymen preferred to teach submissiveness to the poor rather than charity to the rich, and when arguments of a Malthusian kind were widely used to question all relief of distress. He deplores the Highland clearances, which were all too often ignored, or condoned as 'improvements'.[14] His brief critique of laissez-faire market theory is powerful. And above all, with his concept of culture, he offers a way of understanding social bonds that transcends the stale eighteenth-century antithesis of self-love and benevolence.

Report to the County of Lanark, Robert Owen, 1821

Owen's *Report* is a pamphlet addressing the problem of the general depression that followed the Napoleonic wars. Demand had collapsed, the markets were glutted, there was high unemployment. The poor rates had risen alarmingly, and Owen, like many others, was searching for a better remedy than the old Poor Law. He insists that it is a case of poverty in the midst of plenty; the productive capacity of the nation has increased greatly over recent decades, and yet the masses are in want. His diagnosis and recommended cure fall under three headings: a change in the monetary system; the adoption of spade cultivation; the setting up of model communities.

The change in the monetary system – or as Owen calls it, the change in the standard of value – is designed 'to let prosperity loose on the country' (248).[1] Gold and silver have ceased to be satisfactory as the standard of value, for wealth has increased so much that the stock of bullion can no longer represent it. He thinks this became clear in 1797, when Britain went off the gold standard; but now the government is seeking to return to gold, with disastrous consequences. Owen proposes, instead of the 'artificial' standard of gold and silver, a 'natural' standard – labour. Each item should be priced in accordance with the quantity of labour that went into its making. The raw material component can also be valued in these terms, because it cost so much labour to obtain the raw materials. Though he does not indicate this in the *Report*, Owen intends that labour should be assessed not simply in terms of hours; allowance should be made for differing qualities of labour, skilled counting for more. Just as commodities are to be priced in accordance with the labour they contain, so also labourers are to be paid in labour notes, that is, notes worth so many hours of labour, which can be exchanged for the goods valued in hours of labour.[2] The thinking behind these proposals is tangled in the extreme. Apparently a prime influence is the labour theory of value of Smith and Ricardo. But even if Smith is right, that labour is the best measure of value, or if Ricardo is right, that value is determined by embodied labour, this would not support Owen's conclusion that gold and silver should be replaced by labour notes. For this would merely be to alter the medium of exchange and the mode of expressing values; it would not alter the values themselves, which, both before and after the change, would be measured or determined by labour. Another idea underlying the proposal is the belief that the labourer is unfairly rewarded. His labour produces all wealth, yet a large portion of it is pocketed by the rich who do not labour. So, perhaps Owen is thinking that the introduction of labour notes would strip the veil from the face of exploitation, enabling workers immediately to see that they are not receiving the full value of their labour. But Owen has not thought this one through; he is certainly not recommending that the labourer be paid the full value of his labour:

> The landholder and capitalist would be benefited by this arrangement in the same degree with the labourer, because labour is the foundation of all values, and it is only from labour, liberally remunerated, that high profits can be paid for agricultural and manufactured products. (263)

We have still failed to see how Owen could have thought that a change in the standard of value would solve the depression. He was correct in regarding the return to gold as a bad measure of economic policy.[3] It shook confidence, already reeling from the postwar collapse of demand, and thus deepened the recession. It is not clear, however, how Owen's new standard of value would have been a better remedy than a continuance of the issue of paper money, an abandonment of the deflationary return to gold. Maybe behind his labour standard of value lies a confused apprehension of Say's law; the thesis that there can never be a long-term glut, because supply creates equivalent demand.[4] It may be that Owen's new standard is designed, however mistakenly, to make this principle effective, pricing goods in terms of labour, and remunerating labourers in the same terms, thus enabling them to buy, to mop up the supply. But if so, it is a misconceived measure. If Say's law is correct, a glut will solve itself in the long run, without the instrumentality of a new currency. In fact, the postwar recession was a short-term crisis, resulting from a sudden change in the pattern of demand caused by the cessation of military and naval expenditure and from a collapse of confidence. Perhaps it could have been alleviated by Keynesian measures to stimulate demand; but the government of the day had neither the knowledge nor the means to do this, and Owen's new standard of value would not have helped. Finally, to price goods in accordance with the labour they contain is to price them solely in terms of cost of production, ignoring demand. A particular commodity – say, black cloth – is not going to sell at its 'labour' value if the market is overstocked with black cloth. Furthermore, it may not be easy to assign a 'labour' value to a commodity because of differences in the skill and efficiency of labour that cannot readily be quantified. These problems helped to bring about the failure of Owen's plan when Exchange Bazaars and Labour Notes were tried by his followers in 1832 and 1833.[5]

The expansion of spade cultivation is intended as an immediate remedy for unemployment, and as a solution to the longer-term problem of population pressure. Owen calculates that 60 million acres in Great Britain and Ireland are cultivated at present; a change from the plough to the labour-intensive spade method, as well as mopping up surplus labourers (he calculates 60 million labourers could be employed cultivating 60 million acres) would produce enough food to support a population of 100 million in 'high comfort' (259). 'The change from the plough to the spade will prove to be a far more extensive and beneficial innovation than that which the invention of the spinning machine has occasioned' (257). Behind this lies a momentous shift in perception, which distances Owen from, for example, Hall. He knows what technology can achieve, and it has given him a faith that a society dominated by scarcity can give way to a society transformed by abundance.[6] This new perception was to play a central role in much nineteenth- and early twentieth-century socialism. But he has chosen a bad example. Robert Owen, master manufacturer, intoxicated by the explosion of productivity in the cotton industry, overoptimistically supposes that a similarly dramatic technological revolution can be achieved on the land, by turning from plough to spade. The fact that the revolution in cotton was labour saving, whereas that proposed for agriculture would consume *more* labour, ought to have made him doubt the parallel. His case is argued most unconvincingly in the *Report*, comparing unfavourably with the more informed and detailed plans for intensive cultivation provided earlier by Hall and later by Cobbett. A characteristic intellectual failing of Owen's is exemplified here; not only does he use evidence in a slipshod manner, it is also apparent that he has no grasp of what is required to prove an argument. The sole piece of evidence brought forward in defence of spade cultivation is a vague reference to the successes of Mr. Falla of Gateshead. Therefore the reader cannot help feeling that Owen's confidence is unwarranted when he insists that 'These facts being incontrovertible, few perhaps will hesitate to admit them' (255).

The adoption of spade cultivation must be accompanied by appropriate arrangements; by this he means new communities. The communities described in the *Report* are pauper colonies – settlements designed to give accommodation and work to the unemployed – and, at the same time, ideal societies, Owen's blueprint for the future. His account of the colonies, minute and circumstantial on some issues, is fatally vague on all-important questions of finance and economic organization. The population of a community should number between 300 and 2,000 and ideally should come within the 800–1,200 range. No defence of these figures is given; Owen merely appeals to 'many years of deep and anxious reflection' (265). He also specifies the number of acres a community should have; for it must combine industry and agriculture. No labourer should be divorced from his food supply in a factory town or denied the pleasure of cultivating the soil. This is a surprising opinion from the lips of a captain of industry; but Owen is concerned about the damage to mind and body when a worker spends his life shut in a mill, engaged in a mind-dulling repetitive task, returning in the evening to an overcrowded and polluted slum. The *Report* contains hostile reflections on the division of labour reminiscent of Ferguson and Adam Smith (258, 267, 274, 284). The communities, Owen's famous 'parallelograms', are therefore to be spacious and airy, set in the countryside. Living quarters will be centrally heated or cooled 'on the improved principles lately introduced in the Derby Infirmary'; meals will be centrally cooked and communally eaten; even the dress of the inhabitants is planned – loose, light clothes, something between a Roman toga and a Scottish kilt. The operative principle of the communities is to be coopera- tion; to use slightly later language, *social*ism not *individual*ism. This, together with good planning and management, will be the key to economic success. The communities will be immensely more productive and profitable than the old economic order, which is based on 'minute division of labour and division of interests' (283). Their system of education is crucial; for Owen, following (and coars- ening) Godwin, believes that

> principles as certain as those upon which the science of mathematics is founded may be applied to the forming of any given general char- acter, and that by the influence of other circumstances, not a few individuals only, but the whole population of the world, may in a few years be rendered a very far superior race of beings to any now upon the earth, or which has been made known to us by history. (282)

This truly breathtaking claim is based upon his faith that 'the science of the influence of circumstances over . . . character' (271) is the most pregnant discovery in the history of the human mind.

Communities may be formed by different agencies; by landlords, large capitalists, companies, by parishes and counties as a replace- ment for the poor law, or by associations of farmers, mechanics, and tradesmen who wish themselves to adopt the new life (285). Their manner of management will vary according to their mode of inauguration. When landlords and capitalists are the founders, they will put in professional managers; but when communities are es- tablished by their members, they will be governed by committees, say, of members between the ages of thirty-five and forty-five – for Owen does not want the tumult of elections. Present-day con- ceptions of democracy require elections as a defining characteristic. Are we to say that Owen was not a democrat? The issue is not so simple.[7] Political equality can also be cited as a defining charac- teristic,[8] and Owen certainly believes in that, in the sense that ideally everybody should rule in turn. His is a 'paternalistic' conception of 'democracy', suspicious of the unthinking and irresponsible mob, placing power into the hands of the old and wise. It is a 'democracy' that seeks to implement, not the will of the majority, but the right answer, the answer given by those appropriately educated and ex- perienced. The communities will engage in more or less trade with each other, and with the outside world; some trading they will have to do, to earn cash to pay national taxes. Communities will be desirable for any state. Being so productive, their members will be free from want, taking from the common store according to need (289). This, coupled with their scientific formation of character, will eliminate bad and malevolent passions, and therefore crime; they will want no laws, courts, police, or jails. In time of war, the communities will furnish the best soldiers, for their members will be healthy and will have undergone systematic courses of physical education and drilling. But when the communities overspread the world – as they surely will when all humanity envies the superior life they afford – and as they transform human character, eliminating selfishness, greed, aggressiveness, and pride – then war will disappear from the earth.

Owen's proposals were tried out: New Harmony in America; Orbiston, Queenwood, Ralahine in Britain. Their example did not overspread the world, for they failed; Owen lost his fortune at New Harmony. As contemporary critics pointed out, to set up an Owenite community would be extremely expensive; the successful co-operatives of Mondragon in the Basque country today demonstrate the necessity of a solid financial base, which none of the Owenite ventures had. Secondly, a viable community could not be established simply by gathering together a population taken at random, without regard to the balance of knowledge and skills. Owen himself, in the *Report*, recognized that getting the communities organized and going would be no easy matter (285) and his somewhat contradictory assertion that 'the principles being understood, a man of fair ordinary capacity would superintend such arrangements with more ease than most large commercial or manufacturing establishments are now conducted' (286) is wide of the mark. Managing a cotton mill, which Owen did so well, was a small matter beside managing the diversified economy of a community. Thirdly, he failed to appreciate the problem of the internal politics of a community. He naively assumed that the members would see the truth of his proposals, and that there would be no disputes; in practice it was not like that at all, and his paternalistic style caused trouble. Fourthly, as Torrens pointed out, Owen failed to resolve the issue of the relationship of the communities to the wider world. They were meant to be islands of stability and full employment; but if they traded in the national market-place, would they not be disturbed by its fluctuations? And if they did not, how could they adopt the economies of scale and division of labour that both economic theory and practical experience demonstrated were crucial to enhanced productivity?[9]

I now turn from an outline of the argument of the *Report*, to an analysis of its structure and conditions. Owen makes no use of systematic tools of moral theory – concepts of rights, justice, or utility. Nor is there anything to compare with Hall's powerful evocation of moral condemnation by depiction of human suffering. Characteristically, much of the moral argument proceeds by unspecific and unsupported assertion and reiteration; present society produces misery and degradation, Owen's new world will engender happiness and improved characters. Two areas merit further consideration. Scattered hints permit the reader to build up a picture of the qualities of character and behaviour Owen hopes to promote by improved education and environment – I shall look at this later. Most strikingly, Owen recommends a society[10] based on cooperation rather than selfishness and competition. The argument is contained in two passages. The first forms part of his advocacy of a labour standard of value. The true and original principle of barter is to exchange articles that are genuinely equivalent in value, because they contain equal quantities of labour. Barter, however, has given way to commerce, whose principle is to buy cheap and sell dear; not to seek a fair exchange, but to maximize one's own advantage at the expense of another.

> But it has made man ignorantly, individually selfish; placed him in opposition to his fellows; engendered fraud and deceit; blindly urged him forward to create, but deprived him of the wisdom to enjoy. In striving to take advantage of others he has over-reached himself. (262)

The result is the economic instability of the day, the paradoxical situation of poverty coupled with the power to create plenty. The second passage forms part of the description of model communities. He takes to task 'theorists in political economy' who have argued that if each individual pursues private interest, this will result in public good:

> From this principle of individual interests have arisen all the divisions of mankind, the endless errors and mischiefs of class, sect, party,

and of national antipathies, creating the angry and malevolent passions, and all the crimes and misery with which the human race have been hitherto afflicted.

In short, if there be one closet doctrine more contrary to truth than another, it is the notion that individual interest, as that term is now understood, is a more advantageous principle on which to found the social system, for the benefit of all, or of any, than the principle of union and mutual co-operation. (269)

It is plain that the occasion for this passage is political economy, and that Owen is here rejecting its central conception of a self-regulating market system. This is his chief claim to fame as a thinker; this is what makes him a founding father of socialism. How is this departure possible for him? To some extent the answer is obvious; the doctrine of the unregulated pursuit of self-interest is so contrary to the ethical traditions of European civilization that it was bound to provoke reaction. Owen can appeal to a rival image of human relationships in loving and caring family life: 'They will each render to the others the same benefits as are now given, or rather much greater benefits than are now given to each other by the members of the most closely united and affectionate families' (289). Experience of the French wars also suggests the superiority of collective over individual action:

> If . . . experience has proved that union, combination, and extensive arrangement . . . are a thousand times more powerful to destroy than the efforts of an unconnected multitude, where each acts individually for himself, – would not a similar increased effect be produced by union, combination, and extensive arrangement, to *create and conserve?* (270; see also 261)

But the prime source of his ideal of cooperation lies in his experience as a factory manager. Hence he commends the advantages of carefully planned and coordinated activity (268) and likens his model communities to a machine (285) and to a factory (286). Owen knows, from a lifetime of experience, what can be achieved by rational planning within the unit of production; he advocates the extension of the same rational control to the economic system as a whole (or rather, as a collection of more or less independent economically diversified parts). Here he touches a chord that vibrates throughout subsequent socialist thought.

It is possible to detect the frame of mind of a factory manager in the conception of 'good character' that serves as the goal of the education by which Owen places so much store. He writes of 'men trained in the best habits and dispositions'; 'renovating the moral characters of the population', of 'good conduct' rather than 'wretched habits'. The word 'educate' is regularly coupled with the word 'train', and it soon becomes clear that he is thinking of something practical and vocational. He has little time for book learning and wants 'useful knowledge', and a population 'trained to fill every office and to perform every duty that the well-being of their associates and the establishments can require', and 'a working class full of activity and useful knowledge', fitted for 'easy, regular, healthy, rational employment'. Education, in fact, must equip its pupils for the regular and rapid routine of the factory. The drilling and dancing that was so conspicuous and unusual a feature of the education at New Lanark has all the signs of having been designed to this end:

> Bodily exercises, adapted to improve the dispositions and increase the health and strength of the individual, will form part of the training and education of the children. In these exercises they may be instructed to acquire facility in the execution of combined movements, a habit which is calculated to produce regularity and order in time of peace, as well as to aid defensive and offensive operations in war. (291)

His career as a cotton manufacturer is a vital clue in understanding Owen's mind. This is what generates his overweening confidence in the power of science and technology; this is what underlies his supreme self-assurance. He is one of the 'practical men' who know how to do it and who are so much ahead of the 'closet theorist', 'however acute, learned and eloquent', 'who so often leads the public mind astray from its true course' (260, 265–6).

Closet intellectuals might think, however, that Owen could have profited by giving more systematic attention to social theory. He has no orderly and coherent set of concepts for describing society. He writes of ranks, rich and poor; higher, middle, and working classes; landowners, capitalists, and labourers. He insists that labour is the source of all wealth, that a few monopolists have unjustly absorbed the wealth produced by the many; but the nature of this exploitation is not explained, and he suggests that landowners and capitalists will continue to enjoy their incomes, perhaps augmented, under the new system of cooperative villages (246, 258, 263, 267). He is inconsistent in his account of what lies at the root of social ills: sometimes it is the principle of barter; sometimes the division of labour; sometimes the principle of individual interest, from which have arisen 'all the divisions of mankind, the endless errors and mischiefs of class, sect, party, and of national antipathies, creating the angry and malevolent passions, and all the crimes and misery with which the human race have been hitherto afflicted' (269). Sometimes the erroneous belief that individuals are responsible for their own characters (which in reality are formed for them by their circumstances and education) is the source of all hatred and revenge.

If Owen's treatment of society marks a retrogression, conceptually and theoretically, from the achievements of his predecessors, there is a further weakness, evident in his *Report* because of its crudity, which was also present in their writings. This is the claim that social antagonism can easily be eliminated because it rests, quite simply, upon mistaken attitudes. What conceptions of interpersonal relations does he deploy in arguing that social conflict can be eliminated? At first sight, it looks as if he has rejected the Smithian natural harmony of interests, replacing it with the principle of the fusion of interests.[11] But it is not quite as simple as this. Certainly he sometimes advocates a fusion of interests through love and sympathy; but he only rejects the natural harmony of egoisms in its Mandevillian or Smithian form, where public good results as an unintended consequence of the pursuit of self-interest. Owen thinks that human beings are mainly selfishly motivated; but he thinks self-interest is best served by promoting the good of others. The natural harmony of egoisms results from a prudent, rational pursuit of self-interest that consciously aims at the general good. To go for one's private good to the detriment of others is shortsighted folly, self-defeating conduct.

'[T]he happiness of self, clearly understood and uniformly practised . . . can only be attained by conduct that must promote the happiness of the community.'[12] In this easy way, he solves the problem of class conflict and the problem of arriving at a general will. Hence, his proposals to the County of Lanark describe

> an improved practical system for the working classes, highly beneficial, in whatever light it may be viewed, to every part of society. (264)
>
> It calls for no sacrifice of principle or property to any individual in any rank or condition. (297)

This audacious cop-out is to be found, muted somewhat, in Ogilvie, Godwin, and Hall. Maybe it is an afterecho of religious ways of thinking; the good God could not have created a world in which conflict and disharmony are part of the basic order of things; they exist only as results of sin and error.

Owen's *Report* needs excavating, in order to uncover the hidden substructure of religious ways of apprehending experience. We know that he was a deeply religious youth and that he ended his life as a spiritualist. We know that in his preaching of the New Moral World in the 1830s, he drew upon millennialist language to describe the great change. We know that his cooperative communities were inspired by the Quaker John Bellers's *Proposals for Raising a Colledge of Industry* of 1696, and by the living examples of religious communities in America. Such communities are characteristically in the business of dropping out from and repudiating the old immoral world; they bespeak a Manichean frame of mind, which encourages the habit of thinking in sharp contrasts. The antitheses of theology – God-world, grace-nature, salvation-sin, elect-damned – are mirrored in Owen's thought by the sharp contrast between the error, superstition, prejudice, and selfishness of the old immoral world, and the truth, reason, and benevolent cooperation of the new moral one. The same sharply antithetical pattern of thinking is evident in Godwin's *Political Justice*, a book whose roots in a religious culture can easily be demonstrated. To think in this way is at once a strength and a disability for a critic of society. It facilitates the total rejection of the present order and the proposal of a radically new one; but it encourages a naive faith in a once-for-all transformation, a total shift from pure evil to unadulterated good. It discourages any sense of the ineluctably tangled, and only partially tractable, nature of human affairs.

The conception of time and change is partly progressivist, partly 'millennialist'. There is no sense in the *Report* of a long process of evolution and gradual change. The transformation is to occur suddenly and rapidly: 'Yet this extraordinary change is at hand. It will immediately take place' (257), but also peacefully and quietly (271). The pattern for this conception is probably to be found in the technological breakthroughs in cotton manufacturing during the past generation. The change is described by Owen as a transition from error to truth, and also from an irrational, unplanned order – a realm of contingency – to rational planning: '[T]he present state of society, *governed by circumstances*, is so different in its several parts and entire combination, from that which will arise when society shall be brought to *govern circumstances*' (273). Hence the present order has no value, but the order to come is of infinite value. The change is to be achieved through conscious human agency, but not necessarily *mass* agency. Owen's *Report* is addressed to the local gentry: in 1818 he had proposed a committee to consider his schemes, to be composed of the archbishops and bishops; ministers; judges; Dukes of Rutland, Wellington, and Bedford, and numerous other peers; Sir Francis Burdett, Wilberforce, W. Smith, Thomas Babington, Coke of Norfolk, Huskisson, Walter Scott, Dugald Stewart, and Robert Southey.[13] 'He is not now, however, addressing the common public, but those whose minds have had all the benefit of the knowledge which society at present affords; and it is from such individuals that he hopes to derive the assistance requisite' (272).

So much of Owen's thought – the change from error to truth, the evaporation of social conflict and its replacement by consensus, the enormous faith in the ability of science and technology to transform not only production but also human relationships – is underpinned and made possible by an implicit epistemology, one that informs the thought of Ogilvie, Godwin, and Hall also, because it is a structural characteristic of the enlightenment.[14] Owen is a votary of 'Truth'; and truth is a copy of reality, a plain and simple record of facts. Facts are unproblematic to unprejudiced minds. Human faculties of perception are receiving instruments that need contribute no colouring, no structure of their own. Hence mind can discover the general laws by which the universe – including humanity – is regulated. Hitherto the race has not attained truth, because it has been in the grip of superstition and the fallacies of the imagination; once these cobwebs are cleared away, nothing will obstruct the clear light. Truth is correspondence with Nature. This epistemology is implied by such statements as the following: 'These individuals must be left to be convinced by the facts themselves' (275). 'This view of human nature rests upon facts which no one can disprove' (281). 'The principles may be made plain to every capacity. They are simple principles of nature, in strict unison with all we see or know from facts to be true' (285).

It also sustains Owen's educational ideas. He is a perfect Mr. Gradgrind in his enthusiasm for facts, albeit a kindly and charismatic Gradgrind. The children in his schools will be freed from the present defective and tiresome system of book learning (283) and will be brought into direct contact with the facts of nature; in this way they will master all that the human mind has hitherto achieved before they reach the age of twelve (284). This epistemology explains also his curious ideas about dress. There is a measure of good sense in his observations; he proposes a mode of attire that will not constrict or overheat the body. But his supposition that there is one natural or rational mode of dress, which, once adopted, will be in use for centuries and that 'fashion' will only survive, even among the 'most weak and silly', for a very short period (278) is most revealing. In the first place, it manifests a lack of awareness that it is not always appropriate to judge human. conduct right or wrong, rational or irrational; for behaviour – and this is patently the case with dress – is also expressive and creative. Second, it shows how much Owen lacks the idea of culture – the sense that differences of opinion and behaviour may not always be differences between truth, half-truth, and error, but rather, differences between systems of meaning and interpretations of experience; differences that cannot be resolved by appealing to the 'facts', because facts themselves have to be interpreted. It is because they lack these ideas that Ogilvie, Godwin, and Owen can have so much confidence in the eventual triumph of their arguments. Conversely, because these ideas are part of our intellectual furniture, we cannot share their optimism, which seems to us naive and at first sight puzzling.

This epistemology underpins Owen's implicit conception of 'politics'. He is not opposed to politics understood as administration; his new society might well involve an extension of governmental activity. He hopes that communities will be set up by the agencies of local government, the counties and parishes. But he is utterly opposed to politics understood as *party* politics, politics as the articulation of opposed interests and ideologies. Such a 'pluralist' conception of politics is alien to his desire for unity, a unity based upon reason and truth.[15]

Owen was self-taught; his reading, though copious in early life, was unsystematic, and his sense of himself as a 'practical' man led him

somewhat to despise academic learning. It is not surprising, therefore, that the conceptual and theoretical apparatus of his writings
is so weak, and his use of evidence, his intellectual method, so poor.
Nevertheless he was a remarkable man whose thought ran far away
from common channels, and he captured the imagination of working class radicals, then and since. When we read Owen, we feel that
the source of his inspiration lay less in intellectual concerns, more
in his practical experience as a factory manager. But experience
does not come directly into the mind, unmediated through concepts
and assumptions. Owen had picked up enough of the ideas of the
radical enlightenment to enable him to experience his society as
highly imperfect, capable of being bettered. He had imbibed a faith
in science and progress and latched on to associationism as a theory
that promised a technology for transforming and improving human
character. He had a smattering of political economy, which had a
crucial negative influence upon him; he looked upon the theory of
the self-regulating market and saw that it was bad.

Owen, the critic of individualism, is the father of British socialism. In his later descriptions of the New Moral World, he envisages
no distinction between rich and poor. None will seek power; all
will rule in their turn. In spite of this, Owen remains an ambiguous
socialist in twentieth-century terms, and this is especially apparent
in the *Report*. So much of the pamphlet reads like a factory manager's ideology. The audience to which it is addressed is the aristocracy, the gentry, and wealthy manufacturers. This was true of
all of his propaganda effort before 1820. After 1817, he grew notorious as one who scorned religion and whose plans became increasingly visionary; it got harder for him to obtain an audience,
except among the labouring classes. Secondly, the pamphlet idealizes order, coordination, and rational control. It regards the poor
as a resource to be trained and managed – with a view to their own
good, of course – but the bettering of their condition is not necessarily to be initiated by themselves. Thirdly, he is very tender
towards the propertied; in the *Report to the County of Lanark*, at
least, the landlord is to retain his rents and the capitalist his profits.
By common consent he was the leading 'socialist' in the Britain of
his day: today, his 'socialist' credentials are debatable. This indicates the extent to which the meaning of the word has shifted.

A Few Doubts as to the Correctness of Some Opinions Generally Entertained on the Subjects of Population and Political Economy, 'Piercy Ravenstone', 1821

Ravenstone's book belongs to the contemporary debate about the condition of the poor. It begins with a long critique of Malthus's population theory, which Ravenstone thinks is cruel, insulting to God's providence, and erroneous both factually and theoretically. Ravenstone seeks to establish that hunger results, not from the natural workings of the economic order, but from bad human institutions. He begins by attacking the famous geometrical ratio, whereby population is alleged to have the capacity to increase geometrically in periods of twenty-five years. In the first place, the threat of imminent overpopulation is greatly reduced by infant mortality; only eleven females out of twenty born live to the age of marriage. At first sight this does not seem to contradict Malthus, who did not suppose that the geometrical ratio actually operated (except in very unusual circumstances); premature death, often brought on by hunger itself caused by overpopulation, checked the growth of numbers. But Ravenstone maintains that the high death rate among children is endemic to the human condition and is not caused by the occurrence and recurrence of widespread malnutrition. Undoubtedly this argument had some validity in the early nineteenth century, when diseases and illnesses resulting from poor hygiene carried off young lives; but if part of Ravenstone's purpose is to defend the goodness of God, he has been less successful than he thinks. God is on the way to being cleared of the charge of so arranging the system of the world that millions must die of famine, but he stands convicted of fashioning humanity in such a way that nine out of twenty young innocents must perish. Ravenstone is on firmer ground when he makes the simple but devastating point that the number of births is related, not to the total population, but to the number and duration of fertile marriages. 'In every country, in every society, where any statistical tables have been kept' (34)[1] it appears that, of females who reach the age of marriage, nineteen out of twenty marry, and nineteen out of twenty marriages are fertile. But for how long? Given that the period of fertility may be curtailed by the death of either partner, Ravenstone calculates an average fertility period of eleven years. How many children will be produced in that period? Ravenstone subscribes to the belief, widespread then but doubted now, that a mother is infertile while breast feeding and derives the conclusion that the average number of children of fertile marriages will be five and a quarter. Given infant mortality, given the women who do not marry, given the marriages that prove infertile, an average of four per fertile marriage would maintain population at a level; the figure of five and a quarter would permit a doubling in 75 years. So Malthus's geometrical rate of increase over periods of 25 years is impossible; at worst this rate would be over periods of 75 years.

Ravenstone now turns from the general law of population increase, to the facts of history and to recent statistics. He seeks to show, not only that population never has grown with Malthusian speed, but also that its doubling has been in periods of more than 75 years. He draws on the Bible, Greek and Roman history, and the history of medieval and modern Europe to show that in antiquity, population levels were very low, and that there has subsequently been a steady but slow growth. The evidence for modern Europe shows a normal rate of doubling every 110 or 120 years, and he remarks that if the average rate since Noah's flood, 4,150 years ago, had been a doubling every 130 years, this would increase the eight survivors of the deluge to the present population of the world (54). His history of population is an overambitious undertaking; he does not have a sufficient evidential basis to support his conclusions. It is overoptimistic to say, 'Yet no where has any inconvenience been felt from this increase of numbers; nowhere except in England, and that only during the last thirty years, have the means of subsistence been found to increase less rapidly than the number of the people' (77). He is ignoring the fluctuations, such as the peak of the thirteenth century and the decline of the fourteenth century in England, which might support Malthus rather than himself. '"Heaven and earth shall pass away, but my theory shall endure," is the cry of every system-maker' (110). He accuses Malthus of selecting those figures from the British censuses of 1801 and 1811 that fit his theory, while rejecting those that do not. But Ravenstone does the same himself; the censuses show a population growth rate of 1.5% per year, implying a doubling in sixty years, and he insists the figures must be wrong. Modern historians would confirm this rapid growth in these years; and although it is quite exceptional for all periods of British history for which we have adequate records, other societies have since recorded even faster growth – though with the help of medical techniques far beyond those of Ravenstone's day. America, he remarks, is Malthus's stronghold; there, where natural resources far exceeded the needs of a small population, doubling in periods of twenty-five years was recorded. But Ravenstone argues convincingly that much of this increase was due to immigration, a fact that Malthus 'passes over in silence' (125); once a due allowance for that exceptional factor has been made, the rate of increase in America is no faster than in Europe. It would be beyond the purpose of this book to explain all the other arguments against the Malthusian geometrical ratio, some of which employ statistics in a most ingenious manner; Ravenstone evidently enjoyed playing with numbers. But it is worth noting the precise wording of his conclusion:

> Everywhere we find the annual marriages bearing the same propor-
> tion to the whole number of the people: everywhere we see the mar-
> riages renovating the world by almost exactly the same number of
> births; everywhere we perceive the numbers of the people rapidly
> though insensibly increasing in almost equal proportions. (118)

Ravenstone believes that his researches have shown population growing everywhere, as if by an irresistible law, at a roughly equal rate: topography, climate, economy, and social customs do not vary its progress. This orderly and beautiful progress is dictated by the laws of God (148).

He deals with Malthus's arithmetical ratio of the increase of the food supply over periods of twenty-five years more briefly. Like Hall, whom he may have read, he insists that the quantity of subsistence is proportional to the number of hands employed in agriculture; therefore there is no reason why it should not grow step by step with population. He will have no truck with the argument of Malthus and Ricardo, that increasing the food supply becomes progressively harder as population growth compels recourse to inferior soils. The productivity of the soil depends upon the amount of labour applied to it; to all practical intents and purposes, there are no inferior soils. If Malthus's theory were correct, one would expect the masses to live most comfortably in the thinly populated regions of the world. But the converse is generally the case; and the reason is that a dense population permits greater division of labour, greater specialization, which enhances productivity. The relation between population growth and increase of subsistence is a virtuous circle:

> [E]verywhere we find the means of subsistence rising as it were spontaneously from the earth, to meet the wants of its newly-created inhabitants. Increase and multiply was a command not given in vain. . . . He, who has mitigated the storm to what the shorn lamb may bear; He, without whose permission a sparrow cannot fall to the ground, has not neglected the chief work of creation, has not left man without resource. (118)

Widespread and enduring distress and misery result only from bad human contrivances; only if (and here again the resemblance to Hall is striking) an excessive number of hands are diverted by wealth and power away from the cultivation of the soil will there be lasting hunger. This concludes the argument against Malthus and leads naturally to the next stage – property, and the effects of rent, taxes, and capital upon the distribution of wealth and the production of food. Property, according to Ravenstone, is the groundwork or substructure of society; on it are raised power, rank, and all the ornamental parts. True common property has never existed, and it would be most undesirable; if management of property were in public rather than private hands, this would mean big government, that is to say, tyranny – 'the most artificial form, . . . the worst which society can assume' (197). In dealing with private property, Ravenstone follows Locke, draws out the radical implications of his argument much as Ogilvie does, but then invokes other considerations that lead him to a tempered inegalitarianism. The original and natural right of property is based on labour; he who cultivates a field has a claim to the crop, and also to the land that his labour has improved. These rights are sacred, and unalienable even by the express act of their possessor (205). But they do not extend to the whole product of labour. What the cultivators have a sacred right to is as much of the produce of their industry as will afford them a comfortable subsistence. The surplus may rightly be allocated to a leisured class, an aristocracy. Not only *may* this be done; it *should* be done. Society is best if pyramid-shaped. Inequality is essential as an incentive; if all had the same, there would be nothing to struggle for, and natural indolence would prevail (225–6). This argument was tackled sixteen years earlier by Hall, who pertinently asked how the creaming off of part of the fruits of his labour could possibly act as an incentive, either to the despoiled labourer, or to the drone who robbed him. It also conflicts with an earlier passage in which Ravenstone maintained that we are so constituted as to find idleness irksome and employment satisfying (120). Inequality is also defended as a necessary condition of the development of the arts and sciences, and of all the grace, dignity, and ornament that an aristocracy brings to a society (206, 228). An aristocracy has the weight and standing to defend the rights of the whole community against tyranny (237). Finally, a leisured aristocracy is justified in terms of the services it performs, governing, administering, dispensing justice, providing leadership in all spheres. This is the original cause of the emergence of aristocracies. Ravenstone dismisses the suggestion, which we find in Hall, that inequality was originally established by force. Instead, he traces it back to the original patriarchal communities, where the father of the family or tribe was supported by his children in return for his wise government. This is the continuing moral basis of unequal classes; the rights of the rich are accorded to them in return for the performance of certain duties:

> The great body of the nation is content to say to the few: 'Let us but live in peace, protect us from the fury of our enemies, from the consequences of our own internal quarrels, maintain among us peace and justice and good order, relieve us from all the care and anxiety for our condition, and we will endow you with the surplus produce of our industry. We only desire what is necessary to a comfortable existence; all superfluities shall be for you.' This is in fact the original compact between the different classes of society. (238–9)

These defences of inequality are neither very convincing nor systematically set out. Evidently Ravenstone does not feel the need for buttressing arguments at this point, no doubt because he expects few to disagree with him. A wealthy class of nonproducers, therefore, is of benefit to a nation; but only if it is not too large, only if the diversion of resources to it does not trench upon the comforts of the labourers. Ravenstone fears that the normal course of historical evolution tends to upset the balance, so that the shape of society comes to resemble an inverted pyramid, with an excessive number of idle persons supported by an inadequate number of labourers: 'the temple of social happiness sinks under the weight of its ornamental parts' (203). The normal course of social evolution may be summed up as follows. Population growth makes possible the division of labour, which raises productivity; it now becomes feasible to support some who do not work, and at first these are the elders, the wise men, the fathers of the people who in return provide leadership and protection. But with the lapse of time, the original purpose of the institution of inequality is forgotten; aristocrats come to regard their wealth as an unconditional right for which they need make no return. As wealth confers power, they are able to extort a steadily increasing share of the product; as we shall see later, the growth of taxation and capital plays an important part in increasing the share going to the maintenance of idle persons. Consequently, the labourers become more oppressed. In those societies where this imbalance, this corruption, eats most deeply into the fabric, the masses live on the verge of starvation. Now the end is near: either the state will be conquered by a better balanced and therefore stronger enemy, or the people, provoked beyond endurance, will rise and overthrow the system, as happened in France in 1789.

Rent can be paid in two ways: the 'feudal' way, in goods and services; and the modern way, in money. Ravenstone believes that feudal exactions were lighter than modern ones. His account of rent presents a couple of difficulties. He is clear that it has grown; but nowhere does he explain the mechanism of its growth. A central weakness of his book is the lack of any coherent account of the principles according to which the wealth of a nation is distributed. This was a central theme of Ricardo's book, published four years earlier. Ravenstone never mentions Ricardo, and it is impossible to be certain that he had read the *Principles of Political Economy and*

Taxation. His acquaintance with the work is strongly suggested, however, by his espousal of the labour theory of value in its Ricardian form (268). But his argument has ruled out the possibility of a Ricardian explanation of the distribution of wealth. The key, in Malthus and Ricardo, is population pressure on scarce resources.[2] Ravenstone has rejected the Malthusian theory of population, and with it goes the Malthusian-Ricardian theory of rent. In so doing, he deprives himself of one theory of distribution and fails to provide another. His definition of rent, though useful for polemical purposes, does not help with the difficulty. 'Rent, then, may be defined as the idle man's share of the industrious man's earnings. Every increase of it is a conversion of industry to idleness' (225).

This quotation raises the issue of his system of social classification. He sees society as consisting of landlords, farmers, agricultural labourers; professional men; traders, master manufacturers, and manufacturing labourers; government employees and servants. These are then classified into the idle, unproductive labourers, and productive labourers. In physiocratic style,[3] he regards farmers and agricultural labourers as the only productive section of society; on the fruits of their labour all else depends. Servants, and those who are engaged in manufactures are unproductive labourers – sometimes he also groups them with the 'idle', the landlords and government employees. His thinking here appears to be that they are 'idle' in the sense of having to be supported by the primary producers, the workers of the land. But in another place, he looks more favourably upon manufacturing labourers and introduces another system of classification. Those who make wool into cloth, and cloth into coats, are not idle, nor without social value. He therefore divides society into the useful and the useless classes. Agricultural producers and manufacturing labourers are useful; all the rest, including traders, middlemen, are useless. Ravenstone's system of social classification bears a family resemblance to those of Hall and Colquhoun, and also to the physiocratic and Smithian distinction between productive and unproductive labour. Ravenstone's overlapping, poorly articulated and inadequately explained set of concepts is better suited to a moral critique of society than to a scientific analysis. The drift of his argument is towards the conclusion that a society is sadly out of balance when the idle,

the unproductive, and the useless are so numerous as to deprive
the productive and the useful of their comforts and even their
subsistence.

What share does rent have, when compared with taxes and capital, in the blame for this imbalance in society? Ravenstone appears
to speak with different voices on this issue:

> The greater part of the inequality which exists in England, is to be
> attributed to the growth of taxation and capital, those exhaustless
> sources of wealth to the rich, of misery to the poor. (219)
>
> High rents are indeed the greatest grievance which a nation can en-
> dure; they draw on in their train high profits and high taxes. (231)

This contradiction is perhaps resolved by what he says about the
way in which the profits of capitalists are determined. He argues
that the share of the produce of the artisan taken by his employer
follows and is determined by the share of the produce of the agricultural labourer taken by his landlord (326). Furthermore, other
occupations – those of tradesmen, professionals, shopkeepers – regulate their incomes by comparison with those taken by landlords
(330). This is an important and plausible modification of the distribution theory of classical economics; incomes are determined,
not only by the laws of the market, but also by custom. But it is a
chain of reasoning whose first link is unanchored; he has argued
that other incomes are determined by rents, but as already indicated
he has no theory of how rents are determined.

Taxes had grown massively during the eighteenth century and
first two decades of the nineteenth, as explained above.[4] Complaints
about the consequent emergence of a class of wealthy, parasitic
fundholders were common. Ravenstone argues that the overall result has been a massive increase in the number of idle persons supported by the producers. This need not have been so, if taxes had
fallen, as they once did, upon land; but 'wealth is power; and power
is little disposed to listen to the claims of unprotected industry'
(257). The landed interest, dominant in government, has brought
in consumption taxes, shifting the burden from themselves on to
the productive labourers. A tax on land would not have increased
the total burden of idle and unproductive persons; it would simply
have taken from one idle section (the landowners) to give to another
(those in the pay of the state). But when taxes fall on consumption,
they leave the existing idlers undisturbed and create a new class of

idlers alongside them. What about the argument that the labourers will have recouped in higher wages what they lost in increased consumption taxes? First, wages cannot rise unilaterally in a heavily taxed country, for this would price its goods out of the international market. Second, Ravenstone tries to show, from the statistics at his disposal concerning rents and taxes, that while the tax burden has mushroomed over the last hundred years, the income of the land-owning class has risen rather than fallen. Consequently, he infers, the standard of living of the labourers has declined. He is thus an early contributor to the debate about the standard of living in the first decades of the industrial revolution, a debate that still goes on. In the light of modern findings,[5] is Ravenstone right? First, it is plain that his assessment is based on a wholly insufficient body of data; and second, he makes no allowance for increased production and the fall in price of many manufactured goods. There can be no doubt, however, that rental incomes had shown a substantial long-term upward trend, and that the wages of southern agricultural labourers had fallen in real terms; no doubt either that the increase in the tax burden had fallen on the labourers rather than the wealthy. Ravenstone makes the further point that consumption taxes transfer wealth to traders from all other classes of society. The trader's profit is proportional to the selling price; if taxes put that up, they also enhance the profit. The redistributive effects of taxes have brought England to the state France was in before the revolution, a state unusual in the history of human society, in which the labourers receive barely enough for subsistence: 'But, in England, all society may be considered as at an end. The great bond of society, the advantage of all its members, no longer exists, the bands which held it together are burst asunder' (258).

Orthodox political economy had argued for the beneficence of capital, which set labour to work; the quantity of capital determined the quantity of productive activity, hence society's wealth. Ravenstone's purpose is to refute this, to show that capital has 'none but a metaphysical existence', an 'incorporeal nature', that it has no power of its own, that it is an illusion, a false god (293–4). 'As no man is so absurd as to suppose that the mere possession of the land can add anything to the amount of its produce, so neither can the amount of capital add anything to the results of unproductive labour' (311). (By unproductive labour, Ravenstone means labour

in manufacturing industry). But this is a poor argument; agricultural labour must have land to work on, manufacturing labour must
have raw materials, and machines and tools to enhance productivity. Now it might be argued that the landlord contributes nothing
to production; he did not make or find the land, which was a gift
of nature. But fixed and circulating capital is not a gift of nature.
Defenders of capital might argue that the capitalist has performed
a vital service in providing materials and tools, for which he deserves his reward. Ravenstone's claim that capital is parasitic and
illusory certainly needs a better defence than he has provided. He
further maintains that the level of economic activity is determined,
not by the amount of capital, but by the level of demand. A tailor

> will regulate his stock of cloth, not by his capability of buying, but
> by his probability of selling. . . . What is true of the tailor is equally
> true of every tradesman, from the great merchant down to the hum-
> blest shopkeeper. Their trade is not dependent on their capital, but
> the amount of their capital is dependent on the extent of their trade.
> (295–6)

A defender of capital might reply to this that, even if there is adequate demand, the tailor cannot set about producing to meet it
unless he has a stock of cloth or the money with which to buy cloth;
and to suggest that the bank will lend him the necessary money,
recognizing that his prospects are good, merely means that he will
rely on the capital of the bank. Ravenstone has argued that the level
of demand determines the level of activity and the amount of capital; but Say's law puts the reverse case. Capital, by setting labour
to work and causing the production of commodities, creates demand; for the commodities that are supplied can be exchanged for
other commodities, that is to say, can constitute a demand for them.
   Ravenstone distinguishes three kinds of capital and maintains
that all are useless and unnecessary. First, capital can take the form
of merchants' inventories, stocks of goods in transit and in ware-
houses; this form of capital does not cause or promote production.
He is highly critical of trade, which he thinks reduces the wealth
of a nation; the goods it brings in are of no more value than the
goods it sends out to pay for them, and resources are squandered
on transportation. For example, the high excise on beer drives labourers to tea; this has to be imported, and the overall result is
that the nation is poorer than if the home-produced drink had been

consumed. Ravenstone's ideal is an economy with very little trade, either external or internal; were it not for consumption taxes of various kinds, he maintains, trade would be virtually unknown; each landowner would supply his own wants, brewing his own beer, making his own cloth. The obvious reply to this is in terms of the advantages of specialization and division of labour, which Ravenstone himself invoked earlier, when it suited his purpose of defending population growth. Adam Smith argued that international trade permits an international division of labour, so that each country produces those things for which it is best endowed.

The second form of capital is buildings and machinery; these things have no value, according to Ravenstone, apart from the industry that employs them and that they facilitate. But in admitting that buildings and machinery 'facilitate' production, he has presented the capitalist with a weapon of defence. The third form taken by capital is credit, the sums lent by investors and bankers to borrowers. The typical borrower in Ravenstone's eyes is the extravagant landlord who wishes to anticipate his income. Evidently capital in this form does not promote production; it simply transfers wealth from one class of idle persons to another. Therefore he takes issue with Adam Smith on frugality and saving; they are not, as Smith maintained, beneficial to society, they do not create jobs and enlarge the wealth of the nation. The frugality of the man who saves merely enables the prodigality and improvidence of the man who borrows. Ravenstone's criticism of Smith on this issue only works if we go along with his conception of the typical borrower; he has ignored borrowing for purposes of productive investment – to improve land, to start a new business, or enlarge an existing one. It was this kind of saving and investment that earned Smith's commendation.

So what kind of a thing does Ravenstone think capital is? It is, essentially, the power that an idle man has to appropriate part of the wealth of another. He conceives of this power in three different ways. One is the power of the usurer, the frugal man, over the prodigal who needs a loan. Second, he thinks of it as a monopoly. Capitalists control manufacturing and trading operations, and labourers cannot gain access to employment except on terms dictated by capitalists (200).

> To such an extent has capital increased in this country, such are the
> encroachments it has made on industry that the humblest occupa-

tions are become matters of property; the right of supplying a particular neighbourhood with milk, or of blacking shoes in a particular district is only to be acquired by purchase. . . . Where every employment is become a property, it is only by capital a man can acquire a command over the industry of others. Though it adds nothing to the wealth of a nation, it contributes much to the aggrandizement of individuals. It enables them to purchase, indirectly, the labour of so many slaves. It makes rich tradesmen and poor artisans. (335–6)

This is a conception of capital by analogy with landownership; just as the landlord monopolizes the land, so the capitalist monopolizes the factors of production, to use a later term. But the analogy is not entirely convincing. It is obvious how land can be monopolized by a few, not obvious how all nonagricultural productive operations can be so monopolized. How does such a monopoly work, and how did it originate? Ravenstone provides no answers.

His third conception of capitalist power is as the advantage enjoyed by a middleman. In this conception, a capitalist is essentially a trader. He comes between producer and producer, and between producer and consumer; their exchanges are conducted through him, and he creams off a percentage. His capital enables him to transfer wealth to himself from producer, or consumer, or both, wealth that they would have retained if they had exchanged directly with one another. There is a valuable insight here; Ravenstone has added something of importance to the conception of capitalist power, something not found in Hall's analysis of wealth as power. But for this middleman's power to be real and effective, capital must have more than an imaginary or metaphysical existence. Producers and consumers will only exchange via a middleman if they need him, or have been unable to find a profitable way of doing without him. Adam Smith provided a defence of such middlemen. Their capital enables them to buy in bulk, which pleases producers, and to sell in small parcels, which pleases consumers.

The gravest weakness of Ravenstone's critique of capital, then, is that it is not an effective critique of productive capital. He devotes less than a page to the capital that provides buildings and machinery. He ignores the 'circulating capital' that is employed in industry to provide raw materials, and subsistence for labourers while they complete the manufacture of a 'vendible commodity'. Ravenstone has not answered the claims of capital because he has failed to consider some of its strongest claims. The weight of his fire is directed against the capital of the merchant, the shopkeeper, and the usurer. Middlemen are always easy targets.

The violence of Ravenstone's hostility to trade and capital is remarkable. It would be for the good of society if it could rid itself of capitalists (357).

> Capitalists are a species of vermin not easily shaken off . . . Like that other little hopping animal, who too draws all his sustenance from the blood of the people, and who too, in his visions of political oeconomy, probably attributes the life and spirits of his subject to the quicker circulation caused by his continual phlebotomy; they are only to be got rid of by burning the blanket in which they have burrowed. (356)

He also likens the capitalist to a caterpillar on a plant, and to the old man who fastened himself around the neck of Sinbad the sailor. He comments upon the instability of trading society and admits with distaste that England has become a nation of shopkeepers. He would prefer a situation where

> There will be no fortunes suddenly made by trade; none of those transfers of property from old families to new adventurers, which are supposed to add so much wealth to the nation; none of that perpetual turmoil, that constant anxiety in men's minds to change their condition, which is mistaken for industry. As every man's condition will be more accurately marked out, as the opportunities of placing himself in a different class of society will be few, he will rest more contentedly in his own. As there will be fewer great prizes in the lottery of life, the blanks will be less numerous. (324)

This passage is all the more remarkable because earlier in the book Ravenstone rejected equality on the grounds that it would remove the incentive to effort and struggle, the desire to better oneself and therefore to work hard. It is tempting to resolve this contradiction by regarding Ravenstone's argument as ideological; a defence of the landed class that seeks to suppress the claims both of labour, and of aspiring trade.

My summary of Ravenstone's argument is now almost complete. The detail of his attack on paper money is not relevant to our concerns; suffice it to note that he distinguishes between the real, useful trade of the country – that which is concerned with the disposal of producers' surpluses and meeting the needs of consumers – and the harmful, artificial trade of speculators, which is to do with buying cheap and selling dear, withholding and playing the markets. The useful trade could be carried on, he calculates, with less specie than England already has. Paper money is only required for the trade of speculation. Turning to the corn laws, Ravenstone rejects them. When harvests are normal, and provided that labour has not been excessively diverted from the land by rent, taxes, and capital, they can make no difference to the incomes of landlords, for each country can feed its population more cheaply with the produce of its own agriculture than with imported foodstuffs. Corn laws push up landlords' incomes only in times of dearth; and

> This is a consequence of corn bills, too dreadful to contemplate. I will not believe there is a heart capable of coolly desiring this contingency; that there is an Englishman who would knowingly seek to improve his income by the murder of his fellow-creatures. (414)

Any restriction on trade in corn defies the kind contrivances of providence; God so arranges things that when the harvest falls short in one country, it is compensated by an abundant harvest in another .(418).

Finally, Ravenstone discusses the political consequences of different distributions of property. The political constitution of a state is determined by the manner in which wealth is distributed. A state in which nothing is taken from labour in rent or taxes will be a democracy; such a state will not be a good one, for liberty will be insecure (Ravenstone does not explain why). A state in which labour pays rent, but no taxes, will be an aristocracy. Such a state will be highly oppressive. An absolute monarchy – that is, a state in which labour pays taxes, but no rent – will be less harsh for the mass of people. But the best state will be a mixed constitution, a due balance between democracy, aristocracy and monarchy; a state in which labour pays both rent and taxes, but neither to excess. This balance is precarious; it was disrupted during the reign of Henry VIII by the influx of wealth from the New World, which suddenly created a new set of rich men, who used their riches to divert labour from productive to unproductive employments. This occurred all over Europe, and as a result, all Europe experienced social turmoil. The balance was reinstated in England by the reign of Elizabeth; but since then it has been upset once more. The wealthy have monopolized political power, controlling the House of Commons, a house originally intended to represent the interests of labour. They have shifted the tax burden from themselves to the labourers: having achieved this, there has been nothing to discourage them from increasing public spending and raising taxes. The result has been the growth of poverty and crime, England is now on the verge of revolution, and the labourers can only be held down by military force and harsh punishments.

> England has re-assumed the face it wore in the time of the Norman conquerors; on every side fortresses arise, equally for the subjection and punishment of a people, who inheriting something of the stubborn spirit of their Saxon ancestors, cannot be brought to feel grateful for these, the only proofs of their rulers' kindness. (455)

The remedy is to bring down taxes, and to shift them entirely from consumption to property. And in order to secure this, the House of Commons must be reformed; the principle of 'no taxation without representation' implies the desirability of universal suffrage.

An adequate assessment of the factors that made this text possible and determined its argument would discuss Ravenstone's social position. We have already noted ways in which the argument appears to reflect the interests of the landed gentry – the vitriolic hostility to trade, the defence of inequality. If Ravenstone *is* a spokesman for this group, he is also a critic of it; he perceives and deplores an abdication of responsibility on the part of the governors and recalls them to their duty. More than this, he does not think the landed interest can be trusted unless checked; the rights of the people will only be respected if they can defend themselves through a universal suffrage. It would be good to know more about 'Ravenstone's' background; unfortunately our information about Richard Puller is at present scanty. His father's last home was Painswick Court, Gloucestershire – a rural seat. Yet his father was also a director of the South Sea Company, and his grandfather a director of the Bank of England; evidently Puller was deeply rooted in the trade he so much despised.

The book is partly occasioned by the acute distress of postwar England. The way in which Ravenstone responds to that distress, analyses it, and proposes remedies, is formed by classical economy. Political economy, as much as the distress of the time, is the occasion of the work, which sets out to refute Malthusian population theory and the claims of capital. However much it may dissent from the arguments of the economists, the book depends for its very being upon their mode of approaching and discussing society. It is a contribution to a debate, which could not have been made if Smith and Malthus had not spoken first. In more ways than one it is a deeply reactionary book. It reacts against commercial society, advancing in prosperity by the division of labour, which Smith describes and defends. It reacts against the whole project and scientific aspiration of classical economy, on whose concepts and methods it is nevertheless parasitic. In his introduction, Ravenstone advances an epistemological scepticism reminiscent of Burke. He expresses grave doubts about the possibility of a science of economics; if its conclusions are so repugnant to our feelings and so contrary to our moral and religious doctrines, would it not be wise to follow the latter? His criticisms, if correct, entirely subvert Ricardian distribution theory; yet Ravenstone destroys without rebuilding. He ranges over the whole field, like Smith or Ricardo, but fails to provide an alternative theory. In fact, his criticisms are patchy; his critique of capital, though vigorous, is poorly aimed, and he is most effective against Malthusian population theory.

In comparing Ravenstone and Adam Smith, it is useful to ask to what extent each is a dispassionate analyst of economic structures and processes. At first sight, it seems that Ravenstone imports a greater stock of moral and religious considerations into the analysis; certainly they are more in evidence, more on the surface than in the *Wealth of Nations*. But a little reflection modifies this judgment without invalidating it. Ravenstone employs a system of social classification in which moral and economic aspects are inextricably intertwined: productive and unproductive labourers, the idle class, useful and useless classes. But Smith also makes a (rather different) distinction between productive and unproductive labour. Secondly, an assumption of a natural order designed by a benevolent providence, an order whose tendency to produce the general good is often frustrated by class interest, is explicitly present in Ravenstone's thought. Modern scholarship has cast doubt on the presence of such an assumption in the *Wealth of Nations*; but it could be and often was found in Smith's text by selective reading. This metaphysical assumption, or its afterecho, is what sustains a belief in a natural harmony of interests, which we have found also in Ogilvie, Godwin, Hall, and Owen. It is possible for all these thinkers to come to the comfortable conclusion that self-interested agents need not be for ever in conflict – when they truly understand their own good, they will recognize that it accords with the good of the whole – because they assume, openly or tacitly, that providence or 'nature', or 'reason', has built harmony into the system of things. A religious frame of mind does not inevitably lead to such pleasant prospects. It is equally possible to propose an angry God, visiting the sins of the fathers upon the children. Ravenstone's God is one whose yoke is easy and his burden light. There is one further point of interest in the religious dimension of Ravenstone's thought. All have an equal right to life and happiness. Malthus's arguments, which would persuade us to leave the poor to starve, are utterly wicked because

> Whatever difference there may be in the outward appearance of men, or in their habits; however variously they may be endowed with the gifts of fortune, or the refinements of mental improvement, they are still brethren, the children of one common parent, the creatures of God, equally the objects of his favour and protection; he cares not less for the poor; their happiness is not less dear to him than the rich; they are equally the objects of his paternal solicitude. (22)

In my discussion of the factors that conditioned this text, I have highlighted the debate with the economists and the substructure of religious conceptions. I have still to look at the political ideas and the implicit and explicit historical theories. The book reflects a number of standard political ideas of the age: there is a belief in an ancient constitution that once was more democratic and a suggestion that the rich are descended from the Normans, the labouring classes from the Saxons. The argument of the text is more deeply affected, however, by a perception of the current political order as unbalanced, corrupt, and consequently extravagant and oppressive. Ravenstone says quite explicitly that big government is bad government, and that the state should have purely negative functions – protecting citizens against external and internal aggression. The purpose of the representative system is to check the executive, to ensure that no section of the community is oppressed. Ravenstone thinks that the condition of the labouring class is desperate; but the political beliefs to which he subscribes permit him to recommend only limited measures to ameliorate the lot of the people – taxation reform, brought about by a reform of Parliament. After the denunciation of capitalists as a species of vermin and the accusation that landlords have enforced their rights while neglecting their duties and as good as murdered the starving poor, this is a timid outcome. Turning to time conceptions, the argument is scarcely affected by ideas of progress; Ravenstone even has doubts about progress in knowledge and science. He is no primitivist, no admirer of the noble savage, however. There are echoes of the materialist conception of the Scottish historical school. Division of labour and the emergence of property were advances, for they permitted increased productivity, leisure, and the development of the arts, sciences, and comforts of life. The growth of manufactures, up to a certain point, was beneficial for similar reasons. But this perception of economic, social, and cultural advance in the past does not sustain a theory of continuing progress. Ravenstone has a greater admiration for feudalism than any of the thinkers so far considered. Not only is the theory of historical change a materialist one; political superstructures are also explained as having an economic basis. The way in which property is held and wealth distributed determines the distribution of power. So, in the England of his day, landlords and traders have sucked a disproportionate share of wealth to themselves, and consequently they monopolize political power. But the manner in which he proposes to set things right is incoherent with this; indeed, it turns materialistic conceptions upside down. The labouring classes have too small a share of wealth; they are to obtain redress by first obtaining a greater share of political power through universal suffrage. The pattern of social and political change perceived by Ravenstone bears a strong resemblance to neo-Machiavellian and neo-Harringtonian political theory. The good society, the good constitution, is one that is balanced. But the evil of imbalance is not seen to be tyranny or anarchy. Like Hall, Ravenstone supposes that an unbalanced society is one in which the labourers receive too little of the fruits of their labour. Balance is precarious, constantly threatened by corruption. Once the balance has been upset, decline sets in and accumulates. Eventually, the state stands on the verge of ruin, as France did in 1789 and as England does in 1821. There is no gradual and easy way back to equilibrium; France had to pass through the fire and blood of revolution, and England may have to do the same, unless the rulers have a change of heart and remodel the constitution. Corruption is normal: 'Such is the natural and inevitable course of events. The imperfection of all human institutions renders them subject to decay. Every society, from its first formation, bears in its bosom the seeds of its destruction' (203).

In conclusion and assessment, Ravenstone's book is important and impressive in several ways. It is an interesting application of the neo-Machiavellian paradigm; it powerfully argues the 'abdication on the part of the governors' case and recalls traditional society to its duties. Its criticism of Malthusianism is devastating. Finally, it marks another step forward in the developing critique of capital. Ravenstone takes up where Hall left off, echoing so many of Hall's ideas that the influence of the earlier writer seems likely. Hall explored the exploitation of the poor by the power of wealth. But he did not much examine the differences between landed and capitalist modes of exploitation. In his view, monopoly of land was the basis of exploitation, and the capitalist merely shared in the landlord's power. Ravenstone gives much more attention specifically to capital. Like Hall, he sometimes explains capitalist power unsatisfactorily by analogy with rentier power; but he also investigates the idea that the capitalist is a kind of middleman, drawing an advantage from a favourable situation within the processes of production and exchange. He is convinced that there is something fundamentally wrong with the contention of classical economy, that capitalists are the essential progenitors of wealth and growth. There is something *unreal* about capital; it is not as fundamental, or necessary, or worthy, as labour. These are Ravenstone's insights; but they are poorly argued, because he focusses upon the capital of trade and usury, virtually ignoring productive capital. Hall's theory was clear, but inadequate because of excessive simplicity. Ravenstone has a greater awareness of the complexities, but he has not seen his way through them. He is full of good ideas, but has not worked them up into a coherent theory. This is further exemplified by what he says about the distribution of wealth. He destroys without rebuilding. He rejects the doctrine of different qualities of land, and the theory of rent built upon it; he denies that population growth and the consequent increase in the supply of labour has any essential tendency to bring down wages or push up food prices; he insists that the supply of capital has no effect on the level of productive activity. Thus he removes all the supports of Smithian and Ricardian distribution theory, without providing any plausible alternative.

An Inquiry into the Principles of the Distribution of Wealth Most Conducive to Human Happiness; Applied to the Newly Proposed System of Voluntary Equality of Wealth, William Thompson, 1824

Faced with the problems of poverty and inequality, theorists, Thompson insists, divide into two schools: the intellectual and the mechanical. Intellectual speculators such as Godwin, concerned with ideals, favour equality, but they overstress the powers of mere mind; in phrases reminiscent of Marx's later critique of the young Hegelians in the *German Ideology*, 'the intellectual aristocrat . . . [forgets] . . . that without [labour's] kindly and ever-recurring aid in the supply of food, clothing and shelter, the high intellectual energies, of which he boasts, could scarcely for one hundred hours preserve themselves' (v).[1] Mechanical speculators such as Malthus, concerned with material realities, argue that inequality is inevitable and beneficial to production, but they ignore moral considerations. 'Here is the important *problem* of moral science to be solved, "*how to reconcile equality with security*; how to reconcile *just distribution with continued production*"' (xiv). This is the issue addressed in Thompson's weighty volume. The essentials of his solution are furnished in the first chapter, a chapter that would by itself constitute a modest book in late twentieth-century terms. The job is done by the establishment of three principles: first, that labour is the sole parent of wealth; second, that an equal distribution is most conducive to happiness; and third, that production is maximized if each labourer receives the full fruits of his labour, an arrangement that tends to equality.

That labour is the sole parent of wealth is primarily established by defining wealth initially as 'that portion of the physical materials or means of enjoyment which is afforded by the labor and knowledge of man turning to use the animate or inanimate materials or productions of nature' (6) – that is to say, by circular reasoning.

The exchange value of an article is determined by the average quantity of ordinary labour required to make such articles. Thompson has an Adam Smithian answer to the criticism that value is also determined by scarcity; a well of water in a parched sandy country is a source of wealth, having a high value determined by the amount of labour that would otherwise be necessary to bring water from the nearest supply (9).

Equality of distribution is defended on utilitarian grounds; it will promote the greatest happiness. This claim is sustained by two arguments. First, that all normal humans are equally capable of happiness. Different animals have different capacities for happiness: a horse has more sources of enjoyment than an oyster, and a man infinitely more than a horse. But humans are naturally equal in this respect: physiological similarities greatly outweigh differences. If some were more capable of happiness than others, utility would require us to direct the means of happiness their way; but Thompson has a knock-down argument against this − who is to judge?

> Are we to institute a court, and to impanel a jury, in the case of every individual; or, if this be too troublesome, are we to use a judge without jury, and label every man's neck, to say nothing of the women, with tickets of susceptibility of one to one hundred . . . ?
> (23)

Second, he argues that as additional portions of wealth are given to individuals, a law of diminishing returns of happiness applies. The first portion is of infinite value to happiness, as it enables the individual to live; the second affords real comforts; but the third brings only imaginary comforts, meretricious trinkets, and status goods (72). If 1,000 portions of wealth were taken from 1,000 industrious producers and given to one rich despoiler, the happiness he would gain would be proportioned to the happiness they would lose as 1:1,999,000 (75).

Utility, therefore, speaks in favour of equality.[2] Bentham had said as much, but he went on to argue that equality, however desirable at first sight, would be contrary to utility in the long run. For, where the distribution of wealth was concerned, security was vital. If individuals were not secure in their possessions − if there were any kind of interference to promote equality − they would lack the incentive to produce. Bentham therefore concluded that only the most cautious redistributive measures were permissible; for ex-

ample, primogeniture might be abolished and equal sharing between children enforced. Thompson entirely concurs that security
must be sacrosanct; but he insists that the existing distribution of
wealth is a system of spurious security. The rich – government
employees, landlords, large farmers, capitalists – seize a portion of
the wealth labour has produced, thereby violating security. Thompson does not use Proudhon's famous words, but the thought is the
same: 'Qu'est-ce que la propriété? . . . C'est le vol.' The rich have
pulled off a confidence trick: they have mobilized the valid principle
of security in defence of the system of insecurity that benefits them.
And all the dire consequences, predicted by Bentham if existing
property were to be attacked, are already taking place. Labour,
losing its fruits, has no incentive to work well, and productivity is
thereby depressed. In language reminiscent of Marx's 1844 man-
uscripts, Thompson writes, 'To take from them what their arm
guided by their mind has produced, is like taking from them a part
of themselves' (94). If each labourer enjoyed the full fruits of his
labour, production would be greatly enhanced, and the distribution
of wealth, though not equal, would approach much nearer to equality than at present. Hence both morality and economics, both intellectual and mechanical speculation, speak in favour of equality.
But is not the capitalist, who provides raw materials, tools, machinery, buildings, and wages so that labourers can live until the
job is completed, entitled to some remuneration? Thompson, as
Marx was to do later, insists that these factors of production generate no value: 'the additional value proceeds from labor alone'
(166). But he then goes on to concede that these factors contribute
to the productivity of labour (167). The original thesis, that labour
is the sole parent of wealth, is salvaged by the thought that materials, machines, and so on are themselves products of labour: still,
even if they are but labour under another guise, may not the capitalist who furnishes them have some claim to a reward? Thompson
admits this; but the reward should be no more than sufficient to
replace the capital as it is used, plus wages to the capitalist to support him 'in equal comfort with the more actively employed productive laborers' (167). The claims of capital, then, do not entail
any departure from rough-and-ready equality. All of this is thoroughly unsatisfactory. Thompson provides no reasons for fixing
the capitalist's reward at this level: conversely, if, as suggested else-

where, capital was originally extorted by force or fraud from productive labourers, then does capital deserve any reward at all?

If first principles favour equality, what about the remoter consequences of equal and unequal distributions? Thompson argues that the 'collateral advantages' also line up for equality. He discusses them under three headings: moral, political, and economic. Inequality corrupts both rich and poor. His sketch of the life-style of the rich is reminiscent of Turgenev or Chekhov; all their wants being catered for, they lack incentives to the deployment of physical and mental energies; theirs is a life of inaction, listlessness, wearisomeness – in a word, *ennui* – interrupted by bouts of extravagance and sensuality, strong stimulants to awaken the feeling of existence. So far removed are they from the poor[3] that they lack all sympathy for the latter; as a result, their conduct towards their inferiors is characterized by selfishness. This is exhibited by the very different codes respecting 'debts of honour' (gambling debts) and 'debts of honesty' (tradesman's debts). The status system of an unequal society causes the rich to despise work, especially manual work, and this corrupts the whole tone of the nation. The poor are not much better; they are driven by want to dishonesty, the struggle for existence makes it impossible for them to live respectable, orderly lives. Like James Mill, Thompson finds most virtue in the middling ranks. Malthus and even Ravenstone defended inequality as necessary to the production of artistic excellence and magnificence; Thompson gives an emphatic utilitarian no to such arguments: 'If such works were not found by the community to contribute to its happiness, they ought not to be produced or maintained' (152).

Where politics is concerned, a society divided into rich and poor has no common interest; hence the rich, who possess power, pass laws on their own behalf, oppressive to their inferiors. Class warfare results:

> The law punishes the productive laborer who will not work for the regulated hire: the combination law punishes him who dares to work under the wages regulated by the mechanics themselves. Thus is a community converted into a theatre of war. (258)

Equality, by contrast, would mean democratic, representative government; for equality and democracy go hand in hand. 'Without equal security, representative government cannot continue: without representative government, security cannot continue' (267). This is because, on the one hand, the distribution of political power follows the distribution of wealth; and, on the other, equality of wealth will never be established until political power has been wrested from the rich. There is a vicious circle here that Thompson appears not to have noticed. If there can be no equality of wealth without equality of power, and if inequality of wealth necessarily begets inequality of power, there would appear to be no way out. In Thompson's view, equality of political power is of the utmost importance, for it would lead to the death of old corruption, the elimination of unnecessary and oppressive taxation. He is convinced that the extortions of government are worse than the extortions of capitalists: 'Where private plunder abstracts from industry its tens, . . . public plunder abstracts from the same industry its thousands' (224–5). Equality of wealth would mean the virtual elimination of war; for if all were productively employed, they would have no time for fighting, which is undertaken to relieve the boredom of the rich. Finally, equality would lead to the extinction of crime.

Is inequality justifiable on the grounds that a class of rich men is necessary if there is to be accumulation and investment in the capital that sets labour to work and makes it more productive? Thompson's starting point is evidently Adam Smith's argument that the amount of employment depends upon the size of the capital stocks – the materials, machinery, and funds for the payment of the wages to productive labourers – that have been accumulated. Smith also drew a distinction between productive and unproductive spending, productive and unproductive labour.[4] Thompson does not challenge Smith's judgment that the most harmful unproductive expenditure is that of government. But whereas Smith maintained that private individuals would not on the whole squander capital in unproductive spending, Thompson insists that the wealthy spend nine-tenths of their revenues unproductively, on needless luxuries and status goods. But under a system of equality, each worker would be his own capitalist; he would own his tools, raw materials, and subsistence. Holdings of capital would be smaller, but much more numerous, than under a system of inequality; and, as a consequence, the total stock of capital would be much greater. On the whole, manufacturing labourers would not need large capitals, for the period of turnaround in manufacturing is usually rapid; hence the labourer would not need a large sum to pay for his subsistence until the job was completed. And on those occasions when small capitals would not suffice – jobs taking a long time to complete or requiring very large outlays in machinery, buildings, and so on – the need for large *capitals* would not entail a need for large *capitalists*: the small capitals of the labourers, added together through the institution of a joint-stock company, would produce the required large total (245). This is a crucial issue in Thompson's case for equality: how good is his argument? If it can be judged no worse than Smith's, it has to be said that the arguments of both thinkers have weaknesses in common. The basic problem is that both rely upon general reasoning to establish conclusions that have an inadequate basis of evidence. Smith has no statistics to demonstrate that on the average capitalists maintain and increase their capitals: Thompson has no figures to show that the rich spend nine-tenths of their income unproductively. Thompson's claim that large capitals are rarely needed rests upon the assumption that the most important form of capital is that which pays the subsistence of labourers while they complete the task (circulating capital in Smith's terminology) rather than that which buys buildings, machinery, and so on. This assumption, also made by Smith, made better sense for the early industrial revolution in Britain than for the later. Finally, how can Thompson be sure that under a system of equality the sum total of small capitals will be larger than the total of large capitals under inequality? What if the labourer-capitalists develop a propensity to spend rather than accumulate? Given that in an egalitarian society there will be no incentive to get rich for the sake of status, we might fear that spontaneous accumulation would prove inadequate for rapid economic growth.

Thompson's argument that the rich are not needed as capitalists is leaky; his argument that they are not needed as big spenders is rather better. Malthus[5] had taken issue with Smith on productive and unproductive expenditure, arguing that a class of rich, unproductive spenders was necessary to mop up supply.[6] Thompson's simple answer is that the consuming could be done just as well if the wealth of a rich despoiler was shared among the industrious labourers he had despoiled; and he offers, with typically heavy-handed wit, a reductio ad absurdum of the Malthusian argument:

> Suppose that an intellectual ape could speak, and offered his services to become infinitely more patriotic and useful in the employment of

the poor, by consuming ten times the quantity of expensive fruits and wines in a day, that the candidate for excessive wealth could consume; should we not be bound in fair reasoning to give the preference to the ape, as the greatest patriot and most enlightened consumer of the two, as keeping a greater number of the industrious busy in supplying him? (199)

This then is Thompson's argument for equality – or 'equal security', as he prefers to call it. He offers two quite different recipes for societies that will realize this principle: the competitive, individualistic model and the cooperative one.

An individualistic system with equal security would be achieved when each individual received the full fruits of his labour; and the necessary conditions for this state of affairs are free and voluntary labour and exchanges. What are the factors that inhibit free labour and exchanges, and thereby promote inequality? The reader is immediately struck by the great emphasis that Thompson places upon the unrepresentative state and its meddling laws. In the first place, security – the right of the labourer to the full fruits of his labour – is greatly trenched upon by public plunder, that is to say, by all the taxes levied by the state. To this item may be added tithes. Then there are laws that prevent equal access to unappropriated natural resources: game laws, navigation and fishing laws, laws dealing with water and mineral resources. The freedom of labour is curtailed by apprenticeship and guild regulations, monopolies, restrictions on the mobility of labour, and laws that enforce public holidays. Free exchanges are prevented by wage regulations and combination laws, whose effect is to prevent labourers bargaining on equal terms with their employers. Finally, existing inequalities are entrenched by the laws of inheritance. Condemnation of this catalogue of measures of state interference would occasion no surprise in the pages of Adam Smith or Bentham. What *is* surprising is that Thompson believes the removal of these laws would go a long way towards producing equality. The surprise is the greater, because he is so emphatic about the evils of *capitalist* exploitation. In the process of production, all added value is produced by labour (166), but the capitalist, because of his possession of productive resources (a possession deriving from luck more often than from intelligence and virtue) (503) takes on the average at least one-half of the added value as profit (165). Thompson uses the soon-to-be-famous phrase 'surplus value' to refer to this slice taken from the fruits of labour. In the light of this, is it reasonable to suppose that the abolition of his catalogue of restrictive laws will do much for equality? He makes the objection very effectively himself:

> The rule of free and voluntary exchanges would appear, on a first view, to operate tremendously against the mere unprovided productive laborer, with no other possession than his capability of producing: for all the physical materials on which, or by means of which, his productive powers can be made available, being in the hands of others with interests opposed to his, and their consent being a necessary preliminary to any exertion on his part, is he not, and must he not always remain, at the mercy of these capitalists for whatever portion of the fruits of his own labor they may think proper to leave at his disposal in compensation for his toils? (164–5)

Exactly so, we are tempted to reply; and it is not easy to be convinced by his remedy, 'beautiful for its simplicity' (180) – the removal of legal restraints on labour as indicated, plus the widest diffusion of useful knowledge. His vision is of a free, rational, and informed work force, bargaining with the capitalists on equal terms and getting a fair deal (166).

This then is the first of Thompson's recipes for society; the system of freedom and security with private production and private property. But though he thinks its tendency will be towards equality, he perceives serious disadvantages in the system of free competition. First, because each producer is out for self, selfishness is fostered as a leading motive. The evils of selfishness and competition are delightfully illustrated with reference to doctors: 'In medicine, it is the interest of the physician to cure diseases, but to cure them as slowly and with as much profit as the competition of other medical men will permit' (371). Secondly, for the sake of competitive advantage, producers conceal new knowledge and inventions, and this trammels technological advance. Thirdly, an unplanned competitive system will inevitably lead to mistakes in the employment of labour and capital. Fourthly, an individualistic system makes no adequate and wholly reliable provision for sickness and old age. Fifthly, to use modern terms, a system of free competition strengthens the nuclear family, living in self-sufficiency in its own dwelling. This contributes to the servitude of women: they become dependent upon their husbands, they are tied to the drudgery of cleaning and cooking. It also harms the education of the rising generation; being prisoners, as it were, of the home, they have the prejudices of their parents thrust down their throats, and free inquiry is thereby discouraged (369–76).

Thompson therefore turns to his second and preferred solution to the problem of how to reconcile equality of distribution with perfect security. This is the Owenite system of cooperative communities. In them, where property is owned jointly ('joint-stock companies of equals' [488]), security is social rather than individual. Instead of the individual receiving the full fruits of his or her individual labour, the community enjoys the full fruits of its joint labour. Thompson's plans for cooperative communities are avowedly inspired by Owen; but some aspects are explained more fully in his tome than in Owen's short report. For example, the unspecialized nature of the communities, engaging in both agriculture and manufacturing, is more adequately defended: many occupations, especially agriculture, make fluctuating demands for labour, and therefore the ability to move labour from one employment to another will maximize production. Like Smith before and Marx after him, Thompson recognizes the degrading effects of overspecialization (401–2). In addition, there are significant differences between Owen and Thompson. The most important is Thompson's enthusiasm for democracy and liberty, expressed in language evidently derived from Godwin. In his communities there will be no minute and interfering regulations concerning dress and mealtimes (495). Chapter 4 entitled 'Of the acquisition and diffusion of knowledge' paints a very Godwinian scenario of the empire of reason taking the place of the empire of force. Conflicts of opinion can never entirely be eliminated, as long as each individual is allowed to think freely (495); but free discussion in a context from which sinister and corrupt interests have been removed will bring the closest possible approximation to harmony, so that very little government will be required (497). So much faith does he have in the rationality of the inhabitants of his communities, that he predicts universal voluntary abstention from alcohol and tobacco (512). This insistence that communities be perfect democracies eventually caused a rift with the more authoritarian Owen and within the cooperative movement.

Like Owen, he believes cooperative communities will not require penal systems, for it is possible to produce improved characters. Unlike Owen he places little reliance upon education to do this; it is rather the general environment that makes people good or evil. Ninety-nine out of a hundred crimes proceed from the pursuit of individual gain (415): common ownership will eliminate these at a stroke. People are corrupted by bad institutions and will be wonderfully improved by good ones. Democracy will get the business of government done efficiently; it will also elevate the moral characters of the participants. These arguments look back to Godwin and also anticipate one of the major themes of J. S. Mill's *Representative Government.* Following Bentham, Thompson distinguishes natural and artificial sanctions controlling behaviour. Bentham thought that artificial sanctions – punishments – were essential. Thompson believes that in a properly constructed environment, natural sanctions will be sufficient. If you lean too far over, a natural punishment ensues – you fall down. In the same way, if you tell lies, others mistrust you. These natural consequences would control behaviour efficiently and with the minimum of pain; for the natural course of things is for happiness to follow conduct that benefits others, unhappiness to follow harmful conduct. But moralists, legislators, and political economists have attempted to establish and defend an *unnatural* order in the interests of a minority. Hence artificial sanctions are required (448–50). All these arguments play down the need for one human being to control another. But Thompson does not entirely eliminate mechanisms of social control. He provides for the arbitration of disputes (390). Again following Godwin, he proposes to employ the discipline of public opinion, of 'moral inspection and control'. This discipline would be especially powerful in small cooperative communities: since all work for the common prosperity and draw from the common stock, any backsliding will meet with the stern disapproval of those who are pulling their weight.

> Even now, who can bear the averted eye and the altered manner of a single friend? But under the arrangements proposed, where every co-operator is a friend, and an always busy friend, always employed for the benefit of the idle as well as of the rest of the co-operators; who could live exposed to the alienated feelings of such a community of friends, to whose intelligent and interested glance, and to whose mutual inspection and control he must be every day exposed? (395)

Incentives to hard work are required; but it is a crude mistake to think of money as the only possible incentive. Good workers everywhere prove that the esteem of one's fellows is equally potent (470,

514, 517). Finally, absolute voluntarily and viciously idle persons would not be admitted or tolerated in the communities (47). Thompson appears to have torpedoed his own argument. We begin with glad optimism; coercion and control are unnecessary in a natural order where individuals are formed by the environment for goodness. Then arbitration is admitted; next the discipline of public opinion; finally the sanction of expulsion. Jackdaw-like, Thompson has picked bits from Bentham, Godwin, and Owen, but has not welded them into a convincing account of how communities can combine liberty and harmony.

He is altogether more convincing when countering the population trap. Equality and common ownership will not lead ineluctably to overpopulation and starvation, as Malthus predicted: in the first place (and he refers to Poland, Ireland, Russia, Naples, Norway, Switzerland, France, and the United States to back up his point), experience proves that it is poverty rather than prosperity that causes rapid growth of numbers. The fact that the rich manage to exercise prudence proves that the rate of increase is determined by social circumstances rather than by any inexorable natural necessity. But second, the arrangements of the cooperative communities will be such as to control population levels. A community will have a given number of private apartments: a young couple seeking to marry and wishing to remain where they have been born and brought up will have to wait until an apartment falls vacant on the death of its occupants. Thirdly, he decorously hints at the use of artificial contraception (547). In logic this ought to be his chief answer; for, with utilitarian consistency, he praises the pleasures of sex (555) and advocates easier divorce (557). How much pleasure is currently lost to the world when marriage is so often a commercial contract and when unions are determined, not by affection, but by considerations of social rank! The communities will immensely improve the lot of women. Being equal cooperating members, with a share in the joint stock, they will not suffer a degrading dependency upon their husbands. The day nursery and the communal kitchen will liberate them from domestic drudgery, and all occupations will be open to them.

How will a community relate to the wider society? Is it to be a secluded enclave, an expression of a strategy of 'dropping out' from the old immoral world? Thompson appears to think that, by going it alone, communities could escape economic and social oppression, the exactions of capitalists and landlords; but they would be unable to evade political oppression, the public plunder of taxation, which is the worst oppression of all. Setting up communities is therefore not an alternative to public participation, to engaging in agitation for political reform. Supposing success in the struggle against old corruption, supposing that communities overspread the nation and even the world, how will their activities be coordinated? This is a question of some moment in the assessment of the schemes of Owen and his followers. If the communities do not trade with one another, then the benefits of the division of labour and specialization will be lost; but if they do, then have not the despised market relationships and competition been reintroduced? Thompson is dodgy on this one. In one place he evades the issue by maintaining that, the communities being largely self-sufficient, trade will be limited (399). In another, he somewhat naively supposes that the members of communities, each combining the role of labourer and capitalist, will be averse to sharp trading practices and strongly inclined to the fair exchange of commodities in accordance with the labour they cost to produce. This, however, does not rule out the discipline of the market. In a later passage he points out that indolent and inefficient communities will earn less in the market-place, and this will be an incentive to effort (534). So inequality (between communities) is allowable if deserved. What about undeserved inequalities, stemming from such adventitious circumstances as the possession of more or less fertile soil, or a more or less favourable position? In a passage that sits uneasily with his usual condemnation of big government, Thompson suggests that public utilities could be paid for by progressive taxation of communities (577).

How is this communitarian vision to be made into reality? Force is emphatically ruled out (598–9); it would do great harm and in any case is quite unnecessary. The great panacea is universal suffrage: 'The strong holds of insecurity once broken down by simple representative institutions, all its minor ramifications will gradually be rooted out by the diffusion of knowledge, without force or effort' (595). Universal suffrage will mean the end of public plunder, taxation; it will also bring in its train the extinction of all those laws that restrict the freedom of labour and exchange. And universal suffrage is inevitable; the time is coming when education, the diffusion of knowledge, and institutional reform will work together for the victory of *truth* (362). This will set the context for the termination of the exploitation of labourers by capitalists, which itself will be achieved peacefully. Thompson argues that the workers, enlightened and united, will have no difficulty in buying out the capitalists. For fixed capital is not so large, in relation to the powers of production, as is generally thought: he estimates the annual revenue of the country at £400 million, and the accumulated capital at no more than £1,200 million. Since the state currently creams off one-third of the annual revenue, the money saved by the abolition of taxes will be sufficient to buy out the capitalists in nine years (587–8).

Having summarized Thompson's quarter of a million words in a mere five thousand, I am now in a position to discuss, for this text as for the others, its conditions of possibility. What is immediately striking is the extent to which this text appears to have an intellectual context rather than a material one. Almost the whole of his book takes the form of a debate with other writers; it is not a reflection upon his experiences. The theory of human nature occupies less space in this text than it did in those of Godwin and Owen: nevertheless it is indispensable to the argument. The associationist theory of malleability is employed as a critical device – existing individualistic arrangements have corrupted human character – and to sustain optimism for the future. More important, the assumption that all are born equal and uniform, when coupled with the principle of utility, permits Thompson to conclude that wealth, with which all are equally capable of obtaining pleasure, should be distributed equally.

Interpersonal relations are a large issue in this text, and Thompson carries on the discussion from where Bentham, Godwin, and Owen left off. Like his predecessors, he couches the question in terms of the crudely opposed concepts of egotism and benevolence. Benthamite and Godwinian themes sit uneasily side by side. In his Benthamite moments, he insists that all conduct is selfishly motivated. Unlike Adam Smith, he does not believe that the direct pursuit of self-interest by all will lead, as an unintended consequence, to the general good: economic advance requires coordination and cooperation. Following Owen, he argues that self-interest is best pursued indirectly, by promoting the good of others. '[C]omprehensive wisdom, resting on the most enlarged experience' (370) proves this to be the case. These are grand but unconvincing words. This is Hobbes with the edge taken off, a comfortable, domesticated Hobbesianism. Things are so fortunately arranged that the most efficient course of selfish action is identical with the path of benevolence. On occasion, however, he contradicts himself. The evil of private ownership of capital lies precisely in that capitalists do *not* promote the general good; and the real interest of the capitalist is always and necessarily opposed to the interest of labourers (422–3). The very point of cooperative ownership is to *create* a situation in which self-interest and public interest coincide (379). Thompson is in danger of drowning here, and accordingly he clutches at Godwinian benevolence. He descants upon the pleasures of sympathy and comprehensive benevolence (500), which are partly natural, partly reinforced by socialization (421). This is incompatible with the Hobbesian doctrine that all our actions are selfishly motivated, as Godwin was well aware. A possible compromise is foreshadowed, but not developed, when he suggests that conditions of scarcity engender selfishness, while benevolence is more likely to flourish when urgent physical wants have been satisfied. In conclusion, we may say that the concepts available to Thompson for the discussion of interpersonal relations facilitated the contrast between individualism and selfishness on one side, and socialism and benevolence on the other; but they have not readily led him to a convincing solution of the problem of how to create a society of harmony and cooperation.

Thompson's socialism is firmly based upon ethical theory, and the theory on which he draws is almost exclusively utilitarian. He does make use of the language of rights – the 'right to the whole produce of labour' – but such rights are expounded as secondary principles, derived from the primary principle of utility. A producer is entitled to his product because his possession of it will be most conducive to happiness. At the beginning of his book, Thompson pays his intellectual debts, to Helvétius, Priestley, and Paley, but above all to Bentham, in whose house he had resided for several months at the end of 1822 and beginning of 1823. Thompson's most important theoretical achievement is his derivation of egalitarianism from Benthamite utility. The other main theoretical pillar of his system is classical economy. Although Ricardo's *Principles* had appeared in 1817, there is no direct and conclusive evidence that it had any influence upon Thompson's text: he refers to Malthus, James Mill, and Harriet Martineau, but the main input of economic theory comes from Smith's *Wealth of Nations.* Three ideas especially enable Thompson to be a particular kind of socialist. The first is the doctrine that labour is the sole parent of wealth, and the second the Smithian distinction between productive and unproductive expenditure. Thirdly, there is the lack of emphasis upon fixed capital, the capital tied up in machines and factories. Both writers assume that the key to greater productivity lies in setting more labourers to work and in more efficient ways through increased division of labour. Consequently, the capital that matters is circulating capital, the capital that pays wages and buys raw materials. Thompson's kind of socialism, requiring very little state activity, a socialism based upon moderately sized producers' cooperatives, makes better sense for an economy with modest capital requirements than it does for one with very large amounts of capital tied up in plant and distribution networks. It is a prerailway age socialism, and in this way the legacy of the *Wealth of Nations* is a liability as well as an asset. Thompson has taken from his reading of Smith yet another conception of doubtful worth. This is the semireligious belief in a natural economic order, which would always work for the best if the meddling and clumsy fingers of state policy and artificial regulation were kept out. As we saw in an earlier section, Smith himself held this view only with reservations and qualifications. Thompson is less cautious, and he thinks the natural order will produce both prosperity and equality.

Both the conception of a natural order and the Godwinian stress upon rational persuasion rather than coercion dictate a limited role for politics. To be more precise, Thompson is true to philosophical radicalism in his enthusiasm for political reform, but the reform he envisages has a decidedly negative character. Universal suffrage is vital because it will bring in its train a thorough cleansing of the Augean stables. Public plunder is much worse than the exploitation of labourers by capitalists: universal suffrage will extinguish this, along with artificial restraints upon the natural order. These negative tasks having been completed, political activity has no further part to play in the establishment of a just and equal society. Equality cannot be established by law, as is proved by the histories of Sparta, Greece, and Rome (98):

> Reason is the only agent worthy of effecting such a change. The puny and suspicious aid of self-constituted political power, would but mar the mighty work. (579)
> [Genuine security] requires none but the most simple laws and the mildest punishments to preserve the peace and happiness of society; while unequal or spurious security . . . necessarily complicated in its arrangements, requires laws without end to follow those complications. (586)

All this is doubly unsatisfactory. For firstly, Thompson has exaggerated expectations concerning the good to follow from suffrage extension. But secondly, he underestimates the extent to which a new order would need to be created, by sustained political activity. Instead, he leaves the job to 'reason' and 'nature'. Nature dictates three natural laws of distribution: that labour should be free and voluntary, that labour should enjoy its full fruits, and that all exchanges should be free and voluntary. She dictates them in the sense that if they are obeyed, prosperity follows: if they are disobeyed, the natural punishment ensues of 'the loss of the objects of wealth and of the happiness to be derived from them' (178). The diffusion of knowledge will acquaint all workers with these laws, so that they will no longer tolerate exploitation. If government interference is eliminated, therefore, a natural economic order sets in whose workings are benign and that produces prosperity and equality. This indicates the profoundest difference between the economic theories of Thompson and Marx. Thompson thinks that the free market naturally tends to produce equality, but that this tendency is frustrated by law and by the monopoly of knowledge by the rich. Marx, by contrast, insists that a free market in land, commodities, and labour itself naturally tends to produce inequality, accumulations of capital, and hence economic power in the hands of those who occupy favourable positions in the process of production. 'Nature' plays an important part in Thompson's thought, and its chief effect is to permit him to ignore vital problems.

Faith in nature is not accompanied by any nostalgia for the state of nature. He does not admire 'the wretched savages living on the raw fish of the shores of New Holland, or in New Zealand devouring each other' (266). He has a strong and uncomplicated belief in progress; humanity is mounted on a rapidly ascending escalator.

For him, as for Ogilvie, Godwin, and Owen, the doctrine of progress makes the problem of transition to a better society seem to be no problem. There are occasional echoes of the economic theory of progress of the Scottish historical school, but these are swamped by an intellectualist emphasis that reminds the reader of Godwin, and also of the fact that Thompson was in contact with the Saint-Simonians. Accordingly, the Middle Ages are a period of darkness, and at their end 'untutored reason sprang from the cold embrace of the superstitions of a thousand years' (325). Human misery has been produced by unwise institutions (86). There is still misery, in his own age of improved mechanics, chemistry, and the steamship, because of unenlightened laws and institutions, 'the wicker-work and shims of political economy' (135). There are repeated references to 'social science' as the great hope for the future, and its triumph is guaranteed by the wide diffusion of printed publications. All of this is standard for the age, as is the naive expectation of the triumph of 'Truth' that we have noted in other thinkers: Thompson, too, has a strong sense that he stands at a turning-point of human affairs.

> Hitherto mankind have been governed by the unreflecting *habits* formed by *institutions*, with the necessary supplement of *force* always at hand to restrain their aberrations. Henceforth rational beings must be governed by reason. (315; see also 472)

To conclude and summarize, Thompson's book exhibits in exaggerated form the strengths and weaknesses of the radical enlightenment. There can be no doubting he has used the available mental apparatus to distance himself triumphantly from his own society, proposing an alternative socialist vision of harmony, equality (including the equality of women), and sexual liberation.[7] Thompson is manifestly the contemporary of Fourier; he is emphatically out of step with the respectability of the ensuing Victorian generation. His book is a summation of British radical social and economic ideas of the age, stating the Owenite case thoroughly and fully, offering a persuasive egalitarian reinterpretation of Benthamite utilitarianism. But his analysis and criticism of capitalism is not much of an advance upon the work of Hall and Ravenstone. He wisely does not follow Ravenstone in thinking that capital is unnecessary to production; like Smith, he recognizes its economic functions.

These, he thinks, can be performed without a class of large capitalists; workers could set up as their own capitalists, perhaps buying the existing ones out. The difficulties of this proposal are not tackled. Meanwhile, large capitalists unjustly take a portion of the fruits of the labour of others. The capitalist's power over the processes of production derives from two things: first, laws that protect monopoly and restrict the freedom of labour: second, 'ignorance on the part of the labourers', which prevents them from obtaining their due rewards. Remove the laws and the ignorance, and exploitative capitalism will fall. This is highly unconvincing; it ignores, in a way that Marx does not, the entrenched power and adaptability of accumulated capital. Thompson is unduly distracted from social criticism by the preoccupation of philosophic radicalism with parliamentary reform. He unrealistically expects this, plus laissez-faire, to lead to equality. He is led up a blind alley by the myth of a benign natural order.

The argument of the book is excessively theoretical and abstract. Thompson persistently relies upon reasoning rather than upon evidence: his book has much less factual material than does, for example, Smith's *Wealth of Nations*, on which he draws so extensively. The abstract character is reminiscent of *Political Justice*; but Godwin's text is to some extent redeemed by its originality, power, and range. Thompson does not have these virtues. He is eclectic, unsystematic, and pompous; and he never uses one word where twenty will do.

Labour Defended against the Claims of Capital or the Unproductiveness of Capital Proved with Reference to the Present Combinations amongst Journeymen, Thomas Hodgskin, 1825

Summarizing Thompson's argument improves it; but Hodgskin's pamphlet is admirably clear and economical. The first thing to note is the authorial voice; unlike all the writers considered so far, Hodgskin speaks as a labourer to labourers. This voice reflects what he was, only if we accept his definition of labour, which embraces mental as well as manual work. He was the son of a storekeeper in the naval dockyard at Chatham. He went to sea as a cadet, rose to lieutenant, and was discharged when, in his own words, 'I complained of the injury done me, by a commander-in-chief, to himself, in the language I thought it merited; he had unjustly deprived me of every chance of promotion from my own exertions, and that was robbing me of every hope.' Of such stuff are radical critics of society made. There followed hard times; but eventually, he succeeded in making his living as a writer and journalist. Hodgskin was a professional intellectual. In the difficult years after he left the navy, he studied philosophy and wrote a treatise *On Mind*, which failed to find a publisher and is now lost. We may compare him, then, to Ogilvie, Godwin, and Coleridge, also professional intellectuals; but whereas they were products of educational institutions – the Scottish universities, an English public school and Cambridge, dissenting academies – Hodgskin was largely self-taught. In this he resembles Owen; but Hodgskin has a better-disciplined mind.

The occasion of the pamphlet is the parliamentary debates surrounding the repeal of the Combination laws in 1824: Hodgskin defends the right of workers to combine and strike. But the form of the pamphlet is an argument about capital with classical economy. The latter, ostensibly a neutral, scientific study of society, had given comfort to the claims of capitalists, and Hodgskin seeks to

show that these claims, and the theory supporting them, are false.
Like the economists, he distinguishes fixed and circulating capital.
Circulating capital, according to Mill and McCulloch, consists of
a stock of food, clothing, and raw materials or the power to draw
upon such a stock, which the capitalist provides for the worker to
enable him to subsist and work until the commodity is finished and
ready for sale. The defenders of capital argue that without this stock
labourers would be unable to undertake any productive operations
that did not yield an immediate return. Fixed capital consists of
tools, machines, and factories that enable labour to be more productive. In return for these benefits, capital deserves its reward.
Furthermore, according to McCulloch, the quantity of employment
depends upon the quantity of circulating capital. The whole population can be employed only if there is a sufficient stock of food,
clothing, and raw materials. Therefore if the workers, by combining
against capital to seek excessive wages, drive capital out of the
country, they will be losers not gainers. Instead of obtaining higher
wages, they will lose their jobs. These are the claims of capital with
which Hodgskin takes issue.

His discussion of circulating capital is the most impressive part
of the pamphlet. He argues that it is misleading to think in terms
of a stored-up stock of food, clothing, and raw materials, which
the capitalist possesses or upon which the worker can draw with
money provided by the capitalist. To think in these terms lends
credit to the idea of the accumulation of capital; but essentially,
there is no accumulation. This can be illustrated with reference to
commodities such as bread and milk. A stock of these is not stored
up to keep the workers going until their productive task is completed. Milk and bread have to be obtained and prepared every day.
It does not make sense to think of a stored up stock even of clothing:

> There is, it may be admitted, a small stock of clothing on hand; but
> considering what enemies moths are to the materials of which it is
> made, only a very small stock is ever prepared, compared to the
> general consumption. (43–4)[1]

If workers are to set about the task of building a ship or making
a road, they have to be confident of obtaining bread and milk daily,
and clothes when required. Their confidence is justified, not because
there is a stored-up stock, but because other workers are making
bread and clothes and obtaining milk while the first lot of workers

build ships. Specialization is rendered possible not by accumulations of capital but by *coexisting labour* – by the coexistence of
different kinds of productive activity. Proof of this can be obtained
by considering one of the lengthiest productive tasks – the production of a skilled labourer. The parents who rear and train the
future worker from infancy to manhood do this without any stored-
up stock of subsistence goods. They are enabled to do it by labour
– their own and that of other labourers:

> Under the strong influence of natural affection and parental love,
> they prepare by their toils, continued day after day, and year after
> year, through all the long period of the infancy and childhood of
> their offspring, those future labourers who are to succeed to their
> toils and their hard fare, but who will inherit their productive power,
> and be what they now are, the main pillars of the social edifice. (50)

Similar arguments apply to fixed capital. Hodgskin concedes that
by the use of tools and machines the productive power of labour
is wonderfully enhanced. But in the first place, machines and tools
are themselves the products of labour. And secondly, like circulating
capital, items of fixed capital should not be thought of as an accumulated stock, possessed by the capitalist and made available by
him. In order to have tools and machines, all that is required is
another kind of coexisting labour, namely, that of the workmen
who make tools and machines. Thirdly, fixed capital can produce
nothing by itself; it only becomes productive when directed by labour: 'It has been asked, what could a carpenter effect without his
hatchet and his saw? I put the converse of the question, and ask
what the hatchet and saw could effect without the carpenter. Rust
and rottenness must be the answer' (61). Hodgskin does not dispute
the right of the maker of a machine to a reward for his labour. He
denies, however, that the capitalist who neither makes nor uses it
is entitled to a reward merely for owning it.

Defenders of capital have argued that it is entitled to a reward
because it aids production. But it can be shown, Hodgskin maintains, that capital is not rewarded in proportion to the contribution
it makes to production. As far as circulating capital is concerned,
the amount of production is proportioned to the quantity of subsistence and raw materials it furnishes for labour. But where fixed
capital is concerned, the level of production is proportioned to the

quality as much as to the quantity of capital. Hodgskin mentions steam engines in his pamphlet, and different kinds of motive power would serve to illustrate his point. A water-mill costs more to set up than a steam-mill of equivalent capacity; hence a water-mill represents a greater quantity of capital, a steam-mill, capital of a higher quality. In this way it can be shown that fixed and circulating capital aid production in accordance with quite different principles. But the two sorts of capital are not rewarded differently: a capitalist expects to get the going rate of interest, whether he is providing fixed or circulating capital. This shows, Hodgskin concludes, that the capitalist gets his profit, not because of the contribution he makes to production, but because of the power he has over labour.

By these arguments he believes he has shown not only that capital does not deserve the large share of wealth it gets, but also that capital, as the political economists understand it, is not necessary to the process of production. The effects that the economists believe are achieved by circulating capital are in fact due to coexisting labour. And in order to have tools and machines, three things are required – ingenious inventors, skilled labourers to make the instruments, and skilled labourers to use them. If we regard the invention of machines as a species of labour, then all that production requires is labour – especially skilled labour. Hence there need be no fear that combinations of workers, by driving capital out of the country, will destroy jobs and arrest the wealth-generating machine. Money may flee abroad: as long as skilled labourers and inventors remain behind, the productive power of the nation is undiminished.

The capitalist is nothing but a parasite upon labour and production; but he has achieved the marvellous feat of representing himself as the mainspring of production. Public opinion is on his side; even the workers he exploits regard him as a benefactor. He has power over labour, and this power is buttressed by opinion; as a result he is able to make exorbitant claims upon the wealth produced by labour. Hodgskin guesses that the consumer has to pay six times the labour cost of a coat, a pair of shoes, or a loaf of bread. The extra cost constitutes the profits taken by various capitalists and the rents taken by various landlords (75). He illustrates the magnitude of the claims of capital with reference to the iniquities of compound interest. According to the principle of compound interest, what is owed to the capitalist grows greater every year:

> Dr. Price has calculated that the sum of one penny put out to com-
> pound interest at our Saviour's birth, at 5 per cent, would in the
> year 1791 amount to a sum greater than could be contained in three
> hundred millions of globes like this earth, all solid gold. (75)

What Hodgskin aims to prove with this titbit of curious information
is that the claims of capital have a permanent tendency to outgrow
the power of labour to satisfy them. And having proved this – at
least to his own satisfaction – he has forged a useful weapon for
his battle with the economists. For he has found an answer to the
arguments of Malthus and Ricardo claiming a tendency of wages
to fall to subsistence level. Wages remain low, not because labourers
breed excessively, causing population to outrun food resources;
they remain low because the demands of capitalists are exorbitant
and ever-increasing. Furthermore, he uses the same argument to
explain the falling rate of profit, which both Adam Smith and Ricardo had thought was a long-run feature of advanced economies.
Smith thought that the rate of profit would fall because more capital
would have been accumulated than could find profitable investment
outlets. Ricardo argued that the fall would be due to population
increase, which would eat up the surplus out of which profits could
be paid.[2] Hodgskin counters that profit falls off because the claims
of capital for profit go way beyond the bounds of possible repay-
ment, as demonstrated by Dr. Price's penny. Smith had argued that
the natural tendency of an economy was to an eventual stationary
state, Malthus that the natural laws of population led continually
to misery. Hodgskin, on the contrary, maintains that any adverse
tendency is artificially induced by the iniquities of capital; nature
herself is benign:

> In the system of Nature, mouths are united with hands and with
> intelligence; they and not capital are the agents of production; and,
> according to her rule, however it may have been thwarted by the
> pretended wisdom of law-makers, wherever there is a man there also
> are the means of creating or producing him subsistence. (108)

After his critique of capital, Hodgskin turns to the issue of how
wealth *ought* to be distributed. The principle of just distribution is
eminently simple: 'the whole produce of labour ought to belong to
the labourer' (83). But the application of the principle is not so
simple. Hodgskin is fully cognizant of the fact that production of
wealth does not go on in Robinson Crusoe fashion. A commodity

is rarely produced by a single individual; most result from the 'joint and combined' labour of many men, and as society advances and the division of labour is carried further, this becomes increasingly the case. There is no ready way of identifying what a particular individual has produced through his labour when that individual has performed but a part of the 'great social task'. Hodgskin's solution, to use modern terminology, is free individual and collective bargaining in a situation of equality of power and knowledge. When a commodity is jointly produced, the allocation of rewards must be debated and decided by the workers themselves. But labour must be free in this bargaining (i.e., there must be no combination laws); it must be sufficiently enlightened to see through the deception of the claims of capital; and it must be free of prejudices. For example, it must be recognized that intellectual work – designing, planning – is labour just as much as the work of the hands and is equally entitled to reward. Conversely, the labour of direction and management must not be *overvalued* in relation to manual labour. Because managers are often also capitalists, they have succeeded in obtaining higher rewards, and their superior payments have come to be regarded as natural. But Hodgskin doubts 'whether one species of labour is more valuable than another; certainly it is not more necessary' (89). Hodgskin's discussion seems to imply an ideal situation of approximate, but not absolute, equality. Reward is to be proportioned to labour, and those who sow not, neither should they reap. In all this there is no mention of those who *cannot* labour – the sick and aged. But we should not reproach Hodgskin for this. *Labour Defended* is a brief work that makes no claim to have tackled all social questions. Its discussion is limited to the rival claims of labour and capital.

How can society be changed so that labour receives its full reward? Workers' combinations – trade unions – are engaged in practical attacks on the claims of capital (103). Eventually they will succeed, because workers are becoming better informed, through new educational opportunities in schools and mechanics' institutions:

> As the labourers acquire knowledge, the foundations of the social edifice will be dug up from the deep beds into which they were laid in times past, they will be curiously handled and closely examined, and they will not be restored unless they were originally laid in justice, and unless justice commands their preservation. (102)

In their war with capital, labourers have every reason to hope for the assistance of the masters (i.e., professional managers who do not own the company they manage), for masters are in reality a kind of skilled labourer.

As with the others, I shall now analyse the conditions of the possibility and shape of Hodgskin's text and attempt to assess its quality. The latter task is especially important in Hodgskin's case. *Labour Defended* is the culmination of the pre-Marxian critique of capital in Britain; after Hodgskin, Gray and Bray add little of theoretical importance. Furthermore, the rival merits of Hodgskin and Marx have been the subject of earnest debate.

The pamphlet says almost nothing about human nature (the idea that human beings are habit-forming animals plays a significant role, as we shall see later). There is little more about the nature of interpersonal relations. Hodgskin does envisage labourers in the future sharing out the wealth they have collectively created, in a process of free and equal discussion. This process, evidently one of individuals making claims (90), suggests a greater proximity to Godwinian individualism than to Owenite or Thompsonian co-operation; and we know from other writings that Hodgskin *was* an individualist.

The argument of the pamphlet is fundamentally a moral one, concerned with what labourers and capitalists ought to receive. But fashionable moral theories play no part in it. He had connections with the philosophic radicals, and he alludes to the doctrine of utility (82) but he does not employ it in building up his case. There is an echo of Locke – 'the labour of a man's body and the work of his hands are to be considered as exclusively his own' (83) – but the doctrine of natural rights plays no part either. All the work is done by a desert-based concept of justice.[3] Reduced to its bare bones, the argument of the pamphlet is that the capitalist does not contribute to the production of wealth; therefore he deserves no reward. All wealth is produced by labour, and the labourer is entitled to the full fruits. The closing words of the pamphlet urge us 'to do justice, and allow labour to possess and enjoy the whole of its produce' (109). This desert-based concept of justice is not defended, nor are its difficulties explored. The pamphlet is an application of the moral concept, which is simply assumed, taken for granted. The issues are not whether people should get their deserts, or what we mean by desert: the issue is, who is deserving, the labourer or the capitalist? Consequently, although Hodgskin is building up a moral case, the pamphlet devotes very little space to morality; most of it belongs to that discourse we label political economy. Here we need to notice, and discard, a misconception. Hodgskin has been dubbed a 'Ricardian Socialist'; in fact both parts of that title are inaccurate. Hodgskin looks like a socialist from a post-Marxian point of view because he is a critic of capitalism. But, at least in the 1820s, 'socialism' was the opposite of 'individualism', and he is emphatically an individualist, a critic in later life of Owenite cooperation. If he were a 'Ricardian', we would expect his desert-based concept of social justice to be built upon Ricardo's labour theory of value. We would expect him to say, 'because commodities are valuable in proportion to the labour they contain, therefore labour ought to receive all the value it has created'. But *Labour Defended* nowhere contains this argument; and from other sources we know that Hodgskin rejected Ricardo's value theory, preferring to use the 'adding-up' theory of value of Adam Smith, in accordance with which the price of a commodity (supply and demand being equal) is the sum of its costs in rent, interest, and wages. Hodgskin regards labour as the producer of wealth, rather than the determinant of value. It would be more appropriate to call him a 'Smithian' critic of capital.[4]

The central questions in a discussion of Hodgskin's pamphlet are these. How has political economy made his social criticism possible? What is the nature of his departures from political economy? Has he simply added a moral commentary, or has he successfully challenged its concepts and theories? How does his critique of political economy compare with that of Marx? Plainly, without classical economy, *Labour Defended* would be impossible. The pamphlet works with the concepts of the economists – land, capital, labour, rent, profit, wages, fixed and circulating capital, and so on. Its starting point is with doctrines of classical economy that Hodgskin is not prepared to accept – that the capitalist is a benefactor who creates jobs, that wages are kept down by the tendency of labourers to breed excessively, that attempts to raise wages would drive capital out of the country and thus destroy employment.

Hodgskin's most important challenge to political economy is

achieved by a curious transference of an idea, out of the web of argument in which it was originally placed, into a new context. The original idea is Hume's well-known assault upon causal necessity.[5] As Hume observes, when we say that one 'object' or event causes another, we suppose that the first 'object' has within it a power to bring about the second. But in fact we have no direct experience of this power or causal efficacy; all we experience is a succession of 'objects'. This can be demonstrated by a consideration of our experience of a pair of conjoined events. The first time we watched a moving billiard ball about to strike a stationary one, we would be unable to predict that the former would transmit its motion to the latter. We would perceive the moving ball; but we would not perceive any power within it to set the stationary ball in motion, we would have no prior knowledge of a causal or necessary connection between the movement of the white, its impact with the red, and the subsequent movement of the red. However, after we have observed the collision of many billiard balls, we come to expect a certain pattern of events. We speak of the power of one ball to move another, of the white causing the red to go into the pocket, of the necessity of the red moving if struck by the white. But as far as direct experience is concerned, nothing has changed: we have still never experienced the power, causal efficacy, or necessity we talk about; all we have experienced is a succession of events. Our supposition of a causal necessity stems not from objective experience, but from subjective expectation. As a result of frequently experiencing one event following another, the mind acquires a habit of connecting the two together. It is in fact a particular form of the general psychological principle of the association of ideas. But the mind still has no *knowledge* that the events *must* go together. Yet, even though our knowledge is only of co-occurrences and not of any necessary connections, this is sufficient both for science and for the practical business of life. On the basis of our experience of one event regularly following another, we make scientific predictions and practical plans for the future; and the success rate of our predictions and plans is good enough to enable us to continue predicting and planning with a fair degree of confidence.

   Bearing this idea of confidence in mind, let us turn from Hume on causal necessity to Hodgskin on circulating capital. What is the function claimed for it by the defenders of capital? Its alleged function is that it enables the labourer to get on with a specialized task, confident that while he does so his means of subsistence will be forthcoming. The defenders of capital maintain that this confidence rests upon the existence of circulating capital as a stored-up stock of subsistence goods. But Hodgskin has shown that there is no stored-up stock; there is only coexisting labour. The supposed existence of circulating capital has no basis in experience. Specialization of trades is possible, because the human animal is a creature of habit:

> As we expect that the sun will rise to-morrow, so we also expect that men in all time to come will be actuated by the same motives as they have been in times past. If we push our inquiries still further, all that we can learn is, that there are other men in existence who are preparing those things we need, while we are preparing those which they need. The conviction may, perhaps, ultimately be traced then to our knowledge that *other men* exist and labour, but never to any conviction or knowledge that there is a stored-up stock of commodities. (45–6)

Hodgskin's argument here, though it is concerned with a quite different topic, is evidently patterned on that of Hume. The idea of circulating capital corresponds to the idea of causal necessity. Coexisting labour corresponds to co-occurrence of events. Whereas Hume argues that we have no experience of causal necessity, but only of succeeding events, Hodgskin argues that we have no experience of a stored-up stock of goods, but only of coexisting labour. Whereas Hume argues that the events come to be bound together in our minds by the principle of association or habit, Hodgskin argues that different trades are bound into a single economic system by habit. Hume has shown that we deceive ourselves if we suppose we have knowledge of causal necessity; Hodgskin that we are deceived in our belief that circulating capital exists as an object or accumulation of objects. That Hodgskin was familiar with Hume's argument cannot be doubted, though we cannot be certain that he got it directly from the pages of Hume. We know that he was working on a treatise *On Mind* in 1815. The actual wording of the passage in *Labour Defended* is significantly similar to that of Godwin's discussion of causal necessity in *Political Justice* (337); Godwin's phraseology, in turn, follows that of Hume's *Enquiry*, which Godwin acknowledges.

Mere influence studies are tedious things. My excuse for having devoted so much space to Hume's influence of Hodgskin is that this is *not* a mere influence study. We are dealing here with Hodgskin's most important theoretical achievement, the aspect of his pamphlet that most profoundly anticipates Marx. I have shown that he reaches this point by a surprising and creative adaptation of an idea of Hume's from a remotely related field. So Hodgskin has arrived at much the same point as Marx. The capitalist system of exploitation rests upon an illusion. The illusion is the belief that capital is a living economic power. It is in fact no more than a mask that hides the reality – human skill, human labour, a particular set of human relationships, a particular organization of productive activity. These, not capital, are the realities, the living powers:

> One is almost tempted to believe that capital is a sort of caballistic word, like Church and State, or any other of those general terms which are invented by those who fleece the rest of mankind to conceal the hand that shears them. It is a sort of idol before which men are called upon to prostrate themselves. (60)

Human labour and ingenuity have wonderfully transformed the earth, making it fit for humanity to live in and capable of yielding sustenance:

> The instruments he uses to do all this . . . have been called fixed capital; and shutting out of view MAN himself, in order to justify the existing order of society . . . all these glorious effects have been attributed, with a more extraordinary perversion of thought, perhaps, than is to be found in any other department of knowledge, to fixed and circulating capital. The skill and the art of the labourer have been overlooked, and he has been vilified; while the work of his hands has been worshipped. (66)

Is this illusion consciously fostered by capitalists, or do they believe it themselves? The passages quoted above do not enable the reader to be sure of Hodgskin's opinion. If the former is the case, then Hodgskin's account of the deception practised by capitalists resembles French enlightenment assaults upon established religion, as a deception practised by priests in order to line their pockets. The continuation of the first passage supports this parallel: '[W]hile the cunning priest from behind the altar, profaning the God whom he pretends to serve . . . puts forth his hand to receive and appropriate the offerings which he calls for in the name of religion' (60). (Hodgskin himself was a sincere Christian; but that is compatible with a typically eighteenth-century aversion to 'priestcraft'.) But the opening words of the passage, 'One is almost tempted to believe' cast doubt upon an interpretation of the text as claiming a *conscious* deception, and the second passage could easily be read as meaning that the *capitalist* is taken in by the illusion of capital, as well as the labourer. If the latter is the correct interpretation, then Hodgskin's account of the illusion of capital anticipates Marx's theory of ideology.[6]

If we now turn to what *Labour Defended* has to say about how the capitalist system of exploitation has come into being and compare that with Marx, we find once more a simultaneous looking backward to older ideas and anticipation of Marx. Hodgskin maintains that exploitation is possible because the capitalist has power over labourers. Several passages indicate that this power takes the form of a monopoly of resources, which can be traced back to conquest and forcible seizure. Labourers are descended from bondsmen and serfs (22, 39, 70). We encountered this line of thinking in Ogilvie, Godwin, Hall, and Thompson. It is a variation upon the ancient and popular myth of 'the Norman yoke'. The power of this myth to enable and generate radical social criticism is undeniable. Further, it naturally leads to measures for eliminating exploitation of a certain kind – parliamentary reform, changes in the laws of inheritance, redistributive taxation. Such solutions are proposed by political radicals like Bentham, as well as by social radicals such as Hall and Thompson. Hodgskin's *Labour Defended*, however, does not entirely follow this way of thinking. The pamphlet has a solitary footnote that explains that in the feudal era, capitalists were benefactors. They provided employment in the towns for peasants fleeing feudal tyranny. But since then, capitalists have 'reduced the ancient tyrant of the soil to comparative insignificance, while they have inherited his power over all the labouring classes' (67n). The difficulties raised by this passage are of the utmost significance. If capitalists enabled peasants to escape from feudal monopoly and exploitation, then how can their power be based upon the same monopoly? What is the nature of the power of the capitalist over labour? Let us glance at what Marx has to say about the genesis and development of capitalist exploitation. We find, in fact, that Marx himself employs the venerable conquest theory of the origins of exploitation, as well as developing a distinct and more plausible theory. For Marx supposes an original or primary accumulation of capital by violence – the seizure of monastic land at the Reformation, of peasant land by enclosures, of overseas resources by the conquest of colonies: 'capital comes into the world soiled with mire from top to toe, and oozing blood from every pore.'[7] But secondly, Marx shows how the power of the capitalist over labour, and his ability to exploit labour, can arise continually within the process of production itself. The elaborate division of labour, coupled with the institution of private property and a free market in land, commodities, and labour itself, makes it possible for those who occupy key or controlling positions in the productive process to extract surplus value from those who are less favourably situated. Hence the putter-out, who supplies raw wool, and collects the finished cloth to take to market, can pay those he employs less than the value their labour has produced. The 'Norman yoke' theory of exploitation may be valid for an agrarian economy, but this second theory is better adapted to a manufacturing one. Hodgskin has not arrived at Marx's theory of the origins of exploitation several decades before Marx. But *Labour Defended* is groping towards a similar understanding:

> Betwixt him who produces food and him who produces clothing, betwixt him who makes instruments and him who uses them, in steps the capitalist, who neither makes nor uses them, and appropriates to himself the produce of both. With as niggard a hand as possible he transfers to each a part of the produce of the other, keeping to himself the larger share. Gradually and successively has he insinuated himself betwixt them, expanding in bulk as he has been nourished by their increasingly productive labours, and separating them so widely from each other that neither can see whence that supply is drawn which each receives through the capitalist. While he despoils both, so completely does he exclude one from the view of the other that both believe they are indebted to him for subsistence. He is the *middleman* of all labourers. (71–2)

Now if exploitation comes about in this way, then different remedies will be required from those deemed appropriate if it is a legacy of 'the Norman yoke'. It will be necessary for labourers to acquire a thorough understanding of the process of production, and then to establish control over it, so that the outcomes in terms of the distribution of wealth may be determined in accordance with justice, rather than in accordance with chance, custom, and an unequal distribution of power within the process of production itself. Without doubt, Hodgskin is already moving along this road. He wants labourers to become well versed in political economy – his kind rather than the orthodox version – and hopes that mechanics' institutes will promote this. Next, he expects free trades unions to correct the imbalance of power over production, enabling labourers to enforce distribution according to desert. But it must be doubted whether Hodgskin has gone far enough. To have a situation in which enlightened trades unionists put their case is not the same as a situation in which labourers control production and distribution. Such control would need to be exercised at different levels: at the level of the productive unit (e.g., a factory), at the level of the economy as a whole. Hodgskin has deprived himself of the possibility of proposing effective control at the work place level, because, individualist that he is, he will not consider forms of collective or cooperative ownership. At the national level, any solution is precluded by his rejection of politics. He is prepared to contemplate political activity in order to destroy the power of the rich to protect their own interests (106); but this having been done, there is no hint of a need for the state to manage and regulate economic life. 'No statesman can accomplish this, nor ought the labourers to allow any statesman to interfere in it' (90). This is the fatal flaw at the heart of *Labour Defended*. Hodgskin is fully aware that production is no longer individual – if it ever was: 'there is no longer anything which we can call the natural reward of individual labour' (85). His model of productive activity is not the small craft workshop, but the large enterprise with considerable division of labour.[8] Yet he is not prepared to contemplate collective ownership and control.

In developing this criticism of *Labour Defended*, I do not mean to imply that Marx was a great deal better on this issue. Marx certainly insists upon collective ownership and control, but he does not face the very real difficulties of combining control with freedom, efficiency, and genuine democracy. He merely provides generalities, skating over the problems in a fashion that takes one's breath away: 'In communist society . . . society regulates the general production'.[9]

This weakness of *Labour Defended* lays it wide open to attack by advocates of capitalism. Coexisting labour is the reality, Hodgskin says. Circulating capital is an illusion and can be dispensed

with. But once the capitalist has been abolished, who or what will
take on his task of organizing production? Who or what, in the
absence of entrepreneurs, will spot new opportunities and set up
new businesses? Hodgskin the anarchist, foe of politics and collective control, has no answer. This distrust of positive, active politics
is as we have seen so widespread in late eighteenth- and early nineteenth-century Britain as scarcely to require comment or explanation in Hodgskin's case. But it is strengthened by his deepest
philosophical and religious convictions. There is little explicit reference to religion in the pamphlet, but there are enough scattered
hints to reveal that he was a religious man who believed in a wise
and benevolent providence (35, 60, 78, 82, 107, 108). This belief
goes hand in hand with the familiar contrast between nature and
artifice. Like William Thompson, he believes that there is a 'wise
system of the universe', 'Nature's rule', which is 'thwarted by the
pretended wisdom of law-makers'. Given this belief, the aim must
be not to extend state regulation, but to abolish it. It may be that
Thompson and Hodgskin have culled this idea from their reading
of Adam Smith, ignoring the role accorded by Smith to the state
in creating the institutional framework within which economic activity takes place. In this respect they come close to the popularizers
of political economy, the 'vulgar' advocates of laissez-faire.[10] Once
again we find the nature–artifice theme enabling and disabling social criticism. Hodgskin's conviction that nature (God) is good encourages him to reject Malthusian and Ricardian pessimism and
an 'artificial' order of society that promotes unhappiness contrary
to God's intentions: at the same time, it leads him to ignore the
possibility that a better order might require much political artifice
for its creation and maintenance.

A comment is needed on what *Labour Defended* says specifically
about fixed capital. Its importance is played down: given knowledge
and skilled labour, it can be provided as required. Here, too, Hodgskin has laid himself open to counterattack by the defender of capital. For surely he underestimates the extent to which fixed capital
needs to be accumulated over a long period. Factories and machines
cannot be created overnight. To turn forests and marshes into fertile
land, to dig mines, require considerable and long-term capital investment. This is preeminently true of the economic infrastructure
of docks, roads, canals, and railways. Marx at least did not make

this mistake; a familiar passage from the *Communist Manifesto* is a paean to the achievements of capitalism.[11] There is a real and important difference between Hodgskin and Marx here. Marx believes that the capitalist stage, though painful, was necessary and beneficial; it brought about an accumulation of capital, multiplying human productive powers and hence laying a foundation of plenty on which alone socialism could be built. This is not Hodgskin's opinion. He is prepared to concede that capitalists performed a useful service long ago when they provided an urban refuge for fugitives from feudal tyranny. But apart from that, the message of his pamphlet is that capitalists, and indeed capital understood as an accumulation of things, is and has always been unnecessary. It is difficult to defend him on this score. To argue that he was writing during the early industrial revolution before the massive capital accumulations of the railway age is not a complete excuse: agricultural improvement, docks, mines, roads, canals, all conspicuous examples of the accumulation of fixed capital, were salient features of his world and some are referred to in *Labour Defended*.

Just as the neglect of politics weakens his account of an alternative to capitalism, so it deprives him of any plausible strategy for transition. As with the other thinkers we have considered, there is no recognition that a long period of political struggle, with frequent reversals and frustrations and disagreements even among the labourers themselves, might be required. Instead there is the same epistemological overoptimism as in Ogilvie, Godwin, Owen, and Thompson – the belief that Truth has been discovered and that its triumph is imminent.

> No Holy Alliance can put down the quiet insurrection by which knowledge will subvert whatever is not founded in justice and truth. (101)
>
> It is impossible that the labourer should long remain ignorant of these facts, or acquiesce in this state of things. (103)
>
> It is not possible that any large body of men who are acquainted with their rights will tacitly acquiesce in insult and injury. (99)

These are strong, appealing, but perhaps surprising words. They are surprising, because Hodgskin comes so close to what we now denominate the concept of ideology. He has come to see much of classical economy as systematic (and successful) class propaganda, masquerading as science. He has argued that this rests upon a yet deeper delusion, the belief that capital is a thing, an object, a living and beneficent economic power. Yet this awareness of distorted perception does not weaken his faith in the eventual triumph of truth.

Labour Defended is an impressive text. Its argument is clear and orderly, expressed in plain but dignified and vivid prose. It benefits by being more narrowly focussed than any of the other texts we have considered. Its social radicalism is made possible by a number of intellectual commonplaces of the age: the belief in progress, especially progress in knowledge; the nature–artifice antithesis; the ancient conception of justice as desert; the myth of 'the Norman yoke'. These are simply taken on board, unexamined and unexplored. But the most important condition of the possibility of the pamphlet is classical economy, and here Hodgskin's creative work occurs. He does not merely add a moral gloss to the conclusions of the economists; he takes one of their central concepts, *capital*, analyses it, criticizes it, and reformulates it, taking the argument well beyond the point at which it had been left by Hall, Ravenstone, and Thompson. *Labour Defended* is therefore a theoretical achievement as well as a moral argument. He shows that classical economy is not a pure science, value-free. He gets to this conclusion by a route that could not have been predicted, via Hume's critique of causal necessity. *Labour Defended* is not merely a working-out of widespread assumptions, a natural and inevitable development of existing discourses: it is an original achievement, which could only have been written by Hodgskin. Working along his own lines, he arrives at a conception of capital substantially similar to that of Marx. Obviously *Das Kapital* is a richer book, with a much more fully developed account of capitalism; but there seems to be little warrant for drawing the Marxist distinction between a scientific Marx and a prescientific Hodgskin. If he anticipates Marx in his critique of capital, he does not, however, anticipate the Marxian theory of value and of surplus value; unlike Marx, he does not take Ricardo's theory of value as his starting point, but repudiates it, returning in this department to Adam Smith.

Labour Defended is a powerful critique of capitalism; its weakness is that it not only fails to propose a plausible alternative, but also sets obstacles in the way of an alternative. It too readily assumes that if there is labour, then 'capital' – or rather the benefits that fixed and circulating capital are supposed by the economists to provide – will be forthcoming. For Hodgskin ignores the difficulties of creating and organizing a complex economic system. All is to be left to Reason and Nature, politics is to play no part. Justice is to be achieved by a free market, under ideal conditions of equality of economic power and information. But what if the free market spontaneously generates inequality and exploitation? How can this be controlled without political action at several levels?

Rural Rides, William Cobbett, 1830

Cobbett's *Rural Rides* is a diary of his journeying on horseback around southern England in the years 1822–6. He ranged south of the Thames from Kent to Somerset, and north of the Thames in Berkshire, Oxfordshire, Herefordshire, and Worcestershire. He does not treat most of the Midlands, the North, East Anglia, or parts of the British Isles outside England, though some of these areas were covered in other articles in his *Political Register* that were not included in the 1830 collection. *Rural Rides* is a description of and commentary upon what he sees and does. He describes the landscape, the crops, the towns, villages, farms and inns, the country estates, and the people he meets. The description is larded with commentary upon the times, and this is our main concern. But the commentary and the description cannot be disentangled, for his perception is coloured by his moral, social, and political concerns.

The rides begin during the nadir of the postwar agricultural depression. Prices of farm produce have collapsed, as Cobbett demonstrates in his reports of the fairs he visits. For example, at the Weyhill sheep fair of 1822, the turnover has fallen from £300,000 a few years ago to £70,000 (58).[1] This spells ruin for farmers who rent and work the land; for rents, fixed when prices were high, remain high even though prices and therefore farming incomes have slumped. Many farmers who owned their land were no better off; for they had taken out mortgages in the boom period, which they could no longer repay. Cobbett finds general gloom at the farmhouse firesides:

> These fire-sides, in which I have always so delighted, I now approach with pain. I was, not long ago, sitting round the fire with as worthy and as industrious a man as all England contains. There was his son,

about 19 years of age; two daughters, of 15 to 18; and a little boy
sitting on the father's knee. I knew, but not from him, that there
was *a mortgage* on his farm. I was anxious to induce him *to sell
without delay.* . . . The deep and deeper gloom on a countenance,
once so cheerful, told me what was passing in his breast, when turning away my looks in order to seem not to perceive the effect of my
words, I saw the eyes of his wife *full of tears.* . . . How many men,
of the most industrious, the most upright, the most exemplary upon
the face of the earth, have been . . . driven to despair, ending in
madness or self-murder, or both. (91–2)

But the farmers are not alone in their agony. They drag the landlords
down with them when they fail to pay their rents in full; for the
landlords have mortgages, too, and other commitments that they
undertook in more prosperous times. Cobbett catalogues the landlords who have gone under. On a ride of eighty miles, from Reigate
to Burghclere, he passes estates formerly held by twelve of the oldest
and most distinguished families, now in the hands of new men from
the city – bankers, powder-makers, merchants. As he rides down
the valley of the Avon, from Pewsey to Salisbury, he counts eight
gentlemen's mansions where half a century ago there were fifty.
But worst of all in his eyes is the plight of the rural labourers.
Farmers, desperately trying to make ends meet, have squeezed the
wages of their labourers and have laid off hands. The grievous
results are everywhere to be seen: men, women, and children like
walking skeletons, inadequate wages supplemented out of the poor
rates, thousands employed by the parish to mend roads, or even to
dig holes in order to fill them up again. Cobbett scornfully rejects
Malthusian explanations of the growth of poverty and the poor
rates in terms of overpopulation. He seeks to refute 'beastly MAL-
THUS' and 'his nasty disciples' (318) by demonstrating that population levels have scarcely varied since Domesday Book (350, 461),
and the main evidence he brings forward is the size of parish
churches on his route. So many of them would hold several times
the present population of their villages; in many cases the whole
population could sit comfortably in the tower or church porch
(350). Rural population must therefore have been higher in the
Middle Ages when the churches were built.

It is not just that there is hardship at all levels of rural society:
Cobbett also believes that the economic and social structure of the

countryside is changing for the worse. As he sees it, life is being sucked out of the countryside by the wens. The great wen is London, but there are lesser wens such as Cheltenham and Bath. Wealth is created in the countryside, but is not consumed there by those whose labour has created it. Instead, it goes to the wens. His hatred of these places spills over into his description of their physical appearance:

> The soil is gravel at bottom, with a black loam at top near the Thames; further back it is a sort of spewy gravel; and the buildings consist generally of tax-eaters' showy, tea-garden-like boxes, and of shabby dwellings of labouring people, who, in this part of the country, look to be about half *Saint Giles's*: dirty, and have every appearance of drinking gin. (31–2)

Not only do the wens absorb the wealth: they also draw the people to themselves. This is why the country churches are now too large for the village populations. And this is an unhealthy, unnatural state of affairs; people should live close to where their food is produced. Cobbett delights to find country people who have never travelled more than a couple of miles from their place of birth, people whose roots remain in the soil in which they have grown (292, 471).

The expansion of wens is perceived by Cobbett as part and parcel of what we would now call the development of a market economy, and this, too, he deplores. He believes he is witnessing a shift from a 'subsistence' economy, in which necessaries are produced locally, even within the household, to a situation in which the production of manufactured commodities is concentrated in towns and factories. This is evil; for in the first place it impoverishes rural labourers. Domestic manufacture used to provide an employment, for women and children when the men were in the fields and for the men when the weather kept them indoors (117, 318, 394). Secondly, the new factories are unpleasant and unhealthy workplaces:

> Talk of *Serfs*! Are there any of these, or did feudal times ever see any of them, so debased, so absolutely slaves, as the poor creatures who, in the "Enlightened" North, are *compelled* to work fourteen hours in a day, in a heat of *eighty-four degrees*; and who are liable to punishment *for looking out at a window of the factory*! (127)

Third, it creates a class of middlemen – traders and shopkeepers – who are veritable locusts. Formerly, trading was done at fairs; producers exchanged their surpluses directly with one another. Now, it is done in shops; the shopkeeper comes between one producer and another and robs both:

> [N]ow-a-days, all is looked for at *shops*: all is to be had by *trafficking*: scarcely any one thinks of providing his own wants *out of his own land* and other his own domestic means. To buy the thing, *ready made*, is the taste of the day: thousands, who are *housekeepers*, buy their dinners ready cooked: nothing is so common as to *rent breasts* for children to suck. (475)

The worst of the parasitic middlemen are the Quakers, for in spite of their show of otherworldliness, they speculate eagerly in corn, buying when prices are low and withholding from sale until prices rise. Market principles have invaded the countryside. As he passes through a village near Canterbury, Cobbett observes a sign outside a house:

> 'PARADISE PLACE. *Spring guns and steel traps are set here*'. . . . This is doubtless some stockjobber's place . . . whenever any of them go to the country, they look upon it that they are to begin a sort of warfare against everything around them. (207)

It is these grasping attitudes that have caused landlords to rack up their rents and evict small farmers (436). Cobbett's most memorable illustration of these economic and social changes is his account of a farm sale. He goes to look round, and he sees the evidence for the old way of rural living. There is a long oak table, around which the household sat – the farmer, his family, and his labourers, living and eating together. But the table had been disused for some time, for now there was a *parlour*, with carpet and bell-pull, mahogany furniture, decanters, glasses, and a dinner set. There the farmer and his family in recent years ate alone, on 'two or three nick-nacks . . . instead of a piece of bacon and a pudding: the house too neat for a dirty-shoed carter to be allowed to come in.' The farmer aped the life-style of the wens, and his labourers were banished to hovels, there to live on starvation wages – for the farmer could not afford both the parlour and the old, generous, communal style of living (226–9). Cobbett, like Coleridge, thinks there has been an 'abdication on the part of the governors'. The changes at the farm are one symptom: harsh game laws are another. He waxes indignant about the two young poachers, hanged at Winchester in 1822, one of them merely for shooting at (not killing) a gamekeeper (427). Further evidence of the greed and indifference of the upper classes is constantly supplied by the country clergy. Instead of living

among their flock and using their revenues to relieve poverty, many
are absentees, consuming the tithes extracted from their parishes
in the wens. Cobbett is ever on the lookout for abandoned and
dilapidated parsonage houses. At the parish of Draycot Foliot there
is neither rectory nor church, and when a new parson is inducted,
a tent is erected where the church ought to be (397). Many parsons
become justices of the peace, oppressing the poor instead of aiding
them.

What has caused the transformation and distress of the countryside? The immediate cause, according to Cobbett, is the paper
money system. In 1797 the government, in response to the financial
difficulties of the nation caused by the cost of the war had gone
off gold; the issue of paper money not convertible for gold had
contributed to price inflation. After the war, the government wished
to return to gold and took steps to reduce the volume of paper
currency. Cobbett believed this was causing the price fall and consequent erosion of rural incomes. Farmers and landlords had gained
from high wartime prices; but the higher these men had risen, the
further they had to fall when depression came along. The paper
money system brought ultimate disaster to them; but others did
nothing but gain. By the 'paper money system' Cobbett meant not
only the issue of banknotes, but also the growth of the banking
system and national debt. The system had fabulously nourished a
new class – bankers, stockbrokers, and stockjobbers who dealt in
government loans, stockholders who lived on interest. The rise of
the national debt during the war had enabled these to make enormous fortunes. The return to gold promised them yet another windfall; for the real value of what was owed them, debt contracted at
the time of a debased paper currency, would increase. The overall
effect of the paper money system, as Cobbett saw it, was massively
to transfer wealth from the old landed ruling classes to the new
financial interests. In all this he discerned a grim historical irony.
The paper money system had grown because of the war. The government, a government of landlords, had undertaken the war to
destroy freedom in France and prevent it spreading to England. The
war was part of the attempt of the governors to resist reform that
might threaten their wealth and privilege. Yet in the end the war
had destroyed them:

   The DEBT, the blessed debt, that best ally of the people, will break

them all; will snap them, as the hornet does the cobweb . . . the debt
was made to raise and keep armies on foot to prevent *reform of
parliament*, because, as it was feared by the Aristocracy, reform
would have humbled them; and this debt, created for this purpose,
is fast sweeping the Aristocracy out of their estates, as a clown, with
his foot, kicks fieldmice out of their nests. (242)

Tracing the chain of causes further back, Cobbett finds the origin
of the ills of his time in the attempts of a corrupt aristocracy to
maintain 'Old Corruption'. *Rural Rides* is a running commentary
upon the corrupt gains made by members of the ruling classes out
of the public purse and public property:

If you look through the old list of pensioners, sinecurists, parsons,
and the like, you will find the same names everlastingly recurring.
They seem to be a sort of creatures that have an *inheritance in the
public carcase*, like the magots that some people have in their skins.
This family of DAMPIER seems to be one of those. What, in God's
name, should have made one of these a Bishop and the other a Judge!
I never heard of the smallest particle of talent that either of them
possessed. This Rector of Wyly was another of them. There was no
harm in them that I know of, beyond that of living upon the public;
but, where were their merits? They had none, to distinguish them,
and to entitle them to the great sums they received; and, under any
other system than such a system as this, they would, in all human
probability, have been gentlemen's servants or little shopkeepers.
(327)

The war greatly increased the number of those who drew from the
public purse. The 'taxeaters' included not only the financiers, who
received the interest on the public debt (almost two-thirds of public
expenditure was taken up servicing it).[2] The army and navy had
been much augmented by the war, and a large postwar army was
maintained to keep a discontented populace down. Cobbett is full
of indignation over the 'Dead Weight' – the retirement pay of pen-
sioned-off military personnel. Upon the death of the man, the pension continues to be enjoyed by his widow and children. There is
nothing to stop a dying pensioner from marrying a young girl,
conferring upon her a pension for life. Just think of all the pretty
young girls on the look-out for old soldiers! How can Malthus, the
'check-population parson', rail against the overbreeding poor when
the state is maintaining by its pensions two hundred thousand
breeding pairs (161)?

How far back do Old Corruption and the 'paper-money and

funding system' go? The Glorious Revolution of 1688 marked an
epoch: 'this system of Dutch descent, begotten by Bishop Burnet
and born in hell' (153), but Cobbett traces the system further back
than this. The greatest spoliation of public property was by Henry
VIII, who seized monastic land intended for the upkeep of the poor
and gave it to his favourites. As he passes Netley Abbey, Cobbett
remarks:

> The possessions of these monks were by the wife-killing founder of
> the Church of England, *given away* (though they belonged to the
> public) to one of his court sycophants, SIR WILLIAM PAULET, a
> man the most famous in the world for sycophancy, time-serving, and
> for all those qualities which usually distinguish the favourites of
> kings like the wife-killer. (473)

From this original spoliation all the rest followed: the Reformation
was necessary to justify the dissolution of the monasteries; the Glorious Revolution was necessary to defend the Reformation; the national debt, the paper money system, was required to maintain the
Glorious Revolution.

The remedies proposed follow naturally from the diagnosis. Interest on the public debt ought to be reduced. If there is to be a
return to gold (and Cobbett detests paper money) interest reduction
is equitable, in order to compensate debtors for the increased value
of their debts. Public property should be applied to public purposes;
church and crown lands should be used for the relief of the poor,
thereby reducing the burden of the poor rates. Taxes should be
reduced by cutting salaries, pensions and the armed forces. Since
the clergy do not use their incomes as they should to aid the needy,
tithes should be reduced. To make these changes possible, Parliament must be reformed and power wrested from the hands of those
who benefit from corruption. Cobbett thought that the crisis of the
old system made all these changes inevitable and imminent. He had
no time for those who proposed to deal with the disaffected poor
by educating them or making them religious:

> I will allow nothing to be good, with regard to the labouring classes,
> unless it make an addition to their victuals, drink or clothing. As to
> their *minds*, that is much too sublime a matter for me to think about.
> I know that they are in rags, and that they have not a belly-full; and
> I know that the way to make them good, to make them honest, to
> make them dutiful, to make them kind to one another, is to enable
> them to live well; and I also know, that none of these things will

ever be accomplished by Methodist sermons, and by those stupid, at once stupid and malignant things, and roguish things, called Religious Tracts. (137) The upper classes favour education and religion as a way of keeping the poor quiet, indoctrinating them into submission (75). To ascribe the growth of crime to the want of education rather than to the want of food and clothing is comforting to the privileged, who do not wish to relinquish their privileges, but it is to ascribe the misery to the wrong causes (262): 'Education! Despicable cant and nonsense! What education, what moral precepts, can quiet the gnawings and ragings of hunger!' (266).

How accurate was Cobbett's perception and diagnosis of his England and its ills? Any judgments on this have to be tentative: if there is disagreement about our own economic problems today, we can hardly expect to be in a position to give final answers concerning Britain after the Napoleonic Wars. Furthermore, Cobbett's writings are so powerful and familiar that they have coloured the perceptions of subsequent historians right up to the present. It seems likely that the proliferation of paper money contributed to the price rise during the war, and that the attempts to return to gold aggravated the price fall after it. But the price fluctuations were not entirely, or even chiefly, caused by monetary changes. The fact that in 1814 and 1815 the value of gold and silver currency had fallen almost to parity with the value of paper notes argues that government war financing was not uniformly inflationary in its effects. High food prices in the later war years and low postwar prices were caused mainly by poor harvests in the former period and good ones in the latter. Cobbet was correct about the heavy financial burdens of the war, which may have put a brake on economic growth. But it is debatable whether the agricultural depression of the early 1820s was as severe as he (and the farming interest) made out.[3] It is also debatable whether the war and its aftermath caused a catastrophic change in the social composition of the countryside. Cobbett saw farmers going bankrupt and old landed families being replaced by interlopers; but this was always happening in the countryside, and the effect of the war may simply have been to speed up the usual patterns. Certainly recession in agriculture wiped out many small farmers, with the result that small farms were amalgamated into larger ones; but once again this was merely a speeding up of trends discernible throughout the eighteenth century. Aggressive capitalist farming, which enclosed wastes and commons, depriving poor cottagers of an alternative resource, was by no means new. It is significant that *Rural Rides* has little to say about enclosures; the southern countryside around which Cobbett travelled had had its enclosures long ago. The market economy had replaced the subsistence economy long before Cobbett's time.

Cobbett was wrong about population, but not completely off-beam. The population of England may have been as high in 1300 as it was in 1750; if so, the *rural* population was probably higher at the earlier date than at the later. But churches were built large for reasons other than the size of the population. The English countryside of 1300 was *not* prosperous; population was pressing hard upon food resources. And by the 1820s, the population of England was twice what it had been in 1750.[4] There can be little doubt that the poverty of southern villages in Cobbett's day was mainly caused by rural overpopulation, and that diminution of taxes would not by itself have solved the problem. But in other ways Cobbett was right and Malthus wrong. Modern research suggests that relieving the sufferings of the poor did *not* generate a population explosion.[5] But such relief would only have been a palliative. The real solution to the problem of poverty was to lie with economic growth – growth of a market economy and industry, which Cobbett so much detested. Cobbett insisted that reform was inevitable, and the course of events confirmed his prediction. Parliament and the Church of England were both reformed in the 1830s, Old Corruption was cut back, and the economic troubles described by Cobbett played a major part in bringing on these changes. But the changes were not as sweeping as he wanted or predicted – perhaps because the plight of farmers and landlords was not as desperate as he claimed. The teeth of Old Corruption were filed, not extracted, and the New Poor Law of 1834 brought in a harsher regime for many of the old, sick, and unemployed.

It is tempting to argue that Cobbett is a different kind of social critic from Ogilvie, Godwin, Coleridge, or Thompson: that whereas they were formed by current ideas and theories, his social criticism is simply a response to what he sees. Accordingly, to understand Cobbett as a commentator on his times, there is no need to investigate 'mental furniture'; it is simply a matter of relating his opinions to his experience. In corroboration of this thesis, we might draw attention to his brusque dismissal of several of the leading intellectual tendencies of his time. He detests 'Scotch political economy' (362). He does not subscribe to the associationist theory of human nature; with a countryman's experience of animal breeding behind him, he believes that differences have a genetic foundation:

> What would be said of the 'squire who should take a fox-hound out to find partridges for him to shoot at? Yet, would this be *more* absurd than to set a man to law-making, who was manifestly formed for the express purpose of sweeping the streets or digging out sewers? (248)

More generally, he dislikes enlightenment rationalism and science. These qualities are epitomized for him in Unitarians: 'I hate to hear the conceited and disgusting prigs, seeming to take it for granted, that they only are wise, because others *believe* in the incarnation without being able to reconcile it to reason' (236). And he goes on to put seven questions to Unitarians, aiming to show that there are mysteries that human wisdom cannot fathom:

> 3. *Whence* come fish in new made places where no fish have ever been put?
> 4. *What causes* horse-hair to become living things?
> 5. *What causes* frogs to come in drops of rain, or those drops of rain to turn to frogs, the moment they are on the earth? (236)

As he passes Penyard hill, he observes clouds forming on its sides and floating into the air, just as if the hill were puffing a pipe; he remarks that he must 'have a conversation with some old shepherd about this matter: if he cannot enlighten me upon the subject, I am sure no philosopher can' (485). All of these things speak a deep anti-intellectualism, a rooted hostility to professional men of science. Practical experience is what farmer Cobbett values. Of a piece with this is his contempt for educators, moral reformers, and evangelicals.

Indeed, 'farmer' Cobbett tells us a good deal; his can be read as a farmer's outlook. This viewpoint is everywhere in evidence; take, for example, his attitude to landscape. The Cotswold hills, bare, rolling, with their dry stone walls, have no beauty for him; he observes the shallow stony soil and judges it an ugly country, 'having less to please the eye than any other that I have ever seen, always save and except the *heaths* like those of Bagshot and Hindhead'

(404). But as he descends from the wolds, he *does* like the sheltered valleys, with their meadows. The landscape he loves best has

> smooth and verdant down in hills and valleys of endless variety as
> to height and depth and shape; rich corn land, unencumbered by
> fences; meadows in due proportion, and those watered at pleasure;
> and lastly, the homesteads, and villages, sheltered in winter and
> shaded in summer by lofty and beautiful trees; to which may be
> added, roads never dirty and a stream never dry. (411)

This is the perception of a man who proposes to *use* a landscape for crops and animals. Farmer Cobbett's deepest conviction is that they only are truly useful who grow food. He cannot tolerate the pretensions of other social groups who think themselves wiser, or more deserving, than farmers and peasants. Hence his detestation of parasitic middlemen and contempt for the professional intelligentsia of clergymen and 'feelosofers'. Hence his hatred of factory owners and government employees. When he addresses the farmers of Winchester, his own title for his speech is 'RUSTIC HARANGUE'. This title expresses his pride in being of the earth, earthy; and he boils over with rage when he beholds farmers pretending to be other than they are. In a well-known passage he describes his 'education', which consisted of the rough sport of rolling, with his brothers, down a sand-hill:

> This was the spot where I was receiving my *education*; and this was
> the sort of education; and I am perfectly satisfied that if I had not
> received such an education, or something very much like it; that, if
> I had been brought up a milksop, with a nursery-maid everlastingly
> at my heels; I should have been at this day as great a fool, as in-
> efficient a mortal, as any of those frivolous idiots that are turned
> out from Winchester and Westminster School, or from any of those
> dens of dunces called Colleges and Universities. (41)

What map of society is stated or implied in *Rural Rides*? Outside the landed classes there are manufacturers and their labourers. The book has little to say about these, beyond that work in factories is hideous by contrast with rural work and that factories have robbed rural people of their cottage industries. Cobbett's drift appears to be that the manufacturing classes are unnecessary and pernicious; his ideal is of rural self-sufficiency and independence. Instead of elaborate specialization and division of labour, he prefers a society of farming Robinson Crusoes, who meet at fairs and markets to exchange surpluses, but for whom such trading is peripheral. Then

there are traders, the middlemen of a market economy; there are
too many of these, and in a well-balanced society they would be
few. He would pass the same judgment on government employees,
including the armed forces; these are parasites and should be reduced. Financial speculators should be abolished entirely. Clergymen have a function, a welfare function; their job is to guide and
comfort the poor, a job they largely neglect. The landed classes are
the main part of the social edifice, and they divide into three: at
the top, landlords, rentiers who do not farm; at the bottom, landless
labourers, and cottagers perhaps having small plots of land but not
hirers of the labour of others; in the middle, the sector with which
Cobbett identifies and for which he speaks – the farmers, who
superintend and conduct the business of cultivation, hiring agricultural labour. They may rent their land from landlords, or they
may own it, as Cobbett owned his farm at Botley. Cobbett is passionately concerned for the welfare of the bottom section, the rural
labourers; this concern is the most memorable feature of *Rural
Rides*. But still he is a farmer, and no social egalitarian. Throughout
the book, compassion is counterpointed by condescension; Cobbett
cannot but regard rural labourers as inferiors. 'Amongst the labouring people, the first thing you have to look after is, *common
honesty, speaking the truth* and *refraining from thieving*' (45): this
is an employer's view of labour. His opponent Birkbeck fell on hard
times in America; his daughters married '*two common labourers*',
and thereby fell into 'ruin and misery' (301). He sympathizes with
bankrupt farmers, who had brought up their children in the belief
that they were '*not* to be mere *working people*' (424). The rural
hierarchy is accepted; this acceptance is extended to the landlords,
provided that they are kind and charitable, giving good wages, not
rack-renters:

> I know there are some ill-natured persons who will say, that I want
> a revolution that would turn Mr. Drummond out of his place and
> put me into it. Such persons will hardly believe me, but upon my
> word I do not. From every thing that I hear, Mr. Drummond is very
> worthy of possessing it himself, seeing that he is famed for his justice
> and his kindness *towards the labouring classes*. (100)

But when he sees bad landlords, Cobbett explodes:

> There is in the men calling themselves "English country gentlemen"
> something superlatively base. They are, I *sincerely believe*, the most
> cruel, the most unfeeling, the most brutally insolent: but I *know*, I

can *prove*, I can *safely take my oath*, that they are the MOST BASE of all the creatures that God ever suffered to disgrace the human shape. (310)

This goes hand in hand with his dislike of the airs and graces of ladies and gentlemen, parlours, bell-pulls, fancy educations, and social segregation in box pews in churches (186). He insists that the leaders of any reform will be, not the noblemen and gentlemen, but the middle ranks (55).

Apparently, then, there is considerable merit in what Marxists would call a 'materialist' explanation of Cobbett's social thought – in terms of his social and economic environment and his own social position. But the antithesis of 'materialism' and 'idealism' is crude (dare one say, undialectical) and ultimately unacceptable. For Cobbett's social vision is shaped by his experience; and experience is at once *received* and *constructed* by the mind. It is determined from two directions; by the external world, and also by the intelectual tools used to grasp and interpret that world. A close examination of *Rural Rides* bears this out. Cobbett does not just tell it *as it is*, but rather *as he sees it*; and his way of seeing is informed by the mental equipment of his culture.

This can be illustrated by his account of what constitutes the right kind of human relationships. In the technical language of sociology, Cobbett is for Gemeinschaft and against Gesellschaft. That is to say, he favours organic, caring communities and distrusts self-seeking, contractual relationships. *Rural Rides* is a nostalgic book, projecting an image of a happy community life of the past, now lost. But what is the location of the lost community? When and where was it? Is it something Cobbett has known – does his thought merely reflect his environment – or is he constructing a potent myth, selecting, shaping, heightening aspects of that environment? Significantly, the location of his idealized past is not clear. Sometimes it appears to be his boyhood: *Rural Rides* contains warm references to the scenes and events of his upbringing. But we cannot regard this as simply a matter of accurate social observation and commentary. The revolutionary and Napoleonic wars brought great changes, but they did not transform England from a Gemeinschaft into a Gesellschaft. Is the lost community to be found, then, not in general English society of the late eighteenth century, but rather in the close domestic circle – the loving family in which Cobbett was

raised? Is the contrast not between an organic society of the past
and a capitalist society of the present, but between the family and
the uncaring, impersonal wider world? This may be; but there remains a suspicion that Cobbett has idealized his childhood.[6] It was
a happy childhood, he tells us, but twice he ran away from home,
the second time for good. Throughout *Rural Rides* hearth and home
are romanticized. When Cobbett recounts how he sat by the fire
with a bankrupt farmer, he mentions that the unhappy man had
his youngest child upon his knee. He also tells us that 'of course'
the days of his courtship were the happiest days of his life (371).
There is no need to doubt the sincerity of these attitudes to family
life, nor need we claim that the companionate marriage was new;
but to describe and conceive family life in this way, to accord it
such importance, was certainly in keeping with the literary con-
ventions of the time. The compassionate response to the sufferings
of the poor, so much in evidence throughout the book, is typical
of much eighteenth-century literature. One of the most attractive
episodes describes how Cobbett set out one morning with his
youngest son, without breakfast. Hunger made him bad-tempered,
he snapped at the boy, recollected himself, and felt sorry. They
stopped at a cottage, bought bread and cheese, and soon felt better.
This led Cobbett to reflect on the plight of the poor labourer, his
wife, and children. How do *they* cope with *constant* hunger (260)?
Cobbett had read the literature of benevolence; he liked Thomson,
Cowper, and Fielding. He had Goldsmith's *The Traveller* off by
heart.[7] In these authors he could find also the contrast between the
calm, contented life of the country and the hectic, artificial rat-race
of the town.

The benevolism of *Rural Rides* is so much in tune with the literature of the age that it is easy to ignore it, to forget that it is a
culturally specific mode of expression. The medievalism of the book
and especially the admiration for medieval monasticism more readily attracts attention because here Cobbett was more of a pioneer.
The lost community is located, not only in Cobbett's childhood,
the country, and the family, but also in the Middle Ages in general
and the monasteries in particular. He tells us that as they left Winchester Cathedral, his son Richard said to him:

> "Why, Papa, nobody can build such places *now*, can they?" "No,
> my dear," said I. "That building was made when there were no poor

wretches in England, called *paupers*; when there were no *poor-rates*;
when every labouring man was clothed in good wollen cloth; and
when all had plenty of meat and bread and beer." (254)
The sight of Salisbury Cathedral made him feel he lived in degen-
erate times (324). His ride past Beaulieu Abbey inspired reflections
on the goodness of the monks:

> They did spend it all upon the spot; they kept all the poor; Bewley,
> and all round about Bewley, saw no misery, and had never heard
> the damned name of pauper pronounced, as long as those monks
> and templars continued! . . . The monks and the knights were the
> *lords* of their manors; but the farmers under them were not rack-
> renters; the farmers under them held by lease of lives, continued in
> the same farms from father to son for hundreds of years; they were
> real yeomen, and not miserable rack-renters, such as now till the
> lands of this once happy country, and who are little better than the
> drivers of the labourers for the profit of the landlords. (458–9)

Cobbett has anticipated what Pugin was to write in the 1830s, and
Carlyle in the 1840s. There is even a passage that startlingly calls
to mind Pugin's *Contrasts*; Cobbett compares the handsome medieval market cross at Malmesbury with the inferior modern equivalent at Devizes.

What are the sources of Cobbett's construction of the Middle
Ages as a period when society was organic and happy? In Chapter
3, I attempted to trace the growth of medievalism. We have already
seen Coleridge, in a discussion of the highland clearances, contrasting feudal solidarity with the harshness of the spirit of trade.
By the time Cobbett began his *Rural Rides* the poems and novels
of Scott were available. But what can we say with certainty of
Cobbett's specific sources? From 1824 to 1826 he published his
History of the Protestant Reformation, a best-selling work that was
revisionist, in that it painted a more favourable picture of medieval
Catholicism, and a harsher one of Henry VIII's Reformation, than
most Protestant clergymen could find palatable. Cobbett drew heavily on the recent work of the Catholic historian John Lingard. But
Cobbett's conception of the Middle Ages is not drawn solely from
secondary sources. Twice in *Rural Rides* he refers to the fifteenth-
century writer Sir John Fortescue, who describes the English labourers of his day as 'clothed in good woollens throughout' and
having 'plenty of flesh of all sorts to eat' (280). Fortescue was writing after the Black Death, when population levels had fallen dra-

matically. Good land was therefore plentiful in proportion to population, labour was in short supply, and wages were high. The southern labourers of Fortescue's day were more prosperous than their descendants were to be in the early nineteenth century.

Cobbett's overall perspective of historical change is therefore declensionist. He scorns those who, pointing to the new building going on in and around the 'wens', see it as an index of progress. *Rural Rides*, however, does not date the decline from the Norman Conquest. There are occasional echoes of 'the Norman yoke' theme, but these are cancelled and overwhelmed by the high esteem accorded to the whole of the Middle Ages. The declensionism is more concordant with the neo-Harringtonian paradigm; certainly Cobbett's political thought is not alien to that tradition. Decline is conceived in terms of corruption; antipublic interests grow fat and destroy the well-being of society. Independence is idealized – but in *Rural Rides* it is the independence of the yeoman, and even of the cottager, who enjoys a fair measure of self-sufficiency by virtue of domestic industry and allotments of land. *Rural Rides* expresses the belief that Englishmen had liberties in the past (337), which are now being invaded by greedy, corrupt, and oppressive governments. The game laws are part of the attack on English liberties (170); so are the activities of excisemen (286).

> But, mark the consequence; *gaols ten times as big as formerly*; houses of *correction*; *treadmills*; the *hulks*; and the country filled with *spies* of one sort and another, *game-spies*, or other spies, and if a hare or pheasant come to an untimely death, *police-officers* from the WEN are not unfrequently called down to find out and secure the bloody offender! *Mark this*, Englishmen! Mark how we take to those things, which we formerly ridiculed in the French; and take them up too just as that brave and spirited people have shaken them off! (183)

Standard political conceptions of the age lead Cobbett to standard remedies. Political action is required to tame Old Corruption; but it is political action of a particular kind. What is proposed has a once-for-all quality; corruption must be eradicated, government cut back, the health and balance of the body politic restored. *Political* activity is important, to set things right; but subsequent *government* action is not envisaged. The political action he wants is like the activity of a surgeon. Once the cancerous growth has been cut out, the task of the surgeon is over. The subsequent health of the patient is to be left to nature. Nature, in *Rural Rides* as in other texts I have discussed, is an ultimate court of appeal, and here too it has antipolitical implications. Nature is the work of a beneficent providence, all too often disrupted by human contrivance:

> This valley, which seems to have been created by a bountiful providence, as one of the choicest retreats of man; which seems formed for a scene of innocence and happiness, has been, by ungrateful man, so perverted as to make it instrumental in effecting two of the most damnable purposes; in carrying into execution two of the most damnable inventions that ever sprang from the minds of man under the influence of the devil! namely, the making of *gunpowder* and of *bank-notes*! (97)

Rural Rides does not rely upon technical moral theory for its critique, but it is nevertheless a deeply moral book. In keeping with its benevolism, the main moral thrust is the simple and perennial idea that pain and privation – the lot of all too many rural labourers – are bad, and morally evil because they are produced by the greed and hard-heartedness of the middle and upper classes. Apart from this, Cobbett draws upon the language and assumptions of natural rights. The explicit reference comes in the context of a discussion of the game laws, and Cobbett appeals to the authority of Blackstone. All have a natural right, granted by the creator, to catch and use wild animals. Evidently this is grounded in a right of recipience, the right to subsistence, which in turn is grounded in the right to life (431–3). The same idea is sometimes presented without any use of the word 'right'. At Tutbury, Cobbett met a posse in pursuit of a man who had stolen cabbages. He reminded them that the Bible teaches that a hungry man may rightly take food from his neighbour's vineyard (373). The thought underlying this is that every human life is valuable, more valuable than the artificial institutions of property and status. The roots of this idea in Christian culture are indicated when Cobbett praises the medieval church for being free of box pews: 'In short, the floor was the place for the *worshippers* to *stand* or to *kneel*; and there was *no distinction*; no *high* place and no *low* place; all were upon a level *before God* at any rate' (186). *Rural Rides* also invokes a desert-based conception of justice, giving it a biblical foundation: 'We are reversing the maxim of the Scripture; our laws almost say, that those that work shall not eat, and that those who do not work shall have the food' (337; see also 305).

So Cobbett's social critique cannot be understood merely as a response to events. It is informed by the intellectual equipment of the time; moral ideas, forms of sentiment, commonplace political notions, a particular conception of the past, the themes of nature, artifice, and corruption. The form of *Rural Rides* and its method of argument are also important. As he travels down the valley of the Avon, Cobbett makes a careful calculation of wheat, barley, bacon, and mutton produced in the parish of Milton. He then calculates how much the average family requires for a healthy and contented existence, and thus arrives at an estimate of the population that could be supported in comfort. To the modern reader, this is rather quaint, typically Cobbettite, but not otherwise remarkable. It *should* be remarked, however, for the ability and inclination to perform this kind of calculation, the capacity to discuss society with the aid of mathematics, has not always been available. No doubt this kind of thinking has socioeconomic as well as intellectual sources. Cobbett's calculations, of which he is so fond, are essentially balance sheets, accounts of income and expenditure such as a farmer or other businessman might produce. Accounting of this kind was almost unknown in the Middle Ages; the application of such techniques to society as a whole began in the late seventeenth century. Cobbett detests the social statisticians of his day – revealingly, he refers to Colquhoun as COLQUHOUND (368) – but his dislike should not conceal the fact that he is using their methods, often most effectively. *Rural Rides* embodies a conception of what constitutes a good argument. A good argument is backed up with plenty of facts, preferably with figures also. The whole book is an exercise in the gathering of information, similar to and perhaps patterned upon Arthur Young's travels in France and Britain. As a social survey, it lacks rigour by twentieth-century standards, but at least it is an attempt at a social survey, and as such part of the growing ambition to study society scientifically. Cobbett is an inveterate opponent of the leading social scientists of his day, the political economists, and he makes little use of their theories and concepts; but he is engaged in a debate with them, and is addressing their problems. Two of the liveliest and most urgent debates of contemporary economics were population and the bullionist controversy; *Rural Rides* has a great deal to say on both. The reader is continually impressed with how effective a debater and how well informed Cobbett is. He can quote commission reports and acts of

Parliament. He has at his fingertips information about pensions and grants of land to government supporters. He knows the histories of landed and mercantile families, and he can remember statements in Parliament. He can compare the amounts of public money spent on poor rates, the dead-weight, the national debt. Cobbett was not an MP when he wrote *Rural Rides*, and he did not get into Parliament until the end of his career; but in a sense he is already participating in parliamentary debates. *Rural Rides* is part of a growth in communications, which in turn had made social criticism of this kind possible. The growth of the press, the diffusion throughout the nation of information about the doings of Parliament, had extended the debate beyond the walls of Westminster. Cobbett is merely the most famous of those who, outside Parliament, outside the charmed circle of the governing classes and the ranks of privilege, can now discuss national issues in an informed way.

Cobbett's social criticism is intense and passionate; no one is more vehement than he. How did he come to be so distanced from his society? Cobbett the man is so rough-edged, so perennially ready to take up the cudgels against any established wisdom, that one wonders whether a psychological explanation might be appropriate; but this study has not concerned itself with such modes of understanding, where the proof of an interpretation is so tricky. *Rural Rides* responds to crisis in the countryside; it does so from the point of view of a farmer, and through the medium of the intellectual resources of the time.

What is the quality of Cobbett's social critique? The warm humanity of it is moving, the firm rejection of cant and pretension commands admiration. Cobbett was the scourge that Old Corruption so richly deserved. In one respect, his hatred of 'enlightenment' was a strength. There is no hint in *Rural Rides* of that epistemological overoptimism to be found in Godwin, Owen, or Thompson. Cobbett does not think that truth is a recent acquisition of a scientific age, that it is destined to triumph, bringing in its train harmony and happiness. Arrogant, corrupt, selfish men cannot be brought to reason and goodness; they can only be destroyed, swept away by the economic whirlwind they have themselves sown. The forces of evil must be defeated – not by books and ideas, but in the political arena. *Rural Rides* has great strengths, but weaknesses also. Cobbett is disabled by his nostalgic stance. Defenders of progress, and of the market economy he detests, could argue with reason that poverty would only be cured by the growth of industry and commerce. It could be argued that *Rural Rides* is not radical enough, that it plays about the periphery and does not touch the core of social ills. Cobbett accepts social inequality. He sees nothing intrinsically wrong with the relationships of employer to employee, landlord to farmer to labourer, factory owner to factory operative. These relationships (at least the rural ones) are seen by him as *natural*, potentially organic and happy; they are essentially right, but have accidentally gone wrong, because of corruption, high taxation, the growth of middlemen and financiers. Society is a body that has fallen ill; the task is simply to restore it to health. *Rural Rides* is a critique of taxes, of the market economy, and of usury; but it is not a critique of capitalism or of exploitation. It has no strategy for the radical transformation of society, because it sees no need for such a transformation.

14

Conclusion

Looking back over the ten books studied in the previous chapters, we can now sketch in a pattern of change and development. At the beginning, Spence and Ogilvie stand apart, not only because of their agrarian emphasis, but also because their social criticism is rooted in the language of natural rights, a language that has no great importance in any of the later texts. The thinkers who come next, Godwin, Hall, and Coleridge, are in different ways the most seminal. Godwin takes eighteenth-century associationism to the most egalitarian and optimistic conclusions. He offers the prospect of a glorious social future, achieved by a transformation and perfection of human character. The new moral worlds of Owen and Thompson flow from here. Hall's text is a watershed. It is the first of them significantly to borrow from and debate with classical economy; all of those that follow continue this debate. Coleridge's originality lies, in John Stuart Mill's well-known words, in his contribution 'towards the philosophy of human culture'. His cultural critique of commercial society has affinities with that of Cobbett; both stand at the beginning of a tradition that embraces Carlyle, Ruskin, Morris, Tawney, Eliot, and Leavis. A developing critique of exploitation is to be found in the texts, especially those of Spence, Ogilvie, Godwin, Hall, Ravenstone, Thompson, and Hodgskin. It begins as an offshoot of 'the Norman yoke' myth; conquerors monopolize the land and force the dispossessed to labour on highly unfavourable terms. This way of thinking survives right through to Hodgskin; but alongside it other ideas emerge, as the texts begin to grapple with the specifics of *capitalist* exploitation. This development can justly be regarded as leading on to Marx.[1] Both Marx and Engels, in coming to terms with political economy, read and drew upon this critique of it also. The writings of Hall, Ravenstone, and Hodg-skin are not utterly alien in approach and method to Marx's economic 'science'. They are moral critiques, which Marx's mature works claim not to be; but they are also 'scientific' in his sense, engaged about the business of analysing and reformulating the concepts and theories of the economists. Unlike Marx, they do not take as their point of departure Ricardo's labour theory of value; but they anticipate Marx in working towards an exposure of the illusions of capital.

To read the texts in this way, as leading towards what came after, is important but dangerous; dangerous because it runs the risk of ignoring how they differed from later developments. For, from another point of view, these early critics of capitalism are worlds apart from Marxian socialism. In the terms of their own day, only Owen and Thompson would have counted as socialists, and in their socialism opposition to individualism was more important than the critique of capital. Under no definition of the word can Ravenstone and Hodgskin be labelled socialist. If we ask what was the *object* of criticism, only in the case of Hodgskin's pamphlet can we say that it was *capital* exclusively. Hall, Owen, Ravenstone, and Thompson are equally critics of *commercial society*; of production for sale rather than for the satisfaction of needs, of the direct pursuit of self-interest rather than of the common good. This unites them with Coleridge and Cobbett. Another important object of attack is aristocratic wealth and luxury. Sometimes, as in Ogilvie, Ravenstone, Coleridge, and Cobbett, this does not take the form of a rejection of aristocracy, but instead calls upon the wealthy to recognize their responsibilities and restrain their greed. Others go further; Godwin repudiates an aristocratic status system entirely, and Hall can find nothing to redeem inequality and luxury. None of the books anticipates 'state socialism', whether of the Marxist or revisionist kind. In the most radical texts, existing systems of ownership are to be replaced by more equal individual property, or by a decentralized system of communities.

Government and politics, in fact, do not on the whole loom large in these books. Ogilvie's land plan is to be introduced by legislation, and Hall's ideal is a system of equality brought in in the same way. Owen proposes that communities be set up by the state. But what is involved here is a once-and-for-all act of government intervention; there are no anticipations of the bureaucratic state, as in Bentham's *Constitutional Code*. Spence, Ravenstone, Thompson, and Cobbett are opposed to 'big government'; Godwin is an anarchist. Suspicion of government is supported, in some of the texts, by a belief in a benign providence or natural order. The evils under which humanity suffers are perceived as the result of artifice, bad contrivance; they are not part of nature's plan. This is most in evidence in Thompson and Hodgskin. Godwin is undoubtedly a source of Hodgskin's anarchistic tendencies but not of the concept of a natural order. 'Nature' is not an important concept in *Political Justice*; nature is to be overcome by rational control rather than followed. The appeal to nature is general in eighteenth-century thought; specifically, Thompson and Hodgskin probably draw on Adam Smith. According to modern scholarship, this is to misread Smith, who stresses the artificial, legal framework and government intervention more than was once thought; but it is a wholly understandable misreading. There are plenty of passages in the *Wealth of Nations* that, taken in isolation, suggest a natural order; and the text that most forcefully provokes an alternative reading, the *Lectures on Jurisprudence*, was unpublished until this century.

If government is suspected in these texts, politics is often ignored. Politics at best is a necessary evil, a disagreeable means to the achievement of ends established independently of political activity. At worst, it is an evil that might, under ideal conditions, be dispensed with. There is no sense of it as a necessary activity if rival interests and opinions are to settle their differences without bloodshed or brutal coercion; no sense of it as an activity valuable in itself, or as the arena in which ends are evolved and explored. One reason why the desirability of politics is not felt is because most of the texts exhibit epistemological optimism to a high degree – a faith in truth and its victory, ushering in social harmony. Such postenlightenment optimism is not to be found in Coleridge, Ravenstone, or Cobbett; but they conceive of social ills in terms of sin and corruption. What needs to be done is clear; the balance and health of the body politic must be restored. Another piece of mental furniture that constrains and limits conceptions of politics is the habit of thinking in terms of private interest versus the public good – as if the public good were single and unproblematic. Government and politics are inadequately treated in these texts, and this is a major reason why the social ideals they propose so often have an implausible or unattainable air about them. At bᴗᴛᴛom the neglect of politics rests upon metaphysical assumptions. Somewhere – in the past, or the future, or here and now but hidden by the sinfulness of wicked men – lies a harmonious and meaningful order. None of the texts is 'existentialist', informed by a sense of chaos, meaninglessness, tragedy, and irrationality at the heart of things.[2] For all of them, in a sense, God is not dead. They were luckier than we are.

These books are, to a greater or lesser degree, 'original'. The analysis presented here has sought to show that originality became possible where different discourses – moral, religious, historical, political, and so on – met or intersected. For example, *Political Justice* emerges from a fusion of enlightenment and dissent. Hall and Coleridge respond to political economy from the standpoint of literary sentimentalism. Ravenstone finds the arguments of the economists incompatible with religion and with an ideal of a balanced polity derived from the civic tradition. In this period, the cause of private property gains reinforcements from the new science of political economy, but is challenged by older traditions; natural rights, the civic tradition (which influences most of the texts, directly or indirectly, up to and including Cobbett), Christianity. In the late eighteenth century, we find a variety of 'paradigms', 'conceptual frameworks', 'discourses', 'traditions', of varying antiquity, living on side by side, jostling, colliding, interacting; out of this babel of discordant voices, new and radical departures emerge. To read the history of ideas in this way is to follow a different path from those who, like Foucault, have looked for archaeological faults on the map of knowledge, where one great governing 'episteme' gives way to another. It is also to dissent from those 'poststructuralists' who suppress the author, proposing that we think of texts being written, through the author, by the prevailing discourse. If there *is* no prevailing discourse, emphasis is thrown back upon the author, who works creatively with multifarious materials.

Original thought is aided in this period by the fact, which others have noticed,[3] that knowledge is relatively unspecialized. Divergent discourses can clash, because they are not kept apart by rigid discipline boundaries. Moral and factual, 'is' and 'ought' questions, are not strictly segregated, as an influential twentieth-century phil-

osophical fashion has insisted they should be.[4] Nor is religion mar-
ginalized as it is today, kept as a Sunday affair apart from the
concerns of real life. The modern disciplines of history, politics,
economics, sociology, psychology, and philosophy were not yet, or
were only just beginning to be, demarcated. Hence a thinker like
Coleridge could range across them. To us, as a result, the texts
often seem amateurish; but would their radicalism and their challenge have been possible at all, had their authors been confined to
narrow segments of the circle of knowledge?

Notes

Chapter 1. Introduction

1. Information about editions of Spence's lecture is contained in T. M. Parsinnen, 'Thomas Spence and the Origins of English Land Nationalization', *Journal of the History of Ideas*, 34 (1973):135–41. *The Political Works of Thomas Spence*, ed. H. T. Dickinson, Newcastle upon Tyne 1982, collects all Spence's extant political works and has a useful introduction. There is a biography, O. Rudkin, *Thomas Spence and His Connections*, London 1927. The article by T. R. Knox, 'Thomas Spence: The Trumpet of Jubilee', *Past and Present*, 76 (1977):75–98, is to be recommended. Spence, Ogilvie, Hall, Thompson, and Hodgskin are discussed in M. Beer, *A History of British Socialism*, London 1921; see also G. D. H. Cole, *A History of Socialist Thought*, vol. 1, *The Forerunners, 1789–1850*, London 1953. A. Gray's *The Socialist Tradition: Moses to Lenin*, London 1946, includes early British socialists in its sharp and witty survey.
2. London 1782. Latest reprint, New York 1970, is of D. C. MacDonald's edition, London 1891.
3. MacDonald's edition, 243, 305.
4. T. C. Smout, *A History of the Scottish People, 1560–1830*, rev. ed., London 1972, 475.
5. London 1798. The best edition is by F. E. L. Priestley, 3 vols., Toronto 1946. This is of the 3d edition, but it provides all the variations in editions 1 and 2. For secondary works, see B. R. Pollin, *Godwin Criticism: A Synoptic Bibliography*, Toronto 1967. D. Locke, *A Fantasy of Reason*, London 1980, is a good life.
6. Godwin would not have described himself as an anarchist; to him the word meant violence and chaos. It is only subsequent to 1798 that the word has also come to mean an orderly society without government; but this is Godwin's ideal, and so we are entitled to apply the word to him in its modern sense.
7. London 1805; recent photographic reprint, Fairfield, N.J. There is an important article by J. R. Dinwiddy, 'Charles Hall, Early English Socialist', *International Review of Social History*, 21 (1976):256–76.

8. London 1817. Standard edition in *The Collected Works of Samuel Taylor Coleridge*, vol. 6, ed. R. J. White, London 1972. On his social and political theory, see J. A. Colmer, *Coleridge, Critic of Society*, Oxford 1959; and D. P. Calleo, *Coleridge and the Idea of the Modern State*, New Haven 1966. A recent and highly favourable assessment of Coleridge as a thinker is R. Holmes, *Coleridge*, Oxford 1982.
9. Classically by J. S. Mill, 'Coleridge', *London and Westminster Review* (March 1840). Reprinted in *Mill on Bentham and Coleridge*, ed. F. R. Leavis, London 1950.
10. R. Williams, *Culture and Society, 1780–1950*, London 1958.
11. Glasgow 1821. A useful collection of his writings is to be found in R. Owen, *A New View of Society*, ed. G. D. H. Cole, London, 1927. F. Podmore, *Robert Owen: A Biography*, London 1906, is a detailed life. For a recent discussion and bibliography, see K. Taylor, *The Political Ideas of the Utopian Socialists*, London 1982. B. Goodwin, *Social Science and Utopia*, Hassocks 1978, is stimulating.
12. A. E. Bestor, 'The Evolution of the Socialist Vocabulary', *Journal of the History of Ideas*, 9 (1948):259–302.
13. Taylor, *Political Ideas of the Utopian Socialists*, p. 20, makes the same point about Cabet.
14. London 1821.
15. By Piero Sraffa. See his edition of *The Works and Correspondence of David Ricardo*, Cambridge 1951–73, vol. 11, p. xxvii.
16. His contribution to the population debate is discussed in K. Smith, *The Malthusian Controversy*, London 1951.
17. London 1824. Photographic reprint, New York 1963. There is a life: R. K. P. Pankhurst, *William Thompson, 1775–1833, Britain's Pioneer Socialist, Feminist and Co-operator*, London 1954. Thompson and Hodgskin are discussed in E. Lowenthal, *The Ricardian Socialists*, New York 1911.
18. London 1825. Ed. G. D. H. Cole, London 1922; photographic reprint of same, London 1964.
19. Gray, *The Socialist Tradition*, 277.
20. S. & B. Webb, *History of Trade Unionism*, 1896 ed., London, 147.
21. E. Halévy, *Thomas Hodgskin* (English trans., London 1956); J-P. Osier, *Thomas Hodgskin: Une Critique Prolétarienne de l'Economie Politique*, Paris 1976 (a provocative Althusserian interpretation).
22. London 1830. The recent biography by G. Spater, *William Cobbett: The Poor Man's Friend*, 2 vols., Cambridge 1982, has a good bibliography.
23. R. H. Tawney, *The Acquisitive Society*, London 1921.
24. J. Lindsay, *William Morris*, New York 1979, 262.
25. For an explanation and defence of my method, see W. Stafford, 'How Should We Read Utopian Socialist Texts? The Case of the British Pre-Marxians', *Huddersfield Papers in Politics*, 5 (1982).
26. L. Febvre, *Le Problème de l'Incroyance au XVIe Siècle*, Paris 1942.

Chapter 2. General context

1. E. A. Wrigley and R. S. Schofield, *The Population History of England, 1541–1871*, London 1981, Table 7.8.
2. P. Deane, *The First Industrial Revolution*, Cambridge 1965; J. D. Chambers and G. E. Mingay, *The Agricultural Revolution 1750–1880*, London 1966, 111, 115.
3. P. Deane, 'The Industrial Revolution in Great Britain', in *The Emergence of Industrial Societies, Fontana Economic History of Europe*, ed. C. M. Cipolla, vol. 4, pt. 1, London 1973, 161–227. Deane, p. 209, suggests that the coming of the railways ensured that Great Britain continued on the path of industrial growth. Wrigley and Schofield in *Population History*, p. 403, argue 'the historic link between population growth and price rise was broken' by about 1811.
4. Chambers and Mingay, *Agricultural Revolution*, 103, 144; H. Perkin, *The Origins of Modern English Society, 1780–1880*, London 1969, 147.
5. M. Turner, 'Agricultural Productivity in England from the Eighteenth Century: Evidence from Crop Yields', *Economic History Review* (hereafter *EcHR*), 35 (1982):489–510; N. F. R. Crafts, 'British Economic Growth, 1700–1831: A Review of the Evidence', *EcHR*, 36 (1983):177–99; M. Overton, 'Agricultural Productivity in Eighteenth Century England: Some Further Speculations', *EcHR*, 37 (1984):244–51; M. Turner, 'Agricultural Productivity in Eighteenth Century England: Further Strains of Speculation', *EcHR*, 37 (1984):252–7.
6. Chambers and Mingay, *Agricultural Revolution*, 4. The argument of their book is that British agriculture largely succeeded in feeding the growing population in this period; its success was masked by the unusual runs of bad harvests. P. K. O'Brien, 'Agriculture and the Industrial Revolution', *EcHR*, 30 (1977):175, is more critical of the response of agriculture to increased demands.
7. Chambers and Mingay, *Agricultural Revolution*, 98. By contrast, K. D. M. Snell, 'Agricultural Seasonal Unemployment, the Standard of Living, and Women's Work in the South and East, 1690–1800', *EcHR*, 36 (1981):430, 'questions the capacity of enclosure and the new, improved agricultural practices to provide greater and more regular employment throughout the year for the growing male labour force'.
8. Figures from E. Halévy, *England in 1815*, London 1924; and J. Steven Watson, *The Reign of George III*, Oxford 1960. For the rate of change, which he thinks has been exaggerated, see Crafts, 'British Economic Growth'.
9. M. I. Thomis, *Responses to Industrialisation: The British Experience, 1780–1850*, Newton Abbott 1976, argues this; so does S. Pollard, *Peaceful Conquest: The Industrialization of Europe, 1760–1970*, Oxford 1981.

10. Pollard, *Peaceful Conquest*, 24.
11. D. P. O'Brien, *The Classical Economists*, Oxford 1975, 17ff.
12. Crafts, 'British Economic Growth', 194–6. This issue is much debated.
13. P. J. Perry, *A Geography of Nineteenth Century Britain*, London 1975, 25.
14. P. H. Lindert and J. G. Williamson, 'English Workers' Living Standards during the Industrial Revolution: A New Look', *EcHR*, 36 (1983):1–25.
15. Deane, *First Industrial Revolution*, 224.
16. See the Hobsbawm-Hartwell debate in *EcHR*, 16 (1963):119–46.
17. R. S. Neale, 'The Standard of Living, 1780–1844; A Regional and Class Study', *EcHR*, 19 (1966):590–606.
18. M. W. Flinn, 'Trends in Real Wages', *EcHR*, 27 (1974):395–413.
19. Lindert and Williamson, 'English Workers' Living Standards'. See also M. W. Flinn, 'English Workers' Living Standards during the Industrial Revolution: A Comment', *EcHR*, 37 (1984):88–92.
20. Lindert and Williamson, 'English Workers' Living Standards', 12.
21. Wrigley and Schofield, *Population History*, 403. Their thesis is questioned in P. H. Lindert, 'English Living Standards, Population Growth, and Wrigley-Schofield', *Explorations in Economic History*, 20 (1983):131–55.
22. We know very little about changing standards of nutrition in this period. See D. Oddy and D. Miller, *The Making of the Modern British Diet*, London 1976, which highlights the difficulties, and concentrates on the late nineteenth and early twentieth century.
23. Karl Marx and Frederick Engels, *Selected Works*, London 1968, 38, 36.
24. J. Stevenson, *Popular Disturbances in England 1700–1870*, New York 1979.
25. The thesis of E. P. Thompson, *The Making of the English Working Class*, London 1963, challenged by, e.g., M. I. Thomis, *The Luddites; Machine Breaking in Regency England*, Newton Abbott 1970.
26. P. Laslett, *The World We Have Lost*, London 1968.
27. Chambers and Mingay, *Agricultural Revolution*, 144; Perkin, *Origins of Modern English Society*, 126.
28. Laslett in his foreword to M. Mitterauer and R. Sieder, *The European Family*, Oxford 1982, xi.
29. A. Macfarlane, *The Origins of English Individualism*, Oxford 1978.
30. Perkin, *Origins of Modern English Society*.
31. Perkin's thesis is anticipated and supported by A. Briggs, 'The Language of "Class" in Early Nineteenth Century England', *Essays in Labour History*, rev. ed., A. Briggs and J. Saville, London 1967, 43–73.
32. Stevenson, *Popular Disturbances*.
33. C. Calhoun, *The Question of Class Struggle: Social Foundations of Popular Radicalism during the Industrial Revolution*, Oxford 1982.

34. E. P. Thompson, 'The Peculiarities of the English', in *The Poverty of Theory and Other Essays*, London 1978, 35–91, at 71.
35. I. Prothero, *Artisans and Politics in Early Nineteenth Century London: John Gast and His Times*, London 1979; J. A. Hone, *For the Cause of Truth. Radicalism in London, 1796–1821*, Oxford 1982. A useful survey of recent work on radicalism and class consciousness is G. Claeys, 'The Triumph of Class-Conscious Reformism in British Radicalism, 1790–1860', *Historical Journal*, 26 (1983):969–85.
36. R. A. Soloway, *Prelates and People, Ecclesiastical Social Thought in England, 1783–1852*, London 1969, 6–8; G. Kitson Clark, *Churchmen and the Condition of England Question, 1832–1885*, London 1973, 31.
37. W. R. Ward, *Religion and Society in England, 1790–1850*, London 1972, 9.
38. Perkin, *Origins of Modern English Society*, dissents from this view, suggesting that the recessions of the period up to 1848 were no deeper, nor longer lasting that those of the alleged era of Victorian prosperity.
39. Information about trends taken from W. W. Rostow, *British Economy of the Nineteenth Century*, Oxford 1948.
40. This is the opinion of Chambers and Mingay, *Agricultural Revolution*, 27, but Deane, *The First Industrial Revolution*, 191, maintains that 'For nearly a quarter of a century agriculture endured unrelieved misery; the distress affected landlords, tenant-farmers and labourers together'.
41. Perkin, *Origins of Modern English Society*, 345, maintains we should not ignore the 'psycho-economic climate'. He thinks this is the main difference between the period 1815–50, a period of falling prices and money wages, and 1850–75, a time of rising prices and money wages. In spite of the worse reputation of the earlier period, he believes real wages rose faster then.
42. From Rostow, *British Economy*; and T. S. Ashton, *Economic Fluctuations in England, 1700–1800*, Oxford 1959.
43. On the effects of the war, see C. Emsley, *British Society and the French Wars*, London 1979; p. 151 for export of bullion.
44. Rostow, *British Economy*, 15.
45. Emsley, *British Society and the French Wars*, makes this clear.
46. I. P. H. Duffy, 'The Discount Policy of the Bank of England during the Suspension of Cash Payments, 1797–1821', *EcHR*, 35 (1982):67–82.
47. Halévy, *England in 1815*, 370; Watson, *Reign of George III*, 20.
48. K. D. Brown, *The British Labour Movement, 1700–1951*, Dublin 1982, 61.
49. The classic account of the system is L. B. Namier, *The Structure of Politics at the Accession of George III*, 2d ed., London 1967.
50. G. Spater, *William Cobbett: The Poor Man's Friend*, Cambridge 1982, 139–42.

51. P. A. Brown, *The French Revolution in English History*, London 1918; and A. B. C. Cobban, *The Debate on the French Revolution*, 2d ed., London 1960.
52. I. R. Christie, *Wilkes, Wyvill and Reform*, London 1962.
53. J. E. Cookson, *The Friends of Peace. Anti-War Liberalism in England, 1793–1815*, Cambridge 1982.
54. G. A. Williams, *Artisans and Sansculottes*, London 1968.
55. C. Hill, *The World Turned Upside Down*, London 1975.
56. G. D. H. Cole and R. Postgate, *The Common People*, 2d ed., London 1956; Thompson, *Making of the English Working Class*; Stevenson, *Popular Disturbances*.
57. See Thompson and Thomis, n. 25 above. K. D. Brown, *British Labour Movement*, doubts the revolutionary conspiracy theory; E. Royle and J. Walvin, *English Radicals and Reformers, 1760–1848*, Brighton 1982, summarize recent work and find evidence of an underground revolutionary tradition and political content in Luddism.
58. See Emsley, *British Society and the French Wars*.
59. Halévy, *England in 1815*, 381.
60. J. H. Plumb, *The Commercialization of Leisure in Eighteenth Century England*, Reading 1973; and 'The Public, Literature and the Arts in the Eighteenth Century', in *The Triumph of Culture*, ed. P. Fritz and D. Williams, Toronto 1972, 27–48.
61. R. D. Altick, *The English Common Reader: A Social History of the Mass Reading Public, 1800–1900*, Chicago 1957, 62.
62. I. Watt, *The Rise of the Novel*, London 1957, 290.
63. R. Porter, 'The Enlightenment in England', in *The Enlightenment in National Context*, ed. R. Porter and M. Teich, Cambridge 1981, 1–18, at 2.
64. J. H. Plumb, 'Political Man', in *Man versus Society in Eighteenth Century Britain*, ed. J. L. Clifford, Cambridge 1968, 1–21, at 11.
65. R. K. Webb, *The British Working Class Reader, 1790–1848*, London 1955, 38.
66. Taken from J. Hall, *The Sociology of Literature*, London 1979, 122.
67. Altick, *English Common Reader*, 255–7.

Chapter 3. Mental furniture

1. S. Collini, D. Winch, and J. Burrow, *That Noble Science of Politics. A Study in Nineteenth-Century Intellectual History*, Cambridge 1983; M. Ignatieff, 'Marxism and Classical Political Economy', in *People's History and Socialist Theory*, ed. R. Samuel, London 1981, 344–52.
2. H. G. Gadamer, *Truth and Method*, London 1975.
3. *The Concept of Socialism*, ed. B. Parekh, London 1975, 3–6.
4. C. Morris, *The Discovery of the Individual, 1050–1200*, London 1972, 1.
5. A classic statement of this is Kant's doctrine of the 'Kingdom of ends';

see B. Williams, 'The Idea of Equality', *Philosophy, Politics and Society*, ed. P. Laslett and W. G. Runciman, Oxford 1967, 110–31.
6. Morris, *Discovery of the Individual*, 58.
7. As in the parable of the lost sheep, 'joy shall be in heaven over one sinner that repenteth, more than over ninety and nine just persons, which need no repentance'. Luke 15:7.
8. J. A. Passmore, 'The Malleability of Man in Eighteenth-Century Thought', *Aspects of the Eighteenth Century*, ed. E. A. Wasserman, Baltimore 1965, 21–46; W. Stafford, 'Utopianism and Human Nature', in *Politics and Human Nature*, ed. I. Forbes and S. M. Smith, London 1983, 68–85.
9. C. A. de Helvétius, *De l'Homme, de ses Facultés, et de son Education*, 1773.
10. A. Smith, *An Inquiry into the Nature and Causes of the Wealth of Nations*, (1776–8), Everyman ed., London 1910, vol. 1, 14.
11. E. Halévy, *The Growth of Philosophic Radicalism*, London 1972, 437.
12. J. Mill, *Analysis of the Phenomena of the Human Mind*, London 1829.
13. Collini, Winch, and Burrow, *That Noble Science*, 18.
14. J. A. W. Gunn, *Politics and the Public Interest in the Seventeenth Century*, London 1969.
15. Halévy, *Philosophic Radicalism*, 11–18.
16. I. Hont and M. Ignatieff, *Wealth and Virtue: The Shaping of Political Economy in the Scottish Enlightenment*, Cambridge 1983, 11.
17. This is argued in several recent works, e.g., D. Winch, *Adam Smith's Politics*, Cambridge 1978; R. H. Campbell and A. S. Skinner, *Adam Smith*, London 1982.
18. Campbell and Skinner, *Adam Smith*; T. Campbell, *Seven Theories of Human Nature*, Oxford 1981.
19. This has been most thoroughly demonstrated in L. J. Hume, *Bentham and Bureaucracy*, Cambridge 1981. See also R. Harrison, *Bentham*, London 1983.
20. F. H. Bradley, 'My Station and Its Duties', in *Ethical Studies*, 2d ed., Oxford 1927, 160–213.
21. T. Campbell, *Seven Theories*, 97.
22. Collini, Winch, and Burrow, *That Noble Science*.
23. I. Berlin, *Vico and Herder*, London 1976.
24. R. L. Meek, *Social Science and the Ignoble Savage*, Cambridge 1976, 37–8.
25. C. Hill, 'The Norman Yoke', in *Puritanism and Revolution*, London 1958, 50–122, at 58.
26. A. Chandler, *A Dream of Order. The Medieval Ideal in Nineteenth Century English Literature*, Lincoln, Neb., 1970.
27. A. Smith, *Wealth of Nations*, vol. 1, 363–5.
28. See D. Forbes's Introduction to his edition of A. Ferguson, *An Essay on the History of Civil Society* (1767), Edinburgh 1966, xxxix.

29. I. Watt, *The Rise of the Novel*, London 1957, 94–5, 201, 269.
30. D. Lerner, *The Passing of Traditional Society*, New York 1964, summarized in A. D. Smith, *Theories of Nationalism*, 2d ed., London 1983, 89–93.
31. W. J. Bate, *From Classic to Romantic*, Harvard 1946, 48–9.
32. L. Stone, *The Family, Sex and Marriage in England, 1500–1800* (1977), rev. ed., Harmondsworth 1979.
33. Ibid., 80.
34. R. A. Houlbrooke, *The English Family, 1450–1700*, London 1984.
35. From A. B. C. Cobban, *The Debate on the French Revolution*, London 1950, 85.
36. P. L. Thorslev's expression in *The Byronic Hero*, Minnesota 1962. J. Viner, 'Man's Economic Status', in *Man versus Society in Eighteenth Century Britain*, ed. J. L. Clifford, Cambridge 1968, 22–53, at 52.
37. This essentially subjective, occasionalistic orientation is nicely illustrated by Chambers's ironic advocacy of gardens in the 'Chinese Style'. They are to be artfully contrived so as to arouse all manner of sublime emotions: 'For actual "gibbets with witches hanging *in terrorem* upon them"; "forges, collieries, mines, coal tracts, brick or lime kilns, glassworks, and different objects of the horrid kind"; half-famished animals, ragged cottagers, and their picturesquely dilapidated huts: – all these were already common features of the English scene, "particularly near the metropolis". All that was needed was that "a few uncouth struggling trees, some ruins, caverns, rocks, torrents, abandoned villages, in part consumed by fire", should be "artfully introduced and blended with gloomy plantations", in order to "compleat the aspect of desolation, and serve to fill the mind, where there was no possibility of gratifying the senses"'. A. O. Lovejoy, 'The Chinese Origin of Romanticism', in *Essays in the History of Ideas*, Baltimore 1948, 99–135, at 132–3.
38. Watt, *Rise of the Novel*, 270.
39. G. Sherburn, 'Fielding's Social Outlook', in *Eighteenth Century Literature. Modern Essays in Criticism*, ed. J. L. Clifford, Oxford 1959, 251–73, at 252–3.
40. M. Butler, *Romantics, Rebels and Reactionaries: English Literature and Its Background, 1760–1830*, Oxford 1981, 17, 19, 31; C. L. Thomson, *English History in Contemporary Poetry*, London 1928, 63. Radicalism is less common in painting, which is so dependent upon the patronage of the very wealthy. But George Morland paints the poor, sometimes in a manner critical of society. See J. Barrell, *The Dark Side of the Landscape. The Rural Poor in English Painting, 1730–1840*, Cambridge 1980.
41. L. Stephen, *English Literature and Society in the Eighteenth Century*, London 1904, 87–9; B. H. Bronson, 'The Writer', in *Man versus Society*, 102–32, at 106–7.

42. C. Hill, *Reformation to Industrial Revolution*, London 1967, 230–2.
43. Watt, *Rise of the Novel*, 79.
44. Richardson was a nonconformist. As Watt points out, going even further back, medieval saints' lives portray simple people with seriousness and even sublimity, and the New Testament does the same.
45. Butler, *Romantics, Rebels and Reactionaries*, 16.
46. Williams, *The Country and the City*, London 1973.
47. Ibid., 46.
48. Ibid., 82.
49. Barrell, *Dark Side of the Landscape*, 73, 77, 82.
50. *Classical Influences on Western Thought, A.D. 1650–1870*, ed. R. R. Bolgar, Cambridge 1979, 10.
51. References in parentheses are to A. Smith, *An Inquiry into the Nature and Causes of the Wealth of Nations* (1776–8), Everyman ed., 2 vols., London 1910; T. R. Malthus, *An Essay on the Principle of Population* (1978), Penguin ed., Harmondsworth 1970; D. Ricardo, *On the Principles of Political Economy, and Taxation* (1817), Penguin ed., Harmondsworth 1971. Excellent books on classical political economy abound. See M. Blaug, *Ricardian Economics*, Yale 1958; M. Blaug, *Economic Theory in Retrospect*, 2d ed., London 1968; W. Barber, *A History of Economic Thought*, 2d ed., Harmondsworth 1967; R. H. Campbell and A. S. Skinner, *Adam Smith*, London 1982; S. Hollander, *The Economics of David Ricardo*, Toronto, 1979; I. Hont and M. Ignatieff, *Wealth and Virtue: The Shaping of Political Economy in the Scottish Enlightenment*, Cambridge 1983; D. P. O'Brien, *The Classical Economists*, Oxford 1975; A. Walker, *Marx: His Theory and Its Context*, London 1978; D. Winch, *The Emergence of Economics as a Science, 1750–1870, Fontana Economic History of Europe*, ed. C. M. Cipolla, vol. 3, sec. 9, London 1971, 507–73; J. C. Wood, *Adam Smith. Critical Assessments*, 4 vols., Beckenham 1984 (a substantial collection of major articles on Smith).
52. This is well argued in Collini, Winch, and Burrow, *That Noble Science*. Donald Winch points out, however, that Smith dedicated his *Wealth of Nations* to Quesnay and thought of the physiocrats as the only group of authors engaged in the same project as himself. Hont and Ignatieff, *Wealth and Virtue*, 268. Perhaps the boundary was beginning to appear.
53. Hont and Ignatieff, *Wealth and Virtue*. See especially the introductory essay by the editors, 'Needs and Justice in the *Wealth of Nations*: An Introductory Essay', 1–44.
54. Collini, Winch, and Burrow, *That Noble Science*.
55. K. Tribe, *Land, Labour and Economic Discourse*, London 1978.
56. M. Ignatieff, 'Marxism and Classical Political Economy', in *People's History and Socialist Theory*, ed. R. Samuel, London 1981, 345.
57. Adam Smith was not the first to analyse society in this way; the physiocrats do the same.

58. A. Briggs, 'The Language of "Class" in Early Nineteenth Century England', *Essays in Labour History*, ed. A. Briggs and J. Saville, London 1960.

59. G. Claeys and P. Kerr, 'Mechanical Political Economy', *Cambridge Journal of Economics*, 5 (1981):251–72 argue that this distinction is the basis of Smith's reputation among working class radicals.

60. M. Ignatieff, 'Marxism and Classical Political Economy', 349–50. J. Dunn, 'From Applied Theology to Social Analysis', in Hont and Ignatieff, *Wealth and Virtue*, 119–35, at 133–4.

61. O'Brien, *Classical Economists*, 44; Blaug, *Ricardian Economics*, 61.

62. M. Berg, *The Machinery Question and the Making of Political Economy, 1815–1848*, Cambridge 1980, 58, 72. Her interpretation is discussed in Claeys and Kerr, 'Mechanical Political Economy'.

63. S. Hollander, 'The Post-Ricardian Dissension: A Case-Study in Economics and Ideology', *Oxford Economic Papers*, vol. 32, no. 3 (1980):370–410.

64. In Chapter 5, 'Of Property', in the second of his *Two Treatises of Civil Government*.

65. K. I. Vaughn, 'John Locke and the Labour Theory of Value', *Journal of Libertarian Studies*, vol. 2 no. 4 (1978):311–26.

66. J. Tully, *A Discourse on Property*, Cambridge 1980, 140.

67. Berg, *Machinery Question*, 82.

68. Ferguson, *An Essay on the History of Civil Society*, 182–3.

69. T. C. Smout, 'Where Had the Scottish Economy Got To by 1776?', in Hont and Ignatieff, *Wealth and Virtue*, 45–72.

70. K. Marx and F. Engels, *Selected Works*, 40.

71. The orthodox interpretation has been fundamentally and extensively challenged in Hollander, *The Economics of David Ricardo*. See n. 77 below. Hollander thinks that both Smith and Ricardo took full account of modern industry.

72. A. Walker, *Marx: His Theory and Its Context*, London 1978, 36.

73. Bentham apparently read him in this way. See R. Harrison, *Bentham*, London 1983, 123.

74. See, for example, D. Winch, *Adam Smith's Politics*, Cambridge 1978; K. Haakonssen, *The Science of a Legislator*, Cambridge 1981.

75. Haakonssen, *Science of a Legislator*; T. Campbell, *Seven Theories of Human Society*, Oxford 1981.

76. Campbell, *Seven Theories*; Dunn, 'From Applied Theology', interprets Smith as an essentially secular thinker. Winch questions the view of Smith as an optimist, in his *Adam Smith's Politics*.

77. Hollander, *Economics of David Ricardo*. Hollander challenges many of the received views of Ricardo. Not only was Ricardo an optimist; he did not have a labour theory of value, he was not harsh on the poor laws, and he did not use a corn model (the corn model has been seen as central to Ricardo's thought since the work of Piero Sraffa). Hollander's reinterpretation has been challenged; see, e.g., D. P.

O'Brien, 'Ricardian Economics and the Economics of David Ricardo', *Oxford Economic Papers*, vol. 33, no. 3 (1981):352–86, and Hollander's reply, 'The Economics of David Ricardo: A Response to Professor O'Brien', *Oxford Economic Papers*, vol. 34, no. 1 (1982):224–46. The effect of Hollander's reinterpretation, if it were correct, would be to rescue Ricardo from his situation as an exponent of the harsher features of capitalism and as a precursor of Marxism. It is too early to judge whether Hollander's intervention will lastingly modify our understanding of Ricardo. In any event, if Sraffa, Blaug, and O'Brien have radically misunderstood Ricardo, then so did many of his contemporaries.

78. O'Brien, *Classical Economists*, 153; P. Deane, *The First Industrial Revolution*, Cambridge 1965, 177, 179.
79. Blaug, *Economic Theory in Retrospect*, 16, 23, 171.
80. F. Tonnies, *Community and Association* (1887), English trans., London 1955, 183–4; F. H. Bradley, 'My Station and Its Duties', in *Ethical Studies*, 2d ed., London 1927.
81. See especially D. Miller, *Social Justice*, Oxford 1976 (the best treatment of desert-based justice); J. Feinberg, *Rights, Justice and the Bounds of Liberty*, Princeton 1980; *Justice*, ed. E. Kamenka and A. Erh-Soon Tay, London 1979; A. Weale, *Equality and Social Policy*, London 1978; D. D. Raphael, *Justice and Liberty*, London 1980; and J. Rawls, *A Theory of Justice*, Oxford 1973.
82. Feinberg, *Rights, Justice*, 286–92.
83. Weale, *Equality and Social Policy*, 14.
84. But see I. Berlin, 'Equality', *Proceedings of the Aristotelian Society*, 56 (1955–6), 301–26; and B. Williams, 'The Idea of Equality', *Philosophy, Politics and Society*, 2d ser., ed. P. Laslett and W. G. Runciman, Oxford 1969.
85. This is not to contradict the *logic* of Weale's argument.
86. A. O. Lovejoy, *Essays in the History of Ideas*, Maryland 1948, 80, 85.
87. R. Price, *Observations on the Nature of Civil Liberty* (1778), in *Richard Price and the Ethical Foundations of the American Revolution*, ed. B. Peach, Durham, North Carolina 1979, 63–175, at 146–7.
88. Miller, *Social Justice*, 189.
89. R. Tuck, *Natural Rights Theories: Their Origin and Development*, Cambridge 1979. See also Feinberg, *Rights, Justice*; J. Finnis, *Natural Law and Natural Rights*, Oxford 1980; Hont and Ignatieff, *Wealth and Virtue*; D. G. Ritchie, *Natural Rights* (1894), 2d ed., London 1903; *Human Rights*, ed. E. Kamenka and A. Erh-Soon Tay, London 1978; and R. Dworkin, *Taking Rights Seriously*, London 1978.
90. Feinberg, *Rights, Justice*, 151.
91. Quotation from de Tocqueville, taken from *Human Rights*, 34.
92. Quotation from the seventeenth-century leveller Overton, in A. S. P. Woodhouse, *Puritanism and Liberty*, 2d ed., London 1974, 327.

93. For Grotius, Pufendorf, Locke, and their eighteenth-century successors see the works cited by R. Tuck and by I. Hont and M. Ignatieff; also J. Tully, *A Discourse on Property: John Locke and his Adversaries*, Cambridge 1980.

94. Tully, *Discourse on Property*, thinks that Locke asserted a positive community: the introductory essay, and the essay by J. Moore and M. Silverthorne, 'Gershom Carmichael and the Natural Jurisprudence Tradition in Eighteenth-Century Scotland' in Hont and Ignatieff, *Wealth and Virtue*, 73–87, argue that he asserted negative community.

95. Locke's discussion of property in Chapter 5 of the second of his *Two Treatises of Civil Government* (1690). For commentary on his property theory see especially J. P. Plamenatz, *Man and Society*, London 1963; C. B. MacPherson, *The Political Theory of Possessive Individualism*, Oxford 1962; and Tully, *Discourse on Property*. Tully emphasizes the egalitarian aspects of Locke's theory.

96. Paine, for example, asserts both liberty and recipient rights: Tom Paine, *Rights of Man* (pt. 2, 1792), Everyman ed., London 1915, 250.

97. The natural rights tradition is an offshoot of the doctrine of natural law. Natural law is organic rather than individualist, formulating the obligations of the individual to the community. It can be a critical doctrine, but in the late eighteenth century it tended to be conservative. See P. Gottfried, 'German Romanticism and Natural Law', *Studies in Romanticism*, 7 (1968):231–42. For an important corrective, see also P. Lucas, 'On Edmund Burke's Doctrine of Prescription; Or an Appeal from the New to the Old Lawyers', *Historical Journal*, 11 (1968):35–63.

98. *Justice*, 9–12.

99. S. I. Benn, 'Human Rights – for Whom and for What?' in *Human Rights*, 59–73, at 72.

100. On utilitarianism, see L. Stephen, *The English Utilitarians*, London 1900; E. Halévy, *The Growth of Philosophic Radicalism*, London 1928; J. P. Plamenatz, *The English Utilitarians*, 2d ed., Oxford 1958; A. Quinton, *Utilitarian Ethics*, London 1973; and W. Thomas, *The Philosophic Radicals*, Oxford 1979.

101. See Dworkin, *Taking Rights Seriously*; and Rawls, *Theory of Justice*.

102. J. Steintrager, *Bentham*, London 1972, 12–13.

103. Raphael, *Justice and Liberty*, 1–2.

104. E. K. Hunt has argued that utilitarianism is logically consistent with free enterprise capitalist ideology, but not with egalitarianism. See his *History of Economic Thought: A Critical Perspective*, Belmont, California, 1979, 137ff.; and his 'Utilitarianism and the Labor Theory of Value: A Critique of the Ideas of William Thompson', *History of Political Economy*, vol. 11, no. 4 (1979):545–71. But this is a mistake. Firstly, Hunt assumes that utilitarianism entails an indivi-

dualistic and egoistic theory of motivation. But the utilitarian criterion is not necessarily tied to any particular theory of motivation. Bentham, it is true, assumes that the most important motivations are selfish ones; but Hume and J. S. Mill lay greater emphasis on sympathy, and Godwin advocates, and thinks possible, totally benevolent motivation. Secondly, with very little argument, Hunt insists that Benthamite objectivism is utterly untenable. The pleasures of two individuals can never be compared. Hence Bentham's egalitarian argument based on the principle of diminishing returns collapses. Now situations in which individuals or minorities have infinitely greater pleasure capacities than the mass can be hypothesized, and such possibilities cannot absolutely be disproved; but this does not make such hypotheses more reasonable or plausible than Bentham's principle of diminishing returns. Alan Ryan is surely more accurate in his judgment that utilitarianism does not necessarily support private property, and that whether it justifies equality or inequality depends upon the factual suppositions with which it is combined. A. Ryan, *Property and Political Theory*, Oxford 1984, 91–2.

105. I have in this section concentrated on moral concepts and theories around which academic debate has centred. In so doing I have not exhaustively surveyed the moral ideas available at the time. To do this would require a list or map of evaluations in all kinds of literature, a value survey. This would reveal things not so far touched upon – what qualities of character were admired, for example. Systematic value surveys of large numbers of texts are mammoth tasks, and such studies are as yet in their infancy. For an example of a value survey, see M. Billig, *Fascists: A Social Psychological View of the National Front*, London 1978. To do this kind of job on a large scale would require the techniques of content analysis: see O. R. Holsti, *Content Analysis for the Social Sciences and Humanities*, Reading, Massachusetts, 1969.

106. The best general survey of eighteenth-century political thought is H. T. Dickinson, *Liberty and Property. Political Ideology in Eighteenth Century Britain*, London 1977.

107. A useful summary of trends in eighteenth-century political ideology is contained in H. T. Dickinson, 'The Rights of Man – from John Locke to Tom Paine', in *Scotland, Europe and the American Revolution*, ed. O. D. Edwards and G. Shepperson, Edinburgh 1976, 38–48. See also his 'The Eighteenth-Century Debate on the "Glorious Revolution" ', *History*, 61 (1976):28–45.

108. J. Mill, *An Essay on Government* (1821), ed. E. Barker, Cambridge 1937. The utilitarian argument for democracy was first put forward by Bentham himself, in his *Plan for Parliamentary Reform* of 1817. For the argument and its critics, see *Utilitarian Logic and Politics. James Mill's 'Essay on Government', Macaulay's Critique and the Ensuing Debate*, ed. J. Lively and J. Rees, Oxford 1978.

109. J. Mill, *Essay on Government*, 34.
110. J. G. A. Pocock, 'Burke and the Ancient Constitution', in *Politics, Language and Time*, London 1972, 202–32.
111. C. Hill, 'The Norman Yoke', *Puritanism and Revolution*, London 1958.
112. Paine, *Rights of Man*, 49.
113. J. G. A. Pocock, *The Machiavellian Moment: Florentine Political Thought and the Atlantic Republican Tradition*, Princeton 1975.
114. D. Winch, *Adam Smith's Politics*, Cambridge 1978.
115. J. N. Shklar, *Men and Citizens: A Study of Rousseau's Social Theory*, Cambridge 1969.
116. Pocock, *Machiavellian Moment*, 441, 447. See also N. Phillipson, 'The Scottish Enlightenment' in *The Enlightenment in National Context*, ed. R. Porter and M. Teich, Cambridge 1981, 19–40.
117. J. Robertson, 'The Scottish Enlightenment at the Limits of the Civic Tradition', in Hont and Ignatieff, *Wealth and Virtue*, 137–78, at 143.
118. J. G. A. Pocock, 'Cambridge Paradigms and Scotch Philosophers: A Study of the Relations between the Civic Humanist and the Civil Jurisprudential Interpretation of Eighteenth Century Social Thought', in Hont and Ignatieff, *Wealth and Virtue*, 235–52, at 250.
119. For utopias of the classical age, see F. E. and F. P. Manuel, *Utopian Thought in the Western World*, Oxford 1979.
120. On utopianism and time, see R. Levitas, 'Sociology and Utopia', *Sociology*, 13 (1979):19–33.
121. Though rights of recipience are referred to in Blackstone's *Commentaries*, and by Spence, as we shall see.
122. L. J. Hume, *Bentham and Bureaucracy*, Cambridge 1981.
123. B. Crick, *In Defence of Politics*, 2d ed., Harmondsworth 1982, 18–19, 30. The beginnings of this conception of politics can perhaps be found in William Penn. Gunn, *Politics and the Public Interest*, 179, 190.
124. R. A. Soloway, *Prelates and People. Ecclesiastical Social Thought in England, 1783–1852*, London 1969, 62.
125. J. Viner, 'Man's Economic Status', in *Man versus Society*, 47.
126. Though most clergymen took their Malthus in J. B. Summer's modified form. Soloway, *Prelates and People*, 95ff.
127. Ibid., 162–3.
128. Ibid., 123–4.
129. *The Works of William Paley*, London 1838.
130. Ibid., 551.
131. Soloway, *Prelates and People*, 27–28.
132. E. M. Howse, *Saints in Politics*, London 1971, 56.
133. Ibid., 97.
134. Ibid., 96.
135. William Wilberforce, *A Practical View of the Prevailing Religious System of Professed Christians in the Higher and Middle Classes in*

This Country, Contrasted with Real Christianity, London 1797, 489.
See also Howse, Saints in Politics, 100.
136. A. D. Gilbert, Religion and Society in Industrial England. Church, Chapel and Social Change, 1740–1914, London 1976, 82.
137. The Works of the Rev. John Wesley, London 1811, vol. 10, 107.
138. Ibid., vol. 10, 103, 104.
139. Ibid., vol. 8, 57, 58.
140. Ibid., vol. 8, 59 (in his later years Wesley was less radical).
141. Ibid., vol. 8, 52. For the large sums of money given by Methodists to the poor see E. D. Bebb, Nonconformity and Social and Economic Life, 1660–1800, Epworth 1935, 142–3. The relationship between Methodism and working class radicalism has been the subject of much historical debate. Halévy thought that Methodism saved England from revolution by diverting the energies of working men and leading them into the paths of respectability. E. Halévy, England in 1815, London 1924, 424–5. Hobsbawm doubted whether there were enough Methodists to have this effect. He pointed out that, though official Methodism was conservative, many in the rank and file and in breakaway groups were more radical. Methodism and radicalism share the same chronology, growing and declining together. E. J. Hobsbawm, Labouring Men, London 1968. E. P. Thompson is inclined to dismiss the link between Methodism and radicalism; there just happens to be cross-membership. Methodism is 'the chiliasm of despair', a retreatist and defeatist response to the miseries of industrialization. E. P. Thompson, The Making of the English Working Class, rev. ed., Harmondsworth 1968, 428, 433. Perkin and Gilbert are more impressed by the link between Methodism and radicalism. H. Perkin, The Origins of Modern English Society, 1780–1880, London 1969, 344; Gilbert, Religion and Society, 30, 83.
142. Bebb, Nonconformity and Social and Economic Life, 57; Gilbert, Religion and Society, 86.
143. J. E. Cookson, The Friends of Peace. Anti-war Liberalism in England, 1793–1815, Cambridge 1982, discusses the radical implications of 'rational dissent', pp. 3–8, and shows how it became antiestablishment in this period, but not socially radical, p. 28.
144. C. M. Elliot, 'The Political Economy of English Dissent, 1780–1840', in The Industrial Revolution, ed. R. M. Hartwell, Oxford 1970, 144–66, at 155, 163.
145. The Theological and Miscellaneous Works of Joseph Priestley, London 1823, vol. 22, 13, 38, 133.
146. As I. Kramnick does, 'Religion and Radicalism: English Political Theory in the Age of Revolution', Political Theory, 5 (1977):505–34, at 511.
147. I. Sellers, 'Unitarians and Social Change', Hibbert Journal, 61 (1962):16–22, at 20.
148. The Theological and Miscellaneous Works of Joseph Priestley, vol. 22, 125.

149. Price, *Richard Price and the Ethical Foundations*, 75.
150. Ibid., 151.
151. C. Garrett, *Respectable Folly: Millennarians and the French Revolution in France and England*, Baltimore 1975.
152. Ibid., 15, 121. J. K. Hopkins, *A Woman to Deliver Her People: Joanna Southcott and English Millenarianism in an Era of Revolution*, Austin, Texas, 1982, shows the connection between millenarianism and popular despair and aspiration.
153. A. O. Lovejoy, *The Great Chain of Being*, Cambridge, Massachusetts, 1953.
154. C. Becker, *The Heavenly City of the Eighteenth Century Philosophers*, Yale 1959.
155. *The Theological and Miscellaneous Works of Joseph Priestley*, vol. 12, 9.
156. Pocock, *Machiavellian Moment*, 401–5.
157. Garrett, *Respectable Folly*.
158. R. L. Meek, *Social Science and the Ignoble Savage*, Cambridge 1976.
159. Meek, ibid., regards the Scottish historical school as a precursor of Marxist economic determinism; this has been challenged as an oversimplification by, e.g., Haakonssen, *Science of a Legislator*, 182–5; Ignatieff, 'Marxism and Classical Political Economy', 347; and Ignatieff, 'John Millar and Individualism', in Hont and Ignatieff, *Wealth and Virtue*, 317–43, at 318.
160. See his 'Conclusion' (vol. 2, 349–58), Q. Skinner, *The Foundations of Modern Political Thought*, Cambridge 1978.
161. G. E. Aylmer, '"Property" in Seventeenth Century England', *Past and Present*, 86 (1980):87–97.
162. J. Bossy, 'Some Elementary Forms of Durkheim', *Past and Present*, 95 (1982):3–18.
163. R. Williams, *Keywords*, London 1976.
164. K. Tribe, *Land, Labour and Economic Discourse*, London 1978.
165. In this he follows Hume.
166. For the developing eighteenth-century critique of 'certain' knowledge, see D. L. Patey, *Probability and Literary Form. Philosophic Theory and Literary Practice in the Augustan Age*, Cambridge 1984.
167. Locke distinguishes our perception of primary and secondary qualities in things. Primary qualities – e.g., shape, mass – are real properties of the things. Secondary qualities – e.g., colours – are by contrast effects produced upon our senses, the character of these qualities being in part determined by the nature of our sensory apparatus.
168. The 'episteme' of eighteenth-century thought is expounded in this way by M. Foucault, *The Order of Things* (first published in French 1966), London 1970. It is strikingly expressed by T. Sprat in his *The History of the Royal-Society of London for the Improving of Natural Knowledge*, London 1667. For example, see p. 113: 'They have therefore been most rigorous in putting in execution, the only Remedy,

that can be found for this *extravagance*: and that has been, a constant Resolution, to reject all the amplifications, digressions and swellings of style: to return back to the primitive purity, and shortness, when men deliver'd so many *things*, almost in an equal number of *words*. They have exacted from all their members, a close, naked, natural way of speaking; positive expressions; clear senses; a native easiness: bringing all things as near the Mathematical plainness, as they can: and preferring the language of Artizans, Countrymen, and Merchants, before that, of Wits, or Scholars.'

169. The thesis of, e.g., Kant, Hegel, Husserl, the 'Frankfurt School', Habermas.

170. From Butler to Burke there are those who doubt our ability to attain certain truth. These doubts often take the form of a cautious empiricism contrasted with rationalism. They also draw upon the traditions of the discipline of rhetoric, which offers a looser method than logic, more suited to the complexity and opacity of human affairs. See Patey, *Probability and Literary Form*; and M. Einaudi, 'The British Background of Burke's Political Philosophy', *Political Science Quarterly*, 49 (1934):576–98.

171. The 'classics' of the theory of ideology are K. Marx and F. Engels, *The German Ideology* (1845–6); and K. Mannheim, *Ideology and Utopia* (1929). For a good modern survey, see J. Larrain, *The Concept of Ideology*, London 1979.

172. S. I. Benn and R. S. Peters, *Social Principles and the Democratic State*, London 1959, 103.

173. G. D. H. Cole, 'The Rights of Man', in *Essays in Social Theory*, London 1950, 132–50, at 149.

174. R. Nozick, *Anarchy, State and Utopia*, New York 1974.

175. Raphael, *Justice and Liberty*; Miller, *Social Justice*.

176. C. Belsey, *Critical Practice*, London 1980, 7, 14, 122.

Chapter 4. Spence, *The Real Rights of Man*

1. References in parentheses are to T. Spence, *The Real Rights of Man*, as printed in *Pig's Meat* (London 1795), from *The Political Works of Thomas Spence*, ed. H. T. Dickinson, Newcastle 1982.

2. T. R. Knox, 'Thomas Spence: The Trumpet of Jubilee', *Past and Present*, 76 (1977):79.

3. H. T. Dickinson in his introduction to *The Political Works of Thomas Spence*, viii.

4. Ibid., ix; and see Knox, 'Thomas Spence'.

5. *The Political Works of Thomas Spence*, ix.

6. See the title pages reproduced by Dickinson in ibid.

7. This expression was used by Burke in his *Reflections on the Revolution in France*.

8. *The Political Works of Thomas Spence*, v.

9. R. D. Altick, *The English Common Reader. A Social History of the Mass Reading Public, 1800–1900*, Chicago 1957, 30.
10. J. H. Plumb, *The Commercialization of Leisure in Eighteenth Century England*, Reading 1973, 6.

Chapter 5. Ogilvie, *An Essay on the Right of Property in Land*
1. See above, Chapter 3, section 4.
2. References in brackets to D. C. MacDonald's edition (under title *Birthright in Land*), London 1891.
3. Ogilvie began by writing in terms of an equal shareout among all *mankind*; by this stage of the argument, the sharing group has become the citizens of the nation.
4. See MacDonald's introduction in his edition of Ogilvie's text, *Birthright in Land*, London 1891.
5. T. C. Smout, 'Where had the Scottish economy got to by 1776?', 67, in I. Hont and M. Ignatieff, *Wealth and Virtue: The Shaping of Political Economy in the Scottish Enlightenment*, Cambridge 1983.
6. J. Robertson, 'The Scottish Enlightenment at the Limits of the Civic Tradition', in Hont and Ignatieff, *Wealth and Virtue*, 137–78, at 143. Fletcher, like Ogilvie, was a 'visionary', proposing a federal reorganization of Europe modelled on the Achaean league of classical antiquity.
7. See above, Chapter 3, section 8.
8. A. H. Lincoln, *Some Political and Social Ideas of English Dissent, 1763–1800*, Cambridge 1938, 10–11, 19–20. D. O. Thomas, *The Honest Mind: The Thought and Work of Richard Price*, Oxford 1977, 99.
9. See above, Chapter 3, section 8.
10. See above, Chapter 3, section 2.
11. R. Williams, *Keywords*, London 1976, 276.
12. See above, Chapter 3, section 2.
13. See above, Chapter 3, section 5.
14. 'Nations' not 'societies'. The latter would be the normal word to employ today, but Ogilvie does not use the term 'society' or 'societies' in this sense, to refer to specific instances – 'French society', 'British society'. Instead, he uses 'nation', 'country', or 'community'. See above, Chapter 3, section 2.
15. The one history mentioned by name is Gibbon's *Decline and Fall*; we may hazard the guess that he had read Voltaire on Henri IV (49).

Chapter 6. Godwin, *Enquiry concerning Political Justice*
1. References in parentheses are to the Penguin edition, ed. I. Kramnick, Harmondsworth 1976.
2. For his life, see C. Kegan Paul, *William Godwin: His Friends and Contemporaries*, London 1876, and D. Locke, *A Fantasy of Reason. The Life and Thought of William Godwin*, London 1980.

3. For a fuller defence of this point, see W. Stafford, 'Dissenting Religion Translated into Politics: Godwin's *Political Justice*', *History of Political Thought*, 1 (1980):279–99. See also G. Claeys, 'The Concept of "Political Justice" in Godwin's *Political Justice*: a Reconsideration', *Political Theory*, vol. 11, no. 4 (1983):565–84.

4. See above, Chapter 3, section 4.

5. See above, Chapter 3, section 1.

6. B. R. Pollin, *Education and Enlightenment in the Works of William Godwin*, New York 1962, 41. See also Stafford, 'Dissenting Religion Translated into Politics'.

7. See above, Chapter 3, section 4.

8. See above, Chapter 3, section 4.

9. Kramnick incorrectly supposes that Godwin refers here to Spence.

10. Point taken from Ogilvie, and acknowledged.

11. For the changes in the three editions, see F. E. L. Priestley's edition of *Political Justice*, Toronto 1946, vol. 3, 232.

12. Ibid., vol. 3, 198–9.

13. The *locus classicus* is F. Tonnies, *Gemeinschaft und Gesellschaft* (1887), a sociological classic of enduring influence. But the basic idea can be traced back through Marx and Hegel to Herder and to the Scottish historical school.

14. See above, Chapter 3, section 2.

15. On p. 791 there is an echo of Hume and Smith: modern society is more equal than feudal, and commerce was the agent of this beneficial change.

16. From Hume's *Essays*, which he acknowledges.

Chapter 7.   Hall, *The Effects of Civilization*

1. Almost certainly he has Paley in mind here; Paley is quoted later on another issue.

2. Page references in parentheses are to the original edition, published in London.

3. H. Perkin, *The Origins of Modern English Society, 1780–1880*, London 1969, 419.

4. Like Spence and Ogilvie, he makes little use of the term 'society', employing instead country, nation, people, civilized state, community. But the absence of the term does not entail an absence of awareness of 'social' change, or of varying 'social' patterns; like Ogilvie, he can conceive and describe these with the other terms at his disposal.

5. I. Hont and M. Ignatieff, 'Needs and Justice in the *Wealth of Nations*: an introductory essay', in I. Hont and M. Ignatieff, *Wealth and Virtue: The Shaping of Political Economy in the Scottish Enlightenment*, Cambridge 1983.

6. See above, Chapter 3, section 3.

7. J. D. Chambers and G. E. Mingay, *The Agricultural Revolution, 1750–1880*, London 1966, 6.

Chapter 8. Coleridge, *A Lay Sermon*

1. References in parentheses are to the edition in *The Collected Works of Samuel Taylor Coleridge*, vol. 6, *Lay Sermons*, ed. R. J. White, London 1972.
2. See above, Chapter 3, section 6.
3. It should be noted that Coleridge develops this theory without using the term 'culture'. The nearest he came to that word was 'cultivation', and even that is not used in this sermon. Instead, he refers to the 'spirit' or 'genius' of the nation. He does use the term 'society'; but he uses other terms more – country, nation, people, community, state (meaning society). He especially favours 'nation' and 'country', and this is intimately bound up with the strongly patriotic tone of his later writings. Coleridge cannot be a very strong critic of his society; as a nationalist, he loves his country.
4. See above, Chapter 3, section 2.
5. The Fabians, like Coleridge, drew upon continental sources: German idealism and French sociology.
6. See above, Chapter 3, section 2.
7. N. Fruman, *Coleridge, The Damaged Archangel*, New York 1971; M. Lefebure, *Samuel Taylor Coleridge: A Bondage of Opium*, London 1977.
8. This was not new to Coleridge; for example, the stimulating effect of the war is discussed in Colquhoun's *Treatise on the Wealth, Power, and Resources of the British Empire* (editor's note in Coleridge, *Lay Sermons*, 158).
9. *Essays on Politics and Culture by John Stuart Mill*, ed. G. Himmelfarb, New York 1962, 162.
10. J. S. Mill, *Essays on Bentham and Coleridge*, ed. and intro. F. R. Leavis, London 1950; R. Williams, *Culture and Society, 1780–1950*, London 1958.
11. This might be regarded as part of the problem of Northern Ireland, the Lebanon, or Iran today. Richard Hoggart and Raymond Williams have argued that the problem of British society is its lack of a common culture; there are, rather, exclusive and hostile class cultures. See R. Hoggart, *The Uses of Literacy*, London 1957; R. Williams, *The Long Revolution*, London 1961.
12. S. T. Coleridge, *Lectures 1795 on Politics and Religion. The Collected Works of Samuel Taylor Coleridge*, vol. 1, ed. L. Patton and P. Mann, London 1971, 46, 162–5, 351–3.
13. Matthew Arnold, *Culture and Anarchy*, London 1869; T. S. Eliot, *Notes Towards the Definition of Culture*, London 1948; F. R. Leavis and D. Thompson, *Culture and Environment: the Training of Critical Awareness*, London 1933; K. Mannheim, *Ideology and Utopia* (1929), London 1960, 137–8.
14. J. Prebble, *The Highland Clearances* (1963), Harmondsworth 1969, 103.

Chapter 9. Owen, *Report to the County of Lanark*

1. References in parentheses are to the Everyman edition, R. Owen, *A New View of Society*, ed. G. D. H. Cole, London 1927.
2. The full details are not contained in the *Report*. See F. Podmore, *Robert Owen: a Biography*, London 1906, 404ff.
3. See above, Chapter 2, section 3.
4. See above, Chapter 3, section 3.
5. G. D. H. Cole, *Robert Owen*, London 1925, 199.
6. G. Claeys and P. Kerr, 'Mechanical Political Economy', *Cambridge Journal of Economics*, 5 (1981):251–72, at 268.
7. G. Claeys, 'Paternalism and Democracy in the Politics of Robert Owen', *International Review of Social History*, 27 (1982):161–207.
8. J. Lively, *Democracy*, Oxford 1975, 8, 13, 27.
9. Podmore, *Robert Owen*, 266–7.
10. In this text we find the abstract concept of society fully developed and the term frequently employed. He writes of different states or stages of society, of barbarous and civilized society; he contrasts the government of the country with general society, and refers to different stations in society. When he wishes to refer to *a* society, however, he more usually employs the terms 'nation' and 'country'.
11. See above, Chapter 3, section 2.
12. Owen, *A New View of Society*, 17.
13. Podmore, *Robert Owen*, 237n.
14. See above, Chapter 3, section 8.
15. Claeys, 'Paternalism and Democracy', 207.

Chapter 10. Ravenstone, *A Few Doubts*

1. References in parentheses are to the first edition, published in London. 'Piercy Ravenstone', as I indicated in the Introduction, was really Richard Puller.
2. See above, Chapter 3, section 3.
3. Ravenstone is very close to the physiocrats. Like them, he is highly critical of trade, yet he defends free trade.
4. See above, Chapter 2, section 3.
5. See above, Chapter 2, section 1.

Chapter 11. Thompson, *Principles of the Distribution of Wealth*

1. References in parentheses are to the above first edition, published in London.
2. E. K. Hunt has argued that there is a tension, even a contradiction, in Thompson's work between the egalitarian and socialist labour theory of value and the principle of utility, which according to Hunt is more consistent with inequality and free market capitalism. See his *History of Economic Thought: A Critical Perspective*, Belmont, California 1979; and his 'Utilitarianism and the Labour Theory of Value:

A Critique of the Ideas of William Thompson', *History of Political Economy*, vol. 11, no. 4, 1979, 545–71. As I argued in the section on moral theories above, I think this is mistaken; utilitarianism has no necessary connection with inequality and free enterprise and can support egalitarian conclusions, depending on the factual premises with which the moral criterion is combined. Hunt appears to be criticizing Thompson for not being Marx, refusing to recognize that socialism may have other valid theoretical foundations than the Marxist.

3. Once again we are reminded of Marx when Thompson argues that the social gulf is widening: 'The tendency of the existing arrangement of things as to wealth, is to enrich a few at the expense of the mass of the producers; to make the poverty of the poor more hopeless, to throw back the middling classes upon the poor, that a few may be enabled . . . to accumulate in perniciously large masses' (xvi).

4. See above, Chapter 3, section 3.

5. Thompson does not refer explicitly to Malthus's works on subjects other than population.

6. See above, Chapter 3, section 3.

7. B. Taylor, *Eve and the New Jerusalem*, London 1983.

Chapter 12.   Hodgskin, *Labour Defended*

1. References in parentheses are to G. D. H. Cole's edition, London 1922, reprinted 1964.

2. See above, Chapter 3, section 3.

3. See above, Chapter 3, section 4.

4. S. Hollander, 'The Post-Ricardian Dissension: A Case-Study in Economics and Ideology', *Oxford Economic Papers*, vol. 32, no. 3 (1980):370–410; E. K. Hunt, 'Value Theory in the Writings of the Classical Economists, Thomas Hodgskin and Karl Marx', *History of Political Economy*, vol. 9, no. 3 (1977):322–45; E. K. Hunt, 'The relation of the Ricardian Socialists to Ricardo and Marx', *Science and Society*, vol. 44, no. 2 (1980):177–98.

5. David Hume, *A Treatise of Human Nature* (1739), bk. 1, pt. 3. *Enquiry Concerning the Human Understanding* (1748), sec. 7.

6. Osier, who wishes to emphasize the differences between Hodgskin and Marx, to the detriment of the former and the glory of the latter, insists that Hodgskin means *conscious* deception. J. P. Osier, *Thomas Hodgskin*, 69.

7. Karl Marx, *Capital*, vol. 1 (1867), Everyman ed., London 1930, 843. On 'primitive accumulation', see A. Walker, *Marx: His Theory and Its Context*, London 1978. See also M. Ignatieff, 'Primitive Accumulation Revisited', in *People's History and Socialist Theory*, ed. R. Samuel, London 1981, 130–35; M. Perelman, 'Classical Political Economy and Primitive Accumulation: The Case of Smith and Stewart', *History of Political Economy*, vol. 15, no. 3, 1983, 451–94.

8. Probably, given his background, his model is the shipyard.
9. K. Marx and F. Engels, *The German Ideology* (1845–6) London 1965, 44. This criticism of Marx is developed with erudition and wit in A. Nove, *The Economics of Feasible Socialism*, London 1983.
10. G. Claeys and P. Kerr, 'Mechanical Political Economy', *Cambridge Journal of Economics*, 5 (1981):266.
11. K. Marx and F. Engels, *Selected Works*, London 1968, 40.

Chapter 13. Cobbett, *Rural Rides*
1. References in parentheses are to the Penguin edition, Harmondsworth 1967.
2. E. Halévy, *History of the English People in the Nineteenth Century*, vol. 2, *The Liberal Awakening, 1815–1830*, London 1961, 37.
3. See above, Chapter 2, section 3.
4. E. A. Wrigley and R. S. Schofield, *The Population History of England 1541–1871*, London 1981, 208–9.
5. J. P. Huzel, 'The Demographic Impact of the Old Poor Law: More Reflexions on Malthus', *EcHR*, 33 (1980):367–81.
6. G. Spater, *William Cobbett: The Poor Man's Friend*, vol. 1, Cambridge 1982, 11.
7. Ibid., 18.

Conclusion
1. G. Claeys, 'Engels' *Outlines of a Critique of Political Economy* (1843) and the Origins of the Marxist Critique of Capitalism', *History of Political Economy*, vol. 16, no. 2 (1984):207–32; J. E. King, 'Utopian or Scientific? A Reconsideration of the Ricardian Socialists', *History of Political Economy*, vol. 15, no. 3, 1983, 345–73.
2. Albert Camus, *L'Homme Révolté*, Paris 1951.
3. S. Collini, D. Winch, and J. Burrow, *That Noble Science of Politics. A Study in Nineteenth-Century Intellectual History*, Cambridge 1983.
4. For the conservative implications of this separation, see H. Marcuse, *One Dimensional Man*, Boston 1964.

Index

abdication by the governors, 20–1,
173, 253, 271
adding-up theory of value, 57, 235,
239
agrarian law, 110, 112, 115, 151
agriculture, 12–14, 54, 167, 277 n6;
depression in, 22, 250, 257, 279
n40; improvement of, 12, 110–11,
151, 157, 183–4
alienation, *see* division of labour
ancient constitution, 76, 91, 211
Anglican clergy, 21–2, 253–4, 256,
261
aristocracy, 136–8, 199, 271
artificial identification of interests,
principle of, 36–8, 116
associationism, 33–5, 67–8, 94, 169,
185, 240, 259, 270; in Godwin,
128, 136; in Thompson, 222, 226

balls, billiard, 240
beer preferable to tea, 204
benevolism (*see also* sentimentalism)
36, 124–5, 177, 227
Bentham, Jeremy, 36–7, 74–5, 81, 97;
Thompson influenced by, 215–16,
220, 223–4, 226–7
Burke, Edmund, 38, 77, 95, 170, 210

candour, 88, 113, 121–3
capital, critique of, 160; by Hodgskin,
232–7, 246–7; by Ravenstone,
203–7, 213; by Thomspon, 216–
20
capital, defence of, 58–9, 160
capitalists resemble fleas, 207
Carlyle, Thomas, 3, 21, 171, 264, 270
Cartwright, Major, 26, 75, 77, 88
civic republicanism, *see* classical
republicanism
class, *see* social classification
class conflict, 18, 52, 54, 148

classical economy (*see also* economic
theory), debate with: Cobbett, 259,
276; Coleridge, 173–5, 273; Hall,
158–62, 273; Hodgskin, 239–42,
248; Owen, 187–8; Ravenstone,
209–10; Thompson, 228
classical republicanism, 47, 49, 78–81,
91–2, 273; in Cobbett, 265; in
Coleridge, 178–9; in Godwin, 125;
in Hall, 154; in Ogilvie, 117; in
Ravenstone, 212; in Spence, 103
Cobbett, William, 3, 151, 164, 184,
270–3
Cobbett, William, *Rural Rides*:
accuracy of his survey, 257–8;
classical republicanism, 265; debate
with classical economy, 267; dislike
of intellect, 259; growth of reading
public, 268; map of society, 260–
2; moral ideas, 266; organic
community, 262–5; politics, 265;
statistics, 267; summary, 250–7
Coleridge, Samuel Taylor, 3, 253,
270–3
Coleridge, Samuel Taylor, *Lay
Sermon*: debate with classical
economy, 173–5; an ideological
production, 179–80; metaphysics
and epistemology, 179; moral
ideas, 171–3; organic society, 171;
social structure, 176–8; summary,
164–9; theory of culture, 169–71,
175–6, 178; time and change, 178
Colquhoun, Patrick, 48, 52, 201, 267
commerce, critique of, 78, 149, 165–9,
204–5, 210, 271; by Cobbett, 252,
258, 260–1
cooperation, 187–8, 222, 238, 245
copy theory of knowledge, 95–6, 192
culture, 28–30; concept of, 38–9,
169–71, 175–6, 178, 193, 270,
294 n3

democracy, 75–6, 185, 209, 217–18, 222–3, 225, 228
Diggers, 1, 27, 102, 104
discipline boundaries, 31–2, 47–8, 273, 283 n52
disinterested observer, 94, 116, 122, 126
dissent, religious, 25, 87–9, 273; and Godwin, 123, 125–6, 129, 137, 139; and Spence, 104–5
distribution of wealth, 52–4, 200–2, 210, 236
Divine Providence, *see* natural order
division of labour, 57–8, 198, 205, 225; unfortunate side effects of, 58, 147, 184, 222
dress, rational, 185, 193

economic conjuncture, 22–4; agricultural depression, 22; effects of war, 23–4; harvests, 22; trade cycle, 22–3
economic structure, 11–17; agriculture, 12–13; industry, 13–15; population, 11–12; standard of living, 15–17
economic theory, 46–65; capital, 58–60; class conflict, 52–6; discipline of economics, 47–8; labour theory of value, 56–8; monetary policy, 63–5; population, 49–50; right to subsistence, 47–8; theory of class, 50–2; theory of the market, 60–3
economy, concept of, 94
empathy, growth of, 41
enclosures, 13, 258, 277 n7
enlightenment ideal, *see* candour
epistemological overoptimism, 95–7, 114, 145, 151, 179, 192, 247, 268, 272, 290 n166
equality, 2–4, 32–3, 67–9, 75–6, 79, 82–3, 116, 198–9, 237, 261–2, 270; Godwin on, 125, 127–8, 132, 134–8, 140, 143; Hall on, 146, 153–5, 160; Thompson on, 215–21, 225, 227, 228–30, 286 n104, 295 n2
evangelicalism, 42, 85–7, 172
exploitation, theory of (*see also* capital, critique of), 109–10, 182, 243–5, 270; in Godwin, 134–5, 144; in Hall, 146–8; 160–1; in Thompson, 216, 226

factories and factory legislation, 28, 168

falling rate of profit, *see* stationary state
feeling, changes in structure of, 41–5
Ferguson, Adam, 39–40, 58, 79, 114, 117, 119
feudalism favourably evaluated, 39–41, 119, 147–8, 161, 212
Fourier, Charles, 4, 230
freedom of thought and conscience, *see* candour
French wars, 22–5, 27–8, 165, 173–4, 181, 188, 209; Cobbett on, 254–5, 257
fusion of interests, principle of, 36–8, 116, 139, 190

Gemeinschaft, *see* organic community
Glassites, 104
Godwin, William, 2, 106, 158, 169–70, 177, 185, 210, 238, 241, 270–2; editions of *Political Justice*, 2; influence on Thompson, 214, 222–4, 226–7
Godwin, William, *Political Justice*: aristocracy, 136–7; associationism, 128–9; classical republicanism, 125; government and politics, 142–3; ideal of enlightenment, 121–3; influenced by dissent, 123; interpersonal relations, 138–9; justice, 126–8; rights, 130–1; theory of property, 129–38; time and change, 139–42; utility, 124–6
Goldsmith, Oliver, 42, 44, 46, 171, 263
government, big, for and against, 26, 80–1, 129, 162, 177, 211, 245–6, 265, 271–2; Thompson on, 220, 222, 225, 228
Gradgrind, 193
grain trade debate, 47, 159
gratitude, 137–8, 177

Halévy, Elie, 36–8
Hall, Charles, 2, 184, 197–9, 201, 210, 213, 270–1, 273
Hall, Charles, *The Effects of Civilization*: awareness of other societies, 154–5; classical republicanism, 153–4; debate with classical economy, 158–61; government and taxation, 162; religious ideas, 158; rights, 153; science, 155–6, 157–8; sentimentalism, 156–7; summary, 146–52; time and change, 155; utility, 153

Harrington, James, 78, 80, 102–3, 106, 112, 125, 178
Hartley, David, 34, 169
harvests, good and bad, 22, 146, 167, 257
Helvétius, C. A. de, 34–5, 74, 122, 128
Herder, J. G., 39
hierarchical society, *see* traditional society
Highland clearances, 13, 168, 171
historical change, *see* time and change
history, Scottish philosophical, 38, 92, 119, 141, 155, 212, 230
Hobbes, Thomas, 35–6, 38
Hodgskin, Thomas, 5, 270–2
Hodgskin, Thomas, *Labour Defended*: debate with political economy, 239–47; distrust of government, 246; epistemology, 247–8; justice, 238–9; religious ideas, 246; summary, 232–8
human nature and the individual (*see also* associationism; culture), 32–5; associationism, 33–5; individualism, 32–3
Hume, David, 36, 39, 74, 77, 95, 169; influence on Godwin, 122, 140–2; influence on Hall, 148, 153; influence on Hodgskin, 240–3
Hutcheson, Francis, 74, 112, 122

idealism, 92, 141, 179, 230
ideology, presence of conception of, 96, 143, 145, 151, 162, 242–3, 247–8
independence, 88, 117, 129, 133, 138–9, 265
individuals, respect for (*see also* religious ideas: equal worth of every soul), 32, 69
industrial revolution, 13–15, 23; *see also* preindustrial attitudes
inheritance laws, 75, 150, 161, 216, 220, 243
interests, *see* artificial identification of interests; fusion of interests; natural identity of interests; self-interest
interpersonal relations, 35–9, 115–16, 138–9, 170–1, 190–1, 226–7
invisible hand, 61

justice, 66–9, 73, 97, 126–8; desert-based, 68, 97, 238–9, 266; procedural or equity, 67–8, 126–7, 137

Keynes, John Maynard, 63–4, 174, 183

labour the source of all wealth, *see* labour theory of value
labour theory of value, 56–8, 182, 201, 214–15, 228, 234–5, 238–9, 271
laissez-faire, 60–1, 81, 119–20, 175; Hodgskin's defence of, 246, 249; Thompson's defence of, 220–1, 229
Levellers, 27
Lingard, John, 40, 264
literacy, *see* reading public
literature, focus of attention in, 44–5
Locke, John, 33, 56–7, 75; influence on Godwin, 122; influence on Hall, 153; influence on Ogilvie, 107–9; influence on Ravenstone, 198; influence on Spence, 103, 106
long run and short, 63–4, 175
luxury, 78, 117, 122, 125, 132, 135, 271; Hall on, 147–52, 154, 161

malleability of human beings, *see* associationism
Malthus, Thomas Robert, 12, 16, 20, 48–50, 62, 64, 84, 174; Cobbett's critique of, 251, 255, 258; Hall's critique of, 152, 154, 158; Hodgskin's critique of, 236; Ravenstone's critique of, 195–8; Thompson's critique of, 214, 217, 219–20, 224
Mandeville, Bernard, 36–8, 122
Mannheim, Karl, 178, 179
manure, 151
market mechanisms, 60–3, 175, 188, 225
market society, *see* commerce, critique of
Marx, Karl, 59, 63, 115, 170; anticipations of his ideas, 159, 214, 216, 220, 238; compared with Hodgskin, 238–9, 242–8, 296 n6; compared with Thompson, 229, 231, 295 n2, 296 n3; influenced by British critics of society, 5–6, 270–1
materialism, 92, 179, 212
methodology and epistemology, 93–7; abstract concepts, 94–5; confidence in power of mind, 95–7; "Reason" and "Nature", 93–4; theory, 94
methodology of this study, 6–8, 31–2, 97, 156, 194, 248, 258–9, 267, 273–4, 276 n25

Mill, James, 76, 97, 233
Mill, John Stuart, 169, 175
Millar, John, 39, 92, 120
millennialism, 89–92, 104, 164, 191
monetary policy, 23, 63–5, 165, 174,
    181–3, 207; *see also* paper money
    system
Montesquieu, 39, 79, 92
moral discourse, 65–75; 'bourgeois
    ideology', 72–3; justice, 66–9;
    natural rights, 69–72;
    utilitarianism, 73–5

natural identity of interests, principle
    of, 36–8, 116, 187–8, 190
natural jurisprudence, *see* right of
    property; rights
natural order, 90, 158, 195, 197, 208,
    210–11, 228, 236, 246, 272–3; *see
    also* invisible hand
nature, 93–4, 192, 229, 265, 269, 272
Norman yoke myth, 76–8, 81, 91–2,
    104, 209, 211, 243, 265
novels, 29–30, 41–5

Ogilvie, William, 2, 132, 158, 198,
    210, 270
Ogilvie, William, *Essay on the Right
    of Property in Land*: agrarian law,
    110, 112; classical republicanism,
    117; conception of society, 115–
    16; enlightenment ideal, 112–14;
    natural rights, 107–9; summary of,
    107–10; time and change, 118–20;
    utility, 109, 116–17; work of
    agricultural improver, 110–11
old corruption, 24, 26, 211, 218, 255–
    6, 258, 265
optimism in political economy, *see*
    invisible hand; natural order
organic community and individualistic
    association, 17–20, 171, 253, 262–3
Owen, Robert, 3, 70, 210, 222, 224,
    226, 270–1
Owen, Robert, *Report to the County
    of Lanark*: epistemology, 192–3;
    government and politics, 185, 193;
    interpersonal relations, 187–91;
    monetary policy, 181–3; religious
    ideas, 191; summary, 181–7; time
    and change, 191–2

Paine, Thomas, 26, 72, 76–7, 80, 122
Paley, William, 74, 84–5, 97, 153
paper money system, 254–7
patriarchalism, 199

perfectibility of human beings, *see*
    associationism
Petty, William, 57
physiocrats, 47, 51, 54, 57, 158, 201
political corruption, *see* old corruption
political reform, 25–6, 75–7, 105,
    209, 243, 256; Thompson on,
    225–6, 228
political thought, 75–82; conception
    of politics, 81–2; Machiavellian
    moment, 78–80; natural rights in,
    75–6; scope of government, 80–1;
    traditional rights, 76–8;
    utilitarianism and, 76; utopianism,
    80
politics, 24–8; conceptions of, 81–2,
    145, 186, 193, 228–9, 272–3;
    corruption, 24–5; demand for
    reform, 25–7; Luddism, 27; poor
    law, 28; war, 27–8
poor laws, 20–1, 28, 50, 84, 181, 185,
    258
population (*see also* Malthus, Thomas
    Robert), 11–12, 16, 60, 109, 132,
    151, 183, 277 n6
preindustrial attitudes, 59, 120, 163,
    219, 228, 247
Price, Richard, 72, 76–7, 88–9, 95,
    113; his penny, 236
Priestley, Joseph, 72, 74, 76–7, 88–9,
    106, 113, 169
primitive accumulation, 59, 149, 155,
    199, 243–4
primitivism, 91, 117–18, 125, 140–1,
    179, 212, 229; Hall on, 146, 151,
    155
private interest versus public good, *see*
    self-interest
productive and unproductive classes,
    51–2, 158–9, 201–2, 218, 228
progress, 90–2, 118, 139–42, 179,
    191, 212, 229–30
property: concept of, 94; right of, *see*
    right of property

Ravenstone, Piercy, 4, 217, 270–3;
    really Richard Puller, 4
Ravenstone, Piercy, *A Few Doubts*:
    capital, 203–7; classical
    republicanism, 212; debate with
    classical economy, 209–11; debate
    with Malthus, 195–8; labour
    theory of value, 201; politics, 208–
    9, 211–12; private property, 198–
    200; rent, 200–1; social
    classification, 201–2; taxation,
    202–3; time and change, 212

reading public, growth of, 28–30, 106, 141, 268
reason, 93–5, 123–4, 128–9, 142, 229
religious ideas, 82–90; anglican attitudes to poor, 83–5; equal worth of every soul, 33, 68, 128, 172, 266; evangelical attitudes to poor, 85–7; influence of (*see also* dissent, religious; millennialism), 104, 133, 158, 164, 172–3, 179, 191, 273; millennialism, 89–90; old dissenting attitudes to social questions, 87–9; religion and the rise of capitalism, 166; secularization, 90; supporting inequality, 83; supporting social reform and equality, 82
rent, 200
Ricardo, David, 54–6, 57–8, 198, 200–1, 236
right of property, 47–8, 71–2, 97; Coleridge on, 167–9; Godwin on, 133; Hall on, 153; Locke on, 56–7, 71–2; Ogilvie on, 107–9; Ravenstone on, 198–9; Adam Smith on, 47–8, 72; Spence on, 103
right to whole product of labour, *see* labour theory of value
rights, 69–76, 81, 97, 227, 266, 270, 273, 286 n97; of action and of recipience, 70, 76, 80, 103, 107, 266; 'active' and 'passive', 69, 130; Coleridge on, 171–2; Godwin on, 130–1, 133–4, 137; Marxism on, 73; 'objective' and 'subjective', 69, 131; Spence on, 101, 103; traditional, *see* ancient constitution
Rousseau, Jean Jacques, 39, 79, 81, 117–18, 122, 136, 140, 153
rural idyll, 45–6, 117, 154

Saint-Simon, Count Claude Henri de, 4, 230
savagery, *see* primitivism
Say's law, 64, 182–3, 204
science: enthusiasm for, 114, 128, 141, 155, 157–8, 189, 230, 267; hostility to, 210, 259
Scott, Sir Walter, 39–40, 171
Scottish enlightenment, 2, 79, 112–14
secularization, 90
self-interest, 35, 115, 167, 187, 221, 226, 272
sentimentalism, 41–5, 117, 124–5, 156–7, 263, 273

Sismondi, Simonde, 4, 63
Smith, Adam, 92, 94, 218, 220, 272; on class and class conflict, 50–4; defence of capital, 58–9; and Godwin, 122; and Hall, 146, 148, 158–62, 159, 161; and Hodgskin, 236, 239, 246; on human nature, 34; on interpersonal relations, 36–8; on labour theory of value, 57; and laissez-faire, 61, 81; not a bourgeois ideologist, 52–4; on productive and unproductive classes, 51–2; and Ravenstone, 205–6, 210–11; on society, 39–40; and Thompson, 228
social classification, 50–1, 144, 148, 189, *see also* productive and unproductive classes; Cobbett on, 260–2; Coleridge on, 161, 176–7; Ogilvie on, 115, 120; Ravenstone on, 201–2, 210
social contract *see* state of nature
social structure, 17–22; abdication on the part of the governors, 20–2; Laslett on, 18–19; Marx on, 17–19; Perkin on traditional society, 19–20; *see also* organic community
socialism, 4, 32, 185, 188; later socialists influenced by early British critics of society, 6, 183; problems of definition, 6, 194, 239, 271
society and human relations, conceptions of, 35–46; awareness of different societies, 39, 119, 141, 154, 224; changes in sociable feeling, 41–4; commercial society, 39; concept of 'society', 39, 92, 94, 103–4, 141, 292 n14, 293 n4, 294 n3, 295 n10; in country and in town, 45–6; focus on lower levels of society, 44–5; Halévy on conceptions of interpersonal relations, 36–8; lack of concept of culture, 38–9; medieval society admired, 39–41, 263–6, *see also* feudalism; savage society, 39; self-interest and public good, 35–8
Spence, Thomas, 1, 158, 167, 270, 272
Spence, Thomas, *Real Rights of Man*: classical republican echoes in, 102–3; concept of society in, 103–4; doctrine of rights in, 101, 103; Locke's influence on, 103; Norman yoke myth in, 104; outgrowth of expansion of reading public, 106;

Spence, Thomas (*cont.*)
  outline of, 101–2; related to
    political radicalism, 105–6;
    religious influences on, 104–5; in
    utopian genre, 102
standard of living, 15–17, 203
state, concept of, 94
state of nature, 39, 68, 101, 103; *see
    also* primitivism
stationary state, 62–3, 236
statistics, 48, 94, 149–50, 157, 196–7,
    267
subsistence economy, *see* commerce,
    critique of

Tawney, R. H., 6, 270
taxation, 23–6, 143, 243; Cobbett on,
    255–6, 258; Coleridge on, 165,
    174, 177; Hall on, 150, 162;
    Ravenstone on, 200, 202–3, 211;
    Spence on, 101, 105; Thompson
    on, 218, 220, 225
theory, 94, 113, 124, 161, 248
Thompson, William, 4, 246, 270–2
Thompson, William, *Principles of the
    Distribution of Wealth*:
    conceptions of time and change,
    229–30; cooperative recipe for
    society, 222–6; human nature in,
    226; individualistic recipe for
    society, 220–2; interpersonal
    relations in, 226–7; limited role of
    government and politics in, 228–9;
    moral ideas in, 227–8; and

political economy, 228; summary
    of, 214–6; utility and equality,
    215–20
time and change, 90–3, 265; agents
    and mechanisms of, 91–2;
    Coleridge on, 178–9; direction of,
    90–1; Godwin on, 139–42; Hall
    on, 154–5; Ogilvie on, 118–20;
    Owen on, 191–2; pace and
    character of, 91; Ravenstone on,
    212; subject of, 92–3; Thompson
    on, 229–30
trade, *see* commerce, critique of
trade cycle, 22–4, 174–5, 279 n38
trade unions, 27, 135, 232, 237, 245
traditional society, 19, 136–8, 176–7

underconsumption debate, 64–5, 219–
    20
unemployment, *see* monetary policy;
    underconsumption debate
utilitarianism, 73–5, 76, 97, 153, 224,
    227; and equality, 75, 215–17, 286
    n104, 295 n2; Godwin on, 124,
    132–3; Ogilvie on, 109, 115, 116;
    philosophy for pigs, 171
utopianism, 80, 102, 138

war, 150, 154; *see also* French wars
Wesley, John, 86–7, 173
women, servitude of, 221, 224, 230

Young, Arthur, 13, 267

For EU product safety concerns, contact us at Calle de José Abascal, 56–1°,
28003 Madrid, Spain or eugpsr@cambridge.org.

www.ingramcontent.com/pod-product-compliance
Ingram Content Group UK Ltd.
Pitfield, Milton Keynes, MK11 3LW, UK
UKHW010349140625
459647UK00010B/935